MERCHANTS

MERCHANTS

The Community That Shaped England's Trade
and Empire, 1550–1650

EDMOND SMITH

YALE UNIVERSITY PRESS
NEW HAVEN AND LONDON

Copyright © 2021 Edmond Smith

All rights reserved. This book may not be reproduced in whole or in part, in any form (beyond that copying permitted by Sections 107 and 108 of the U.S. Copyright Law and except by reviewers for the public press) without written permission from the publishers.

For information about this and other Yale University Press publications, please contact:
U.S. Office: sales.press@yale.edu yalebooks.com
Europe Office: sales@yaleup.co.uk yalebooks.co.uk

Set in Garamond Premier Pro by IDSUK (DataConnection) Ltd
Printed in Great Britain by TJ Books, Padstow, Cornwall

Library of Congress Control Number: 2021940106

ISBN 978-0-300-25795-3

A catalogue record for this book is available from the British Library.

10 9 8 7 6 5 4 3 2 1

CONTENTS

List of Illustrations		*vi*
Acknowledgements		*viii*
	Introduction: In the Footsteps of William Turner	1
1	The Art of Merchandising	14
2	Many Bodies Corporate	57
3	Living Together, Working Together	96
4	Monopolists and Interlopers	130
5	The City and the Court	173
	Conclusion: The Business of Empire	207
	Notes	*229*
	Bibliography	*314*
	Index	*341*

ILLUSTRATIONS

All chapter head crest illustrations are from Hazlitt, W. Carew, *The Livery Companies of the City of London, their Origin, Character, Development, and Social and Political Importance* (London: Swan Sonnenschein & co, 1892).

Introduction: Merchants of Spain
Chapter 1: Merchants Adventurers
Chapter 2: Merchants of East India
Chapter 3: Merchants of Russia
Chapter 4: Merchants of the Levant
Chapter 5: The African Company
Conclusion: The Virginia Company

PLATES

1. Portrait of Thomas Gresham, by Anthonis Mor, *c.* 1560–5. Rjiksmuseum, Amsterdam.
2. A ewer, formed of a jug of İznik ware (1585), mounted with spout, cover and foot of silver in London, 1597–8. © The Trustees of the British Museum. All rights reserved.

ILLUSTRATIONS

3. Portrait of a Greek street vendor in Constantinople, by an anonymous artist, 1618. © The Trustees of the British Museum. All rights reserved.

4. The 'Fremlin Carpet', *c.* 1640. © Victoria and Albert Museum, London.

5. *Jahangir Preferring a Sufi Shaikh to Kings*, by Bichitr, *c.* 1615–18. Freer Gallery of Art, Smithsonian Institution, Washington, D.C.: Purchase – Charles Lang Freer Endowment, F1942.15a (Detail).

6. Plan of Richard Bill's shop and home, by Ralph Treswell, 1612. Image published with the kind permission of the Clothworkers' Company, London.

7. *Bishopsgate with Sir Paul Pindar's House*, photograph by William Strudwick, mid–late nineteenth century. © Victoria and Albert Museum, London.

8. 'Londinium' from *The Arches of Triumph erected in honour of the high and mighty prince James the First at his entrance and passage through London*, by William Kip, 1603. British Library.

9. Torture and execution scenes from *A True Relation of the Unjust, Cruel and Barbarous Proceedings Against the English at Amboyna*, by an anonymous artist, 1665. © British Library Board. All Rights Reserved/Bridgeman Images.

10. Portrait of William Windover, by an anonymous artist, 1634. Image published with the kind permission of the Clothworkers' Company, London.

11. Eating vessels from England's colony in Virginia, *c.* 1609–18. Courtesy Jamestown Rediscovery Foundation/Preservation Virginia.

12. East India Company ballot box, 1619. Image published with the kind permission of the Worshipful Company of Saddlers. Photograph courtesy of Prof. Tracey Hill.

13. *Byrsa Londinensis, vulgo The Royall Exchange of London*, by Wenceslaus Hollar, 1644. Art Institute of Chicago.

ACKNOWLEDGEMENTS

This book has grown from years of research and writing and would not have been possible without the support and guidance freely offered by a wide community of scholars who have shaped my work. To start, though, I would like to thank the archivists and curators whose incredible work preserving and sharing records is absolutely essential for our research as historians – without them the lives of the merchants in this book could not be written. Also, bringing this book to life with the team at Yale University Press has been a pleasure, and I am grateful to the anonymous reviewers, Julian Loose, Katie Urquhart, Rachael Lonsdale, Sophie Richmond and Lucy Buchan for their keen eyes and helpful notes.

I have been lucky enough to work alongside some brilliant people in my academic career to date, and this book owes debts to them all. During my studies, I was grateful for the support of Alexander Kazamias, Richard Drayton, William O'Reilly, Sujit Sivasundaram, D'Maris Coffman, Philip Stern and Phil Withington, all of whom provided invaluable advice and encouragement. Since graduating, my professional life has been buoyed by some fantastic colleagues, starting with William Pettigrew, who gave me my first academic job at Kent and let me conduct full-time research for the first time – thank you. Here, I was privileged to

ACKNOWLEDGEMENTS

work alongside Misha Ewen, Peter Good, Liam Haydon, Emily Mann, Tristan Stein and David Veevers who, with shared interests and wildly different ideas about corporations, served as the perfect sounding board for developing this research. In this role, I was also able to supervise Aske Brock and Haig Smith during their own PhDs, which remains one of my most fulfilling experiences in academia, and I have been fortunate enough to have worked with them both since as colleagues and collaborators. I have also been fortunate to work with some wonderful colleagues, mentors and managers in the private sector, especially Juliet Knight, Jessica Thorpe, Miranda Seath, Laura Duguid and Emma Glatman, who were amazingly flexible and supportive as I studied and worked part-time while completing my PhD. The final stages of this book were completed after I joined the University of Manchester, and here I again find myself working alongside some lovely people; I can already see traces of conversations with Georg Christ, Philipp Rössner and Catherine Casson shaping my work and this volume.

One of the great things about working in academia is the chance to be part of a much larger community of scholars than any one institution. The chance to present parts of this book at workshops, seminars and conferences has been invaluable, and I am grateful to everyone who asked me questions at these events. Across these events, I have become part of a tight-knit community of scholars interested in questions of trade, empire and economic history more broadly, and many have become familiar faces, friends and commentators on my work as it has developed and grown. I would especially like to thank Jennifer Bishop, Emily Buchnea, Nandini Das, João de Melo, Derek Elliot, Karwan Fatah-Black, Charlotta Forss, Elisabeth Heijmans, Lisa Hellman, Mélanie Lamotte, Simon Layton, Adrian Leonard, Tom Leng, David Ormrod, Edgar Pereira, Julie Mo Svalastog, Siobhan Talbot, Joris van den Tol, Guido van Meersbergen, Margaret Willes, Kaarle Wirta, Lauren Working, Koji Yamamoto and Nuala Zahedieh for their impact on my work. Richard Blakemore and John Gallagher, especially, have always been happy to burn the midnight oil, arguing about this or that,

– ix –

ACKNOWLEDGEMENTS

and each will recognise the products of these early hours musings here (alongside stories of accidental monkey imports ...). Finally, despite our never working together formally, I have found in Cátia Antunes a remarkable mentor, who since she first saw my research in New Orleans back in 2013 has given me her generous support and encouragement, and whose research continues to be an inspiration.

Finally, I would like to thank Rachel Smith, who not only read and improved every word of this text, but who continues to make life beyond this book absolutely brilliant.

INTRODUCTION
In the Footsteps of William Turner

On a cold, wet December day in 1606, the English merchant William Turner sent a frustrated letter to his business partner John Collett. Time and time again, a series of storms, gales and unpredictable wind patterns had forced Turner and their ship, the *Susan*, to turn back from a voyage to Spain. A new peace had suddenly opened access to Spanish ports and private merchants like Turner were frantic to make the best of new opportunities in the Iberian Empire, but twenty-five days since first setting sail, the *Susan* was still stuck in the English Channel and losing valuable time.

After departing from Brownsea, near Poole on the south coast of England, the wind shifted so that the *Susan* was 'forced to put back again'. The ship then 'came to an anchor in Hurst', where it was kept by the weather for six days. Protected by the rocky promontories at Hurst and sheltering behind the Isle of Wight, the ship was joined by 'some 50 sail of Flemish merchant men' and numerous local vessels that sought to ship fish to Spain and Portugal 'because it will yield them nothing at home'. Together, this veritable armada of multinational vessels sheltered from the storm and waited for a change in the weather. When this finally came, Turner made 'ready to put out to sea', but no sooner had they raised anchor than 'the wind came again to the south so that we

MERCHANTS

were forced in the dark to go moor our ship again'. The next day, 'we had but a small gale of wind and smooth riding yet both our old cables being out, broke one after another' and they were forced to anchor again as they desperately repaired the damaged ship. Yet, no sooner were these repaired than 'there came such extreme foul weather with the wind at south and south west that we had great doubt whether our ground tackle would hold the ship to ride it out or no'.

'This storm and foul weather' continued for the best part of the next week, and it was only when the weather improved that the full extent of their predicament became clear. After surveying the damage to the ship's cables 'our men bid us provide another cable or else they say none of them will go to sea in the ship'. Turner had only recently returned from a voyage to another new commercial opportunity, the fisheries of the North Atlantic, and believed this recent trip to 'Newfoundland was the spoil of both the old cables', but in his haste to make the most of the booming trade in Atlantic fish in Spain he had ignored the need for more cautious preparation. Rushing to resolve the problem, Turner and his crew 'laboured to all places where we hear are any [cables] to be had', thinking they had got lucky on the Isle of Wight where they heard that 'choice 7 or 8 great cables which were bought off diverse Flemings' were available in Newport. Unfortunately, before they could reach this scarce commodity some local men had already sold them.

After surely getting more and more desperate, Turner eventually had a change of fortunes when one of his associates, Samuel, sent news that he had tracked one of these cables to Hamton, where he had bought it and shipped it to Turner, 'which I hope we shall receive the next fair day'. The cordage arrived just in time – the ship's master believed even a single day more riding the storm would have destroyed their remaining good cable. Yet, while the voyage was back on track, Samuel had to pay £20 for the scarce resource, an unexpected cost that undercut the expected profitability of the voyage. To pay for it at all, Samuel had been forced to ask a certain Mr Cornelius, another business associate of Turner's, to pay for the cable, a charge that was added to an ever-shifting

– 2 –

INTRODUCTION

balance sheet between these two merchants. However, with the new cable in place Turner was hopeful that they would depart soon and was only waiting for the 'good pleasure of God for good winds which I beseech him to send'. Finally, it seemed, Turner's voyage to Spain would get under way, hopefully still in time to beat competitors to its booming markets.[1]

Turner was caught out by the myriad of uncertainties that were part of early modern merchants' everyday lives. Changeable weather, shifting market conditions, controlling servants overseas, exchanging information, buying goods, and navigating diverse jurisdictions were just some of the issues confronting these commercial actors. So why did merchants like Turner pursue these trades when everything seemed set against them? Why did Samuel continue to go to such lengths on Turner's behalf? And why did Cornelius risk £20 of his own money to support a business associate on a project that appeared doomed? It was not simply individual boldness, self-assurance or self-interest that underpinned their success. As England's merchants set out for dangerous new worlds, it was their extraordinary sense of community, shared endeavour and the trust in their partners that they depended on to bring them home.

This is a book about William Turner's world. It is about the people he collaborated with, the people he competed with – the merchants who together changed England's relationship with the world. In the century after 1550, English trade blossomed as thousands of merchants launched and participated in ventures across the globe. At the heart of England's commercial expansion were so-called 'mere merchants' – a group who believed they alone were capable of leading the country to wealth and power.[2] These merchants had a distinct professional identity, resting on their training and place within tightly knit commercial communities, and they took care to maintain their control and influence over much of England's overseas activities.[3] Their efforts contributed to England's development from a peripheral power on the fringes of Europe to a country at the centre of a global commercial web, with its merchants' interests stretching from Virginia to Ahmadabad and Arkangelsk to Benin.[4] Some of those merchants participated in colonial ventures and brought about considerable, sometimes forced, human migrations, placing foreign lands under direct territorial control. More still dedicated themselves to trade, exporting English goods and importing products from around the world back to England, sometimes for re-export. Individual traders and small partnerships undertook many of these activities, but innovative forms of commercial organisation – most famously the joint-stock corporation – drove others. In their day-to-day lives, merchants like Turner were consumed by broken cables and capricious winds, but as a community, their efforts would come to reshape England's place in a globalising world.

How then did merchants like Turner come to take a leading role in the making of England's international commercial activities? What was so unique about this community? How did the ways in which they worked together and lived together make it possible for merchants to strike out so successfully to build new trades across the world? This book traces the commercial lives of merchants at the heart of England's global engagement – who they were, how they operated and what they did to try to come to terms with their rapidly changing environment. First, it will show how England's commercial development was a cultural and social phenomenon as much as an economic one. Merchants depended on common values and practices to do business with each other, and this was by no means lessened as the risks and novelty of ventures increased. Second, it will illustrate that the foundations of England's commercial development can be found in the activities of individual merchants and corporations, and that these were connected, collaborative and crossed different geographies. If we were to look for the origins of a 'global' Britain, we would find it in the lives of merchants whose livelihoods depended on traversing borders, building relationships and working effectively with people of other cultures and customs in Europe and beyond.

INTRODUCTION

Historians have paid a great deal of attention to the implications of growing global interaction during this period, but the origins of England's trade and empire remain deeply contested, with many studies considering only a small part of the country's overseas activity or presuming that the state was the driving force behind expansion.[5] In the popular imagination, this has contributed to visions of England's history that have more to do with buccaneers, pirates and explorers than the lives of the people who actually got the job done – the merchants who travelled overseas, interacted with strangers in distant lands and worked collaboratively to establish enduring commercial relationships. This focus has undermined the significance of many of the economic, social and cultural developments that we can see in the early modern period, which is problematic – both in terms of contemporary debates about Britain's role in the world and in the way we understand global economic change. Rather than being brought about by the buccaneering sea dogs of popular imagination, the origins of a globally connected, commercially successful Britain are found in the collaborative activities of the merchant community that are at the heart of this book. By illuminating the histories of individual merchants, and their community, this book offers a new history of this transformative period and, in the lives of England's merchants, it traces the foundations of our modern, capitalist, global world.

It seems unlikely that, when Turner was stranded in freezing gales at Hurst, writing apologetically to his business partner, he had such lofty ambitions at the forefront of his mind; he was probably thinking about what he could do to mitigate the uncertainty that was a constant companion for early modern merchants. The vagaries of weather, pirates, foreign rulers and other threats could turn success into failure at the drop of a hat. For England's merchants, the trials and tribulations of international trade were simply part of everyday life, and the ways in which they went about their business were intended to provide as much security as possible in uncertain times.

Most importantly of all, merchants needed to depend on each other, for contracts and agreements to be honoured, and for partners and

– 5 –

agents to cooperate regarding shared interests.[6] Working within a carefully calibrated and enforced cultural system that bound them together in England and overseas, merchants depended on 'unwritten rules and social norms' that were common across the commercial community and 'generated, if not trust, at least firm expectations about behaviour'.[7] This in turn 'rendered expectations more predictable and created the necessary incentives for cooperation' among family members, business partners and even between strangers.[8] Over time, shared commercial experiences, education and corporate governance generated 'a regularity of behaviour' through rules, beliefs, norms and organisational practices that made it easier for merchants to work together.[9] The common commercial culture that this created was a central pillar of the merchant community that led England's interactions with an increasingly connected world. To meet the demands of international commerce, merchants created new structures of daily life in England that helped sustain relationships in the face of greater distances, complexity and risk than their trade had ever seen before.

To maintain these standards, entry into the ranks of England's merchant community was carefully controlled and restricted – and consequently contested by those left out. Young aspirants were expected to have spent years living and working in the households of senior merchants, where they were shown how to behave just as much as they learned the practical skills of merchandising. It is no surprise, then, that Turner's career had begun in this traditional setting; he entered into an apprenticeship at an early age in the Haberdashers' livery company where he learned the skills necessary for business.[10] This education included learning not only how to keep accounts or maintain correspondence, but also how to develop soft skills – the practices and customs of being a merchant. These were considered essential foundations for a young merchant and were buoyed further during years spent working as a factor and conducting trade on their master's behalf either in London or overseas. In doing so, Turner would learn how to bargain, assess goods, organise transportation, use credit agreements and under-

INTRODUCTION

take all the other activities needed to trade profitably. It also contributed to the development of skills that would serve merchants well in managing people, corporations and colonies. Merchants' education made them uniquely capable of undertaking overseas trade. Their careers depended on their ability to work together and, as England's commercial interests grew, merchants' skills would lend themselves to the organisation of commercial activities across the globe.[11]

In order to regulate these practices and oversee trade more effectively, English merchants adopted and adapted a range of innovative business models to facilitate their activities overseas, notably through the use of the corporation.[12] Essentially, corporations supplied a means for members to act together towards common goals, providing 'a framework, or structure, for continuous and systematic public activity' by their members.[13] As well as allowing merchants to group their capital together, these organisations were responsible for regulating the behaviour of members and employees, and they allowed them to act as a single body during interactions with the English and foreign states. This made it possible for merchants to pool their resources and contribute to the upkeep of essential infrastructure such as ambassadors, warehouses, ships or even military forces.[14] Companies were also able to restrict interference from outside the organisation, including from the crown, and sometimes took on responsibilities that were otherwise monopolised by the state, such as punishing criminals or making treaties with foreign powers.[15] It has been suggested that traces of England's corporations can be found as far back as the *societas*, the organisation of Italian financiers in England in the thirteenth and fourteenth centuries, and corporate organisation was certainly vital to the guild system that had regulated many trades in England from the thirteenth century onwards.[16] New corporations therefore drew on long-standing traditions and accepted norms of social organisation even as they created innovative approaches to the government of people, trade and behaviour.[17]

It is important to remember that in early modern England, corporate bodies were key parts of the daily lives of people in the commercial

-7-

community. They were not distant, impersonal institutions in which people simply invested money, but deeply social organisations. Members invested time and energy on behalf of the public community that the corporation represented.[18] In the case of Turner, after completing his apprenticeship, he became a freeman and citizen of the City of London urban corporation and a member of the Haberdashers' livery company, through which he obtained the privileges necessary to participate in local politics, enter into partnerships and join corporate bodies active in overseas trade and colonisation.[19] In joining a corporation, merchants became part of its internal social network, gained access to whatever rights and privileges a company offered (such as access to a particular market or participation in a joint-stock investment) and were bound by its rules and regulations.[20] Of course, these rules were not always followed to the letter, and corporations spent considerable efforts on maintaining standards. Turner himself had run afoul of the Merchant Adventurer's decrees (a company that oversaw the trade of English woollen cloth to northern Europe), and alongside several other merchants he had 'been disenfranchised by reason of their marriages with women strangers'. He was only readmitted in 1606, possibly following the death of his wife, and he never married again.[21] Regulations regarding sexual and marital relationships were common, as were rules relating to civility, religion and the recording and sharing of information. By providing common standards for those participating in commercial activity, corporations were able to better regulate the behaviour of their employees and ensure people were held to account when they failed to abide by the expectations set by the community.

Relationships between merchants across the commercial community depended on trust between individuals, and reputation and creditability were vitally important.[22] Indeed, 'credit was a public means of social communication and circulating judgement about the value of other members of communities' that helped people assess who to do business with.[23] The early modern economy was a system of cultural as well as material exchanges, in which the central mediating factor was credit or

INTRODUCTION

trust – without it, commerce would have been impossible. Across the commercial community, participation in organisations provided a means for merchants to expand their personal networks and develop new commercial ventures within a set of shared, creditable practices. In turn, as arbiters of disputes and regulators of behaviour, corporations helped solidify relationships and facilitate creditable transactions across England and internationally.

Living amid the bustle of business in early modern London, first on Fleet Street in a shared apartment with John Palmer and later in All Hallows Barking, near the Tower of London, Turner lived and worked in an intensely corporate environment.[24] In these neighbourhoods, he lived alongside his business partners and competitors, passing their places of business and pleasure as he rushed about London's winding streets. The glorious, richly furnished halls of London's livery companies stood out as symbols of the city's corporate foundations and many merchants would have seen these organisations as the heart of their daily lives – often living in property rented from them and working closely with other members. In the sixteenth and seventeenth centuries, as possibilities for overseas trade and empire grew dramatically, this already densely populated urban centre attracted more and more merchants and their wealth.[25] In such an environment, it is easy to see how merchants grouped together, shared ideas, gossiped, built relationships and launched innovative new ventures to distant seas.

Turner's first experience of overseas trade, like that of many merchants, had been trading as part of the Merchant Adventurers company, which he probably joined soon after completing his apprenticeship.[26] The Merchant Adventurers had been founded in the fifteenth century and was regulated to export English undyed woollen broadcloth, principally to trading entrepôts in northern Europe.[27] Yet, although he began his commercial career in this traditional setting, Turner was far from hidebound and tried hard to take advantage of new opportunities throughout his career.[28] Even within the Merchant Adventurers, Turner was willing to go against the grain; he was one of

– 9 –

the first members to embrace plans to export dyed cloth to the continent after 1614. By 1617, he was one of only 140 merchants engaged in this activity, albeit on a rather modest scale.[29] He would continue to participate in the trade of woollens throughout his career, but Turner's most profitable successes came through activity in newer, more innovative organisations. In 1599, he was among the first subscribers to the newly formed East India Company, investing £300 in partnership with his cousin and uncle.[30] Soon after, in 1605, he joined the Levant Company, and by the end of the decade had joined the Irish Society and Newfoundland Company too.[31] Turner also invested heavily in attempts to develop the alum industry in England and owned numerous properties across London, including a house in St Katherine's parish that he bought from one of the Tower of London's lion tamers.[32] These activities, coupled with his cloth exports, investment in Atlantic fisheries and attempt to beat the rush to Spanish markets, suggest a merchant eager to take advantage of opportunities across the full range available. Turner, like many other merchants, was not constrained by ideology and engaged in enterprises irrespective of whether they were colonial or commercial, domestic or global.[33]

Much like Turner, few merchants were members of only one single corporate body and interested in only one single commercial endeavour. Most were part of a wide variety of communities in early modern London through different institutions, activities and relationships.[34] A 'tangled, messy, skein of overlapping and intersecting social networks' made up English society, and within this environment, individuals relied on a variety of different communities in their daily lives.[35] This atmosphere enabled merchants like Turner to meet and work with partners across a number of networks, to join a number of companies when it suited them and to operate outside specific corporate jurisdictions when necessary.[36] Individuals' relationships across these different interactions could easily influence how they thought about the world and how the world thought about them.[37] England's commercial activities across the world were not directed by a single hand, but by thousands of merchants, each of whom brought with them their own ideas, interests and priorities – meaning that even as they established ways of doing business together effectively, the ideas they held about how best to profit from new opportunities were often contested. A common commercial culture helped provide a means for these individuals to operate together despite their differences, and through corporations, the multiple interests of members could be more easily directed towards increasing their common wealth.

Working together in a corporate body gave merchants much greater powers when it came to organising their enterprises, but they were still dependent on states and legal structures for recognition and support. How the corporation interacted with the state, with the wider public and with their own members could be the deciding factor in whether a company was successful – or if it could even get off the ground.[38] Corporations were political and social bodies in their own right, and rather than functioning simply as business concerns, companies created 'institutions and ideologies that condition political authority, obedience, coercion, and negotiation'.[39] Indeed, the relative weakness of the English state during this period, seen in particular in the piecemeal state apparatus, created a constant need for corporations to adapt their legal, commercial and financial institutions rapidly.[40] Rather than providing an arm of the state or a substitute for state involvement in overseas activities, the development of strong corporate organisations was influential in the formation of a more centralised state during the early modern period.[41] Although merchants did require state support in areas like licensing and diplomacy, the state was dependent on merchants to increase shipping and provide customs revenue, goods and expertise in administration. This relative freedom from state control allowed corporations in English cities to undertake activities designed to improve the commercial environment and better compete with commercial centres in Europe.[42] At the same time, the corporate form provided a means for merchants to group their finances and to present a united face to the crown, the public and other merchants.

Merchants similarly depended on corporate structures when they needed to engage personally with markets overseas to buy and sell goods – or rely on factors and servants to do so on their behalf. Many travelled personally, especially in the early stage of their careers, and experienced the challenges of living and working in other countries. Their success was often built on their ability to operate effectively in 'cosmopolitan' environments and develop relationships with local agents and states. As trade took merchants further and further from England's shores, skilled merchants followed cross-cultural practices that had been successful elsewhere and applied them across the globe. The 'overlapping and intersecting worlds of commercial and colonial enterprise' were brought together in merchants who represented substantial connectedness across ventures in spite of limited state involvement or imperial centralisation throughout this period.[43] Merchants and their agents spun a commercial web that crisscrossed empires, oceans and continents, and tied England into rapidly maturing global networks of trade and exchange.

Turner's, and other merchants' activities across these ventures, contributed to the 'trial-and-error' efforts of English traders, explorers and colonists up to the middle of the seventeenth century that built the foundations of the British Empire and embedded the country within global networks that would shape it for centuries to come.[44] Territorially, the Atlantic world was host to a range of ventures by English colonists, from the colonisation of Ireland to the development of settlements on the North American coast and in the Caribbean – territories that were later joined by territorial possessions in Asia and Africa.[45] The interconnected ventures of English actors in the Atlantic were developed in part for commercial reasons but were also motivated by religious and political concerns that were attractive to non-merchants and merchants alike.[46] Although not the sole protagonists of colonisation in the Atlantic, merchants were central to its development and were far from peripheral actors in colonial endeavours. In many cases, merchants became leaders of colonial ventures and were otherwise investors, supporters and essen-

INTRODUCTION

tial suppliers for these new settlements. The Ulster plantation in Ireland, for example, was organised and governed by the Irish Society, a company whose membership was largely made up of merchants and citizens of London.[47] Additionally, commercial activities in the Atlantic and North America were closely tied to activities elsewhere.[48] Across the globe, merchants were participating in the growing English empire. As colonies developed, they gained access to new markets and established links with trading circuits throughout the world.

The global expansion of England's commerce in this period was driven not by the state or a centralised authority, but by numerous overlapping interest groups of merchants and non-merchants, who sought profit and power through ventures overseas. For the merchant community, new opportunities in international trade went hand in hand with possibilities for investment in land, property and empire – even the development of new industries and crafts – all were fair game.[49] As a result, it was corporate institutions and individual actors, rather than the state, that had a great degree of control over burgeoning commercial and imperial endeavours. The state provided support or leadership for some ventures, but commercial interests, particularly chartered companies, undertook many more, at times operating beyond the state's authority. As Turner desperately rushed to get his ship ready to go to Spain, his footsteps echoed across a country undergoing rapid transformation. He and other merchants were the driving force behind England's emerging global trade and empire, and it was this community that defined English engagement with the world.

– 13 –

ONE

THE ART OF MERCHANDISING

Abandoned in Africa on the banks of the Benin River in 1553, the first English merchants to travel to the region could only look back and reflect that, perhaps, their organisational strategy had not been very effective. The voyage had started well, leaving Portsmouth in England with little in the way of trouble and progressing rapidly down the African coast through tropical seas and under a scorching sun. On arrival, they had been lucky enough to have been invited before the King of Benin in his 'great huge hall long and wide' and learned that he spoke Portuguese, which 'he had learned as a child'. Communicating through their Portuguese pilot, they explained how they 'were merchants travelling into those parts for the commodities of his country in exchange of wares which they had brought from their countries'. The king was impressed and proposed an exchange of pepper for their European goods. He even offered 'to credit them to their next return' should they need it. Within thirty days, the English merchants received 'four score tons of pepper' and were hopeful of receiving more. The merchants must have been overjoyed: not only had they found a viable market in Benin, but also they had encountered a local economic culture that played by the same rules as they were used to, with a supportive monarch and a shared language. Their joy was not to last though, and

THE ART OF MERCHANDISING

even as the deal was finalised, they received some devastating news – the crew of their ships had mutinied, and they had been stranded, left to fend for themselves in a strange land.

Where did their plans go so awry? 'Certain merchant adventurers of the City of London' had funded the venture, and they had done their best to ensure to find 'two good ships' that were 'well furnished . . . with men of the lustiest sort' as well as 'ordinance and victuals requisite for such a voyage'. They had even found and employed 'a stranger called Antoniades Pinteado', who had served the King of Portugal in Africa and Brazil, to act as 'expert pilot and politic captain'. However, problems arose when Pinteado was 'matched with an unequal companion' in the form of the second ship's captain, Mr Wyndam. A man 'with virtues few or none adorned, with vices diverse and many', Wyndam obtained the appointment as a 'kinsman of one of the head merchants' even though, one angry writer remarked, 'happy was the man or woman who knew him not'! Without clear articles or instructions, the lesser captain was able to obtain more and more authority throughout the voyage, leaving 'him to command all alone, setting naught both by captain Pinteado' and 'with the rest of the merchant factors'. Where the voyage should have been 'ministered in a common wealth', it was instead 'tormented with the company of a terrible hydra'.

Rather than working in sync with the community on board, Wyndam ignored their input, 'sometimes with opprobrious words and sometimes with threatening'. Desiring to push further and further along the African coast, the cantankerous captain overruled first the factors when they identified spices available on 'the great river of Sesto' that could 'be sold for great advantage for the exchange of other wares', and then Pinteado who advised they stop at São Jorge da Mina to 'make sale of their wares such as they had for gold, whereby they might have been great gainers'. Wyndam would hear none of it. Unwilling to take advice, 'the un-tame brain of Wyndam' led the voyage astray, as he ignored the 'council and experience of Pinteado' and drove them onward to Benin. Arriving very late in the season, things started to fall apart. While the

– 15 –

merchants continued on to the court of the welcoming king, the irascible Wyndam stayed with the ships, watching on as the mariners, eating 'the fruits of the country, and drinking the wine of the palm trees', quickly fell ill. The disordered men 'in such extreme heat' bathed in the river and were soon laid low with 'swellings and agues'. Three, four, or five men were dying each day. Eventually, news reached Wyndam from the merchants, 'certifying him of the great quantity of pepper they had already gathered' and asking to have only a few more days to collect more. It was the last advice they would see ignored. Wyndam angrily demanded they return immediately 'or else threatened to leave them behind'. The querulous captain died before he could carry out the threat, but in his absence the mariners carried out his final order, sinking one of the ships and taking the other to return to England.[1]

TRAINING, EXPERTISE AND DISCIPLINE

The episode in Benin is illustrative of the English experience of trading beyond Europe's borders in the middle of the sixteenth century – it was dangerous, experimental, and depended on foreign experts and brokers to have any chance of success. Whether in Africa, the Mediterranean or in America, doing business meant operating within very different commercial frameworks. These were not imposed by England on the world; merchants could only operate profitably by adapting to local conditions and adopting the economic practices and behaviours of their trading partners overseas.[2] Yet, as the merchants discovered in Benin, the practicalities of trading face to face with people across the world was not necessarily the biggest barrier to commerce – it was what they were trained to do. The greatest challenge instead lay in establishing the institutional structures that could be depended upon to deliver merchants and their goods to global destinations and bring them home again.[3] By maintaining strict standards and regulations about training, employment, accountability, reporting and discipline across the commercial community, merchants sought to ensure that doing business on a global stage would not break the bonds that held them together.[4] Through these means, innovations and novel approaches employed by corporations and private traders alike were grounded on mercantile practices that remained secure, resting on decades of tradition and common practice. Over the coming hundred years, these institutional arrangements, grounded through common education and training in what it meant to be and what it meant to act like a merchant, helped create more stable arrangements that underpinned English commercial activity across the globe.

Apprenticeships were a vital route for young merchants (who were almost always men) to obtain the skills necessary to become fully fledged members of this community, providing training on the job as servants and factors for more senior merchants.[5] Simply put, this system of training centred on contracts whereby apprentices would work for minimal wages, usually for some years, in exchange for instruction.[6] Through these arrangements, they obtained the practical and social training that made it possible for them to join England's commercial community. In England, the 1562 Statute of Artificers sought to regulate the terms and structure of these agreements, but different livery and trading companies, as well as individual merchants, undertook training in ways that were deemed most productive for their specific demands. This statute had three key tenets – that those conducting training were householders over twenty-four years of age; that apprenticeships lasted at least seven years; and that participants would be over twenty-four years old on completion. Although apprenticeship contracts were agreed privately, they were normally undertaken within corporate frameworks whereby apprentices were enrolled with relevant authorities and obtained their 'freedom' from these organisations at the completion of their training.[7] In this way, apprentices could become citizens of their local urban corporation – such as Bristol or London – and were able to participate in a wide range of political, social and economic activities.

The need to secure an apprenticeship was therefore of paramount importance for a young merchant in training.[8] It was not uncommon for apprentices' families to secure such a placement with the payment of a 'premium' to their children's new master, sometimes also paying bonds to guarantee good behaviour, or even subsidising costs for clothing or accommodation.[9] As this suggests, obtaining an apprenticeship with a well-connected master could be considered a sensible form of long-term investment. Apprentices were not only trained in the specific skills required for conducting trade, such as writing letters or keeping accounts, but they were also tied into their employer's client, credit and supplier networks. This relationship was also essential for many senior merchants who required trusted apprentices and servants to operate on their behalf overseas. While an apprentice might become a rival to their master later in their careers, they could also be a means of establishing long-standing relationships that merchants might depend upon throughout their business lives.[10] Importantly, apprenticeships also served to educate young merchants about the cultural and behavioural norms of doing business in the early modern world. Such tacit knowledge, acquired through imitation, observation and experience, was most effectively obtained through an apprenticeship immersed in the practice of trade.[11] Looking back after a long career, Lewes Roberts dedicated his book *The Marchants Mapp of Commerce* to his former master Thomas Harvey in acknowledgement that he was 'as a child first bred under your roof, and since nourished and educated abroad for many years at his and your charges' – through which he had learned the skills to become a successful merchant.[12] It was a sentiment shared by William Windover (Plate 10), who was careful in his portrait to commemorate his family, livery company, and first trading company that had each supported him during his youth.

In usual circumstances, participation in crafts and trades in England was restricted to those who had undertaken an apprenticeship specific to that field, or who had trained while working as a factor or servant overseas. In part, these restrictions helped exclude competition from manufacturers and traders operating outside the corporate systems that regulated so much of England's non-agricultural economy.[13] Further regulations by specific corporations also served to limit the number of people who could enter

THE ART OF MERCHANDISING

particular communities. For example, Eastland Company members were permitted to have two apprentices every seven years.[14] On the other hand, while it was common to use the standards of the apprenticeship system to limit access to companies, merchants were quick to condemn companies when they felt their regulations unduly limited the training opportunities for young merchants. In 1591, merchants protesting the incredibly small membership of the Levant Company, which they claimed had only six active members, argued that so few merchants could not possibly train enough young men to continue the trade.[15] However, despite the restrictions of corporations such as the Levant Company, the number of apprentices in England's commercial centres was significant. In London, for instance, roughly 10 per cent of the city's population were apprentices, and around two-thirds of its adult male population served as apprentices during their lives.[16] That being said, not all apprentices completed their training and not all those who did became freemen or citizens of the town or city where they had trained.[17] Becoming a member of a company, whether urban, livery or trading corporation, required the payment of fees and sometimes other forms of approval. Not all apprentices could, or sought to, meet these criteria.[18]

Vitally, 'the completion of an apprenticeship marked a man out as trustworthy and dutiful'.[19] Through the process of apprenticeship, young merchants were able to demonstrate their suitability for joining a community that depended on common behavioural norms to maintain the bonds of trust and creditability that made long-distance trade possible. For instance, when John Clayton was apprenticed to John Bolton, a Dublin merchant, in 1647, the expectations of what the training experience should deliver were carefully laid out. Bolton agreed to 'teach and instruct, or cause him to be taught and instructed by others, in the knowledge, science and experience of a merchant', as well as providing 'sufficient meat, drink, lodging and apparels'. In return, Clayton would serve his new master faithfully and protect his interests. Rather that agreeing to undertake specific activities, the new apprentice was instead expected to behave in an appropriate manner – he was

– 19 –

forbidden from marrying, committing adultery, playing 'dice, cards or any other unlawful games', or entering 'taverns or alehouses' unless 'it be about his master's business'.[20] The young apprentice would learn the skills necessary for a merchant over time, but he was expected to behave in the manner of a merchant from the start.

Such behavioural standards were vital when merchants from England were placed into the contested cultural spaces in which they would operate overseas. In the *Merchants Avizo*, an experienced merchant, John Browne, offered a series of recommendations to English merchants setting out overseas that could be applied both in 'Spain and Portugal or other countries'. Browne recounted how his own entry into Spain had been 'troubled with difficulties, for want of such pattern as this, for ease of our tender wits'. Highlighting the importance of building relationships, a core tenet of his advice was that all merchants 'show yourself lowly, courteous, and serviceable unto every person', 'yet assuredly (it is well known by experience) that there springs of no one virtue so great fruit unto us, as of gentleness and humility: for it will both appease the anger and ill will of our enemies, and increase the good will of our friends'. It was not the place of English merchants to impose their own expectations onto others – they should be 'circumspect touching your behaviour when you be in the country of Spain or elsewhere', and should 'learn what be their civil laws and customs, and be careful to keep them'.[21] The inculcation of cultural values during apprenticeships was therefore a necessary first step in ensuring that English merchants could operate effectively both within their own community and within cross-cultural environments overseas.

Embedding themselves in the ports and cities where they did business gave English merchants a unique opportunity to sustain relationships with locals and helped them to understand the specific commercial cultures found in different parts of the world. For instance, merchants trading to Morocco confessed they needed more time to learn the customs of the region and the best places to conduct trade before they would be able to outperform French and non-European competitors.[22]

– 20 –

THE ART OF MERCHANDISING

In the entangled empires of the Iberian Atlantic, where English merchants operated across Spanish and Portuguese imperial boundaries as well as within the specific contexts of colonial and trading port towns in Africa and America, these processes of adaptability were commonplace.[23] As merchants spread further from their traditional routes into Spain and northern Europe, they carried these behaviours into new ventures – whether undertaking business in Livorno, Smyrna or Surat, forming working relationships with local traders was essential.[24] In order to operate in the contested spaces of international trade, merchants 'combined social incentives, shared norms about the conduct of commerce, and legal commitments to secure their agents' cooperation', and this was only possible with a deep understanding of local spaces.[25]

Ensuring that merchants remained committed to these practices was an important undertaking for English corporations that sought to ensure the disorderly manner of one member would not be detrimental to others. Charters granted to corporations emphasised the belief that 'no commerce or intercourse can be maintained or continue without order and government', and proponents of such oversight argued that, by working in concert, merchants, 'by their orderly trading and selling', were able to 'gain many privileges' and enable the participation of many more merchants overseas.[26] Corporations quickly tried to impose themselves when these privileges were threatened, so when the factor Martin Kentish was reported to the Levant Company 'in regard of his irregular and disorderly trading', it would probably have been no surprise that he was immediately dismissed from the role.[27] Even where corporations were not active, the behavioural and commercial standards they sought to impose remained ubiquitous and individual merchants similarly sought to distance themselves from poor behaviour. Having been 'bred' in such corporate environments, both apprentices and factors were expected to be dependable. Thus, when the young merchant William Cockayne junior wrote from Elbing to William Cockayne senior seeking employment from his 'loving and kind uncle', all he could do was beg forgiveness for 'my former youthful foolishness, which I must needs

– 21 –

confess I have too much used to your worships discontent'.[28] Even a close family connection was not a panacea for incompetence.

Safeguarding against disorderly conduct, both during and after a merchant's apprenticeship, helped ensure that factors could be trusted to act without constant intervention from their employers. At times, of course, agents might receive specific requests from their employers, such as Lionel Cranfield's order that his factor obtain 2 tons of Spanish wine or the appointment of Maurice Thompson as John Gregory's proxy on a voyage to St Kitts, but for day-to-day business they were expected to operate autonomously.[29] Richard Archdale, for instance, had a number of apprentices: Nicholas Tench and Charles Parker, who entered into servitude in 1603; Pope Alvie (who was his nephew) and Robert Boules in 1608; Samuel Davis in 1614; Lyson Seye in 1617 (who paid £500 for the privilege); and Alexander Shepherd from 1622.[30] His son Matthew also likely served as his factor overseas and received 'stock of trading which is at London, Bordeaux and Leghorn' in 1638 when Richard died.[31] Without the confidence that these young merchants would act effectively on his behalf, they would have been a hinderance rather than a help. When servants were trusted, such as the factor Richard Sheppard, whom William Cranfield and William Halliday shared in Stade, an array of responsibilities could be delegated, most commonly day-to-day trading and business administration. In this case, the factor kept accounts, issued bills of exchange and collected debts, as well as managing the exchange of English woollens for European manufactures.[32] Similarly, when William Cockayne appointed Simon Fryer as his factor in King's Lynn, Boston and Hull, Fryer was expected 'to take account and reckoning of and for all such sum and sums of money' he received and transferred on behalf of Cockayne's businesses in the three ports.[33]

Simply keeping track of trading activities in complex, overlapping international markets would have been impossible without a well-formed and trusted network of employees and partners. A single merchant, like Edward Wollaston, would in a single year import silk, felt, cotton, satin, silver and gold from ports across Europe, and required on-the-ground assistance from factors based in numerous locations to provide local expertise and oversee the conduct of trade.[34] Even for a fairly small, niche market, such as the twenty-six ships that exported calfskins from England in 1615, transporting goods to Livorno, Lisbon, Naples, Messina, Bilbao, Seville, Alicante, Dansk, Malaga and Rouen, required merchants to have factors at each port to receive, sell and record the transactions.[35] For long-term trading engagements, where factors might live overseas for years, they were also key interlocutors between English and local merchant networks, building relationships with local traders, officials and even rulers. William Byron's work for Daniel Harvey in Rouen, for instance, included trading with French merchants like David le Montomier and Peter Bodin, from whom he purchased silk, as well as with English ship masters who transported these goods to England. This was undertaken mainly through credit and debt arrangements, meaning that Byron was required to assess and understand the creditability of each partner as well as administer transactions. In October 1632, he reported that the 'bills, debts and moneys resting in my hands' were worth £27,826 15s 2d; serious sums of money were being given over to the management of overseas agents.[36]

Recruiting apprentices, factors and other agents was therefore not a decision to be taken lightly. For trading companies that employed their factors directly (rather than through individual members), the decision about who to select was not always clear-cut, especially for specific roles or when unfamiliar individuals applied. No matter what specific tasks a role might include, such as translation or religious government, employees were expected to operate in a manner acceptable to the merchant community. The East India Company, for instance, depended on an array of employees to operate in England as well as overseas. Competition for roles within organisations could be fierce, as well-placed factor positions could be a stepping stone to wealth and influence. When the East India Company sought sixteen factors for its first voyage to Asia in 1600, it received enough applications to employ a full complement of skilled merchants, and for one unsuccessful applicant to

MERCHANTS

petition to be allowed to work for the company for free (at least until one of the other factors died). Roger Stile, who made this generous offer, was the son of one of the company's directors, Oliver Stile, and was desperate for the opportunity. Assuring the company he was 'content to be left in the country of the East Indies until the return of the second voyage', he even promised to 'apply himself to learn the language'.[37] This offer was 'well liked' by the company's directors, and he earned his place.[38] In the end, the company's first voyage carried twelve paid factors and seven others 'admitted to go without salary' who would take over if other factors died.[39] In meetings where potential employees were discussed, directors were just as concerned with the character and reputation of applicants as their skills. For instance, when the company sought to employ a preacher to serve their employees in Asia, three applicants were discussed in detail – the company had employed two of them previously and the third had been 'commended to the company as a very fit man'.[40] In this instance, and following standard practice, it was decided that a recommendation could not outweigh the specific experience of preaching in the Indies.[41] Having worked with the company before, the directors knew their first choice was creditable and his experience simply outstripped that of his less-travelled competitors.

An abundance of worthy candidates was hardly something to worry about though. The challenge came when it was necessary to weigh demands for expertise and character against the risks of leaving posts unfilled. Sometimes applicants were just not good enough, such as one Jonathan Smith, who, despite having completed his apprenticeship and presenting a strong recommendation, was deemed 'not fit for service' by the East India Company after admitting 'he had never been at sea'.[42] A reputable character was not a substitute for basic experience. Thomas Offley, on the other hand, was employed by the company despite never being employed as a merchant factor. He was commended for 'his sufficiency in accounts [and] that he writes a good hand' and because 'he has always been of a very civil carriage'. It probably helped that his father was a director at the time.[43] For Offley, a combination of social capital

– 24 –

THE ART OF MERCHANDISING

and the effective demonstration of sought-after skills and character was enough for the company to overlook his dearth of overseas experience. A similar strategy worked for Hatton Farmor, who wrote to his father-in-law William Cockayne to thank him for 'how worthily you have solicited my business' and earned him employment.[44] Social connections were not a guaranteed way of influencing employment decisions, but, from the perspective of early modern merchants, a young merchant's links to trusted, respected and creditable members of the community were a good guide to how well they might integrate into commercial society.

Writing, accounting and trading expertise were all sought-after skills in factors, and all employees in this role would be expected to hold at least some level of competence in each of them. Something that could really set applicants apart, however, was knowledge of languages. Business was conducted in multilingual and cross-cultural environments and the need to communicate with merchants, manufacturers, brokers and officials in markets across the world meant that mastery of languages, or even competence, was in great demand, whether using Latin, such as in the agreement between 'Humfridum Thomson' and 'Arthuro Robinson', both from London, for payment of £10, or the will of Henry Shanks that was recorded in Dutch in Batavia.[45] Similarly, bonds agreed between merchants in York, London and Bristol were written in both English and Latin, while regulations regarding the manufacture and trade of new draperies in Norwich were produced in both English and Dutch to meet the demands of the large migrant population in the town.[46] In other cases, correspondence in the language of key overseas markets was a perfectly suitable means of communication. In Bristol, where merchants had been travelling to France for decades, no challenge was presented when Wannoir la Nord wrote in French to 'Monsieur le Mayor de Bristol' complaining about privateering and loss of goods.[47] When 'Cidi Abdulla Dodan' who was 'Andalusia born, speaking naturally Spanish and Italian' visited London, he had no difficulty in finding merchants who could converse with him.[48] Richard Cocks similarly

– 25 –

embraced his linguistic expertise to send a bilingual Japanese–English letter to his compatriot William Adams, while correspondence regarding the Levant trade between the Ottoman Sultan Mehmed III and Elizabeth I was in English, Latin and Arabic.[49]

Finding merchants able to operate in these different linguistic environments was not always easy, especially in trades where English was never likely to be helpful. The East India Company, for instance, was reliant on Spanish- and Portuguese-speakers to engage with Asian rulers, and 'Richard Temple who had the Spanish tongue' was propelled to a position of great importance when he was appointed to act as an interpreter between Paul Canning and the Mughal Emperor Jahangir in Agra.[50] Demonstrating the effective application of language in a business context, usually learned while merchants were living abroad during their training, could be a sure-fire way of obtaining a position.[51] In the case of Mr Brund, a merchant initially overlooked by the East India Company for the post of principal factor, his linguistic expertise was so widely admired that the corporation's members protested the decision. Insisting that Brund was 'a grave and discreet merchant and one which hath the Arabian, Spanish and Portugal languages', they argued that his exclusion could only mean the directors themselves misunderstood the demands of the trade.[52] In the face of a linguistically fuelled shareholder rebellion, Brund's appointment was quickly confirmed at their next meeting.[53]

Languages were held in such high regard due to their scarcity, and making sure that would-be traders really had the necessary skills to conduct negotiations in another tongue was not always easy. For example, when the East India Company sought to employ 'writers skilful in the Dutch tongue' as representatives in the United Provinces, they were so disappointed by the initial applications that they set a subsequent applicant, Edmond Baynham, a test to ascertain the quality of 'his writing and speaking Dutch'.[54] Where possible, merchants sought to train skilled linguists from among members of their community. Efforts were made to provide instructional texts, such as William Strachey's 'dictionary of the Indian language for the better enabling of such who shall be thither employed' and Richard Hakluyt's material for learning the rudiments of the Malay language that the East India Company thought would be 'very fitting for their factors', but these were probably not all that helpful.[55] Companies tended to rely on language learning during apprenticeships instead, as this could be validated more easily through recommendations. For instance, John Major was apprenticed to John Guillam 'to be instructed in the said art [of a merchant] and the French tongue'. Similarly, in order to obtain a loyal and English, but linguistically capable administrator for their activities in the Ottoman Empire, the Levant Company considered 'whether it was not meet to breed up an Englishman in the ambassador's house [in Constantinople] to be the secretary after Signor Dominico'.[56] Other merchants obtained language skills and experience of living in different lands through less structured educational experiences. The London merchant Lewes Jackson, for instance, who left England in the *Little Hopewell* 'bound for the Amazons', found himself diverted to 'Wyapoko' where he stayed for fifteen months before returning to England via Barbados.[57]

Linguistic skill was respected, but it was the ability to communicate effectively that was essential for early modern merchants – and this was not just a matter of language. It was with this in mind that George Best wrote a detailed account of his travels to North America, offering advice about 'how to proceed and deal with strange people' and detailing the ways 'trade of merchandise may be made without money'.[58] In different contexts, working with and accepting local commercial practices was important, such as in Massachusetts where Richard Foxwell 'do cause myself to owe and stand indebted unto Francis Johnson' not cash but 'one hundred twenty and five pounds of good marketable beaver'.[59] It did not matter if these practices were not the ones merchants might have learned in England; when working in overseas markets, it was a merchant's job to adapt and get the job done.

Unclear communication between merchants could have deleterious effects on both personal relationships and the effective execution of trade. Thomas Kerridge and Mr Brown, two traders in India, were deeply frustrated by their colleagues in Surat who failed to respond to their detailed, clear letter in kind, instead returning one full of 'many good words almost past our understanding'. The accused party had chosen 'to enjoy the licence poetical', which was entirely unhelpful given that Kerridge and Brown had 'no Latin' and were 'unacquainted with the language'.[60] While in this instance poor communication mostly just annoyed their colleagues, a similar failing by an East India Company employee had much more chaotic effects. In 1636, one observer, with some delight, wrote a 'good tale' about how 'a merchant of London that wrote to a factor of his beyond the sea' was undone by his own poor handwriting. While the merchant had 'desired him by the next ship to send him "2 or 3 apes"', he forgot the "r" and then it was "2 o 3 apes". His factor has sent him four score and says he shall have the rest by the next ship, conceiving the merchant had send for two hundred and three apes!' Quite what a spectacle the arrival of a troop of apes at London's waterside might have caused has not been recorded, but the story, which the author claimed 'in earnest . . . is very true' highlights how even the smallest error might lead to quite unexpected consequences.[61]

Without effective and reliable forms of communication, distributing authority to employees distanced by months of travel left merchants and corporations struggling to enforce their wishes.[62] As well as relying on communal governance through shared expectations and practices, many companies sought to alleviate this challenge by creating their own specific regulations that members and employees had to follow.[63] The privilege to make laws was often found within corporate charters, giving these private organisations considerable amounts of legal authority.[64] The East India Company's charter, for instance, specified that the corporation could 'make, ordain & constitute such & so many reasonable laws, constitutions, orders and ordinances' that it deemed necessary 'for good government of the said company'.[65] In turn, corporate conceptions of bad mercantile behaviour could quickly become punishable activity.[66] By establishing 'laws and standing orders', each company could establish a distinct 'governing regime over its own servants' that could be adapted to the specific conditions of their overseas activity.[67] Thus, when the Merchant Adventurers insisted their 'ordinances were enforced in all places where the Merchant Adventurers had privileges' and only 'where there is no ordinance in the fellowship the law of England shall take place', no one batted an eyelid.[68] Similarly, any merchant who joined the New England Company, or who sought to trade to the American colony, placed themselves under the authority of directors who could 'correct, punish and govern all sorts of people', whether simply 'adventurers in any voyage thither or inhabiting there'.[69] Imposing such regulations was a constant challenge for corporations, but they did offer some means of mitigating issues of time and distance between employer and employee.

Expected to oversee the orderly conduct of English merchants, corporations often spent considerable efforts attempting to manage precisely where, when and how their members did business. Sometimes this could take the form of specific requirements for conducting trade, such as the Levant Company's insistence that the merchant Edward James could not carry any woollen cloth to Petra or Smyrna, and at other times it related to the monitoring of standards.[70] Such prescriptions could be very detailed, such as when the Eastland Company chose to establish a mart town at Elbing. This meant that members were forbidden to 'transport, convey or deliver any goods ... directly or indirectly to any other place than the town of Elbing' in Poland, but could still 'trade and traffic into and with the Kingdoms of Denmark, Norway and Sweden and the towns of Rye and Revel' so long as they returned directly to England afterwards. Contravening this order would result in fines to the 'value of 6s 8d sterling upon every pound sterling of all such goods'.[71] How standards were enforced also varied in strictness and coverage, from Southampton's urban corporation punishing John Sanders for selling low-quality 'tall wood' and 'the evil marking of the same wood' to the Spanish Company's attempt to make its consuls monitor members across the entire Iberian Empire and ensure all goods 'which shall have any likeness with the goods of Holland' be registered with Spanish authorities.[72] Overseas, this meant employees were being monitored by senior figures appointed by corporate groups resident in key trading regions. By appointing overseers in foreign ports, companies sought to assist their members with their trade and ensure they did not act in a manner unbecoming to the corporation. Officers in the Eastland Company, for example, were expected to inform the governor and deputy about bad behaviour by other members.[73] In this way, corporations could offer a means to 'reform the abuses' of private traders who mixed good and bad quality products.[74] Through corporations, apprentices, factors and fully fledged merchants alike were monitored to ensure orderly trade and maintain standards.

Agreeing to work for a merchant, join a company or enter an apprenticeship meant agreeing to abide by the expectations of the commercial community regarding good mercantile behaviour, as well as following the specific orders that your employer, corporation or master might issue. This was reflected in contractual agreements and social efforts to enforce standards. For instance, in the Eastland Company, any sons, servants or apprentices deemed disorderly could immediately be dismissed from service; while the young William Harte lived under threat that if he was 'obstinately disobedient' or did not 'fully and duly fulfil the whole term of his service', he would lose out on a £500 inheritance.[75] Other factors operated under conditions specified in bonds, whereby they would forfeit a specified sum of money if they failed to undertake business as instructed. In the East India Company, upon their appointment, factors would 'give in bonds for their truth and good behaviour' that ranged from £500 for the first level of factors who would lead the expedition to 100 pence for the most junior fourth sort of factor.[76]

When regulations and orders were not followed, corporate oversight meant that perpetrators were quickly disciplined – whether overseas or in England – and fines, dismissal and imprisonment were all common punishments. For example, during a concerning string of napkin thefts from the Mercers' livery company, its directors initially

THE ART OF MERCHANDISING

concluded that the butler did it, but after further investigation discovered that one Oliver Cogram was the culprit and 'he was dismissed from the service of the company'.[77] Samuel Grosse faced worse punishment after he committed fraud in Great Yarmouth, and having 'counterfeited the towns best brand of herring', the offending trader was immediately imprisoned.[78] Another merchant, William Craddock, was apprehended while transporting 270 kerseys (coarse woollen cloths) from London to Hamburg and on to Middelburg by the 'Society of Merchant Adventurers there residing', who accused him of trading contrary to the company's charter. To Craddock's great disgust, he was 'imprisoned in the common gaol among felons and criminal offenders', where he would wait until he had paid £180.[79] Senior merchants were not immune either and when John Robinson was found 'in contempt of the good rules and ordinance of his said company and of this city' after refusing to act as warden in his livery company, the City of London had no qualms about imprisoning him at Newgate 'until he shall conform himself'.[80]

Failing to meet the behavioural standards of the community was similarly a punishable offence. In Southampton, the port's corporation chastised Thomas Jackson 'about certain reproachful and slanderous words which his wife should speak unto Mr Dalby against Mr Nevey and his wife'.[81] Similarly, Daniel Veale was fined 7d after he 'called the said John Bigges knave', an uncivil action 'contrary to the ancient orders and customs of this town'.[82] In London, in one dramatic instance, during a dispute over a cart, William Merrick 'with the help of others his assistant' had 'assaulted the said Master and Wardens of his company', threatening 'to draw his knife upon them, and through violence and by force took the cart away from them'. The incident was reported to the City of London and Merrick was imprisoned in Newgate.[83] Worse still, when Edward Beadle, the apprentice of Humphrey Clarke, was caught acting 'very insolently and contemptuously against the authority of the Lord Mayor', vandalising city proclamations with 'a picture of a gallows and of a man hanging on the same, and also used unfitting speech', he was whipped as punishment.[84]

– 31 –

When a servant of Stephen Thomson complained about his master 'for hard usage, namely by keeping him in prison' for three weeks, he was in turn condemned for 'misspending of his goods, from absenting himself from his service, for lying out of his house' and, worst of all, 'for keeping lewd women's company'. After a long debate, the Clothworkers' livery company's directors agreed that the servant should 'submit himself to his said master, acknowledge his faults, and ask forgiveness of him for his lewd behaviour'. Their only request of Thomson was that in future he bring his complaint to the company first before imprisoning his servant.[85] It seems likely, in this circumstance, that the 'lewd' behaviour of the servant was a deciding factor in the company's justification of his punishment – such activity could reflect badly on the whole society.

Ensuring members did not damage the corporate relationship with local actors meant strict measures were taken against members who acted poorly while overseas. Members of the Merchant Adventurers were discouraged from playing 'either at dice or cards or tables', and gambling in public elicited large fines. They were further forbidden to fight or quarrel '(except in his own defence) with any stranger', and here, too, the punishment was sizeable; a freeman of the company would be fined £20 and servants and apprentices banned from practising the trade overseas for three years and only readmitted after paying a fine of £100. Beyond offending local sensibilities and damaging commercial relationships, immoral activities were also seen as a direct cause of bad business. Thus, in response to what was likely a widespread practice, the Merchant Adventurers enacted a rule that none of their members 'use unreasonable or excessive drinking' to provoke others to pledge. In a similar vein, the company combated the temptations many members might have felt, living for years or decades overseas, by insisting 'no married man of this fellowship shall keep or hold any harlot, light or evil disposed woman or abuse himself with any such'. If a married member was caught three times in this position he would be expelled from the company. Unmarried members would not be expelled but would face fines increasing with each offence 'and be further punished at the discretion of the court'. Any

THE ART OF MERCHANDISING

merchant who dared go further and actually 'married a foreign woman' was immediately disenfranchised from the company. In this case, it was not the threat of offending the host community that concerned the company, but the risk of the merchant joining it.[86]

As corporations evolved to take on extensive military, administrative and imperial roles on the global stage, they took care to ensure their ability to enforce their will did too. They obtained privileges both to broaden the parameters of their control (which could mean bringing whole populations under their government) and to increase their authority to create and enforce their orders.[87] When it was chartered in 1600, for example, the East India Company obtained privileges to punish transgressors through 'pain, punishment and penalties', and the only restriction on the company's actions was that they be 'reasonable and not contrary or repugnant to laws, statutes, or customs of this our realm'.[88] This was later deemed insufficient and in 1610 the company obtained commissions from the crown for fleet commanders to have 'the power to execute martial law during the voyage' in order to punish serious offences such as murder or mutiny.[89] In 1613, when this, too, was considered inadequate, the company's governor Sir Thomas Smith wrote to a judge of the Admiralty, Sir Daniel Dunn, arguing that disobedience and lack of order risked entire fleets, with ships, men and goods liable to 'be utterly cast away, to the great loss' of the company and, without greater control, of the public more generally.[90] By 1615, the company had obtained permission to grant 'martial law'-type commissions to their employees independently of the state and in 1623 granted the same authority to leading merchants overseeing factories in Asia.[91] Over time, these practices were extended further, sometimes alongside the acquisition of territorial possessions that would be administered by the corporation. By 1650, East India Company rule over populations in sites such as Fort St George in India led to the imposition of this one company's law not only over its English employees, but also over a growing population of local people.[92] Having been intended initially to mitigate the disorderly actions of English merchants damaging relations

– 33 –

with trading partners overseas, efforts to regulate people across the world increasingly blurred the lines between trade and empire.

WRITING, RECORD KEEPING AND ACCOUNTABILITY

For merchants, apprentices and factors living overseas, ensuring that they operated effectively within the administrative apparatus that constituted international trade was a vital part of their day-to-day experience. In addition to needing to manage, regulate and control behaviour, English merchants depended on accurate information – both in corporate environments and in the operations of individual traders. Keeping track of mercantile activities was only possible through sophisticated book-keeping practices, and accounting records were vital for the functioning of corporate and private trade in early modern England.[93] A strength of corporate management was its effectiveness in supporting institutions to maintain, comprehend and control vast networks of correspondence, commercial accounts and ordered lists of stock, prices and other market data.[94] To manage their activities effectively, merchants developed systematic approaches to the generation and control of information, primarily to ensure easy access to records but also, to varying degrees, to maintain effective monopolies over material related to their trades.

With this in mind, as well as advising how to operate in overseas markets, the *Merchants Avizo* took care to provide young merchants with a guide to the vital administrative tasks of writing letters, bonds, receipts, certificates of lading and other essential paperwork. Such items could be very thorough: when Henry Addes released George Mortimer from 'all and all manner of actions, suits, pleas, costs, charges, debts, debates, quarrels, trespasses, reckonings, accounts, sum and sums of money, bonds, bills, specialties, judgements, executions and demands', he did so 'from the beginning of the world until the day of the date hereof' – but more often than not they followed fairly standard patterns.[95] Key responsibilities for agents included dealing with the administration of overseas trade,

– 34 –

THE ART OF MERCHANDISING

a duty that was essential for merchants to be able to operate effectively on a global scale.[96] William Appowell, for instance, delegated the essential task of accounting in what was a fairly limited trading operation to his apprentice, who noted in the ledger 'payments paid by the hand of my master'.[97] Even for relatively simple commercial ventures, such as those of a single merchant, it could be difficult to micro-manage all aspects of business and apprentices were expected to contribute to commercial administration.

Keeping accurate accounts was essential for merchants to keep track of their international operations, and common standards were maintained across the commercial community.[98] Such material could be kept in relation to a single voyage, such as Jarvis Wylde's accounts of a trading voyage to Andalusia (he employed a fairly simple technique detailing what he 'owed', what he was 'due' and his 'charges'), or serve an individual's or company's business over years or even decades.[99] Thomas Gresham's (Plate 1) accounting records reveal much about how merchants operated.[100] Carefully collated from numerous journals and placed 'into the great book called the ledger', Gresham's wide-ranging activities were detailed in 'pounds, shillings and pence of money of England'. To ensure their accuracy and creditability, Gresham recalled how they were 'written with my own hand, or else with the hand of my apprentice Thomas Bradshaw'. In this way, Gresham drew together records from diverse geographies covering different types of activity, thereby providing a holistic view of his business and demonstrating the ways commercial endeavours across the world came together and related to each other in early modern London.[101] In addition to the exchange of goods, effective accounting could also keep track of financial arrangements – even if, as in the case of one Mr Martin, it could only do so much as allow a division between good and 'sundry bad debts'.[102] Accounts might not always be pleasant reading for their owners, but it was impossible to live without them.

Richard Archdale, a London merchant and draper, kept particularly thorough accounts for his wide-ranging trading interests that allowed him to monitor his far-flung affairs carefully.[103] Running continuously

– 35 –

from November 1623 to June 1630, Archdale's accounts reveal the complexity of early modern commercial operations and show the large amount of paperwork required to take advantage of international opportunities.[104] In addition to purchasing goods from other merchants to sell in London, Archdale participated in organising voyages himself, sending numerous ships to ports across the European Atlantic seaboard, the Mediterranean and to Asia through his investment in the East India Company.[105] To oversee these interests, Archdale managed his accounts judiciously, with records of not just the movement of goods between Archdale and other merchants but also transfers of cash across different parts of his business and the payment of taxes and impositions. For every transaction, he noted the people involved, the volume and quality of goods, financial arrangements and value in the local currency, while the total value for each transaction was recorded in a separate column, in pound sterling. Whether the purchase of thirty-seven pieces of Welsh cottons from John Griffiths of London, two Kentish cloths from Stephen Austin or sixty-six northern kerseys bought off Henry Wilson, recording standards remained the same.[106] To keep track of profits and losses over time, Archdale settled his accounts every few months by converting all of his receipts into cash outgoings and all payments into cash. This allowed him to keep a single 'cash account' that collated information from across his extensive trading organisation.[107] With large numbers of usually small transactions as well as the occasional larger financial move, keeping track of goods, cash, debit and credit across a diverse portfolio of interest was essential. When used properly, documentary material like this provided all the information necessary for a merchant or company to oversee even the most complex trading arrangements and relationships, but maintaining such high standards could be challenging.

Lying at the heart of commercial enterprises in early modern England, accounting records were monitored carefully to ensure standards were met and bad practice avoided – at least in theory. Standards were an important measure of creditability within the commercial community, and private merchants might share their account books with trusted partners to demonstrate their good business practices. For example, Nicholas Osborne agreed to 'make and give a just, true and perfect account or accounts' that would be available to his partner 'at all times and from time to time within one month next after demand'.[108] Similarly, when the London merchant George Mole agreed to invest £1,000 in Benedict Webb's rapeseed oil manufacturing operation in Kingswood, their articles of agreement specified that a 'just, true, plain and perfect reckoning and account in writing' must be kept throughout their partnership.[109]

The same held true in corporations, where it was treasurers' responsibility to ensure accounts could be presented for perusal, usually to select directors but sometimes to the generality.[110] The Clothworkers' livery company, for example, kept different volumes for recording the varied forms of information deemed necessary for the company's interests. These included 'the accounts of the quarter and renter wardens', a book specifically to record 'loan money and the bonds thereupon' and a black book that was kept to record all debtors.[111] In the East India Company, the organisation's *Lawes and Standing Orders* stated that treasurers should 'keep fair books of accounts' that would be 'audited once every quarter at the least'.[112] The first General Accountant of the company was chosen for his highly esteemed reputation, and his replacement, Christopher Lanman, was 'applauded as one of the most perfect and sufficient accountants in London'.[113]

In normal circumstances, these stringent practices meant that merchants could easily demonstrate that their conduct had been creditable. For instance, following the death of the Manchester merchant William Buckley, whose estate included numerous shared obligations with his partner Thomas Rode, 'all the particulars whereof are mentioned and comprised in their books of accounts', it was a fairly easy task for the executors of his will to reach an agreement about the division of assets.[114] Similarly, when the Earl of Carlisle entered into a partnership with the four merchants 'Mr Johnson, Mr Thomson,

MERCHANTS

Mr Roberts and Mr Tucker' in 1640 and complained that 'being absent and not satisfied with their proceedings desired to have an account', they were able to produce one.[115] Through the establishment and application of high standards of recording and reporting vital information, the commercial community was able to function effectively.

Failing to produce valid records, by contrast, could often be damaging. In one striking example, Robert Draper's accounting was as best poor and at worst fraudulent. A merchant accused of owing money to fellow trader William Harwarde and his wife, Draper agreed to supply his accounts for perusal – at which point they were discovered to be 'all differing the one from the other' and drawn from 'new books of account' he had made 'in the space of three weeks whereas the old would have served'. This was exacerbated by the new accounts being 'tedious and difficult' to read and unsuitable for presentation to the commissioners who were overseeing the dispute. Yet, no resolution was forthcoming; Draper maintained he would make no payment until they could prove the debt, which the Harwardes maintained 'we by no means can do without the books of account'.[116] Draper's failure to produce the valid material made the Harwardes instantly suspicious, and while it made it difficult for them to prove their case, it would have damaged his reputation and standing too.

Fraud was also alleged during a dispute between the East India Company and the Muscovy Company treasurer Benjamin Discrowe, who had received bills for £740 11s 8d from John Kirby and William Harrison. While both sides in this case had access to the original documents, disagreement emerged due to ambiguity in precisely what the exchange had been intended to pay for. Kirby and Harrison, with support from the East India Company, insisted that the funds had been intended for payment into a new joint-stock fund they were operating with the Muscovy Company. They said that Discrowe had approached them 'privately and without the knowledge, privity, consent or allowance of either of the said companies' to receive bills that should have been paid directly to the joint stock's treasurer, Robert Batemen. This action had

– 38 –

THE ART OF MERCHANDISING

encouraged Kirby and Harrison to pay their shares, unnecessarily, for a second time, and they condemned Discrowe for 'some secret plot and combination' for which the merchants demanded restitution.[117]

Discrowe was not cowed by the accusation and, taking the fight to the two companies, argued that it was the East India Company rather than himself that had tricked the Muscovy Company and its members into participating in a joint stock, 'which was to the great dislike of diverse of the said Russia Company'. He condemned the agreement as 'done by some direction from his Majesty but not by the voluntary consent of the said company'. This left dissatisfied members ('the old adventurers'), including himself, in a position whereby selling 'most of their goods as well in Russia as in Greenland together with their house here in London to the said joint company' was the only option. This deal, he asserted, had been worth '£37,000 or thereabouts', details of which appeared in the 'journal book of the said joint company' – a sum that included the funds owed by Kirby and Harrison, 'so that the East India Company have no just cause to complain of the assigning out of the said bills of debt'. While the East India Company might claim the sums were part of their new joint stock, Discrowe was adamant that he had received them as the long-standing treasurer of the independent Muscovy Company, 'that these bills were made in this defendants own name for the use of the said Russia Company' and that Kirby and Harrison had 'willingly signed and sealed the said bills'. By insisting that 'he did make out these bills lawfully and honestly without any respect to his own lucre or gain, and without any intent to defraud', Discrowe left the East India Company little room to manoeuvre.[118] In writing at least, it seemed clear that Discrowe had done nothing wrong, and in the merchant community it was what could be proven in writing that mattered.

The Merchant Adventurers to Greenland, an association of forty-one London merchants, found out exactly how difficult providing proof could be when a sale of whale oil fell apart. Having appointed three members, John Williams, William Cockayne and James Young, to oversee the transaction, they met with the soap boilers Thomas Overman

– 39 –

and Edward Whitwell 'to further treat and conclude for buying of the same' – eventually agreeing a £14,500 deal. Following standard practice, 'for the better settling the said agreement [the group] did reduce their said bargain into writing'. However, rather than each side keeping a copy, on this occasion the contract was kept only by Overman and Whitwell. This arrangement turned out to be a mistake, and when the first payment was due, the two soap boilers refused to honour the agreement, denying the contract had been made at all.[119] Having failed to maintain their own records of the transaction, the London merchants had little recourse but to ask the Chancery Court to force the documents 'to be relieved therein according to justice and equity' and for Overman and Whitwell to deliver 'the said agreement: in writing, or otherwise set forth upon their oaths where the same is, whether in bag sealed or in chest locked'.[120] Inability, or unwillingness, to produce material relating to commercial transactions could make it very difficult for actors to enforce contracts without the other party's cooperation.

Proof was not lacking in another case, when the Clothworkers' livery company were left with no doubt about the fraudulent accounting practices of a former warden, William Hunter. The company's leadership received a report that Hunter had received an 8s bribe from another member, William Troman, to incorrectly report that his membership fees had been received. Rather than denying the accusation, Hunter 'used diverse frivolous allegations to excuse himself' and was found guilty of 'a thing very unseemly for a man in his place, disgraceful to the company and a foul misdemeanour'. In addition to punishing Hunter by forcing him to publicly acknowledge his crime, the company altered its regulations, agreeing that all future wardens would have to enter into a bond of £50 upon appointment as a guarantee for keeping 'true accounts'.[121] The reputation of the company was at risk from the former warden's misbehaviour, and it was vital to show that it could self-regulate more effectively to regain lost trust.

Incompetence and poor accounting standards could be as damaging as outright fraud, making it impossible for organisations or individuals

THE ART OF MERCHANDISING

to effectively monitor and understand their commercial activities. For instance, when the Mercers' livery company sought to respond to requests from Richard Vernon, their agent for its plantation in Ireland, they were forced to postpone discussions about the colony after the company's clerk admitted they could not find the necessary information about the corporation's holdings in its books.[122] Similarly, during a long-running dispute with Mr Mellyn about what he deemed excessive waste of corporate funds, the East India Company discovered its treasurer, Mr Robinson, was unable to present the account books to the court.[123] If this was not bad enough, another accountant admitted that the accounts had not been updated for the previous five months.[124] The corporation's inability to present its accounts made this dispute more difficult to resolve, damaging the company's image in the process. Here, too, efforts were made to protect against future errors: accounts were more carefully audited, and faults quickly addressed. Thus, when one of the company directors reported an issue a few years later, the new treasurer, Mr Woodall, quickly found all his records under scrutiny as they were reassessed.[125]

Without ensuring the quality of records, it was impossible to maintain effective oversight of activities or defend decision-making processes. This was made clear in another dispute within the East India Company, when news reached the directors, from the treasurer of the company, that some members of the corporation were unhappy and questioned whether the treasurer's accounts were trustworthy.[126] With the officers of the company themselves under suspicion, the distrustful members suggested that some members of the generality should be invited to audit the accounts on the generality's behalf. This was deemed too great a risk, as giving access to privileged information that could be 'divulged abroad' might result in damage to the company. Instead, supporters of the company's current practices argued that the auditors already appointed to review the books were 'gentleman of such sufficiency and without exceptions of partiality' that they would 'satisfy any reasonable person'.[127] Quite reasonably, the company's membership were not

– 41 –

satisfied with this answer, raising the issue again at a consequent meeting and eventually agreeing a compromise. Four or six members of the generality would be given permission to assess the accounts – enough to confirm their validity without removing the protections in place to keep information safe.[128] Even within a corporation, trust between merchants sometimes had to be reinforced and renewed.

In the early modern period, merchants depended on their written records and accounts, not only to understand their own business but also to reassure partners, resolve disputes and demonstrate their creditability to the wider commercial community.[129] It is therefore unsurprising that they took great pains to regulate record-keeping processes effectively. Audits and other forms of review were regularly applied to ensure the validity of accounts. For instance, the Merchant Adventurers of York appointed assessors about every five years who would record errors in the company accounts, such as missing payments for freedoms, impositions and debts, as well as items missing from the shared stock.[130] In the Mercers' livery company, an audit was undertaken 'from year to year' on 'the 4th and 5th of November to the end [that] there may be a day of examination of all particulars concerning the accounts and [a] report to be made the second day unto the company according to custom'.[131] Following a case where members of the Eastland Company believed funds were being misspent, they demanded that in future the accounts should be displayed publicly at least once each year.[132] Through these means, corporations and merchants alike hoped to demonstrate the validity of their accounts and, consequently, their own trustworthiness.

The auditors who undertook these assessments could be appointed in various ways. In the Levant Company, they were chosen from among the corporation's directors, while in the Merchant Venturers of Bristol, members of the generality reviewed accounts.[133] In the Drapers' livery company, senior members were selected, such as Mr Garraway, Mr Goddard and Mr Moore who undertook this role in 1588, all of whom would later serve as wardens or masters of the company.[134] Less regularly,

– 42 –

external auditors were appointed, although these could be expensive and would gain access to potentially privileged information about a company's activities.[135] Sometimes intensive affairs, audits required considerable time as well as financial skills, especially when cross-referencing information across an array of different records. For example, when Mr Heard and Mr Bishop audited the Mercers' livery company, they reported 'that having taken pains therein' they had found errors with the previous treasurer's cash book and 'declared that they found the reconciliation of the said books to be a matter of great labour' and required more time. After two more days of work they agreed that a payment of £409 18s 9d was required to settle the difference between the books.[136]

As well as maintaining standards, auditors might be expected to oversee financial disputes between members by drawing on their expert knowledge. For example, when Mr Gorsuch overpaid his rent, the Mercers' livery company ordered that 'the difference between Mr Smith and Mr Gorsuch touching 40s demanded by the said Mr Gorsuch' should be 'referred to the auditors'. Smith was a company officer and acted on their behalf with tenants, and perhaps in defence of this company man, Gorsuch was accused during the audit of a litany of misdemeanours that caused the delayed payment of 40s – most notably that he had not moved his corn from the company's warehouse which was 'endangered to be tainted with the weevil'. Eleven months after the first complaint, they concluded that Gorsuch was indeed owed 40s, but also, handily, discovered that Smith too was owed 40s by the company due to the cost of his travel to Horsham in the intervening months. In the end, 'Mr Warden Bladwell now paid unto Mr Smith for his said charges 40s which the said Mr Smith presently paid to Mr Gorsuch whereby he is satisfied'.[137] As this case suggests, records were maintained to ensure accountability, but they were interpreted within an environment whereby preserving behavioural standards and good reputation could mitigate or aggravate the way in which they were applied. As well as sources of information, such records represented a textual character of early modern traders, able to reveal to the world whether they were creditable, behaved well, and where they sat within the wider community.

As well as being subject to systems that ensured their accuracy, the records, accounts and legal documents that underpinned the privileges and creditability of individual merchants and their companies were carefully protected. When Sir Thomas Heath and Nicholas Heath, who traded to Spain and northern Europe, became partners, they elected to deposit their shared records 'into the custody of the [Mercers'] company [in] one box of writing'. Their agreement specified that the 'box is locked with two locks and keys, whereof either of them hath one key' and could 'not to be opened till both of them or their assigns come'. To ensure its safety, the Mercers' livery company agreed to keep the box in the corporate treasury 'where the common seal is'.[138] The same livery company undertook a similar role for the Merchant Adventurers by allowing them to deposit 'a white box to be kept here in safe custody' that contained a copy of an indenture signed by officers of the trading company. It would be kept 'in the chest with the [Mercers'] company's common seal' and opened only for those with 'sufficient reason for the viewing of the same'.[139]

For corporations, the charters that confirmed their particular powers and privileges, including permission for them to act as a company in the first place, were perhaps the most important document they possessed.[140] Access to, and the security of, these items was controlled very carefully. While they were occasionally used publicly, such as when the Spanish Company's new charter 'containing five skins of vellum' was 'was openly read in presence of the assistants and generality there present', more often than not they were locked away.[141] Accordingly, Bristol's Merchant Venturers presented its new charter to the generality only briefly before it was deposited in a secure chest.[142] Here, it joined a collated volume of all legal documents relating to the company in a book that 'contains the copies of the charters, ordinances and acts of the master, wardens and commonality' from 1373 onwards, which was used for regular reference rather than the original documents.[143] Other companies had

– 44 –

THE ART OF MERCHANDISING

similar strategies: the Eastland Company decided to keep its great seal and charter in a chest while allowing the deputy to hold the common seal for day-to-day use, and the Merchant Adventurers of York allowed the company's master to keep important texts personally before passing them directly to his successor.[144]

Alongside charters, a merchant's or corporation's power stemmed from their seal and identifying marks; these lent validity to their bills of exchange, orders and letters through which wide-ranging commercial interests were managed.[145] So, when George Hyde requested William Cockayne 'deliver to this bearer, my servant Thomas Garret, the sum of six thousand pounds', he was careful to highlight the authority of an attached seal and 'this my handwriting' that together would be enough to demonstrate the validity of the request.[146] Such seals were chosen carefully, as they were, in some respects, the face of a corporation. When the Spanish Company chose a new seal, it made sure it 'was liked and allowed' by the generality before a design 'made only with the escutcheon of the company's arms' was approved.[147] To stop them being used erroneously, corporations kept seals under similar conditions to their charters. The Company of Merchants Inhabiting in Kingston upon Hull ensured theirs was 'kept in the hands of Mr Governor', whereas in the Drapers' livery company, when meetings requiring important items ended, 'the said common seal was put again in the chest in the treasury and the same locked according to order'.[148] Merchants and corporations alike depended on their seals to lend credence to the documentation that underpinned early modern commerce.

Seals, signatures and other identifying markers helped facilitate trusted communication between employers and their agents. For corporations, this might be given further weight through the presentation of correspondence as originating from the whole company, rather than a single member. In the Spanish Company for instance, rather than being sent from an individual merchant, letters were often 'sent as from the whole body politic', to lend weight and demonstrate the communal structure of corporate organisations.[149] Attempts were also made to ensure

– 45 –

effective communications by asking senior merchants in towns or factories overseas to write letters together; the Eastland Company ordered 'no letter shall be written from Elbing from the company there' unless it was 'subscribed by the deputy and 6 or 4 of the assistants at the least'.[150]

However, writing to their agent John Rowley in Ireland, for instance, the Drapers' company revealed the challenges of maintaining contact with employees overseas despite efforts to ensure the reliability of any individual letter. After Rowley had 'wrote unto us that you marvelled that of long time you have not heard from us, nor have received any answer of the several letters which you have sent', the company grew concerned. Having sent three letters in the previous months, they worried whether their correspondence had been 'miscarried or been interrupted'. They had entrusted the delivery of the letters to the directors of the Irish Society and hoped that Rowley would 'think us not so careless in a matter of such moment, as either to neglect or not to regard our charge' in writing to him, assuring him that in future they would take measures to ensure the delivery of letters, choosing to send 'them by a special messenger of our own who is recommended to us for a very honest man'.[151] Similarly, merchants in Morocco were outraged when John Symcotte, on reaching the region, had opted not to deliver letters, 'most or all were opened and delivered a long time after their arrival'. The abused parties went so far as to request aid from the privy council 'for preventing of evil manners and doings against the commonwealth'.[152]

To avoid such abuses, in the Merchant Adventurers it was not permitted for members to 'withhold, embezzle, or keep by him any letters, request or writing directed or sent or otherwise pertaining to the fellowship' and any such correspondence was expected to be passed to the company without fail. Any member who 'shall of malice or evil intent intercept or break up the letters of any other of the fellowship' was fined £50 and expelled from the company immediately.[153] Similarly, any member of the Eastland Company found to have withheld company books faced immediate expulsion.[154] Ensuring a steady flow of information was essential for individual merchants and corporations alike, and while protecting privileged information was commonplace within companies, the rights of members and private merchants to safely correspond was vigorously protected.

Sending letters, accounts and other forms of written information was key for English merchants seeking to undertake trade overseas or at home.[155] These letters often followed a similar format, including information about a merchant's travel, local news, market conditions, current activities and, of course, gossip about other merchants. For instance, while travelling into Russia on behalf of the Muscovy Company, the merchant Thomas Smith took on the part of factor for Sir John Leveson, who had asked him to sell pearls on his behalf. On arrival Smith wrote 'I understand there is little sale for them in this place' but promised to try again in Moscow. Expanding on this problem, he reported that many of the prices Leveson was expecting were too high, as the market preferred 'bored' pearls. Smith suggested that he would have more luck having them bored before selling them. In either case, Leveson would have to deliver them by the end of April the following year so that they 'may be sent me by the first ships'. If further information was required, Smith assured Leveson that he could be reached through 'my man either at Nettlestead or at Mr Crispe's house . . . in London from time to time'.[156] In the same way, when John Cockayne wrote to William Cockayne in 1624, he detailed how he had delivered a letter on behalf of his uncle, and that the recipient had enquired after William's health. As well as providing updates about business in London, the young merchant suggested his cousin – another William – would be suitable for employment, in part because of his ability to provide 'all the news out of Poland'.[157] Even when they served no commercial purpose, the exchange of information through letters helped reassure and strengthen social bonds. When Elizabeth Smith wrote to her son asking that he 'will not forget a mother that longs to hear when you endured to your journey's end', she was clear she expected a reply that included 'observation of all things worthy note as if you were a traveller in a foreign country'.[158]

– 47 –

MERCHANTS

Letters from Thomas Rogers sent over three years from Surat, Masulipatnam and Golconda to his uncle William Hurt, reveal how merchants' letters blurred the lines between the personal and professional.[159] Rather than maintaining a single, principal–agent relationship with the East India Company in England, Rogers was part of a much more dynamic network of communication and exchange. Through his letters, the young factor shared his personal experiences with Hurt. For example, he apologised for not writing sooner 'but being unaccustomed to the seas it pleased god that I was recently afflicted with sea sickness which continued with me almost three months'.[160] Three years later he informed his uncle that he was 'in good health of body and want for nothing, yet destitute of Englishmen's company, by reason that God called from the misery of this sinful world my second, one Mr William Favour'.[161] As well as sharing information about his health and happiness, Rogers told Hurt how 'in my letter to my mother I have wrote to entreat her to send me, by the first opportunity, a case of paper books fitting for a journal and ledger'.[162]

Yet, alongside this personal correspondence, Rogers also carefully maintained his duties to the company and its investors, taking care always to record the specifics of his business activities. Thus, his uncle was able to learn that after taking on a role overseeing the company's trade between Persia and Surat, Rogers had sought to build on relationships with local actors, having been 'solicited by the Duke of Shiraz'. He also learned of the challenges of maintaining these relationships – in this case because the Persian 'King, being discontented with some action of the Duke's, caused him to be cut in pieces'.[163] Over the following two years, Rogers oversaw the transport of 40,000 ryalls worth of gold and goods and had a further 20,000 ryalls worth in Persia, and complained that the company must send more ships to Persia to take advantage of the privileges granted by the Safavid Shah. After Hunt 'wrote to me for some carpets and quilts', Rogers warned he 'would gladly send you but truly you would not be contented at their prices' and would therefore wait for further instruction.[164] Letters like these

– 48 –

contained an array of valuable business information as well as serving as a means of maintaining structures of trust and reputation upon which the commercial community depended.

These same writing traditions were maintained within corporate environments, where agents were expected to undertake carefully monitored communication regimes with their employers. As William Baffin put it, after spending time in the employment of the North West Passage Company, 'seeing I have been employed and have reaped some profit from your purses, I might be counted a very bad servant if I grace not in some account how we spent our time'.[165] In other circumstances, letters might reflect general opinions regarding the state of trade. The factor of James Gibson, a Scottish merchant, wrote from London towards the end of the Civil War that, in spite of recent difficulties, 'the greatest part of honest persons believe now business in all places [is] in a reasonable good condition'.[166] Perhaps more practicably, when Thomas Kerridge wrote to the East India Company from Ahmadabad in 1613 he covered topics that ranged from local weather and politics to the impact of decreased Portuguese shipping on indigo prices – 'their best flat indigo that was worth to be sold for 18 rupees now offered for 14 rupees'.[167] As this kind of information was received, employers could reassess market conditions, make decisions and send out yet more letters to issue new instructions to their agents overseas.

In most normal circumstances, merchants were able to share their own letters, journals and other documents as they pleased, but restrictions were in place to ensure that those operating within corporate environments did not reveal secrets or harm trading advantage. In early modern England, news could travel very quickly through spoken communication and developing networks of written news.[168] Controlling what was said and written by private individuals was a considerable challenge and corporations used various methods to try to do so. Alongside instructions for trade in Asia, new factors in the East India Company, for instance, were instructed to keep written accounts of all their activities, taking care to ensure that they were legible. On their return to England,

– 49 –

these materials were immediately deposited at company facilities in London.[169] Letters from factors were never opened in public, and the company was concerned with the possibility of letters being read publicly – especially at the Exchange.[170] Instead, letters were read in closed meetings of the directors, quickly copied into the company books and stored in the company headquarters where access was carefully restricted.[171] Even letters for third parties were seized and assessed by the company before being passed to their intended recipients.[172] Companies that opposed openly sharing information were able to control the release of information about the trade not only to the public but also even to the corporation's own members. Such levels of secrecy were useful as a means of control but were predominantly informed by fears that interlopers or foreign competitors would benefit from a more liberal attitude. Secrecy was a form of protection and reduced the possibility that people outside the trusted network at the heart of these organisations could access competitively sensitive business information.[173]

Once this information was collected, corporations took care to ensure it remained in the hands of the company and its members. Trade, whether local, regional or global, depended on an incredible array of written documentation.[174] To ensure the 'better and more safe keeping of the books, records and writings' returning from overseas, the Eastland Company ordered 'the same books and writings shall be from time to time put and kept in a sufficient chest'. This chest would have 'three several locks and keys to be severally kept by our deputy, treasurer and secretary' and would be kept 'in some convenient place in the deputy's house'.[175] For the Clothworkers' livery company, the corporation's counting house provided space 'where the writing, bonds and evidence belonging to this company be bestowed and laid', a site that could be accessed with a key passed from senior member to senior member at the time of their deaths.[176] In Southampton, during a dispute between the city's corporation and the Levant Company, it was agreed that copies of acts of parliament, 'and all other writings and papers which Mr Long [had] touching the sweet wines', would 'remain in

THE ART OF MERCHANDISING

Mr Longs hands till the suit between this town and the Turkey merchants be ended'.[177]

Access to these records was carefully restricted, to ensure that records were not misplaced or lost, but also to ensure that competitors were not able to obtain access to privileged information. The Mercers' livery company imposed regulations to ensure records were only viewed 'when it shall be behoveful, expedient for the company's service', related to bonds and debts, or when 'assistants, auditors, viewers and committees' had the specific consent of a warden to view specific documents.[178] When such items were accessed, they were quickly returned to their secure homes. The Eastland Company's well-locked chest, for instance, was kept sealed 'unless at any court there shall be occasion to use them, the which being done they are to be put back into the said chest again without any further delay'.[179]

As well as physical copies of information being kept under lock and key, efforts were also made to restrain the speech of corporate members. For instance, new East India Company directors were instructed not to speak of company matters when in public and the company's secretary was required to take an additional oath not to disclose any 'of the secrets of this company' or to copy any records for any individual director or member except 'by the authority of the [company's] court'.[180] Only the most senior members of the East India Company were allowed to borrow the books that recorded correspondence from its factors, although others were granted access within the company offices.[181] Yet, even with these restrictions, the company still felt it necessary to issue further warnings, reminding directors that no privileged information should be left in locations where a member of the generality could see them.[182] It was not always possible for the generality to gain access to these records even when they went through the appropriate channels, as members were sometimes denied access to restrict the possibilities of information being shared with the broader public. Over time, the records were restricted only to those with written permission from the directors, and even then, the directors decided that particularly important information could be

– 51 –

redacted in order to protect the trade.[183] Similarly, incoming secretaries of the Eastland Company swore under oath not to share sensitive information and to 'keep secret all matters had or talked and conferred in any court'.[184] Sharing this sort of information might make it more difficult for directors to enact new strategies or to prosecute court cases and it could damage the creditability of members and the corporations.

The generality was similarly expected to help ensure privileged information was not shared. Members of the Eastland Company were ordered not to 'utter or disclose any matter, motion, act or determination of any court either in England or beyond the seas to any one that is not of the assistants'. Anyone who did would face a £5 fine.[185] More strictly still, in Bristol the Merchant Venturers' regulations stated that 'if any brother of this society shall reveal or disclose any matter treated of, or passed, in court either general or assistant, to any person not being free of the company, to the hurt or annoyance of any of the company', they would face fines of increasing severity on each occasion.[186] In the Merchant Adventurers, members were restricted from making 'any retailer or unfreeman perfectly privy to his buying, or show him his letters of advice, invoices or accounts, or give advice of the price of foreign wares'.[187] The East India Company even appointed guards at general courts, who were responsible for ensuring the smooth running of meetings as well as deterring eavesdroppers and stopping intruders.[188] Monopoly privileges allowed many companies to set rates for goods in England, and it was unacceptable for members to undermine this market dominance. Merchants were expected to uphold the common wealth of the full membership, and sharing information with outsiders, whether socially or as part of a business deal, could undermine the value other members might be able to obtain for their goods or damage the reputation of a company and all its members. Such demands for secrecy were even more important where a company's control of information was central to their ongoing control of a market.

The East India Company struggled to come to terms with this dilemma when its own efforts to control sensitive information proved insufficient.

In one case, for example, it became clear that 'the business of these courts are published, and cannot be kept secret'. Fearing that competitors were learning important secrets, the company ordered 'the truth of these things examined and searched that it may be discovered by whom or by what means they have been published'.[189] Eventually, it was revealed that Thomas Mun, a key proponent of the company during public disputes about England's trade policy, had shared the information – though he was adamant that he had not released the information to damage the company.[190] Mun insisted he had acted to protect the company from damaging rumours about its business strategy and had only shared the information with a single contact, Mr Polsted, who then released the information to the broader public.[191] Polsted also defended his activities and reassured the directors that he, too, had passed this information to a single person and that they could retain trust in the organisation as 'it appeared that the business hath been carried fairly here'.[192] Although, in this circumstance, the fear of losing privileged information to competitors proved unfounded, the company's willingness to investigate its own members suggests the importance of controlling information in the early modern commercial community. Paradoxically, for a commercial community that relied on trust to function effectively, by carefully controlling information, merchants strengthened their relationships with partners while simultaneously maintaining security against competitors.

Publication of information by company members or associates that might damage relations with foreign rulers or merchants was also worthy of suppression. For the Muscovy Company, the 'fear a book lately set out by Mr Doctor Fletcher, dedicated to her majesty', would 'turn the company to some great displeasure with the emperor' was taken as a real threat. Concerned the publication would 'endanger both their people and goods', the company requested that all of the books be recalled and 'some course held therein signifying her majesty's dislike of the publishing of the same'. If the book was not withdrawn, the company thought the emperor might 'utterly overthrow the trade forever'.[193] The company's concern was not whether their former agent's book was

MERCHANTS

accurate or not; simply sharing information obtained within the privileged world of their activities was crime enough.

Despite the best efforts of merchants and corporations, poor judgement or lack of effective controls could mean that these records might be misplaced, destroyed or become inaccessible. This might be the result of foul play, such as the discovery in Southampton's corporate records 'that certain leaves of a book, part whereof the new orders concerning this town were written, were torn or cut out', but more commonly simply indicated poor administrative practices or accidental damage.[194] For instance, the governor of the East India Company, Thomas Smith, was forced to write an embarrassed letter to the timber supplier Henry Neville, as the company 'cannot as yet find the writing wherein you covenanted to deliver them 100 load of timber' but acknowledged that the goods had been received and payment would be issued 'as soon as they can find your note [and] send it to you'.[195] In a more dramatic breach of corporate security, it was discovered in 1619, when the New Merchant Adventurer and Spanish trader Thomas Dalby died, that he was in possession of 'diverse books' of the Mercers' livery company he had been keeping 'in his own house'. They were only identified by 'a note upon it showing that the same is belonging to the company' and were quickly taken back under the corporation's control.[196]

In 1630, a long-term breach of standards came to light when George Bruen, an East India Company factor, was accused of defrauding the estate of Henry Shanks for five years – keeping funds for himself that had been intended 'for the use and benefit of the hospital in Leith'. Although Shanks, in 1625, 'dying in Batavia entrusted' his estate to Bruen, depending on his fellow merchant to return his will and funds to England, this had not been done.[197] Instead, it was not until the return of another merchant, Thomas Robinson, from the region, that documents were delivered to the East India Company that demonstrated how Shanks' 'will and estate was for the space of 4 years concealed'. The corporation's failure to ensure the transmission of vital records between Asia and London had, in this case, effectively led to a situation where the merchants involved had been

– 54 –

THE ART OF MERCHANDISING

adversely affected, as had 'the poor of the said hospital', who now desperately sought restitution.[198] The inability of Shanks to communicate his wishes back to England effectively, and Bruen's unwillingness to conform to expected forms of behaviour regarding such information, resulted in a situation that, if allowed to happen too often, would have damaged the operations of English merchants the world over.

Through their efforts to maintain high standards of record keeping and information gathering, English merchants and companies could usually draw on an array of evidence during disputes. For instance, when the Mercers' livery company was approached by Mrs Bennet, who demanded 'copy of divers orders mentioned in a paper now by her exhibited', the company was able to instruct 'that the books shall be searched whether there be any such orders' and ascertain the veracity of Bennet's claims.[199] When Dutch commissioners claimed an historic right to impose a monopoly in the Spice Islands, the East India Company was quick to deploy material backing their own claims – starting with an account of Francis Drake's exploratory voyages in 1577. The final resolution delivered to Dutch envoys included testimonies from a number of witnesses who had been present on the earliest English voyages to the East Indies and their trade at Bantam and Ternate.[200] During a dispute between the Barbary Company and the King of Spain, whose ambassador had seized the English company's goods in Morocco, the merchants received additional material to support their case from Mulley Peydan, the King of Morocco. The African monarch wrote directly to James I, offering his testimony that dismissed Spanish claims that the goods were stolen and explained this 'indeed is not so, these men have gotten them by the true manner of trading'.[201]

That being said, holding the necessary information did not guarantee an easy ride. Richard Middleton, who shipped Silesian linen to Malaga, sent it 'with certificate out of the custom house of London in the form accustomed', but authorities in Seville rejected it for not having been underwritten by Pedro de Weitts, the King of Spain's agent in Hamburg. Malaga was also the destination for Joseph Brand's Essex-made

– 55 –

cloth, but despite a certificate of manufacture it was condemned as a Dutch product and seized.[202] In both cases, the changing dynamics of trade – brought about by renewed war between the United Provinces and Spain – led to sudden shifts in what was deemed acceptable certification by authorities overseas. Even following all the rules of merchandising, sometimes the luck of an early modern merchant could only go so far.

TWO

MANY BODIES CORPORATE

After almost twenty years of sending successful, hugely profitable voyages to Asia, the East India Company had become the stand-out corporation in early modern English trade – and some of its members were not happy at all. Yes, the company had reported profits on some voyages that surpassed 600 per cent. Yes, its factors had broken into markets ranging from Persia to Japan. Yes, its directors sat in the highest positions of power across London's civic and urban institutions. It did not matter. In one vital respect, the company's leadership had failed in the eyes of these members – it had kept them out of the corporation's highest echelons of power. In 1619, these members sought to have their due and demanded changes to the corporation's approach to management.

In the lead-up to the company's annual elections, normally decided by the raising of hands by members present, demands to change electoral procedure, including the time and place of the election to allow 'their friends to be present', were met with consternation and derision by the corporation's leadership. Rather than presented by fellow merchants, the appeal had been made by gentleman members, outsiders who had only 'been taken into the company by courtesy' and who seemingly failed to understand just what it meant to be part of a corporate organisation. To make matters worse, the group had demanded the use of a ballot box, an 'innovation and alteration in the government of the company' that was condemned as serving nothing but 'the endangering and subversion thereof' (Plate 12). The box was an opaque means to make decisions within a community built on trust between members. Decrying the disorderly gentlemen as too 'inexperienced to manage business' and unsuitable to govern, the company's directors made it their mission to ensure that their efforts to reform the company failed. Ensuring the corporation remained free of non-merchant influence was of paramount importance to them.

Later the same day, when the members of the company assembled for their 'General Court', their directors presented a united front. Sir Thomas Smith, the governor, welcomed the members and requested they 'be very considerate, and well advised in the elections to make choice of such as shall be fit to manage so great a business' – a not-so-subtle reminder of the experience and expertise of the current board. The meeting continued as a well-executed piece of political theatre. After opening the room for debate, Smith was met immediately by a request from John Digby 'to deliver a message from his Majesty'. The king, as luck would have it, was also concerned by the prospect of disorderly election and wanted to remind the generality that they were a collection of 'private merchants', who, together, were 'a great ornament and strength unto his kingdoms'. Rounding off with an endorsement of Smith and the current directors, who 'have been hitherto very good', the king's message was delivered with impeccable timing. The gentlemen dissenters' hopes for wholesale reform were quickly undone, but the generality was not entirely convinced on all counts. In an ensuing debate, questions about who was suitable to serve as director and for how long revealed deep divides. Some members argued that the board would benefit from the perspective of shopkeepers and gentlemen, others that too many shopkeepers were directors already. More still maintained that the lifestyle of a gentleman was not conducive to managing the business and that 'merchants, whose knowledge is most proper in merchandising affairs, can best judge of those things which may concern the good of the trade'. Concerns about how young members would gain vital skills as directors if not allowed 'to grow up with the rest in experience' gained traction, and proposals to ensure that more young merchants could take up the role were accepted. What had started as an attempt by gentlemen to seize authority ended with plans to safeguard the merchant community's greatest asset – their unique experience.

Despite their best efforts, gentlemen remained restricted from the highest management positions in the company. Although the company suggested this was because they lacked commercial nous, what they were really missing was an understanding of how the corporation functioned as a social organisation. The leaders of the East India Company and most of its members had been raised in corporate worlds, trained as merchants and lived as part of a commercial community that had its own customs, behaviours and accepted ways of doing business. For a while longer at least, the corporation would remain a place for merchants to conduct business as they saw fit.[1]

MERCHANTS AND CORPORATIONS

At the heart of England's trading and imperial activities was a merchant community that lived and worked in environments dominated by corporations. Whether in London, Bristol or Southampton, long-standing corporate traditions, promulgated through urban and livery corporations and trading companies alike, were an integral part of merchants' lives. Being part of a company was not just a job or a means to obtain dividends. It meant access to a whole world of social activities, business relationships, civic responsibilities – a whole new way of life.

In early modern England, corporations like these were not faceless, monolithic institutions imposing their singular will on the world. Corporations functioned as communities, with trust, reputation and good relationships essential for their success, and their members were not just investors or passive participants – they were engaged and proactive members of corporate communities that were an important part of their daily lives.[2] Even when corporations operated as functioning 'company-states', imposing their authority over employees, members and others, they were restricted and directed by individuals within the complex web of social interactions and relationships that made up their memberships.[3] Indeed, corporate bodies, and even looser associations of merchants forming partnerships, were all part of, and grew out of, a multiplicity of networks in early modern England.[4] It is unsurprising that newly formed entities emerging from this environment included members with a diverse range of interests, experience and expectations; the corporate form was designed to cater to this very range of interests.[5] Corporations functioned as both formal institutions and informal communities.[6] Just as directors of trading companies might seek to impose their will on the wider networks of members, so too did individuals from across these communities seek to influence their corporations.

Commercial ventures into new markets from the sixteenth century onwards served as a means for English merchants to experiment with the institutional models they would depend upon as they established trade with peoples further and further afield.[7] They allowed people to invest in, and experience, the long-distance organisation that transcontinental trade required – and the risk that this involved. They also helped merchants understand the global interconnectedness of the early modern economy and reimagine the possibilities of trades from Hamburg to Senegal or Iceland to Siam.[8] Taking advantage of structural changes in the European and global economy, England's merchants adapted rapidly to find the funds, support and expertise necessary to launch numerous risky ventures. While new organisations relied on the support from the state – especially for patents and charters that defined their privileges – it was primarily merchants who drove and governed them, seeking as they did new means of organising trade to take advantage of the possibilities on offer in an expanding world. Commercial participation across different ventures helped create networks of merchants in England whose interests were linked, whether for a single venture or over multiple

MANY BODIES CORPORATE

ventures during this period.[9] Gaining similar or complementary experiences and expectations of overseas ventures, these individuals could go on to develop improved plans for each new project. Members of the mercantile community increasingly worked together to spread their risk and produce structures of governance for trading that enabled them to participate in increasingly risky and complex overseas projects.

Drawing on corporate traditions from England's numerous urban and livery companies, as well as commercial organisations such as the Merchant Adventurers and Merchants of the Staple, merchants adapted existing ideas to suit the particular needs of new projects.[10] In creating corporate structures to organise overseas activities, merchants obtained numerous privileges to assist in the effective management of their various business activities. Organisations like the East India Company were established as 'one body corporate and politique in deed as in name'.[11] As a corporate body, these organisations formed private communities with their own governance, laws, customs and membership criteria.[12] Authority over each corporation belonged to its members and their elected representatives – not to the crown.[13] These organisations were founded in a number of different ways. The Muscovy Company, for instance, was created with a royal charter to oversee and monopolise trade to newly discovered regions, whereas the mayor and burgesses of Hull took it upon themselves to agree that the merchants of the town 'shall be a fellowship of themselves incorporated'. Much like any other corporation, the newly formed 'Company of Merchants Inhabiting in Kingston upon Hull' was given the right to elect representatives and to 'order and make amongst themselves all such acts and ordinances as shall be most convenient and requisite for the maintenance of the said company'. These powers were limited only by the city's insistence that they should not impinge on the laws of England or the privileges of the Merchant Adventurers or other chartered companies.[14] Whether as part of the Muscovy Company, Hull's new trading corporation or any other commercial institution, merchants chose to participate in these organisations as a means of more effectively engaging in commercial activities.

– 61 –

The precise privileges of trading companies could vary considerably as they were adapted for different purposes, but there were many commonalities.[15] Corporations could make their own laws and orders (so long as they were not contrary to the laws of England) and punish, through imprisonment or fine, members of the company who failed to abide by them.[16] Further privileges meant they could 'sue and be sued, plead and be impleaded, answer and be answered unto, defend and be defended in whatsoever court and places' as they sought fit.[17] Thus, when Thomas Pullison and Thomas Russel wrote excitedly to their compatriots in York that Elizabeth I did 'incorporate us, the merchants trading to the east parts, into one body politic by the name of governor, assistants and fellowship of merchants of Eastland', the details of the new charter – apart from the geography – would not have been unfamiliar. As with their corporate precursors, the Eastland Company could regulate trade within a specific region and forbid 'all others to traffic and occupy the commodities of her majesty's dominions into any of those parts' unless they became members of the company.[18] Once part of a corporate organisation, merchants were expected to follow its rules, meet its behavioural expectations and commit to working for the common good of all its members.[19]

While most merchants would have been familiar with the traditions of livery or urban corporations, joining a trading company could be a more difficult affair.[20] Some, like the Turkey Company, were incredibly restricted in terms of membership, while others, such as the Spanish Company, welcomed hundreds of merchants in a very short time. In most cases, people could join a corporation through ancient right (that they had belonged to the trade before the founding of the company), patrimony, service or redemption.[21] At just one meeting of the Spanish Company, for instance, fifteen new members were admitted, three by right of patrimony, ten after completing apprenticeships and two by redemption.[22] In this kind of traditional, large-scale commercial activity (generally, any kind of trade with Spain, France or northern Europe), many merchants would meet the necessary criteria to join such organisations.[23] However, in a small company conducting a new trade, such as the Turkey Company, no one could claim ancient right and there were not many opportunities for apprentices and factors to obtain the necessary experience to join the corporation. In either case, experience of commercial activity overseas was highly sought after and expected in members. The French Company welcomed applicants who were sons of members or apprentices 'employed in that trade by the space of two years' and the Levant Company charged only 20s for apprentices who had served the company for three years (compared to £50 for those entering by redemption).[24] Even when people were willing to pay high charges to enter through redemption, this option was often only available to those 'being all mere merchants and free of other companies'.[25] Every trading company built further interlocks across England's early modern corporations, strengthening the corporate bonds that held the commercial community together.

For many trading companies, merchants were not only the predominant party but also the only one. This was made clear in the Eastland Company's Acts and Ordinances, for instance. These insisted 'that none be admitted unless he were a merchant', defined as someone who had 'of some good countenance not less than three years trade at home and abroad beyond the seas merchant like'. Simply having completed an apprenticeship was not enough – joining the company required demonstrable evidence of having 'traded merchandises by crossing the seas'.[26] Furthermore, by maintaining standards regarding a member's 'good countenance', the Acts and Ordinances sought to ensure certain behavioural standards from brothers of the company. The Spanish Company applied a similar definition, declaring that only someone who had 'dealt and traded as a merchant, without any retailing or shop-keeping, the full space and term of eight years (in which time an apprentice by his service may attain to the freedom) shall be accounted a mere merchant'.[27] When the Company of Merchants Inhabiting in Kingston upon Hull was chartered, it too restricted membership to those 'using the trade of merchandise from Hull into the parts beyond the seas'.[28]

To ensure that such high standards were maintained, would-be members of trading companies had to provide evidence that they met these strict criteria. Where this proof was available and forthcoming, the process of joining a company was not too strenuous; between 1550 and 1650, thousands of merchants were admitted to companies without incident. It was particularly straightforward for apprentices and members who were recorded carefully as part of corporate administrative procedure, in which cases additional proof was not required.[29] As a result, when the Spanish Company learned that numerous suitors 'being mere merchants by ancient trade' had been left out of the charter by mistake, the directors simply ordered that their names should immediately be written on the back of the document.[30] Similarly, in Bristol the merchant John Smith provided a list of over a hundred individuals 'such as be merchants and have sprung of merchants' who he 'think not to be denied to be of the mystery'.[31]

In other cases, letters, contracts and recommendations were accepted as evidence. Thomas Burgh, the apprentice of George Hanger, was granted admittance to the Spanish Company after presenting the relevant indenture.[32] The same company admitted Ralph Edmunds, who had completed his apprenticeship with the draper Sir Thomas Pullison and was 'also recommended by letter from Don Jon de Taxis' – the ambassador of the King of Spain.[33] When Alderman Johnson recommended his apprentice William Ashwell to the Levant Company, it immediately granted his freedom.[34] The same company admitted Robert Fettiplace, the apprentice of Robert Chambers, after he had 'served out his time and being every way capable of this freedom'.[35] In Bristol's Merchant Venturers, James Croft gained admittance after completing his apprenticeship and appearing before the court with his former master, Richard Holworthy, and paying the standard fine, while William Willets was admitted 'for that he was born in this city and always bred in the way of a merchant'.[36]

Other corporations might also provide recommendations, especially where a young merchant had completed their apprenticeship through a livery company. Within the Drapers' livery company, for instance, it was common practice for members of the company to write letters of support

MANY BODIES CORPORATE

on behalf of their apprentices who sought employment as merchants overseas. Henry Bowdler, for example, wrote to 'Mr Deputy and Company of Merchant Adventurers resident at Middelburg in the favour of Francis Hampton his late apprentice to be admitted and registered to trade'. Richard Daniel, Arthur May, Thomas Flower, Thomas Talbot, Henry Smith, Thomas Blarkley, Thomas Woodrowe and Anthony Young were all given similar support to obtain a position in Emden and Middelburg by their former masters Charles Bond, John Wheeler, Richard Hill, Henry Butler, Robert Smith, Richard Bowdler, Richard Goddard and Lawrence Goff. In each case, the Drapers' corporate leadership used their own reputation to strengthen the weight of these recommendations. For instance, the company's wardens verified Thomas Cross's letter to English residents in Zeeland – they 'subscribed the same with their own hands'.[37] Normally, then, determining who could be accepted into a trading company was no more complicated than double-checking existing records or taking the word of senior merchants who had first-hand knowledge of the validity of an applicant's case.

When proof was not available or was doubted by corporate leadership, it could be very difficult for a merchant to demonstrate their suitability for admittance. For instance, the son of Mr Tyler was delayed entry into the Levant Company after 'it was alleged that his said master [Mr Faulks] has somewhat to object against him'. His freedom was therefore suspended until word was received regarding his master's objections.[38] In other instances, senior merchants who had failed to notarise their relationships with apprentices effectively could endanger those apprentices' entry into a trading company. For example, due to the ongoing war with Spain before 1604, many merchants 'did omit out of their apprentices indentures the words (merchant of Spain and Portugal)', without which their apprentices struggled to gain access to the Spanish Company. In this case, however, the company agreed it would be unfair to punish the apprentices for the oversight of their masters and agreed to admit them so long as they presented the case to the court before the next Christmas.[39] On occasions where merchants

– 65 –

disputed corporate decisions regarding membership, they were invited to 'set down their claim in writing' for consideration, though without evidence complaints would have little chance of success.[40]

However, completing an apprenticeship or bearing patrilineal lineage was not necessarily a guarantee for acceptance into a trading company. In addition to providing proof of their good standing, would-be members had to be wary of other restrictions. The Eastland Company, for instance, forbade entry to the children of members and apprentices who were currently disenfranchised or indebted to the corporation.[41] Similarly, one Henry Cocks was denied membership in the Levant Company, even though he 'did serve one Andrew Stones deceased the full term of his apprenticeship', including spending 'four years and more out of England' as the company prescribed. While the City of London and Clothworkers' livery company accepted his apprenticeship as valid, the Levant organisation adjudged that he owed £37 10s in dues for goods imported to England from after the end of his apprenticeship – he had not, they argued, been either servant or member of the company during this time. Until the dues were paid, he would not be welcomed as a free brother.[42] It did not serve companies to allow access for young merchants who were already indebted or otherwise discredited to take up a position within the organisation.

Merchants, too, might be forbidden from participating in a trading company if their non-trading economic activities were deemed to potentially subvert trading by fellow members within the corporation. For example, the Merchant Adventurers of York forbade members from 'keeping shops of retail in London' because it brought down prices and therefore took 'the living from their brothers'.[43] Similar restrictions were maintained in Bristol, where 'no retailer or artificer, whilst they remain retailers or artificers, shall be received or admitted in to the freedom' of the Merchant Venturers.[44] In the Merchant Adventurers, no member of the company trading in cloth was permitted to participate in the retail of any products transported by the company.[45] Levant Company regulations stated that at a general court the company could 'remove, expel and put out of the said company any of the said company which they shall

– 66 –

MANY BODIES CORPORATE

know or by good testimony made before them find to be retailers and not mere merchants'.[46] The same company simply rejected the entry of Nicholas Dickens, informing him 'it was neither thought fit nor allowable by the charter to admit of any master of ship or common mariner because they are specially excepted out of the charter'.[47] Entry into the Spanish Company was also restricted on these grounds. When the mercer Thomas Dalby and merchant tailor Edward Davenant sought entry in 1604, they were refused 'by reason they are supposed to be retailors and keepers of warehouses'. Attempting to overcome the rejection by agreeing to pay £10 for their membership, this offer, too, was dismissed by the generality who 'agreed that they are not capable' as merchants.[48]

This is not to say that these restrictions were never lifted, but such occasions were few and far between. For example, merchants from outside London might find these restrictions reduced to make up for their limited access to the capital's giant markets. As such, the Eastland Company specified that 'it shall be lawful for such persons as are or shall be free of this fellowship and do inhabit within any city or town (except the City of London) being merchants and not retailers to sell the commodities of the East parts in any of the cities or towns wherein they dwell', but they were limited to selling goods in bulk and could not employ workers to finish products before sale.[49] The same company was similarly willing to allow some level of foreign participation, believing that working with strangers could often be more beneficial than not. Fifty-seven English members of the company and eighteen foreign merchants signed one petition to Robert Cecil for support. These included Ottavio Gerini, David Samin, Robert de la Barra, Nicholas Houbelon and John van Stolt – suggesting involvement with people from across Europe.[50] Membership could also be used to bridge competing commercial groups. For example, the Levant Company invited interloping tin exporters to attend their court and obtain their freedom in order to end a long-running dispute.[51] Despite hefty charges for joining the company, the tin exporters acquiesced, and William Cockayne, John Bland, William Woleston and John Joanes were 'admitted into this society to trade only in tin for the fine of £25'.[52]

– 67 –

MERCHANTS

However, this was certainly uncommon and was not encouraged. In other cases where companies faced pressure to welcome non-merchants, they were not forthcoming. The attempts of Lord Chief Baron to get the Spanish Company to welcome 'certain merchants of Southampton', who were shopkeepers and officers of the customs house were rejected, with Baron informed 'how dangerous a precedent it were and how inconvenient for the company to yield to his lordships request'.[53] Unless the benefits were immediate and substantial, corporations like these thought it best to ensure they remained the domain of merchants alone.

Over the course of this period, many companies were forced into widening access (but only to other merchants) through liberalising policies introduced by parliament or the crown, or because of pressure from the wider merchant community.[54] For example, James I suggested the Levant Company 'enlarge the liberty thereof to all our merchants in general' in order to overcome challenges facing the Levant Company because of 'the discovery of the East Indies'. In order to ensure his plan succeeded he requested that twelve senior merchants and courtiers meet to offer advice regarding 'the establishing of sure a government of the said trade as may be both honourable and profitable for us and tend to the general liberty of all of our said subjects'.[55] In the end, the company was forced to accept 'the admittance of every mere merchant into their freedom' as part of the crown's attempts to revive England's trade.[56] Similarly, when the French Company was chartered in 1611, its membership was open 'to all using only trade of merchandise' and it was forbidden from denying access to merchants who sought entry.[57] In both cases, trading companies were forced to lift their most restrictive practices regarding access, but the expectations that members would be merchants, and therefore trained within the same community and corporate frameworks, endured.

Prescriptive practices such as these were in part a consequence of vested interests: they kept lucrative access to overseas trades in the hands of a smaller number of traders.[58] However, they were also intended to keep standards high and ensure no member behaved in a manner that

– 68 –

did not reflect well on the wider corporation. This meant swift action when people sought to fiddle or defraud the system action. In one such instance, the merchant Raph Hamor informed the City of London corporation 'that one John Lamott who is the son of an alien' obtained his freedom by using 'a counterfeit certificate'. This action reflected poorly not only on Lamott, who immediately lost his citizenship, but also on those who had made his fraudulent activities possible, knowingly or unknowingly. William Whitwell, who had supported Lamott's application for freedom, was discharged and imprisoned, even though there was little evidence of collusion. Instead, Whitwell's punishment reflected the principle that, by recommending and supporting Lamott's application, he had placed his creditability and reputation on the line, and each of these were found wanting. A few days later 'Thomas Clarke who is accused to be a principal actor in the procuring of John Lamott's freedom' was arrested and imprisoned 'until further order be taken'.[59] Once again, it was vital for corporations to maintain the impression that their members were all acting appropriately – if their ability to maintain orderly behaviour was in doubt, the whole system could come under threat.

THE GENERALITY

The 'mere merchants' who joined these trading companies were the bedrock for many of the enterprises that defined England's trade and empire during the sixteenth and seventeenth centuries. Known as free brothers, brethren, citizens, members, adventurers or investors, they took on a new role as part of the corporation's generality.[60] Within corporations, they provided the personnel, funds and expertise necessary for these organisations to function effectively. Outside them, common customs, values and cultural standards helped to ensure that merchants could work together.[61] In both cases, the commercial community relied on its members contributing towards ensuring the overseas activities on which they depended for their livelihoods were managed effectively – both as business and as social organisations.[62] Across different commercial activities and organisations, therefore, merchants were connected through a dense network of shared experiences and expectations about how they should behave and operate. The influence of ideas and practices drawn from such contexts informed the ways they, and in turn their companies, made decisions.[63] In doing so, these institutions adopted forms of governance, commercial practices and economic cultures that reflected their members' interests. Simultaneously, they formed yet another layer of contact between merchants that helped reinforce existing traditions while allowing the sharing of new information, experiences and ideas.

Once they became members of a company, merchants were expected to fulfil obligations of service and to participate in corporate affairs. Probably the most meaningful of these obligations, in terms of management, was to attend general courts and participate in votes regarding 'the choosing of principal officers' or breaches 'of the orders and acts of the company'.[64] Governors, directors and other senior positions in corporate government were subject to election, usually at annual meetings where the whole generality of a company was expected to be in attendance.[65] For much of this period most companies undertook elections 'made by lifting up of hands according to usual manner', but there were variations.[66] In the Somers Island Company, for example, officers were chosen 'by the greater part of the voices of the said company' present at quarterly general meetings, or 'by the voice of the greater part of the assistants' if necessary.[67] Such public votes, while not allowing members privacy, did enable members to leverage their relationships across the commercial community more easily. It also helped to validate selected leaders and demonstrate the trust between members of the organisation.

As we saw earlier, alternative practices, such as the use of ballot boxes, could be judged as subversive practice, and when the East India Company faced a similar request a few years later, the ballot box was again dismissed as an 'Italian trick' that had no place in the corporation.[68] However, other corporations had adopted ballot boxes much earlier, especially in livery company contexts.[69] In the Mercers' livery company, a revealing debate prior to their implementation of balloted voting in 1581 highlighted perceived benefits and limitations. While the company acknowledged that 'where of long time of mind . . . usual proceeding has been by voice and holding up of hands openly', it revealed a number of concerns about such public voting. These 'open dealings' had caused disagreements between 'many good brethren and well willers to our common and general estate' and 'great persons' who had held 'grudging malice' as a consequence of voting decisions. To rectify 'the great displeasure of almighty god and hindrance of the common estate of this our company' that this caused, the company ordered that 'henceforth no matter whatsoever, whether it be for lease or leases, fine or fines, office or office fee or fees, pension or pensions, gift or gifts, grant or grants or any other things or matter whatsoever, that shall be given, granted or allowed of not to pass as an act until the same be first tried by balloting'. A balloting box was provided and during any vote was placed in front of the wardens. On 'the top side of the box shall be set the question in writing' and members would 'put their ball or ballot into one of the boxes *pro* or *contra* as god shall move them'.[70] Anonymous voting might remove the opportunity for votes to strengthen social and business links between members, but it also removed the threat of breaking such bonds when members disagreed. Similarly, when the Levant Company adopted the ballot box in 1623, the decision was made specifically because the validity of votes was called into question when some members were 'so remiss not to hold up their hand either one way or other'.[71] Both key decisions and the election of officers were made through such votes, and whether by ballot box or raising of hands it was important that the process reassure members that the corporation was acting in their best interest and listening to their voice.

Although officials elected through these electoral processes undertook day-to-day management of early modern corporations, regular events throughout the year were open to all members of the generality and served as a means for ongoing dialogue across corporations. In the

East India Company, these meetings were rigidly governed by the company's own regulations. The corporation's *Lawes and Standing Orders* specified that these meetings, known as 'general courts', must be held on the last Tuesday in May, where the regulations of the company and the auditor's report would be read publicly, and in July for elections, and each time ships returned from Asia, at which point the directors would 'deliver and debate the affairs of the company' with the generality.[72] Meanwhile, the Levant Company's charter specified that the general court must include a majority of assistants and be a 'public assembly'.[73] In Bristol, too, merchants only undertook company business during 'a general meeting of the whole society and company', when they were 'in ample number assembled in their common hall'.[74] Although convening only occasionally, these meetings gave all members the opportunity to participate in the organisation and governance of their corporations, providing an essential conduit for internal communication between the directors and other members. However, general courts were not always easy to arrange. Merchants were busy people and it could be challenging for corporations to secure their attendance. When numbers were insufficient, meetings might be delayed or cancelled, such as when only seventeen members attended a Spanish Company meeting and 'for want of sufficient appearance the said general court could not be held'.[75] In an attempt to avoid such problems, the Mercers' livery company assessed the reasons given by members who failed to attend meetings and those without acceptable excuses were fined and recorded in a black book.[76] Similarly, in Bristol, the Merchant Venturers recorded which members arrived 'after the glass was run out and turned again', while in York lateness was fined at 6d for a first offence and could increase as high as 10s if someone was unpunctual on four or more occasions.[77] Merchants might have busy lives as individuals, but as members of a corporation, they were expected to make the time to fulfil their obligations.

Most of the time, the generality did take an interest, did show up and did demand that company directors demonstrate that they were acting in their members' best interests. At general courts, governors and directors of corporations were required to update members on key strategic issues and provide information regarding their company's financial state – all topics that could elicit a strongly negative response if things were going badly. Members, after all, risked winning or losing their livelihoods depending on how well directors managed the trade. This meant the relationship between directors and the generality could be tense, although when attacked, directors were quick to point out that they, too, were heavily invested and risked just as much as anyone else.[78] Through general courts, members got a rare opportunity to directly engage with their elected representatives and, when necessary, make clear their feelings about perceived failings. Decisions about how a company should be organised and how it might more effectively engage in global trade were made through a process of constant negotiation. Sudden changes could be destabilising and directors were more likely to err on the side of caution than quickly embrace innovative ideas. At these meetings, the leaders of corporations had to justify their decisions to potentially hundreds of members; bringing the entire company together as a single body in a single space gave less influential members of the community the opportunity to pressure the strongest.

That being said, directors rarely sat back and took members complaints. Instead, they managed general meetings carefully to ensure that the social and economic bonds of trust that tied members were not weakened. This was especially the case when members critiqued directors personally, because if members could not trust their directors then the whole edifice could fall apart. In one illustrative example, the East India Company directors called an extra general court to demand that members of the generality who had not paid their contributions to the company's joint stock did so – up to £50,000 was owed. Rather than cowing the members into submission, this quickly turned the general court into a platform for complaint. One debtor, Mr Mellyn, railed against the company's leadership, insisting the problem was not late payments but that their bad decisions had led to £100,000 of losses. Accusations of mismanagement were serious and, unless remedied

– 73 –

swiftly, could result in investors losing faith in the organisation. Not surprisingly, the company's leadership were quick to argue that Mellyn had 'spoken seditiously, and scandalously' and should be 'thrust out' of the organisation. Governor Thomas Smith suggested that Mellyn lacked 'charity and judgement' and should be expelled to ensure that the corporation did not 'suffer by cruel division', which would 'bring ruin to the whole company'.[79] However, expelling Mellyn was beyond the directors' powers; company law only permitted the expulsion of a member if he failed to obey the general court.[80] The directors needed to prove Mellyn's guilt to the wider community to secure his dismissal and re-establish their trusted status. To do so, the company appointed auditors to investigate the accusations and present their findings, first to the directors and then to the generality (although this proved harder than expected when it became clear that the treasurer had failed to keep the books for the previous five months).[81] As well as seeking to prove their own trustworthiness, the directors sought to undermine Mellyn's. Pointing to his 'violent and fractious' behaviour, the directors suggested Mellyn was seeking 'the ruin and subversion of the trade' by undercutting their authority 'and disturbing the general proceedings of the company by his bold and uncivil behaviour'. They questioned how it was possible that such a minor investor could have such a negative impact on larger investors, who relied on the company to 'uphold the business and not suffer it to be disturbed'. Although they accepted that a small investor could put their opinion forward 'peaceably and quietly', ultimately the company concluded that Mellyn's bad behaviour showed his inability to function as part of corporate society, and he was banned from attending future meetings of the company.[82] Having the opportunity to complain and hold directors to account did not mean the behavioural standards that underpinned the commercial community could be ignored.

In order to avoid fractious behaviour undermining the stability of the corporation and the effectiveness of their meetings, speech was carefully regulated. In Bristol, the Merchant Venturers insisted that only one

MANY BODIES CORPORATE

person was permitted to speak at a time and serious charges were brought against any member who used 'unseemly or reproachful speech'.[83] Similarly, in the Merchant Adventurers, the company's laws asserted that it 'shall not be lawful for any brother of the fellowship to interrupt another in his speech unto the court, or to speak when another is speaking, or to direct his speech at any particular man or person that spoke last before him'. Members were not permitted to prompt or verbally support speakers, nor were the close relations of members allowed to attend meetings where their colleagues were being questioned. In cases where this was ignored, or where debates became raucous, the governor could 'by a stroke of the hammer' insist that 'no person shall speak loud or hold talk with another, but be still and silent'.[84] When attending general courts, members of the East India Company were expected to 'stand up and be bareheaded' when addressing the company and were only permitted to raise any single topic on three occasions. They were expected to direct their speeches at the governor and private speeches or those 'directed to particular persons' were forbidden. Only the governor or deputy could interrupt speeches, but even they were only allowed to do so in order to 'put any to silence, for impertinency or other unseemly speaking'.[85] These restrictions on the behaviour of members of corporations were intended to ensure open communication, sustain the reputation of each organisation and encourage positive relationships between members of the community of which they were composed.

Maintaining social networks was essential for the effective practice of business. That being the case, companies were careful to maintain the illusion of unity in their public activities, swiftly condemning members who failed to contain their grievances to the privacy of company meetings. For instance, Richard Nelson was imprisoned in Bridewell after he made 'vile and unseemly speeches' against the Lord Mayor to the detriment of London's city corporation.[86] Similarly, when William Caswell was called before the Clothworkers' livery company's court regarding 'indecent and uncivil speeches by him spoken and uttered at the

– 75 –

Guildhall' and 'due proof against him by two sufficient and credible witnesses' was presented, he was found guilty and fined £3.[87] When William Wright was 'summoned to appear' before the Merchant Tailors 'for many peremptory speeches' towards the company's wardens, he was condemned not only for aggressive, uncivil language but also for threatening 'that he would talk with him [the warden] in another place' and declaring the company's clerk a 'sorry knave and scurvy fellow'. Numerous witnesses were available and the court agreed Wright had committed an 'offence deserving greater punishment than could be inflicted upon him' internally and sought the Lord Mayor permission to imprison him.[88]

The reasons for this stern approach to public discord were made clear during a dispute between the East India Company and Mr Burke, a recalcitrant merchant who was accused of discussing what he perceived to be the directors' failings while attending 'a public dinner, amongst many other merchants and others of good account'. Burke's complaints were perceived as a risk to the 'credits and reputations' of the company's directors and therefore required a quick, forceful and public response.[89] Rather than simply fining or chastising Burke privately, the company called the unruly merchant before the generality who were informed how 'a brother of this Company, a grave man, hath offered a great disgrace unto their Governor, deputy and committees'. In the ensuing debate, the generality were reminded of 'the many enemies this company have' and how negative speeches gave 'such an advantage to their adversaries' that it risked their shared investment – following which, they quickly agreed to punish Burke. Leaving no room for Burke to manoeuvre, the company used the communal venue of the general court to highlight the transparency and creditability of its leadership. Public transgressions required some form of public justice. By involving the generality in the dispute, Burke's punishment was far greater than a simple fine, damaging his standing within the merchant community. At the same time, it helped to reinforce bonds within the organisation as members came together to impose a shared judgement.

These institutional regulations among trading organisations mirrored England's wider corporate environment, with both urban and livery corporations prepared to act strongly against individuals who impinged on the community's expectations of civility. Perpetrators of such misdemeanours were quickly brought to account. Sometimes, for instance in ending a 'controversy between Mr Backhouse and Mr Leveson about uncourteous words passed betwixt them at Pauls School', the reaffirmation that they would abide by common standards was enough, and in this case the Mercers' livery company resolved they 'they were both here reconciled and made friends'.[90] However, this was not William Leveson's only offence and after a similar dispute with William Smith when 'uncourteous words delivered unto the other', each man was forced to apologise and pay 20s to the poor.[91] Similarly, when 'Edward Ward and Robert Jennings two brethren of [the Drapers' livery] company have broken the order of this court for reviling each other' they were fined.[92] In the Merchant Adventurers, members who called 'any other of the said fellowship not being his servant a knave, false knave or any other vile or opprobrious name in dispute or malice' would be fined £2. If they 'strike, beat or wound' another member – including servants – members were fined £10.[93] Similarly, after 'Mr Henry Garraway at this assembly did utter very unfit and ill befitting words against Mr Deputy in open court', the Levant Company fined the offending merchant £10.[94] When members of the Eastland Company were found to 'revile, miscall or term any other brother of the company with indecent speeches or words of reproach or discredit', they were fined 20s for each offence. Violent attacks were fined at £5 per blow and the offending party had to apologise in open court or face a further fine of £20.[95] When merchants refused to pay these fines, they faced the prospect of being cast out of the corporate body.[96] The Spanish Company even appointed John ApJohn, the Crier of the City of London, as an officer specifically 'to commit disobedient brothers that shall offend contrary to the orders of the company' – a poorly chosen word could land an uncivil merchant in prison.[97] These strict punishments demonstrate just how seriously uncivil behaviour was treated in early modern corporations.

Fulfilling commercial obligations regarding behaviour was an expectation maintained within and beyond the merchant community. As new overseas ventures were launched outside the hands of the merchant leadership, the behavioural structures that had underpinned corporate projects across the world remained integral in colonies across America's Atlantic seaboard. In New England, where funds from a wide array of investors, including but not limited to merchants, helped launch a colonial enterprise under the direction of Ferdinando Gorges and the Council for New England, early difficulties had led to a breakdown in trust between management and participants in the joint stock. Yet, much like contractual arrangements between individual merchants or with mercantile corporations, the decision to back out of an agreement led to accusations of dishonourable behaviour. When one disgruntled investor, Hugh Smith, wrote to Gorges in 1623 about his wish to renege on his support, he was quickly shut down. Smith believed that the venture had been misrepresented prior to his purchase of the stock, which gave him grounds for withdrawing. Gorges wrote of his surprise in being contacted directly, suggesting it would have been more appropriate for Smith to write to the council itself, but because 'the subject does much concern myself in every way', he felt moved to respond. He angrily told Smith that the stock had been launched not through 'tales of I know not what' but 'a free relation' of information regarding a colony 'wherein I had already spent many hundreds of pounds'.[98] Striking to the heart of the matter – emphasising his own reliability juxtaposed with Smith's failure to behave appropriately by subverting corporate hierarchy – Gorges' response reinforced the council's shared communal interests and Smith's position as an aberrant outsider.

As Gorges went on, he continued to emphasise the threat posed by Smith's decision to leave the company both to the common good and to his own position within commercial circles, stating 'if all should do as you desire to do' then all the investors' fortunes would quickly be ruined. By breaking his contract and letting down the whole community, Smith would deserve no merit 'in honour, honesty or equity'. Considering how damaging that would be to Smith's reputation, Gorges expressed his hope that the letter was a mistake of his secretary rather

MANY BODIES CORPORATE

than a true representation of his intent – providing a helpful excuse for Smith should he recognise his error and return to the fold. Signing the letter as Smith's 'kinsman and true friend', Gorges left no doubt as to how poorly anything other than capitulation on the part of his chastised business partner would be received.[99] Gorges followed this up with a second letter a week later, which reiterated his condemnation and told Smith he was 'sorry you have cashiered yourself out of so pious and so hopeful a business' and that after breaking the contract he would ultimately 'understand the wrong you do yourself'.[100] These letters clearly demonstrate the prevalence of expectations regarding commercial conduct in the New England company. The repercussions of breaking them – lost faith in Smith's honour, honesty and equity – were used as a means to try to enforce behavioural standards.

CORPORATE GOVERNANCE

As organisations came to command considerable resources, to govern people and undertake radical new projects in a search of profits, the challenges of managing such complex groups grew. English corporations brought together communities of individuals with diverse interests and personalities to operate as a single corporate body directed towards the execution of operations – whether trade, industry or empire. As communities of individuals, with different interests, expectations and risk-profiles, these corporations were far from monolithic, homogeneous institutions, and catering to the expectations of members was just as important as drawing on their support. Even if they had been trained and operated within frameworks with common standards about how to do business and how to behave, merchants still had different ideas about how specific projects should be managed. Should a trade be maintained and managed through a common stock? Should corporations act as shipping concerns, carrying goods to and from foreign markets but relying on local representatives to organise the purchase and sale of goods? Were mart towns detrimental to innovation or a key means of regulating

– 79 –

commerce? Would it be good practice to raid foreign shipping? Should they engage in diplomacy with foreign states? Should corporations be used to plant colonies and fortifications overseas as well as trade with local peoples? The answers to these questions varied dramatically across the range of activities undertaken by merchants and every corporation contained members whose views on these questions would differ. It was the responsibility of the directors to answer these questions.

In most cases, corporations were led by a governor assisted by a board of directors, often called 'committees', 'assistants' or 'wardens', who would undertake day-to-day operations. Together, they managed the business on behalf of the generality, which trusted them to execute company business effectively. In this context, officials within corporations were expected to understand 'their official business to be that of "public affairs", which constituted both commercial and political duties, distinguished from the "private interest" or particular affairs of their own personal trading concerns'.[101] In the East India Company, for example, the corporation's charter specified that an elected body consisting of twenty-four directors and a governor would undertake the government of the company, having been chosen during an annual general court and with a 'one whole year' term.[102] Likewise, in Bristol the Merchant Venturers were governed by a master and wardens who were supported by the company's treasurer, clerk and twelve 'of the most discreet, wise and worthy men of the society elected and chosen yearly to be assistants and helpers'.[103] The Levant Company adopted a similar approach, where 'eighteen of the best and discreetest persons of the said company resident and remaining within the City of London' would act as 'assistants of the said company for all things, matters, causes and businesses of the said company in all things touching or concerning the good rule, state and government of the same'. However, in this case, they would be joined by deputies chosen to represent every town 'wherein any merchant free of the said company shall be inhabiting'.[104] The Spanish Company was also governed through a decentralised structure, with a president and directors in London and thirteen deputies each representing a port town across England.[105] In the Merchant Adventurers, efforts to strictly regulate trade overseas led to the governor or deputy and directors meeting 'on that side of the seas [in Europe]' as a means of effectively imposing control. To enforce this management structure, the company's laws and orders imposed a £50 fine on any member who refused to live abroad while acting as director.[106] Corporate governance could be adapted, but the basic tenets remained consistent.

No matter the precise structure, directors in these corporations were expected to be able to represent the generality effectively and it was anticipated that they would be able to draw on considerable experience as merchants, and likely as leaders within their livery companies or urban corporations, before becoming directors.[107] In the East India Company, they were expected to have 'the best experience in merchandising', while the 'Company of Merchants Inhabiting in Kingston upon Hull' sought 'one sober and discreet man to be the master of that company'.[108] Directors were occasionally co-opted when trusted outsiders held expertise deemed essential for company business. Presenting expertise effectively in early modern England was important for professionals and merchants alike.[109] The Spanish Company, for example, asked the solicitor Richard Langley 'to undertake the office of secretary to the said society' after the lawyer had proved invaluable while offering assistance during the renewal of the company's charter.[110] In a similar vein, the East India Company sought to include the merchant John Watts in its board of directors, despite him joining the company too late to be elected through standard procedure. Watts was alderman for Aldersgate ward in London, had been master of the Clothworkers' company and possessed considerable experience of privateering activities, having sent ships to Cádiz, Pernambuco and Puerto Rico; he was also a major ship owner.[111] It was these skills, 'in respect of the great experience of Mr Alderman Watts in shipping and other directions', that encouraged the company's existing directors to agree 'there may be great use of the opinion of the said Mr Alderman Watts in the further proceeding of this voyage' and 'all things concerning the business'.[112] Later, Watts would face the general court and be elected

– 81 –

director and governor through normal means, but his initial admittance into the corporation's management was justified by his great experience.

Merchants were also willing to look past their suspicions of strangers from outside their corporate structures when they could see they would provide specific, necessary skills. This was especially common for pilots and masters of ships, but could also include lawyers, linguists, preachers and others with specific skills required by the organisation. Merchants who were engaged in lobbying activities or embroiled in court cases often required legal expertise. The Clothworkers' company, for instance, kept a lawyer on the corporation's payroll, paying them £2 annually.[113] Legal support could also be obtained by admitting non-merchants as members of corporations. For instance, when Mr Bayley, the Clerk of the Alienations, sought to enter the East India Company in 1609, he was granted admittance because his expertise 'may be beneficial and helpful unto the company'.[114] In 1617, another legal professional, Henry Hobart, met with governor Thomas Smith to discuss his potential membership.[115] Reporting to the directors, Smith said that he had questioned Hobart about some legal concerns, and Hobart's expertise was utilised again after the company approved his membership.[116] In both cases, the prospect of obtaining legal expertise was key in the company's decision to accepting them as members. By offering specific expertise, non-merchants might obtain significant positions of authority and influence, even if they would never be fully accepted into the commercial community. Thus, in spite of competition between whalers from England's northern towns and the Muscovy Company, the corporation's fleet that wintered in Pechora had two Hull seamen as chief pilot and ship's master.[117] Similarly, the Guinea Company placed a huge amount of trust in Captain Brocket, whom they hired to explore and establish trade in the River Senegal region. Brocket was expected not only to trade on the African coast and in by then well-known commercial centres, from which he had already 'sent home a rich return', but also to conduct exploratory ventures into the African interior seeking even better returns. By travelling to 'Tungubutu [Timbuktu] and Gago [Gao], the richest towns for gold in the whole universe', it was

– 82 –

hoped Brocket would 'procure there for the Guinea Company a richer trade than that of the East Indies'.[118] When the need arose, welcoming expert outsiders into the corporate fold could be a risk worth taking.

While seafarers, linguists, lawyers and preachers were deemed essential employees, members of the gentry who sought employment by merchants were less likely to succeed. In part, this reticence stemmed from fears that non-merchants who owed positions to noble or gentry patrons would be less loyal, but it also reflected how merchants understood their unique training and experience as suitable preparation for conducting trade overseas. When merchants faced pressure to employ non-merchants, they were careful to specify precisely why they turned away individuals who sometimes bore recommendations from highly influential members of the court. For example, when the East India Company was preparing for its first voyage, the Lord Treasurer sought to nominate the fleet's commander, and the fledgling corporation was forced to inform him that it would employ no gentlemen and that he should 'give them leave to sort their business with men of their own quality' so as not to dissuade investors.[119] A few years later, another would-be employee was rejected because the company, again, 'resolved to employ none in their affairs but merchants and mariners'.[120] When the Lord Admiral sought to influence the appointment of another commander, the company decided the man was unsuitable because they required 'partly a navigator, partly a merchant . . . and partly a man of fashion' – a gentleman simply did not possess the necessary skills.[121] Similarly, Lord Buckingham's proposal to employ Augustus Fowle as a factor in the Levant Company's new joint stock for currants caused considerable consternation among the corporation's directors.[122] While early modern corporations respected and sought external expertise, they were unwilling to hand over too much responsibility to people whose loyalty might be questioned and who might be unfamiliar with working in mercantile, corporate conditions.

Merchants who obtained positions of corporate authority were expected to swear oaths to act on the behalf of the corporation and its members rather than for their private interest.[123] The laws and orders of the Merchant Adventurers specified how the company's governor and deputy would, 'to the utmost of his or their power, support and maintain the fellowship of the Merchant Adventurers, and the privileges of the same'. In doing so, they would be expected to 'indifferently and uprightly execute the statutes, laws and ordinances of the said fellowship'. Directors were instructed to 'be indifferent and equal between all manner of parties' and give their 'best advice and council, supporting and maintaining the common weal of the fellowship'.[124] The Company of Merchants Inhabiting in Kingston upon Hull also enacted ordinances to ensure that assistants 'shall be sworn to do and execute their affairs truly'.[125] Similarly, directors of the Merchant Venturers in Bristol swore oaths to 'oversee, rule and govern the said mystery and commonality, and all the men, occupiers, dealers, factors, wares and merchandises of the same' while ensuring they 'do right and justice to all persons, in all matters and questions . . . without favour or affection, malice or displeasure'.[126] In the Eastland Company, the secretary was expected to 'show yourself friendly unto every one of the said company'.[127] A company officer took on responsibility to act in the best interests of a wider community, and corporations only functioned so long as members believed they would do so.

This expectation to serve the company's interest at all times could be problematic in the overlapping corporate worlds of many merchants. When Alderman Robert Jones approached the Spanish Company for membership in 1604 his request was immediately accepted, but he was advised 'to hear read the oath of a freeman by redemption' before joining. On hearing 'the reading whereof he refused to be sworn thereunto and so departed and ceased his suit'.[128] For Jones, the limitations placed on him by the corporate oath were too great. Meanwhile, the appointment of Hugh Hamersley as governor of the Levant Company, while he was also governor of the Muscovy Company, presented its own challenges. The two organisations were locked in a dispute about payments for an expedition against pirates and 'in regard of his interest

– 84 –

in both the companies', the Levant Company's members demanded that he would 'carry such an equal and indifferent respect between them when the business should come into question'. Hamersley agreed that if either company took exception to his participation he would excuse himself from representing either regarding the dispute.[129] However, these challenges were uncommon and directors were normally able to take up their positions without too much difficulty.

Once in post, directors' day-to-day management responsibilities often involved little more than overseeing basic administrative tasks and a plethora of small payments relating to issues ranging from labourers' wages to improving a meeting room's décor. In the East India Company, for instance, directors convened regularly each week, attending meetings that usually began at eight o'clock in the morning or two o'clock in the afternoon and could last all day – especially when ships returned from Asia and directors stayed 'until all the said letters be openly read by the secretary'.[130] Although the number of meetings fluctuated during busier periods, in the three months following its first election on 27 October 1600, the company's directors met fifty-two times – an average of more than twice a week.[131] The topics they discussed ranged from strategy for the company's first voyage to interactions with the privy council, but most commonly related to financial issues: payments, the provisioning of ships, the employment of servants for the voyage, the acquisition of bullion. A similar analysis of meetings between August and December 1624 suggests that the stability of long-term organisation reduced demands on directors, but they still met on thirty-two occasions.[132] By this time, specialist committees were appointed to oversee specific tasks, with directors free to spend more time discussing relations with the crown, foreign states and other merchants in England. As this suggests, while the specific challenges faced by companies might change over time and the role of a director evolve away from basic administrative duties, being a director remained a time-intensive enterprise.

Many directors were busy merchants in addition to undertaking corporate responsibilities and they often complained about lost time

MERCHANTS

when taking part in company business – they were expected to attend meetings as often as possible and could be punished for non-attendance. Where a quorum was required for meetings to be valid, demands on directors' time could lead to difficulties. Lack of attendance could seriously delay company business, such as the East India Company's efforts to appoint preachers that were 'put off to a fuller court' after numerous meetings were cancelled due to lack of quorum.[133] Similarly, during discussions about a loan to Charles I, the Mercers' livery company agreed that the matter was too important for the small numbers in attendance to ratify and a further general court was called for the following Saturday morning. It was ordered that those present at the first meeting kept details of the discussion secret until the next meeting 'according to their freeman's oaths'.[134] Corporations did try to mitigate the demands on members and directors, such as the Eastland Company's decision that if a meeting ran past eleven o'clock at night members could depart 'without longer stay to the hindrance of their other either public or private affairs', but such efforts were not always fruitful.[135] When they failed, punishments could be imposed – after being forced to cancel two meetings in less than a year due to low attendance, the Spanish Company took strong measures, immediately discharging all directors who had not been present.[136] Non-attendees also ran the risk of losing a chance to influence decisions, and when 'the greatest number, and those whom the business chiefly concerned, did fail to make their appearance' at a meeting of the Guinea Company, the directors who had bothered to turn up elected to act on their behalf.[137] Managing a corporation required dedication, and it was considered the collegial responsibility of senior merchants to share their time and expertise for the good the wider community.

For companies with decentralised government structures and deputies or directors based outside London, these challenges could be even more acute. For example, in the Eastland Company, in addition to directors in London, the corporation's government was undertaken by deputies from York, Hull, Newcastle and Ipswich, each of whom was given £10 to assist with their duties.[138] Thus, when the company sought to

– 86 –

clarify and update its acts and ordinances, new orders were 'agreed upon at diverse general courts' that brought together 'the governor, assistants and generality of the said company resident at London' as well as 'the brethren of the coast towns'.[139] When the Society of Merchants of the Staple, which regulated England's trade in woollens, decided that 'staple markets of wools shall hereafter be kept at diverse cities and towns within this realm', the newly decentralised structure meant participating towns were required to 'authorise some one or more of your discreetest persons of the brethren of your city to advise with us for the better ordering of the said staple business within your jurisdiction'.[140] For the Spanish Company, decisions were made by the governor and directors in London alongside representatives of the 'privileged ports': Bristol, Exeter, Hull, Barnstaple, Southampton, King's Lynn, Newcastle, Plymouth, Ipswich and Chester.[141] Directors could be 'chosen out of the country' from towns that submitted nominations, but few did – the requirement to attend regular meetings in London was simply too great a demand.[142] For merchants residing across England but belonging to companies managed from London, the lack of representation at meetings was a significant challenge. While they could send letters that would be read publicly to the directors or generality, this offered little in the way of immediacy or opportunity to participate in consequent discussions.[143]

As London's merchants came to dominate England's overseas commerce, particularly through the development of London-based companies, they faced pushback from merchants who resisted the increasing concentration. In one illustrative case from 1579, the newly formed Eastland Company sought to impose its authority on members across England by insisting they travel to London to take their oaths. Merchants in York immediately refused, asking to be sent 'the copy of the oath together with such articles as those who shall be admitted to the society shall be examined upon' and the appointment of a deputy in York who would act as witness.[144] The Eastland Company's directors, arguing that too many members were in a similar situation to those from York, were less than amenable and declared the 'request altogether disagreeing

– 87 –

to our proceedings' and that they could not 'accomplish your desires therein contained'.[145] Yet, while rejecting the proposal on the basis that too many members from across England would seek the same, the very breadth of membership strengthened the York merchants' position. They soon received news from the governor of Hull's merchant corporation that they, too, were similarly opposed to the proposals.[146] Merchants from the two towns agreed that they should send representatives together to argue their case in London. Attempting to build a consensus among merchants in northern England, they had also sent letters encouraging Newcastle's merchants to join them.[147] Roger Raw, the governor of Newcastle's merchants, quickly acquiesced and two representatives from Newcastle joined the growing northern delegation.[148] In the end, with little room to manoeuvre in the face of the Eastland Company's new privileges, they were not able to obtain adjustments to the oath-taking process, although they were successful in obtaining reduced entry fees.[149] In this case, and in a sign of things to come, even when smaller towns and cities came together to demand action, attempts to reduce the London merchants' influence over commercial regulation were rarely successful.

Over time, the challenges of providing representative governance within decentralised corporate structures would be a recurring issue. More than three decades after their first attempts to restrain the influence of London merchants within the Eastland Company, further complaints were made 'on behalf of themselves and others of that society not residing in or near the City of London'.[150] Seeking reduced membership fees, the northern merchants complained about the great expense faced by apprentices required to travel to London to obtain their freedom, that the company seized their goods too freely, and that officers in the northern towns were not rewarded appropriately for their efforts. They also believed payments made to the company 'are not always disposed of for public use' and insisted money should be spent for the benefit of the northern towns as well as London. Although the Eastland Company agreed to adjust its regulations, it did so only after insisting that the towns in questions ensured all debts and membership fees were paid in full and on time.[151] They might have obtained some relief for high fees, but in return, the northern merchants gave the Eastland Company greater reach for enforcing its impositions. The agreed changes did little to assuage the underlying concerns that the company was too London-centric, and consequent disputes highlight how lack of access for merchants outside the capital led to 'much disorder among them for want of appearance at meetings' because they could no longer find members willing to travel to London. The company offered 40s to members who would undertake the journey, but this did little to reduce divisions that stemmed from a lack of real power or influence on the part of the northern towns.[152] Trading companies concentrated more and more power and wealth in London, and the corporate structures in place could only do so much to reassure members from across England that their interests and concerns were receiving the attention they demanded.

Members' anxieties about their effective representation and ability to hold directors to account were often less about the day-to-day management of the corporation and more about the occasions when directors made decisions about big strategic or governmental changes. Corporations established acts and ordinances that they expected members to follow, and although many of these rested on common cultural standards and norms that ensured members acted in ways that would not be damaging to the common good, choices about precisely what to ordain and enforce still had to be made. This process could be inclusive, and when the Spanish Company considered the 'laying down of good orders and constitutions for the government of the society', they sought advice from their members across England.[153] In this case, a preliminary discussion was held in London where thirteen members 'spent the forenoon in perusing the ancient oaths and diverse of the old ordinances anciently made for the government of this company' and suggested alterations, and these were then shared among the generality for comment.[154] However, other companies' directors could be more forceful in imposing their own vision. When the Levant Company sought to overhaul the company's laws and orders, for instance, the task was left in the hands of a mere eight directors, who were instructed to consider any issues that 'may any way concern the good of this company, for the maintaining and upholding thereof, and what they shall do therein'. Despite this incredibly broad remit, the directors were told in advance 'the company will approve of their proceedings'.[155] In each case, the processes by which new regulatory parameters were developed reflected the current relationship between each company and its generality. The Spanish Company directors were seeking to build consensus and establish trust across the new enterprise, whereas in the Levant Company the directors had already earned the members' trust and had free rein to do as they saw fit.

Bad decisions could lead to even the most experienced directors facing the wrath of members – trust could be earned over time but lost in an instant. In the East India Company, annual votes for directors gave members an opportunity to show their displeasure and to have their say in the future direction of the organisation.[156] Disagreements had been brewing for a while as company directors invested more and more in non-trading activities, and parts of the generality were concerned that the costs and challenges of expanding into new markets were not given due consideration. One commentator, Dudley Digges, described how these disputes had 'almost torn that body in pieces'.[157] By 1625, following a series of misfortunes, such as conflict with the Dutch and Portuguese, including the conquest of Ormuz and the notorious 'Amboyna massacre', as well as declining profits, the corporation's generality used their voting powers to enforce a change in leadership. Following this, directors with known affiliations to colonial enterprises like the Virginia or Irish plantations were much less likely to be chosen, and stalwarts of more traditional trades, such as Henry Garraway, Job Harby and Robert Ducy were thrust into leadership positions.[158] These votes were the generality's way of commenting on the overarching strategy of the company. They were no longer willing to endorse such a risky, expensive approach, having seen the ill effects that non-trading activities could have on the bottom line. By electing directors with a particular set of experiences, members were forcing, or at least encouraging, the company to adopt a more peaceful approach to company strategy. By participating in the decision-making process of corporations through such votes, merchants could wield considerable influence. It also allowed differences to be voiced and solutions to be found within a framework that sustained stability and long-term interests in overseas activity. Individual directors might face their members' ire but the corporation endured.

When disputes about how a trade should be managed happened outside an existing corporate structure, disagreements could be more difficult to contain and overcome. This was especially the case when merchants faced the prospect of losing control over their own regulatory frameworks. This was clear during intense disputes about how commerce into Morocco should be structured, an important question amid attempts to reinvigorate trade to the region.[159] As civil wars there seemed to be coming to an end, the new king, Mohammed esh-Sheikh es-Seghir, quickly reached an agreement 'with the King of Great Britain' whereby English merchants obtained rights to traffic freely within Morocco and were protected from local laws and imprisonment.[160] With the treaty in hand, and the promise of increasing trade to the region, English merchants did not take long to launch new projects for improving trade in the region. However, rather than establishing a corporation open to all merchants with claims to ancient privilege, patrimony or service, Charles I elected to reform the Barbary Company 'for the better advancing of the said trade' under the leadership of Robert Russell, a man with little authority or support within the wider commercial community.[161] Although it had a wide-ranging monopoly covering goods like wax, feathers, gum, almonds, dates and goatskins, the new company restricted participation to those willing to invest in a joint stock. The actual management of the trade would be left entirely in the hands of the inexperienced Russell and Charles I's appointed directors.[162] Unsurprisingly, this plan did not sit well with many merchants. Arguing that the new company failed to appreciate the current climate in Morocco, and that Safi and Agadir were

MERCHANTS

'the only ports under [the new king's] obedience', merchants led by William Courteen demanded that opportunities in other parts of the region, including privateering, not be restrained. They saw no reason why violence and leaving 'factors lying ashore at Morocco and Safi in peaceable trade' could not be part of the same commercial strategy.[163] When civil war in Morocco resumed shortly after, another merchant, Robert Black, argued that the Barbary Company's unwillingness to trade with the rebellious faction was risking a potentially valuable opportunity and sought 'with some friends' to send a ship in contravention of the corporation's monopoly.[164] In trying to force merchants to comply with the new Barbary Company's regulation without their input or consent about how it should be managed, Charles I had done little to establish an orderly and profitable trade.

Soon, objections were levelled at the enforcement of a joint-stock model, especially as it demanded that investors place their money in the hands of untrusted directors. Some merchants requested that 'if it be his majesties pleasure that a company be incorporated' then it should at least allow 'those merchants which have used the trade for that country' to join as members and 'that the business be not managed in a joint stock'.[165] As the dispute continued, Charles I called in three senior members of London's commercial community to offer assistance: Paul Pindar, Henry Garraway and Anthony Abdy.[166] However, rather than supporting the crown's company, they backed their fellow merchants whose long-term interest and participation in the trade would ordinarily have secured their ongoing access to the trade, and whose expertise they believed should have been drawn upon for the establishment of a new corporation in the first place. After meeting both investors in the joint stock and the 'old traders', Pindar, Garraway and Abdy recommended that the trade, 'which is now managed in a joint stock ... should be dissolved and a company erected to trade in several'. They encouraged an expansion of the trade from Safi to the entire Moroccan coastline and suggested that current investors in the joint stock be given four months 'to settle their estates' after which time their strict monopoly would be

– 92 –

revoked.[167] Despite this input, 'merchants trading in a joint stock for Barbary' continued to insist their privileges were valid – but their efforts were ultimately in vain.[168] Merchants outside the joint stock quickly prepared ships in contravention of the company's now defunct – in their eyes at least – patent.[169] Charles I's attempts to promote the trade through his chartered joint-stock company had clearly failed. Despite support from the crown, the joint-stock *modus operandi* of the Barbary Company had failed to provide an effective form of governance for trade to the North African coast. Attempting to impose a corporate structure that had not been agreed by a wider cross-section of the commercial community was untenable. A charter or patent alone was not enough to impose authority and, without buy-in from traders themselves, it was hard for any company to succeed.

In the colonial context of English plantations in North America, efforts to regulate commerce were similarly stymied by mercantile unwillingness to support enforced corporate oversight. In the case of the New England Company, the managing council – that included directors from gentry and noble backgrounds as well as merchants – struggled to impose any level of control over merchants trading to the region. After attempting to alter the company's regulations to obtain greater control over the colony's commerce, they complained that while 'his Majesty's letters patent have freely given way to any merchant or others to become adventurers with them', too many had 'already attempted and are in further preparation to assume a liberty to themselves to trade, to the prejudice of the said plantation'.[170] For merchants across England, the new corporation offered little in the way of the structure that they required; so many elected simply to ignore it. In response, the company sought to impose its authority by using strategies utilised by other trading companies. Officers were appointed in Bristol, Exeter, Plymouth, Dartmouth, Weymouth and Barnstaple to oversee and regulate trade to the colony, and each year two general meetings would be held in Tiverton, an inland market town in Devon, where members of the company could participate in the decision-making process. However, apart from being highly inconvenient for merchants to attend, these gatherings did not include an election for members of the council, meaning that no merchant representatives were likely to gain much influence anyway. Worse still, any decision not agreed at the meetings would be referred directly to the managing council rather than being revisited for further discussion. Instead of embracing the communal culture of decision making, delegated authority and equal voting rights among participants, the New England Company model sought to impose a hierarchical structure that left merchants with little recourse. The idea that merchants would consent to investing 'together with the rest' in a trade that would 'be managed by the treasurers and commissioners' of the company, often people who were not practising merchants, was never likely to work.[171]

Instead, the company's merchant members simply and very politely ignored the council's request. The mayor of Bristol wrote to Ferdinando Gorges, the company's president, explaining how the city's merchants had discussed the proposal but found 'the said articles so difficult that at present they cannot conclude in regard of the shortness of time to them allotted'.[172] In the meantime, they sought a copy of the New England Company's patent to assess how far they could challenge the restructure.[173] Until a more satisfactory agreement could be reached, Bristol's merchants concluded they had no option but to continue sending voyages to the plantation.[174] The following year the New England Company wrote back insisting they would 'prohibit any [merchant] from frequenting or visiting the coasts of New England or meddling with the trade or commerce with the natives without licence'. However, in the same letter they were also careful to assure Bristol's merchants they would not 'debar any regular or honest [merchant] from a free recourse to those parts'.[175] By refusing to participate in the New England Company's governmental reforms, Bristol's merchants were able to protest the attempted changes without breaking any prior agreement. In doing so, they both highlighted how difficult it would be for the company's leadership to impose their will on a recalcitrant merchant community and obtained tacit agreement for the maintenance of the status quo.

Good practices in corporate government were meant to ensure that rules were created and maintained, and also that members had the opportunities necessary to undertake trade and make a living. When directors failed to manage corporate activities effectively, the consequences could be severe. For instance, attempts to reinvigorate commerce between England and trading networks in the Gulf of Guinea were beset by issues of governance.[176] Competing conceptions about who should manage the trade and how it should be accomplished led to a severe breakdown between directors and investors in the enterprise. The 'Company of Adventurers of London Trading into Gynney and Bynney', under the leadership of Sir William Saint John, was condemned for failing to effectively oversee the trade after a disastrous voyage. Michael Best, who, after being introduced to 'diverse gentlemen and merchants', had been persuaded to invest £100, reported how he could only watch on in horror as 'the same is utterly lost'. The causes, Best believed, were obvious. First, the 'negligence and improvidence of the said Governor and Company' led to delays that meant ships reached Africa 'at such a late and unseasonable time of the year' that they could not participate in seasonal trade. Second, a ship was lost 'by reason of the dissent and disagreement of the gentlemen and merchants who were committees and adventurers in the same'. Best believed, and was 'credibly informed and doubts not', that fractious gentlemen were 'aiming more at their own private ends ... than the general success of the said voyage'. He maintained that these gentlemen, 'known to be very debauched and disordered persons at home', had imposed their rule over the voyage in spite of their lack of skills and experience.[177] From the highest levels of the company down to on-ship disputes between its agents, poor corporate practice, lack of mercantile control and the inability of members to follow the orderly procedures of England's commercial culture meant that these efforts were doomed from the start.

– 95 –

THREE

LIVING TOGETHER, WORKING TOGETHER

A few days after his election to the highest civic office, the new Lord Mayor of London Thomas Middleton emerged from the Guildhall to find a city transformed. A lavish show, designed and executed by the playwright Thomas Middleton – no relation – had transformed the cityscape into a spectacle that honoured the new Lord Mayor, the mercantile community and the City of London. It left no onlookers in doubt that they were at the very heart of England's commercial wealth and power. Serenaded by trumpets and song, and surrounded by merchants, citizens and other well-wishers in their finery, Middleton's elevation to the highest civic office was a cause for celebration. As he travelled from the Guildhall to Westminster and back again, the new Lord Mayor, and the city's population, would revel in what it meant to be part of the country's greatest city, a trading port with links to the distant corners of the world whose wealth was unparalleled across the breadth of England's emerging empire.

This was no mere party, and Middleton's triumphal procession through the city was interrupted, time and time again, by costumed actors whose carefully choreographed performances presented the new Lord Mayor with visions of the trials and tribulations that lay ahead of him. First, 'after a strain or two of music', he was met by 'a grave femi-

LIVING TOGETHER, WORKING TOGETHER

nine shape' that emerged 'from behind a silk curtain, representing London'. Invoking a 'motherly salutation' in his honour, the figure tasked the Lord Mayor to undertake 'the just government, of this fam'd city, whom nations call their brightest eye'. Later, Middleton was confronted by personifications of *Truth*, *Zeal*, *Ignorance* and *Error*, who each proclaimed that his tenure would be saved (or undone) if he embraced them. These were no dry proclamations but dramatic calls to action. *Zeal* wore 'a garment of flame coloured silk, with a bright hair on his head, from which shoot fire-beams', while *Error* was accompanied by an owl, a mole and a bat, 'symbols of blind ignorance and darkness'. Later, a personified *Envy* joined the parade riding a stylised rhinoceros while eating from a bloody red heart. If these were too subtle, a further encounter at St Paul's Cathedral spelled out what was required from the man at the helm. Here, 'a strange ship' passed by the Lord Mayor 'having neither sailor nor pilot, only upon a white silk streamer these two words set in letters of gold, '*Veritate Gubernor*' ('I am steered by truth'). Early modern communities depended on trust between their members to succeed, and they expected the same from their leaders.

As well as looking inward, the city-wide festivities were an opportunity to celebrate the bounty that good government had brought to London. On reaching the Thames, Middleton was presented by an incredible spectacle – five artificial islands 'artfully garnished with all manner of Indian fruit trees, drugges, spiceries' and other exotic commodities. London's merchants, including Middleton, owed their wealth to bringing such goods to London's docks, and people were unlikely to forget that the prosperity of the capital rested on links with distant lands and peoples. Indeed, not long after viewing these global riches in the Thames, the show's crowd was presented with another spectacle, four more actors playing 'a king of the Moors, his queen, and two attendants of their own colour'. Leaving their ship, the richly and (we can expect) exotically dressed figures gazed in surprise at the London crowd and proclaimed to Middleton:

– 97 –

'I see amazement set upon the faces
Of these white people, wonderings, and strange gazes,
Is it me? Do's my complexion draw
So many Christian eyes, that never saw
A King so black before? No, now I see,
Their entire object, they're all meant to thee.'

Of course, a 'King so black' did not transfix the merchants of London – their new Lord Mayor had treated with kings, emperors and governors across the world during his tenure in the East India Company! Indeed, the Moorish king explained that 'English merchants, factors, travellers' had brought him to London's markets. Through 'truth' and 'good example', England's traders not only brought wealth, but also 'oft hath power to convert infidels'. Finally, after proceeding down Cheapside, Middleton came upon the show's grand finale – *London's Triumphant Mount*. Shrouded in mist and guarded by monsters that faded away at *Truth*'s approach, this grand display celebrated 'this cities grace'. Once again, 'that grave feminine shape, figuring *London*, sitting in greatest honour' was present, flanked by '*Religion*, the model of a fair temple on her head, and a burning lamp in her hand' and '*Liberality*, her head circled with a wreath of gold'. From this last figure, who bore 'in her hand Cornucopia, or Horn of Abundance, out of which rushes a seeming flood of gold', Middleton received his final lesson of the day – wealth, faith and good government were intertwined and interdependent, and the new Lord Mayor would do well to remember it.

After banqueting at the Guildhall and participating in a service at St Paul's Cathedral, Lord Mayor Thomas Middleton emerged once more and was led in a grand procession back to his house, newly trimmed and decorated for the occasion. If he had been in any doubt before, the day's events would have left him with no illusions about the expectation laid upon him – by his good government, truth and zeal, the wealth of the world would continue to flow into London.[1]

LIVING TOGETHER, WORKING TOGETHER

ENTANGLED TRADES

The annual Lord Mayor's show presented an opportunity for merchants and trading companies to join with the wider commercial community to celebrate the benefits of trade, overseas expansion and the civic foundations on which they rested.[2] By presenting London as an imperial city, they provided a public demonstration of the benefits delivered by the city's merchants and corporations and reaffirmed the behavioural and social expectations that made them possible.[3] Early modern merchants depended on collaborative relationships to achieve their business goals. Whether working alone, in a partnership or as part of a larger corporate body, they relied on connections with other traders for issues ranging from obtaining credit to accessing the most up-to-date information about distant lands. The stability of the networks between them was strengthened by corporate structures and the increasingly common standards imposed across different strands of England's international commerce.

By the middle of the sixteenth century, English merchants were already judiciously connecting disparate markets throughout Europe as a means of maximising their trading opportunities. Thomas Gresham's interests, for instance, included trading velvet, satin, damask, sarsenet, camlets, tapestry, raw silk, taffeta, Dutch cloth, English cloth and kerseys – fabrics that were transported in over '20 diverse and sundry ships' to destinations across Europe. When preparing a single voyage in September 1548, his ship carried £588 11s 8d of cloths, £3,397 6s 8d of kerseys, £260 13s 3d of lead and £57 7s 4d of damask. Alongside lead, Gresham exported tin, and his largest imports in terms of value were metals, including £4,843 13s worth of silver that he had imported from the continent. While some transactions with fellow merchants would have barely dented Gresham's capital reserves, such as the purchase of a single cloth from Thomas Andrews, others were much more substantial and could only have been supplied on credit, such as the purchase of 596 pieces of tin from John Elliot for £3,567 13d.[4] Although Gresham was exceptional regarding the scale of his wealth, his interests were

– 99 –

MERCHANTS

not atypical for an early modern merchant – he leveraged his finances to great effect, diversified his investments and built relationships with traders in ports across as many markets as possible.

Gresham's wide-ranging interests were indicative of a wider process of diversification in English commerce that would continue over the course of the following century. During this period, increasing imports, exports and re-exports, combined with broader economic and population growths across England, meant that the total economic output from trade rose steadily, quadrupling between the 1550s and 1650s.[5] Much of England's export trade remained tied to the country's woollen cloth manufacturing industry, but access to new markets expanded the destinations of these products as well as introducing an array of new imports.[6] London, especially, took advantage of this rapidly changing commercial environment and, by the early seventeenth century, was responsible for as much as 80 per cent of total exports from England.[7] The intra-European trading circuit that connected English merchants with consumers across Portugal, Spain, France, the Low Countries, Germany, Poland, Scandinavia and Italy dominated much of this trade – importing exotic commodities from other continents could be highly profitable, but the day-to-day conduct of English business was deeply integrated with its nearby neighbours in Europe and the Mediterranean.

Through their merchants, England's ports, towns and cities 'offered unique opportunities for encounters with the exotic' by traders and consumers alike, and numerous commodities from across the world were enthusiastically sought after to sate the demand of the domestic market.[8] Merchants lived up to expectations. In Bristol, imports increased by 564 per cent between 1560 and 1640, while in London they rose from £900,000 in 1600 to £1,900,000 in 1640.[9] Some high-value products, such as raw silk and pepper, contributed to this increase, but this scale of growth was not achieved through the work of only a small number of merchants or engagement with one or two previously unconnected markets – it represented a broad shift across English commercial activities.[10] In Southampton, for example, larger-scale imports from Saint-Malo,

– 100 –

the Channel Islands and Morlaix in Brittany were supplemented by goods coming from other parts of France, Spain, Portugal, Morocco, the Low Countries, Germany, Newfoundland and Virginia.[11] These links meant that when Peter Prylaux and Paul Mercer purchased forty pipes of oil in Seville or paid £534 for ginger at Sanlúcar in Spain, they were able to transport them through transnational transport networks to Lübeck and Calais before they were loaded onto English ships returning to London.[12] English merchants in Morocco, too, sought to access a diverse range of goods from across North Africa, including sugar, wine, ambergris, ostrich feathers, wax, dates, almonds and a 'store of gold from Timbuktu and Gao'.[13] As global activities became more common, merchant communities would include members with interests across England's trading and imperial activities. Bristol's Merchant Venturers, for instance, included an East India Company factor, sugar refiners, ship owners, explorers, the governor of Newfoundland, traders to Virginia and the Caribbean, salt makers, members of the Spanish Company, the owner of an iron works, a banker, wine merchants and even an employee of the Dutch West India Company.[14] Broadening interest in geography and products obtained enabled English traders to access goods from across the world. A price list of goods available in London in 1601 reveals that shoppers could obtain English and Russian wax, raisins from Málaga, wood from Galicia, rice from Milan, sugar from São Tomé and Brazil, dates and almonds from Morocco, ginger from Asia and wine from Bordeaux – a cornucopia of commodities that would only grow more varied over the coming century.[15] Increasing imports meant customers in early modern England were presented with a global marketplace.

While imports into England were very varied, exports throughout this period remained dominated by the wool and woollen cloth trade, although the destinations, volumes and types of fabric shipped overseas did change to reflect the growing diversity of the country's international trade.[16] Richard Archdale, for instance, oversaw trading operations that exchanged English wool for wines from Bordeaux, the Canary Islands and Málaga, sugar from Lisbon and raisins from the Mediterranean.[17]

– 101 –

Similarly, building on a strong domestic trade for lead and coal, merchants from York and Hull embraced opportunities in international markets ranging from Spain to Poland.[18] Further afield still, English merchants were quick to seek opportunities in Spain's Caribbean colonies, exporting vital supplies in return for precious American silver.[19] These efforts took place in a commercial environment that remained dominated by the export of woollen cloth to northern Europe, via the Low Countries and Germany.[20] Concerns about the cloth trade were common in early modern England, and while exports in so-called 'old draperies' from London had risen from just shy of 20,000 cloths in 1485 to over 127,000 by 1614, this would decline to some 86,000 by 1640.[21] Waning international interest in traditional English woollens, especially in the form of undressed cloth, was mitigated by the introduction of new commodities and the integration of new markets. For instance, between 1600 and 1640, exports of high-quality cloth made with Spanish wool increased from 0 to over 13,000 per year, while the sale of cheaper, colourful 'new draperies' increased fivefold and soon matched the value of 'old draperies'.[22] In London, the value of exports other than 'old draperies' increased from almost £200,000 in 1609 to upwards of £600,000 by 1640.[23] Similarly, total exports from Bristol rose from around £7,500 to just over £48,500 per year between 1560 and 1640.[24] Following rapid increases in wool exports during the sixteenth century, diversification into new markets and new commodities provided ample opportunities and sustained export growth. As imports skyrocketed, the wider English economy slowly adjusted to reflect global demands, and merchants took full advantage of innovations in domestic manufacturing to supply markets across the world.[25]

For many merchants, combining import interests with export business contributed to their trading cycles and long-term profitability. This framework was essential for merchants like Henry de Laune, from Barnstaple, whose livelihood depended on his ability to cross between different regions, first to obtain fish from Newfoundland and then to export them to Cádiz.[26] Similarly, sixty-seven merchants in Hull relied on

LIVING TOGETHER, WORKING TOGETHER

carrying domestic produce like cloth and iron between the northern city and London for their day-to-day business, but supplemented this activity by re-exporting produce like sugar.[27] Recognising the value of these circuits, one contemporary commentator waxed lyrically about how new trades saw 'superfluous commodities transported out of this realm and plenty of needful foreign wares returned', and that England had become so 'abounding with native and foreign commodities [it was] serving for a staple to neighbouring nations'.[28] Merchants were well aware of how their commercial interests related and sought to take advantage of such opportunities. For instance, the Levant Company highlighted how they transported currants in volumes that easily sustained the English market while leaving a surplus 'transported from hence to Middleborough, Amsterdam, Stade, France and other places'.[29] At the more niche end of the scale, hawks imported from Russia by the Muscovy Company found their way onto East India Company ships to be given as gifts to the Mughal emperor.[30] Thus, when Raphe Preston purchased 'some fine calicos' in Bharuch, he wrote to the East India Company in London explaining that they were 'too fine for England but will go for Barbary' – a recommendation dependent on understanding how the markets interlinked.[31] Trade to 'Barbary' was indicative of how international and domestic produce were brought together; traditional exports such as English lead were carried alongside Polonian cloth, Indian calicos, paper, benzoin, almonds, wax, opium and ostrich feathers.[32] England's connected commercial ventures across the world gave merchants greater opportunities to re-export produce, and they were quick to take advantage.

As overseas trade increased, both in terms of volume and geographical diversity, merchants exploited links across different markets, integrating new opportunities into their existing activities as and when they arose. For example, when the Turkey Company was founded to regulate English trade with the Ottoman Empire, the Merchant Adventurers encouraged its own members to join the new organisation. The company highlighted how existing trade with Italian merchants in Antwerp exported a great number of cloths that eventually ended up in Mediterranean markets,

– 103 –

just as the same trade provided access to 'Turkey commodities'. Drawing the northern European and Mediterranean markets closer together could only be a benefit.[33] For George Hanger, whose predominant activity was re-exporting exotic Asian commodities from England to Spain, links with English merchants operating in global markets was essential. His career, and that of 'many other English merchants', depended on bringing a 'great store of calicos, cloves, nutmegs, and other East India commodities to Spain' – a business that relied on the East India Company to ensure a stable supply of goods from Asia.[34] Such links could help ensure the movement of information as well as goods, and when the Levant Company 'had intelligence of 3 French ships, men of war, that were going down into the Red Sea', they had little difficulty in communicating the information to the East India Company, to prevent 'any danger than may ensure unto the English thereby'.[35] Cooperation and connections between merchants across different strands of overseas activity were vitally important, and merchants were careful to sustain relationships across the commercial community – privately and through corporate activity – to bring together diverse activities.

As a means of facilitating activity that cut across different markets and commercial activities, partnerships were a common collaborative tool for early modern merchants. In addition to helping reduce risks and limit transaction costs, such as the twenty-eight merchants who invested £4,225 13s 4d with Thomas Gresham to make use of space on his ships, it might also contribute to sharing expertise or unique market access.[36] Thus, when Daniel Burrish and Adrian Fry, merchants from Southampton and Bristol respectively, joined together to undertake trading voyages to Nantes in France, their ability to access essential markets successfully was strengthened by combining the skills and contacts of the two partners.[37] On a larger scale, the East India and Muscovy companies agreed a wide-ranging joint venture to manage a shared joint stock of £80,000 'to be employed in merchandise and trade in Russia and Muscovy and other parts beyond the seas', for which each company would 'receive half the return and proceed of the wares or

– 104 –

LIVING TOGETHER, WORKING TOGETHER

merchandises which should be returned to England'.[38] The same principle applied when the Manchester merchant William Buckley entered into a 'joint trade or copartnership' with Thomas Rode, a London-based merchant and draper, for the 'buying and selling of Manchester wares and other commodities'.[39] As well as agreeing to exchange goods, the agreement included shared stock and debts – each merchant contributed their local expertise and skills, shared financial responsibilities and stood to profit equally. Interlocks like these enabled merchants to share skills and best practice as well as pooling resources.

The details of these relationships could be complex, especially when partners brought different skills, goods or market access to the table. When Nicholas Osborne and John Osborne, draper and merchant of Norwich and merchant of London respectively, signed an indenture to become partners, their particular roles were carefully delineated. A member of the East India, Somers Island and Muscovy companies, John was part of international trading networks that gelled well with Nicholas's access to Norfolk's manufacturing industries and regional markets. In addition to strengthening a symbiotic trading relationship, their partnership put 'their stocks and estates in money and other wares together, as heretofore they have use to do in trading, merchandising, buying, adventuring and selling' whereby 'in the parts of England as in the parts beyond the seas' they would operate as 'partners with stock of wares and money'. As well as shared stock, John, 'his servants, factors or assigns' would purchase Norwich wares from Nicholas at the best rates and undertook to 'deal faithfully, truly, justly and honestly' with him.[40] Responsibilities for regional and international trade were divided between the two merchants to fit their particular expertise, but they acted in common interest and profited from a common stock. Partnerships like this allowed individual merchants to gain access to goods or markets that complemented their independent assets, making it possible for them to take on larger, more complex undertakings and employ their common resources more efficiently.

In taking advantage of trading opportunities overseas, merchants obtained new streams of income that could be invested in other commercial

– 105 –

ventures at home. This might take the form of purchasing or improving land or property, investing in manufacturing or even purchasing patents from the state to extract commodities like alum, copper or brimstone.[41] For instance, William Towerson and William Cockayne, who had worked together in trading ventures across Spain, France, the Low Countries, Germany, the Baltic and in Asia, pooled their wealth to obtain a seven-year lease for fisheries in Banne and Ulster in Ireland.[42] Similarly, Nicholas Crispe, the son of prominent London merchant Ellis Crispe, used wealth obtained in part from East India Company investment to establish a brickworks in Hammersmith – a facility that likely profited itself from overseas trade by supplying building materials to fellow merchants.[43] Overseas trade was understood to make positive contributions to the domestic economy. Merchants trading to Newfoundland, for instance, claimed that their supply of oil was a key reason for the growth of soap manufacturing in England and the launch of the 'New Company' of soap makers.[44] Similarly, supporters of the Levant Company claimed that imported cotton was 'so good [and] cheap that 20,000 persons are yearly set to work by spinning and making the same'.[45] On a smaller scale, the East India Company took care to highlight how domestic manufacturers would benefit from access to Asian markets, and had undertaken 'a little trial' to export black-dyed woollens.[46]

To undertake such ventures, merchants drew on a range of skills and expertise from within the merchant community and further afield. For instance, when King's Lynn, which had 'anciently been a town and source of good trading', sought to reverse a 'decay' brought about 'through the decrease of trade and loss of ships to pirates', the town's civic leaders sought to establish manufacturing of 'stockings and stuffs of new drapery'. To do so, they sought permission for 'bringing into their town some honest strangers' who would undertake the same.[47] Similarly, when London merchant George Mole invested £1,000 towards the production of rape(seed) oil in Kingswood, he turned to the Wiltshire clothier Benedict Webb to provide the necessary expertise. Webb's 'best skill, knowledge, industry and endeavour' would be used to undertake 'the whole managing, government and ordering of

– 106 –

LIVING TOGETHER, WORKING TOGETHER

the said stock', while Mole could simply sit back and await a return on his capital.[48] Similarly, when the Merchant Adventurers faced accusations that they were ignorant of how to dress and dye cloth, the company's members denied the charge because of their wide-ranging commercial interests and experience elsewhere. They stated, 'there are some of them which know much in that point' through participation in the Muscovy Company, where there 'have been for sundry years Merchant Adventurers, and that company has had the business of cloth buying, dressing and dyeing well performed'.[49] Expertise obtained in the latter organisation could be transferred through common personnel to the former.

Whether looking within or without the commercial community, at home or overseas, merchants were reliant on other people to be successful. Between 1550 and 1650, they oversaw dramatic increases in both imports and exports, and established commercial links with far-flung markets while maintaining, and in many places increasing, the flow of goods between England and Europe. Collaborative methods of working were ingrained in mercantile activity and had their roots in the civic structures that had underpinned economic activity for centuries. They remained essential for regulating commerce in the ports, towns and cities that were at the centre of England's trade and empire.

LIVING IN THE CITY

Early modern merchants depended on a multiplicity of networks for their business and relationships obtained through common experiences, participation in the same trades or formal partnerships were all important means for them to take advantage of England's commercial development.[50] However, entangled business interests were only one form of interaction between members of the commercial community. The common locations of merchants' everyday contact were work, worship and social interactions. Alongside their business relationships, merchants 'intermarried, belonged to the same congregations, lived next door to each other or had many friends in common', which, 'taken together, raised expectations of rectitude'.[51] Through these activities, relationships between merchants were strengthened, information could be shared and behavioural standards enforced.[52] This was vital, as early modern merchants 'depended on a collective truth-economy' and relied on their peers' creditability to underpin transactions, build business and develop trades.[53] In this way, kinship, social and institutional ties across the commercial community helped create and sustain relationships between merchants. Such practices were sustained overseas, where, 'considering the diversity of languages and customs that merchants had to master and the uncertainties they faced', relationships with other English merchants were essential 'because they shared a community of meanings and overlapping social ties'.[54] The formation and practice of business in this environment helped incentivise collaborative activity, creating multiple channels that could reinforce social surveillance and maximise benefits to individuals' positive reputation and creditability. These ties were not maintained through corporate oversight alone, but through merchants living and working cheek by jowl in an environment of significant, ongoing interaction through their families, livery companies, parishes, neighbourhoods as well as their business activities.

In early modern England, urban centres, especially port towns and trading centres, were environments where merchants were able to easily congregate and share ideas, and it was in such spaces that new commercial and colonial ventures were conceived, designed and executed.[55] After centuries of commercial tradition, innovation, governance and experience, towns and cities were sites where 'trade had become part of everyone's daily experience'.[56] They were also home to the urban, livery and trading corporations that contributed to a commercial atmosphere that was, despite many companies' restrictions on membership and centralising features, more connected. Within and across these institutions, merchants could share information, develop new partnerships, spread risk and pool resources more effectively than ever before.[57] Many port towns also had long-standing international connections, or even populations, whereby England's merchant community could absorb Europe's most innovative commercial practices.[58] Indeed, the social and cultural fabric of the commercial community was altered by the experience of international travel and exchange, whether through returning merchants, the movement of exotic goods, the exchange of news or the impact of profits from their global activities.[59]

The new trading ventures that emerged in England in the sixteenth century were fuelled by the rapid expansion of the City of London, growth that helped propel innovation and new approaches in the commercial community.[60] Other urban centres provided similar benefits to local merchants, and ports such as Bristol led the way in reaching markets in the Mediterranean and Atlantic, but the capital's financial capacity, market depth and the sophistication of its corporate structures were unsurpassed.[61] In the sixteenth century, London was the central point of organisation for numerous attempts to expand overseas trade, and it was undergoing a rapid process of development that would make it a global port by the mid-seventeenth century.[62] During this process, investment in manufacturing, mills and mines, as well as essential infrastructure such as roads, bridges and ports, had contributed to increasing productivity and efficiency across the domestic economy.[63] Here, too, London had a greater capacity for international trade, with larger dockyards and warehouses, a larger pool of experienced sailors and captains and access to bullion through the Mint contributing to its attractiveness to merchants.[64] Common interest contributed to 'investment in new skills and industry' and the effective application of 'useful knowledge' that was vital for supporting new ventures.[65]

The growth of cities like London, coupled with the growing wealth of their merchants, contributed towards a process where attempts to develop global trading opportunities led the commercial community to develop the city's facilities as well, obtain greater powers for the control of trade at home and abroad and change the way English people thought about, participated in and understood their role within the domestic and global economy.[66] By participating in broad networks in such densely populated urban areas, in business and socially, merchants within the commercial community contributed to the creation of dense webs of contact and experience – not just relating to a single trade or corporation, but part of a connected, globally focused system.

In early modern England, most merchants would have belonged to at least one corporation, but often took part in numerous organisations.[67] In London, all the major livery companies included merchants as members – for many, this was the main route for the completion of their apprenticeship and their being welcomed into the citizenship of the city. These organisations remained important throughout the lives of many merchants, enabling them to form and strengthen bonds that underpinned their commercial activities in overseas trade and empire.[68] In the East India Company, for example, members of all twelve major livery companies in London had invested in the company by 1613, including almost seventy drapers, forty-two mercers, over thirty grocers, goldsmiths and clothworkers, and between six and twenty-seven members of the Fishmongers', Skinners', Merchant Tailors', Haberdashers', Ironmongers' and Vintners' livery companies.[69] The company's trade with Asia was not these members' only interest in overseas commerce, and the typical merchant and livery company member was an investor in multiple other ventures. Sometimes investments related to the traditional trades of their livery organisation – such as clothworkers supporting trading activities promising new markets for woollens or goldsmiths seeking mineral wealth in colonial ventures – but many merchants had wide-ranging, diverse portfolios. Members of the Skinners', Ironmongers' and Grocers' livery companies were especially likely to invest widely and over time became increasingly likely to maintain senior positions in trading companies.[70] By drawing on investment from members across London's livery companies, trading companies could raise the funds necessary for far-flung ventures. They also provided another avenue through which merchants could build on existing economic interests, social relationships and business networks to support and influence the development of England's commercial and colonial activities.

LIVING TOGETHER, WORKING TOGETHER

Participation in international trade brought money flowing into England's towns and cities, especially London, but most of the time merchant's lives were lived on a much smaller scale – in the home and in the workplace. Merchants lived and worked in spaces where the lines between business and social activities were often blurred, and individual buildings might contain shops, homes, meeting places and other spaces for conducting business.[71] For example, a property on 'the high street called Cornhill' leased by the Clothworkers' to the grocer Richard Bill was set up in a fairly standard fashion. From the street, a visitor would enter Bill's shop, which was 16 by 21 feet, and then pass through into the warehouse, then a yard and finally a kitchen. Bill also leased the property's second, third and fourth floors, as well as the cellars beneath, space that included a counting house (Plate 6).[72] Similarly, Francis Hodgson's purchase of a property at Fresh Wharf in London included living space, cellars and warehouses.[73] Francis Wright's shop and tenements on Catteaton Street were an even more impressive commercial complex. Nestled between two other large enterprises, the Maiden's Head and the King's Arms, Wright's shop was 43 foot long and 30 foot wide and connected to a warehouse and counting house. A further four stories above the shop and a cellar beneath provided considerable living and work space – more than enough to conduct business, raise a family and provide room for apprentices to live in as they learned their trade.[74] Properties like these were spaces where merchants interacted with fellow traders in both social and business contexts.

Congregating especially around markets, warehouses, wharves and centres of administration, merchants often chose to live in places that were conducive to their work. They might easily find themselves living in close proximity to numerous people who were also part of their business networks – whether colleagues, business partners or competitors. For example, St Dunstan-in-the-East and St Michael Bassishaw parishes in London were both popular areas for East India Company merchants, located close to important commercial sites near the Thames and the Guildhall respectively.[75] The former was a notable mercantile parish; John

– 111 –

Stow, in his *A Survey of London*, noted that it was home to 'many rich merchants, and other occupiers of diverse trades'. Similarly, areas close to the Royal Exchange and Leadenhall Market were also popular and possessed 'many fair houses for merchants, and artificers'.[76] This neighbourhood was home to both the Cockayne and Garraway families, prominent merchants who took part in an array of overseas activities. William Cockayne, for instance, rented from the Drapers' livery company, for £9 per year, a property in St Peter-le-Poer parish; a location he shared with merchants Thomas Lowe, Henry Garraway, Isaac Jones, William Garraway, William Towerson, William Callie and John Williams.[77] Living alongside each other, working together on projects and each contributing to the administration of the parish, these merchants would have met regularly, reinforcing bonds of trust and creditability that brought together their commercial worlds and day-to-day lives.

Neighbourliness could help individuals cross the boundaries between different institutions and trades. At one site in London, between St Nicholas Lane and Abchurch, a property owned by the Clothworkers' livery company bordered land belonging to the Drapers' and Grocers' livery companies, the parish of St Augustine, and the private owner Edmund Pretty. The buildings were not only close together, but people living within them shared certain spaces – in this case, a main gate and courtyard.[78] Similarly, the layout of a 'great mansion' leased to Richard Fishbourne starkly revealed the communities that developed around the richest merchants in the city. Fishbourne's personal property included dozens of rooms, such as warehouses, a shop, kitchens, buttery and parlour, and a 127-foot-long garden that stretched back behind the main building. His property was surrounded by similar grand houses in the possession of Sir Thomas Hewett, Sir Thomas Lowe and Alderman Johns. Within Fishbourne's own complex, numerous rooms were rented to other merchants, with Lancelot Johnson and John Cooke both having tenements that could be entered from Throgmorton Street and rooms across all three stories of the complex.[79] Living so closely together did not necessarily mean these men were friends or even business associates,

– 112 –

but these arrangements did help to form and strengthen ties and contribute to the formation of a tightly knit community.

Larger houses, with large halls on their lower floors rather than shop and warehousing space, were signs of civic and economic status within the commercial community and were sites where the accoutrements of commercial achievement could be displayed.[80] For instance, the Bristol merchant John Smith converted his townhouse in Small Street into a veritable urban palace, funding the expansion of a central hall that would later be furnished with tapestry, wooden panelling and wall hangings.[81] Similarly, in London, the merchant Richard Astell used displays of weapons, armour and antique furnishings to demonstrate his family's legitimacy, honour and lineage at the heart of the city's elite.[82] Corporations also made efforts to ensure that senior figures lived in appropriate dwellings. For instance, when the mercer Thomas Bennet was elected to the office of Sheriff, he was granted 100 marks 'towards the trimming of his house' as well as 'use of the company's plate' to ensure he was suitably presented to the wider commercial community.[83] Merchants understood the importance of these spaces for their business activities and that the houses and other properties they used reflected their creditability, sociability and status within the community.

Such grand spaces were meant to be used, and social activities, including dinners and other events, were important opportunities for merchants to come together. For instance, at a meeting at Sir William Romney's house, a group of merchants with interests ranging from investment in the East India Company to trading with Spain and exploration in Guiana 'went to dinner where they had bountiful cheer'. Just over a week later many of the same group met again and 'had great good cheer' at the house of another merchant, Sir Thomas Middleton.[84] Among those present, all of whom were members of the Drapers' livery company, were figures whose businesses overlapped, complemented and competed with the others – it is hard to imagine that trade was not a topic of conversation. Corporations, too, used social occasions to expand and strengthen their networks. When the Mercers' livery company invited the Lord Mayor of London and his son-in-law to dinner, as well as the city's Sheriffs and their wives, they were confident the £30 cost of the event was well worth it, 'being for the worship and credit of the company'.[85] Similarly, the mayor of Southampton invited Henry Sherfield to 'my feast' so that the two could resolve an ongoing dispute about the payment of fees for merchants importing wine into the port.[86] Having spaces available to meet, whether for good cheer and a tipple or for political machinations, was important for merchants, as face-to-face interaction remained the most important means of establishing and sustaining relationships in the early modern period.

Merchants' grand halls were ideal for holding larger gatherings, including corporate activities. Many meetings for the Spanish Company were 'held at the dwelling house of Mr Thomas Wilford', while the Levant Company's directors met at Sir Thomas Lowe's house during his period as governor.[87] In the case of the East India Company, while it did lease a number of warehouses in London, including in the Royal Exchange and Leadenhall Market, as well as operating a major dockyard at Blackwall, the majority of corporate business was conducted in the homes of members.[88] Even after members of the generality complained that the hall in Sir Thomas Smith's house was too small to accommodate them all, and that a larger venue should be found, the directors refused and continued to use the space until the long-serving governor's death.[89] When a venue was needed to host a Dutch delegation for a conference about the East India Company's trade, it was decided that they, too, would meet in Smith's house on account of it being 'the most convenient place (especially in regards of the nearness of them)'.[90] When larger spaces were required, for meetings of the whole generality for example, there were numerous spaces that were available – the Spanish Company held general meetings at Pewterers' Hall, while in Hull, the Company of Merchants Inhabiting in Kingston upon Hull met in 'the Company's Hall (called the Merchants Hall)'.[91] As both social and business events, these meetings of the generality sometimes included dinner or led into sumptuous feasts.[92] The lines between different parts of England's trade and empire were blurred, and the lives of merchants took place across numerous corporate, business and social networks.

In the Grocers' Hall, just over the road from the Royal Exchange, the close connections between the company, its members, the city and the state were laid bare on a grand scale. On entering, a visitor would have passed through the great parlour, an entranceway that bore all the hallmarks of luxury. It was decorated with numerous carpets, including rare specimens recently imported from the Ottoman Empire, new tables, a clock, cushions of tapestry and numerous books. From here, they would pass into the great chamber, a room bedecked with reminders of the history of the company as much as its current position. Although fairly sparse in terms of furnishings, with the eye drawn to the 'chair of crimson velvet' bearing the coat of arms of the master of the company, the chamber was more impressive for the vast array of banners and streamers that hung all around. The largest bore the arms of the king, and this was joined by smaller hangings bearing the arms of the Grocers' livery company, Elizabeth I and senior grocers. Over a hundred smaller trumpet banners and streamers brightened the room further, the largest being 14 yards in length and bearing the image of St Anthony, the others being slightly shorter and decorated with griffins and camels – the latter a reminder of the trading caravans that brought spices from distant lands to grocers' shops.[93]

As sites of constant activity, corporate buildings required regular upkeep and repair. Usually, this would be to deal with normal wear and tear, but it could also be because of accidents, such as the City of Norwich's 'lamentable mishap that befell at the last Guildhall by reason of fireworks'.[94] As demonstrations of their occupants' leadership and standing, corporate buildings were maintained in a manner that ensured their suitability as a meeting place, administrative centre and status symbol. At Drapers' Hall, on Bishopsgate in London, efforts were made not only to keep the property in good repair but also in keeping with the fashions of the day, such as taking down the old parlour's ceiling with 'a fair fretwork to be erected in the place thereof'.[95] The same company

MERCHANTS

approved funds 'for the beautifying of the garden for the delight and comfort of the company' and the 'making of two small summer houses in the garden'.[96] Similarly, members of the Mercers' livery company were tasked with the 'providing and painting of such streamers and banners', the purchase of 'hangings of tapestry' and Turkish carpets, and even installing a clock.[97] When the painter Henry Lilly was hired to repair the company's banners, he was instructed to 'paint the banners with the arms of the City, which is to be painted half over with silver, and the like in the banner with the Merchant Adventurers arms'.[98] The Drapers' livery company similarly celebrated its history and links to the City of London, and statues or paintings of prominent members were displayed proudly in the company's hall.[99] The wealth and exotic commodities brought by new trades helped to realise these improvements. William Garraway 'presented and gave unto the [Drapers'] company a fair and large carpet of Persia, which was right thankfully received of him'.[100] Important displays of corporate wealth and authority, these sites gave members an opportunity to escape from the hubbub of the city and congregate together in a space where the corporate structures of their lives could not be clearer.

Outside their homes, shops and corporate halls, the business of trading companies and merchants in terms of provisioning ships and selling goods took place in more public settings such as markets and docks. In cities and towns, marketplaces were regulated to encourage good business practice, and efforts to stamp down on the 'great deceits and abuses' that traders faced in 'inns and other places' were common.[101] In London, the Royal Exchange, especially, became a centre of commercial activity at the heart of the city.[102] The importance of the Royal Exchange, both practically as a place of business and communication, and reputationally for the City of London, meant that it was maintained with precision.[103] Turrets were repaired with new stones, walls were whitened and painted, gates were repaired, the cellar renovated, statues were erected, and the sundial was kept in fine working order.[104] The activities of its residents were carefully controlled too to make sure

– 116 –

the building was kept in a good state. For example, senior merchants were appointed to oversee John Carpenter's plans to build new stairs to ensure the work 'may not breed any annoyance or inconvenience'.[105] Thus, when Thomas Firth and Thomas Price had the cheek to build ovens and a chimney in the walls of the bourse, 'whereof the north end is brought into great decay', the offending structures were immediately pulled down and the offending tenants charged for 'their presumptions and unadvised attempt [as] the whole monument might have been brought to ruin'.[106] Even the olfactory experience was regulated – users of the vaults and cellars were forbidden to 'stow or lay therein any commodities which may be noisome or offensive to any the merchants or others frequenting the walking place in the said Royal Exchange'.[107]

Ensuring that the Royal Exchange was well looked after was important. As well as serving a practical purpose for the storage and exchange of goods – the East India Company kept warehouses here during this period, for example, and members of the company were present every day – it was a gathering space.[108] Built as a 'burse, or a place for merchants to assemble in', the Royal Exchange represented a vibrant, international environment where merchants from London and beyond could interact with one another (Plate 13).[109] Communicating with diverse figures from across the commercial community, merchants would come to trade and to 'find out who was credit worthy and who was not and to hear the latest news'.[110] It was also here that members of the court delivered proclamations or speeches to the commercial community.[111] Reflecting these diverse roles, when the site came under threat from proposals to construct a similar establishment to the west of the City of London on the Strand, residents petitioned the Mercers' livery company to try to halt the development, arguing that any decline of the Royal Exchange would 'hinder the whole course of trading within this city'.[112] Commercial sites like this were of great importance for English merchants. They were a place for networks to develop across their community and somewhere that new ventures could attract, or repel, future investors, employees and partners.

MERCHANTS

Merchants, then, interacted across diverse locations, including the docks, markets, guildhalls and churches that dominated the urban landscape as well as in each other's homes. These spaces were maintained – as far as possible – as commercially friendly environments where merchants, retailers and manufacturers were expected to follow certain common rules and standards to ensure the ongoing, efficient conduct of business. Accordingly, when the City of London's officers judged that shop stalls were straying too far into the road 'to the annoyance of the passengers through the streets', the offending retailers were quickly reprimanded.[113] Likewise, Robert Wood, a tenant in East Smithfield, received orders that the pavement in front of his house be 'sufficiently repaired and amended', while the Mercers' livery company made efforts to 'compel strangers and hackney men which have stables [in London] to contribute toward the carrying away of dung'.[114] Corporations took care to ensure the tenants in their properties abided by the common standards expected of urban society.

Efforts were also made to ensure that buildings were maintained or, even better, improved by tenants. In the case of Mr Simpson, a tenant of the Haberdashers' livery company in New Fish Street, his request to lease a garden next to his house was denied until a damaged gutter was repaired.[115] Equally, Thomas Rankin was instructed to 'new floor the lower rooms, empty the vault, mend the chimney and flues, and bestow such other needful repairs as are requisite' before he could receive a new lease for a property in Cornhill.[116] Many buildings served commercial as well as residential purposes, whether the Haberdashers' livery company's property in Finsbury Field that included housing and a windmill or the Muscovy Company's in Botolph's Wharf that had 'tenements and warehouses' as part of the riverside property, and it was important that these assets could be utilised effectively.[117] In 'the great house lately erected by Sir William Cockayne' in St Peter-le-Poer parish, three warehouses 'lying one directly over another in the first, second and third stories' and a crane had been built as part of the complex and were leased to fellow merchant Henry Garraway.[118] In other cases, residential space could be

– 118 –

LIVING TOGETHER, WORKING TOGETHER

sacrificed to make way for assets that were more productive. For example, when the Mercers' livery company declared a row of properties in Katherine Wheel Alley derelict, enterprising would-be tenants were invited to propose novel ideas for the use of the land. Over three years, competing offers from Simon Houghton and John Bennet were discussed, the former offering to build an extensive commercial and residential space with a new stone wharf, before Bennet was eventually leased the property. Agreeing to pay £20 annually for rent and to spend 500 marks on rebuilding, Bennet converted the space into 'a dye house and warehouse necessary for a dyers use' – a suitable choice to meet growing demand by merchants for undyed cloth to be finished in the city before export.[119] In a similar vein, the City of London ordered that 'certain old rooms and decayed buildings being now called Worcester Hall' be destroyed so that a new site could be built to more effectively monitor the city's haulage. Although this was an expensive undertaking, the city authorities believed it was 'very necessary and convenient to be done as well for the ease and commodity of the merchants and buyers'.[120] Through efforts such as these, the built environment of early modern London was maintained and actively improved to match increasing demands stemming from demographic and economic change.

Living and working alongside each other in such urban environments, it is no surprise that merchants in early modern England were often drawn together in business. In one illustrative example, merchants, neighbours, business partners and family members were brought together to fund the construction of an ambitious project – London's New River.[121] Designed to 'bring a fresh stream of running water to the north parts of our City of London', plans for the New River were driven forward by a group led by Hugh Middleton, a goldsmith and citizen, whose strong personal links with London's commercial community were essential for the project's success.[122] Major investors in the project included senior merchants like Robert Bateman, Rowland Backhouse, Thomas Middleton, Henry Neville and Marmaduke Rawdon, who were able to provide the funds and organisational experience to undertake the vast engineering project.[123]

– 119 –

Initially founded as a partnership between Hugh Middleton and his investors, the grant of a new charter allowed the formation of the New River Company as a joint-stock corporation.[124] Sites across London soon benefited from access to the new supply, from the Mercers' livery company that obtained 'fresh water taken into Gresham house out of the said Mr Middleton's water works' to Hugh Merrick and Hugh Coloe, who leased 'a quill or branch of lead containing half an inch of water' that would be delivered 'into the yard and kitchen' of their dwelling house.[125] Once the New River had been constructed, 'the great and extraordinary benefit and service this city receives by the water brought through the streets by the travail and industry of Sir Hugh Middleton' was recognised by London's civic authorities and he was given 'a chain of gold set with diamonds and the city's arms thereunto appending' as thanks for his 'worthy and famous work'.[126] As with so much of a merchant's life in early modern England, in the New River Company lines between business and community were blurred. The organisation's investors were brought together not only through expectations of profit but also common social networks. They were interested in increasing their own wealth as well as serving the city's population by providing an essential resource. Their customers were also their neighbours, business associates, family and friends. For England's merchants, separating their social and economic lives would have made no sense, and the urban environment provided plenty of opportunities for them to come together and interact in ways that could reinforce the networks of credit and trust that they depended on to get business done.

REGULATION AND ORDER

In early modern England, merchants shared the same spaces, working, living and socialising together. Busy urban environments in cities like London were ideal for facilitating the face-to-face interaction and strong communal bonds that were essential for business, but they also represented a challenge – how could merchants enforce high standards

LIVING TOGETHER, WORKING TOGETHER

and behavioural expectations across such a fast-changing trading landscape? In part, they achieved this through the common practices inculcated in their lives, but constant regulatory oversight was also required. This vital institutional framework was provided by a range of corporate actors, both at home and abroad, and helped enforce good practice when communal pressure was not enough to make merchants toe the line.[127]

Primarily though, merchants would expect to be able to do business with creditable members of their community without the need to turn to institutional structures for support. Possessing an array of tools for documenting agreements and living within an environment of tightly connected personal and business networks, keeping things personal was suitable in most circumstances – even during disputes. Thus, when Gerard Malynes sought the repayment of a £265 debt from William Cockayne, he did so privately, sending a letter to the senior merchant. Asking Cockayne to 'pardon me to put you in mind thereof', Malynes explained how 'were it not that the ending of differences in accounts is part of my profession and living, it may be I would not have troubled your worship with these few lines'. However, having done so, he hoped the debt would be repaid quickly and without further trouble as 'I do not love to be too troublesome, neither too officious, against my friends.'[128] As long as Cockayne played by the rules, Malynes could be confident that his polite letter would move their disagreement towards a friendly resolution.

When merchants were unable to resolve disputes independently, early modern corporations employed a number of tools to regulate disagreements, and they expected members to use internal structures for arbitration and judgement to resolve disputes in the first instance.[129] For example, in the Eastland Company, 'for the avoiding of charge and tedious suite and for the increase in unity amongst the company' it was 'ordered, concluded and fully agreed that from henceforth all manner of variances, controversies and strife ... shall first be brought before the deputy and assistants.'[130] Directors and senior members in corporations

– 121 –

provided oversight to ensure that common standards were met and to avoid 'diverse abuses and disorders in the company'.[131] Thus, in the Drapers' livery company, when a dispute arose between Mitchell Pemstoy and Henry Wolostoy over 'forty shilling or thereabout', it was 'committed unto two indifferent men of this company' who would 'determine the said controversy'.[132] The Mercers' livery company employed a similar approach when directors 'Mr Cordell and Mr Baptiste Hicks' were 'entreated to deal in the matter Mr Trott and Thomas Dalby' and resolve their dispute through 'some such composition between as may be for the company's good'.[133] In Bristol, a 'difference between Philip Love merchant and Edward Lake, servant to William Yeamans' was decided by Michael Hunt and Hugh Griffiths, who agreed to review and judge the dispute on behalf of the Merchant Venturers company.[134] Similarly, when 'a petition exhibited by certain merchants' of Great Yarmouth was submitted to the town's leaders concerning 'certain abuses, misdemeanours, miseries and wrongs offered to them by the searcher', the corporation quickly ordered 'interrogations to be ministered' to resolve the issue.[135] For Thomas Rogers, a factor of the East India Company in Golconda, a corporate inquiry was deemed his only recourse after a fellow merchant, Mr Barry, had taken 'my beaver hat and band with the paper books' and 'sold them and made an adventure thereof to China'.[136] By overseeing disagreements such as these internally, corporations provided institutional frameworks for ensuring the good conduct of their members, away from prying eyes.

Regulatory oversight was just as much about strengthening cultural standards as it was punishing specific misdemeanours. Accordingly, when the actions of Launcelot Peacock landed a young member of the Haberdashers' livery company, Lambert Olbolton, in prison, he faced the brunt of the corporation's regulatory ire. Olbolton was certainly not blameless – he owed Peacock £70 – but the response of his creditor was deemed excessive, disordered and uncivil. Rather than giving the younger merchant some leeway in paying his debt or bringing the dispute to the corporation's directors for resolution, Peacock instead looked

LIVING TOGETHER, WORKING TOGETHER

outside the organisation for satisfaction and charged Olbolton at the King's Bench. He had also threatened the wife of another merchant who had acted as surety for Olbolton, who had paid the interest owed to Peacock 'to her great grief and vexation'. The Haberdashers' came to Olbolton's aid and entreated Peacock to accept the interest paid and withdraw his suit or else accept the company's appointment of mediators to resolve the issue independently. Peacock, in spite of 'all the entreaties and persuasion' of senior members, refused; worse, 'in very uncivil terms both of scoffing and threatening, [he] abused not only the worshipful Sir John Garrard' but also some of the directors. Peacock's 'most indiscreet, uncivil and disordered manner' emerged during a dispute with another member. Rather than siding with Peacock and ensuring Olbolton's debts were paid, this outburst refocused the company's discussion on Peacock's 'former misdemeanours' and his 'cruel and hard dealing not only with the said Olbolton as aforesaid but also with diverse of those who have been his apprentices'. Peacock's lack of participation in the community's positive development, together with his perceived poor character and lack of creditability, led the company to conclude that he was 'unfit to be of the livery of this company or to bear any office of the same'.[137] The dispute may have begun with Olbolton's poor financial creditability, but it ended focused on Peacock's inability to act within the strictures of early modern London's social business environment. Rather than concentrating simply on contract enforcement or specific rules, corporations took care to regulate their members' commercial activities and behaviour in a manner that was conducive to the communal standards expected of merchants.

As the expected first point of recourse for merchants, corporations were willing to employ imaginative strategies, when necessary, to impose their decisions on members. Over the course of a nine-month dispute with Humphrey Street, which began in April when the recalcitrant shopkeeper refused to pay increased rent for two shops at the Royal Exchange, the committee that oversaw the site on behalf of the City of London and the Mercers' livery company used all the tools at their disposal to bring him to heel. First, they wrote to 'Mr Chamberlain of this City and Mr Renter Warden of the Company of Mercers', who were 'entreated to demand rent at the shops tomorrow, and if he [Street] refuse or do not pay them same it is thought fit that some speedy court in the law be taken against him for his expulsion'. When Street refused to budge, the shops were rented to Thomas Dalby, a mercer, who was encouraged to take Street to court for access to the same. The threat of a suit from Dalby, who now legally held a competing lease to the two properties, brought Street to the negotiating table, and ten days later the committee offered to have the suit dropped should he 'offer to pay for the said shops after the rates of £5 a shop per annum'.[138] By December, Street was back in the Royal Exchange – now paying £8 for each shop.[139] In this instance, Street was unable to stand against the combined authority of the committee, which in this negotiation at least, held all the cards. In this kind of way, corporations might impose their will without needing to actually go to court. Their control of so many aspects of the city's commercial environment – such as leases for shops – allowed them to undertake creative, albeit probably underhanded, strategies without much fear of being overturned.

This did not mean that corporations were always the dominant party during disputes; individuals could certainly defend themselves and their interests. One wide-ranging dispute following the seizure of the ship *Pearl* reveals the limitations of corporate oversight in situations where specific privileges were considered alongside crimes against members of the wider commercial community.[140] Carrying goods worth up to £20,000, obtained during a voyage interloping within the East India Company's monopoly in Asia, the seizure itself was not questioned so much as who should receive a share of its stock.[141] Although the ship's owner, Captain Castleton, was clearly at fault, investors in the *Pearl*'s voyage insisted that they had only participated in the belief that it was intended for legal destinations. One investor who believed it had been intended for the Mediterranean complained he had received 'no penny worth of anything for my long trouble and charge', despite investing in good faith, and therefore had equal claim for the proceeds of the ship.[142] Another investor, the Norwich merchant John Ramsey, claimed he had been persuaded to invest £550 in the belief the voyage had been intended for Guinea and Benin on the West African coast.[143] In either case, the purported destination would not have contravened the East India Company's monopoly, and Castleton's fraud against his investors meant they, too, were deserving of compensation.[144] In short order, investors, including Ramsey, Robert Mansfield, Thomas Edmonds, the Lord of Worcester, Lionel Cranfield, John Morris and Ellis Sotherton, were all awarded compensation.[145] However, while defrauded investors were compensated, the East India Company did not achieve the same positive outcome. In spite of the ship interloping into their markets, and surely undercutting prices and damaging relations overseas just as much as any other, it was not awarded funds from the sale.

For corporations and individuals alike, looking beyond the boundaries of the commercial community to resolve disputes was no guarantee of success. When Arthur Garraway, the son of one of London's most affluent merchants William Garraway, was charged with obtaining diamonds worth £11,000 through private trade – in contravention to the Levant Company's privileges – the corporation seized the gems until fees were paid. The Garraway pair, deeply unhappy, refused to accept the company's high valuation and quickly sought support from the privy council. Yet, the council was unwilling to support either side and resolved that there were insufficient records about transactions associated with the diamonds to make a decision. Despite the Levant Company's best efforts, after multiple meetings the privy council remained undecided.[146] By looking beyond the corporation for arbitration, the Garraway pair had made public a dispute that should have remained within the commercial community.

As these examples suggest, while 'going to court was frowned upon' as a distraction from the practicable conduct of trade and damaging to the social fabric of commercial communities, merchants were willing to employ the full range of legal options available when necessary.[147]

Sometimes this was undertaken with corporate approval, such as when the Drapers' livery company 'gave leave unto Mr Dummer to take the law against Jerome Champion for a certain debt that he owed him' or the Clothworkers' livery company's decision to permit Richard Waltham to sue Thomas Ingram after the latter had refused to participate in internal arbitration.[148] In other cases, the decision to use the courts was taken independently, for example when John and William Bourman arranged to have Richard Levesey arrested 'for the debts of Robert Levesey his son'.[149] This approach was especially likely when a dispute was between an individual and a corporation. For instance, when Timothy Willis struggled to obtain payment from the Muscovy Company he had little choice but ask for the privy council to intervene, who wrote to the corporation insisting that 'some good order and end to be made betwixt them' and their former employee.[150] Similarly, if an individual moved physically beyond the reach of corporate oversight, for example when the linen merchant Peter Moffett 'departed from his dwelling house and absented himself to the intent to defraud and hinder' after becoming bankrupt, merchants were comfortable asking for aid from the state to ensure the debts were repaid.[151]

In addition to overseeing disputes between members and acting as regulators in England, trading corporations also made efforts to ensure that the trading activities of their members, or on their members' behalf, were conducted in an orderly manner.[152] In some cases, such as the decision by Great Yarmouth's corporation to impose new ordinances in response to complaints of disorderly trading, this could be little more than simply restating and more vigorously enforcing existing regulations and practices.[153] Similarly, when members of the Levant Company complained that silk had 'greatly fallen in price' and sought to establish trade in Marseille, the corporation's directors told them that it was not their responsibility to oversee specific trading decisions but instead to provide a forum where interested parties could 'confer together and agree in friendly manner' about commercial decisions.[154] The Merchant Adventurers and Eastland Company likewise employed strategies to maintain orderly practices among their members – the former forbade members to act 'against the standing orders' of the company 'for private profit' and the latter ensured no serious company business was undertaken 'at the exchange, nor at any tavern or such like indecent place'.[155] As a result of such strategies, when Richard Barne, a former member of the Muscovy Company, sought to establish a rival venture in Russia, the corporation were especially concerned that 'this Barne, being a quarrelsome young man' would 'breed such confusion and disorder' in the region that their good trading relations would be undermined.[156] Merchants required stable, orderly trading environments to do business, and corporations sought to provide the institutional frameworks necessary to make this possible both at home and overseas.

Where trading companies did seek to engage directly in decisions about where, when and what should be traded by their members, the most common practice was to establish a joint-stock fund related to a specific area of commercial activity. For instance, when a Hamburg merchant approached Bristol's Merchant Venturers about purchasing wines, almonds and fruit, the company opted to undertake the transaction communally – all members were welcome to participate in the purchase as part of a joint stock, an offer that attracted sixty-four subscribers.[157] The fruit was divided among them and the wine was sold 'for the common benefit of all the merchant undertakers' to the grocers of Bristol.[158] For joint-stock companies such as the East India Company, the entire business was conducted using this model. The company's agents in Asia were expected to operate on behalf of common good, and the corporation took care to try to ensure its servants presented an orderly front even if they privately disagreed about particular policies. For example, when factors Mr Oxwick, Mr Farewell and Mr Ball, based near Bharuch in India, were discovered to be acting against each other to obtain the best deals for indigo, they were quickly admonished. They were reminded by senior merchants in Ahmadabad, William Edwards, John Aldworth and Edward Dadsworth, that 'you are all there for the general business, and so should all join together for the general good thereof'. Rather than trying to outdo each other, the young traders were told to stop acting 'secretly' and instead 'with a mutual consent and with clear facts openly'.[159] When overseeing distant trades, joint-stock organisations had to place faith in their agents and hope that the structures they put in place to encourage orderly, responsible trading would hold up in the face of distance time and changeable commercial conditions overseas.

It was in response to these challenges that the Levant Company's generality agreed 'for selling that commodity [currants] in a joint stock' as a means for 'setting a reasonable price' and 'for the better government and managing of the sale of their currants' – even as the rest of the company's business remained outside the joint stock and was managed by individual members. Appointing 'Mr Deputy, Mr Morris Abbott, Mr Ralph Freeman and Mr Henry Garraway' as managers, the generality were confident these senior merchants would ensure that the 'account should be managed and governed for the good of the company'.[160] Yet, these managers quickly found out how difficult it was to impose their authority in a region where factors representing dozens of different Levant merchants were also active. These issues were exacerbated by long-standing relationships between local merchants in Zante and merchants from Bristol, who had persuaded their Greek counterparts to withhold currants from the Levant Company's factors until 200 tonnes of tin could be dispatched from their home city.[161] Worse still, William Langhorne, a member of the Levant Company, had committed 'disgraceful, contemptuous and malicious scandals' and turned 'the Greeks against them, and principally against Richard Beresford to the endangering of his life'. Although Langhorne was immediately disenfranchised from the company, the episode revealed the difficulties of imposing centralised management over the trade.[162] In an attempt to restore the company's effective regulation of the trade, the Levant Company quickly became more willing to listen to dissenting members of the company who argued that the joint stock was unfair, both in terms of who was able to access it and the imbalance of shares within it.[163] Led by George Conquest and Richard Wiseman, a group of merchants sought inclusion in the joint

– 128 –

stock 'for that they were free brethren of the company and some of them traders'.[164] A more inclusive joint stock was quickly introduced, and the Levant Company returned to more traditional methods of regulating its members and factors overseas.

As well as maintaining regulatory control over its members, the Levant Company elected to increase its direct engagement in trading activities, but it did so without attempting to centralise all commercial decisions. For example, by choosing to hire ships that would carry the goods of any member so long as they paid freight charges, more members were able to benefit and directly managed voyages became less contentious.[165] Consequently, when 'Mr Moyer, master of the *Royal Merchant*' was given clear instruction about where and when but not what to trade, there was little in the way of complaint. Moyer was instructed not to travel to Livorno or Zante but instead 'travel directly to Smyrna, for 20 days, then to Constantinople for 50 days, then back to Smyrna for 60 days, before finally returning to England'. Merchants who wished to return goods on the same ship were required to subscribe for a specific tonnage in advance of the outward departure.[166] Providing this framework facilitated the orderly conduct of trade by members; it did not remove their agency over decisions about what to sell, to whom or at what prices, nor did it diminish their control over specific relationships with partners. In doing so, the Levant Company returned to the essential role of corporations in early modern England – providing institutional structures that strengthened relationships, mediated disputes and safeguarded stability in markets at home and overseas.

FOUR

MONOPOLISTS AND INTERLOPERS

After a decade of working with Mamotack traders on the fringes of England's settlements in North America, William Pynchon had proven himself a key part of the commercial system. Whether buying furs for export to England, selling corn ground at his newly built mill or arranging transport to navigate the winding waterways of Massachusetts, he was the man to go to. In his own words, Pynchon dominated the market because he used 'the best of his skill and judgement' and a deep understanding of how, where, when and for what his Amerindian counterparts traded. It was, he insisted, a strong, positive and long-lasting relationship with local traders that would 'improve this opportunity to the best advantage of the public' and ensure 'a better way for speedy supply' of goods to the colony. By relying on Pynchon to undertake the difficult task of trafficking in this challenging border region, all colonists could access 'this Indian fur trade at equal rates', he argued, without having to go to the trouble of establishing commercial links of their own.

Not all were convinced. Rather than seeing Pynchon as a useful broker, competitors presented the senior merchant as a detrimental, monopolistic presence on the border who stymied their own attempts as trading directly with Mamotack markets. The leading critic, Captain

Mason, described how his own attempts 'to trade some corn with the Indians' had been rebuffed due to what he perceived as Pynchon's undue influence. He reported that local traders had told him they 'dares not [trade with him] without leave' as they were 'afraid of [Pynchon] as also are the Indians on the other side [of the river]'. These claims were reinforced by another trader, Mr Hooke, who stated that 'Mr Pynchon knew that the Indians being afraid of him would not bring down any corn' to trade with other colonists, a situation that resulted in him having 'all the trade to himself and have all the corn in his own hands'. As Hooke and Mason would have it, Pynchon had come to dominate trade across a considerable region through intimidation and fear. Thus presented, rather than acting for public advantage, Pynchon's monopolistic behaviours were damaging to other traders who found themselves locked out of the market.

To justify his position, Pynchon argued that his success had nothing to do with fear or intimidation but was simply because of his more effective trading practices. Not only had he, unlike Mason or Hooke, taken the effort 'in respect of expense of time and victuals and gifts of knives' to effectively build cross-cultural relationships with Mamotack traders, but he had also built up the necessary infrastructure to support the trade, such as warehousing 'for keeping the corn until he had a freight' and canoes for transport. More importantly still, Pynchon suggested that his competitors were simply less attractive partners for local traders. While Mason insisted that he had 'traded some at Woronoto' in the past, Pynchon believed more recent failures reflected his competitor's poor understanding of local customs and inability to establish good relationships. Explaining 'that he did not approve of the Captain's way of trading as the best way to bring in corn and for our safety', Pynchon condemned Mason as both incapable as a trader but also a threat to his own commercial operations. Choosing to 'neither make nor meddle' in his less skilled compatriot's affairs out of concern that the Mamotack 'may bear me a grudge', Pynchon's defence of his privileged position rested on Mason's inability to abide by expected behavioural standards that risked damaging not only his own reputation but also that of the wider English community in Massachusetts. On the fringes of England's emerging empire in America, the risk of disorderly trade was enough to justify the maintenance of essentially monopolistic control over the fur trade – for Pynchon and the colony's commercial future to be successful, not everyone could be a winner.[1]

RESTRAINING OUTSIDERS AND MAINTAINING MONOPOLIES

English commercial culture was often collaborative, with merchants depending on each other to follow common business practices that ensured they could work together. This was reinforced by institutional arrangements that helped regulate activities across the globe. Despite this, individual merchants and corporations still found themselves in competition with each other. Corporations might make efforts to be more inclusive and to allow a broader range of merchants to take part, and their memberships could be dynamic and fluid, but at their core they were restrictive organisations. They demanded certain standards of education from their members, denied access to non-merchants and imposed strict regulations on the practice of trade overseas. Many merchants probably agreed with these parameters – they helped maintain the behavioural standards of the community and merchants' own professional privileges and identity. Companies existed to give their members an edge, whether against competing merchants at home or in challenging trading environments overseas.

However, when corporations used their privileges to target non-members who were merchants, and denied the same merchants access to the corporations, competition between insider and outsider, company and interloper, often came to the fore.[2] For instance, this dynamic was clear when the Levant Company sought a charter from Elizabeth I to merge the Turkey and Venice companies into a single corporate body that would have monopolistic privileges over England's trade with the

– 132 –

MONOPOLISTS AND INTERLOPERS

Mediterranean. These were two of the smallest companies, yet were trading to an incredibly profitable region, so the new proposal was met with dismay by many merchants who would remain excluded. Condemning the corporation's structure as inefficient and damaging to the commonwealth, these merchants complained that only four members of the two existing companies had undertaken significant trade and that the trade of other members was 'no matter of importance'. Questioning 'how far the same may improve the common wealth', they suggested the newly chartered company should welcome 'the rest of her majesty's merchants that have travelled within the Straights, Spain, France and other parts'. Comparing the proposed organisation unfavourably to the larger Merchant Adventurers and Muscovy Company, they proposed that mimicking the regulated structure of the former or (preferably) the joint-stock model of the latter would be more effective. Widening participation in the company, they argued, would give it the strength to prosecute England's interests more effectively and increase the wealth of the kingdom.[3] In the end, the company was expanded, from six to over fifty members – its monopolistic privileges maintained at the price of competing merchants forcing their way into the organisation.[4]

From the perspective of established companies, opening access to new members in this way was perceived as a real threat, not just in terms of undermining the opportunities and wealth of current members who would face greater competition in markets overseas, but also to effective corporate government. Thus, when Elizabeth I ordered that all English merchants would be permitted to trade in the Elbe and Weser regions in Germany, in contravention to the Merchant Adventurers' traditional privileges, the company was dismayed. Richard Gore, the company's deputy-governor, quickly wrote to the privy council to raise his concerns. He complained that even if the new entrants remained in Emden and Stade as instructed, they would still undercut prices for English wool. Worse, many of the new merchants were not following this order, and Gore accused them of smuggling goods directly to Hamburg – a direct violation of his company's monopoly. By altering the corporation's

– 133 –

privileges, Elizabeth I had weakened their bargaining position and risked undermining the good reputation and behavioural standards that the company had taken such care to maintain.[5]

In the early seventeenth century, during debates in parliament about the efficacy of the corporate, monopolistic structure of England's overseas trade, these same questions about wider access versus good government remained at the fore.[6] Especially targeting the Merchant Adventurers, a bill for 'free trade' was presented in 1604 recommending that the organisations that did not conduct an essential service – defined as when 'merchants are at charge in sending presents in maintaining ambassadors, consuls and agents' or operating a joint-stock financing structure – should not maintain their privileges. The bill argued that 'the engrossing and restraint of trade' by corporations reduced exports and that the freedom to trade would help create a 'more equal distribution of wealth of the land'. Although presenting 'the rich merchants of London' in opposition to 'all the clothiers, and in effect all the merchants of England', proponents of the bill hoped that weakening corporate demands on members would provide jobs for young sons of gentlemen: any person willing and able should be allowed to trade overseas, not just merchants.[7]

For merchants, the threat was clear. Not only were their existing monopolistic privileges at risk but also their role in society, their distinct professional identity and their ability to effectively maintain behavioural standards across the English commercial community overseas. To counter the proposals, the Merchant Adventurers argued that limiting cloth exports to their mart town in Middelburg had numerous benefits. A 'ruled trade', rather than commerce undertaken 'in a disordered and straggling manner by all that will', was 'far better for the public good' for several reasons. First, it helped maintain 'orderly trade' that 'has been formed by good experience sundry times' and helped maintain both high volumes of exports as well as keeping prices for English goods high. Second, 'having built many good and serviceable ships', the company helped reduce transaction costs by sending ships in convoy, as well as sharing charges for maintaining their privileges in Germany. Finally, the Merchant

MONOPOLISTS AND INTERLOPERS

Adventurers suggested that the Spanish sought the dissolution of the company, so keeping it around made sense simply as a means of frustrating them.[8] Without these structures in place, they argued that English merchants in Germany would face the same difficulties as their counterparts in Morocco and France, where no company currently operated to stop the imposition of severe duties on English goods. In addition, in what was considered a finite market where 100,000 cloths were already exported, it was believed an increase in merchants would simply result in a situation where 'many men will trade with little or no profit, and so be unable to perform services to his majesty and country'.[9] Proponents of corporate government argued that, by restricting access to markets to those who would follow the rules and work together, companies helped both their own members and the wider commonwealth.

It was in this environment of fevered debate that the Levant Company's charter was reissued by James I in 1605 – and it included changes that made clear the shifting dynamic of state support for corporate privileges. The company maintained its rights to act as 'one fellowship and one body corporate and politic in deeds and in name', and to monopolise England's trade to 'all the other parts of the Levant', Turkey and Venice, but with more strings attached. The company was expected to alter its approach to trading overseas 'not only to uphold and maintain the trade and traffic' already obtained but also 'by the best means we can . . . to advance and enlarge the same'. It was no longer acceptable for the company 'to appropriate the said trade of the Seignories of Venice and Turkey to any limited number of merchants nor to any one city, town or place'. Instead, membership would 'lay open the same to all our loving subjects using only the trade of merchandise' – so long as they abided by the laws and regulations of the company. In this way, the company remained the privileged space of professional merchants, even if it could no longer restrict access to those from towns and cities across England. At the first meeting to discuss the new charter, attended by merchants who intended to join as well as current members, it was agreed that 'contributions should be levied, rated and collected upon all

– 135 –

and every of the merchants which should enter into the privilege and freedom of this trade'. An initial sum of £25 was promised by all merchants entering the trade 'upon the desire of many' present at the conference. The entrance fee would soon increase to £50 as new members sought to protect their own new-found position in the company.[10]

The *quid pro quo* evident in these discussions, between a public, common good brought about by regulated and well-governed trade, and the oversight and restrictive access that enabled this, was a common theme for defenders of corporate privilege. When the French Company was founded in 1611, for example, its charter specified how the organisation was empowered to address complaints that 'trading without any order, society or government amongst themselves had bred very many inconveniences' to the 'great damage and prejudice' of English merchants in France. It balanced these privileges to impose a common governance structure with expectations the company would not 'appropriate the same trade neither to any city town or place, nor to any limited number of merchants, nor to suffer it to be used at all in any degree of monopoly'. Any merchant could participate so long as they paid their fees to the new corporation and abided by its rules.[11] Other companies maintained support by highlighting both the positive benefits for the operation of orderly trade and their role in paying for the 'charge of ambassadors from time to time'.[12] In either case, companies were expected to deliver positive benefits to the state and wider economy of England if they wished to retain their privileges for long.

Quite how to balance these conflicting perspectives was never fully resolved, and similar arguments were presented each time debates about the value of corporate involvement in overseas trade re-emerged throughout the seventeenth century. For example, during the Civil War, one anonymous author targeted the Merchant Adventurers, condemning the company's monopoly as acting 'like an ulcer upon the body politique of this Kingdom' that must be eradicated at once. The author said corporate concern that 'a general freedom of trade might give liberty to become merchants without an apprenticeship' was false, equating it to the absurd

MONOPOLISTS AND INTERLOPERS

idea that 'young gentlemen should be kept from their lands for want of experience to manure them'. Would it not be better, they argued, if 'all active and industrious spirits, to seek more ports, and make quicker returns' were able to do without the shackles of corporate restraint?[13] Conversely, a tract signed by thirty-four merchants trading to Bilbao, and presented to parliament's Council for Trade a little later in 1648, reflected on the decay of trade with Spain and argued that 'regulation and government' was necessary to restore it. A vital port town, Bilbao reputedly imported 'more English manufacture and fish, than any one port in Christendom, for tis the inlet to all Castile'. Trade had declined, the merchants argued, because poor regulation in England had resulted in lower-quality products, which had damaged the creditability of factors in Spain and been exacerbated by 'want of regulation' and involvement by 'some who were not skilled in it'. The tract beseeched parliament to restore a corporate government over the disorderly trade and help English merchants regain their position at the heart of Spain and Portugal's commercial interests. Even if parliament insisted on 'a more open and free trade, than that of companies and societies', it was hoped they would 'take care that government and order in trade may be preserved and confusion avoided'.[14] As these two conflicting perspectives make clear, the relationship between merchants who insisted they were necessary for regulating behaviour and those who supported deregulated access to trade remained fraught throughout the early modern period.

As well as limiting who could join trading companies and thus partici-pate (legally at least) in restricted trades, corporations also made efforts to ensure that non-members were not able to take advantage of corporate privileges through partnerships with members. In the Clothworkers' livery company, for instance, Henry Simpson was fined £20 'for joining in part-nership with [Mr] Griffin contrary to the ordinance of this house'.[15] By joining in partnership with non-members, individuals might obtain a competitive advantage over their brethren and risked sharing trading secrets with outsiders. In the case of John Wright, the clothworker was accused of working directly with a patterner, which was forbidden, and he

– 137 –

MERCHANTS

was ordered to cease work immediately and take measures to ensure that his former partner 'shall not learn the said trade to the detriment of this company'.[16] Similarly, in Bristol, the Merchant Venturers ordered that 'no person free of this company shall join or deal in partnership with any person not free of this company' in any commercial venture.[17] Efforts to crack down on non-member participation in the Spanish Company led to strict enforcement tactics. Here, members 'which have already joined with any partner or partners not being free of the company' were commanded 'presently [to] make relation thereof in writing to the secretary of the company, signifying with whom, and in what manner he has so joined'. 'Besides the infringing of his oath', members who were not forthcoming would be fined. Non-members currently with goods in Spain and Portugal were granted six months 'for returning their wares and merchandises' but after this time members would be banned from partnering 'with any retailer, artificer, inn holder, farmer, common mariner or handicraft man' – those who were caught doing so would forfeit 20 per cent of their goods.[18]

Restricting outsiders was a concern for many corporations, and numerous activities were deemed a threat to the established corporate order. In York, for instance, many individuals were punished for undertaking operations not permitted by the city's merchant corporation. Thomas May, Robert Ellis and John Lodge were fined between £3 and £10 each for selling groceries without a licence, while Richard Both and William Wood were fined for trading while not members of the company, and Mr Breerdy and Mr Eastford were charged £3 12s for a voyage they had undertaken to London without permission.[19] In Yarmouth, news that 'certain strangers do come into this haven and here buy fresh herrings . . . to the great hurt of the inhabitants of this town' was met with the strict application of regulations that denied access to the town's market to such traders in future.[20] In Norwich, however, access to outsiders was denied on the basis that they undermined standards. Here, 'for the help, repair and amendment of the decayed estate of the city', the corporation petitioned the privy council

– 138 –

to protect their 'trade of new draperies' that was 'the chiefest maintainer of all our other traffic and commerce, the nourisher of all others [of] our mechanical occupations and a notable means for the maintenance of many thousands', by forbidding strangers who 'do not yield nor submit their stuffs of new draperies to be governed by the laws of this city' from manufacturing goods.[21] In each case, members and non-members alike were punished for activities that undermined the boundaries between insider and outsider.

Corporations were sometimes willing to put these differences aside, especially when the risks of competition threatened current members – or worse, might lead them astray. For instance, the Merchant Adventurers lifted their restrictions on members joining other companies after the foundation of the Turkey Company. In part, their willingness to do so stemmed from an appreciation that goods purchased by the company's members via the northern European market towns, especially Antwerp, were tied into pan-European trading networks that were strongly linked with the Mediterranean, but it was also a means of ensuring that members were not tempted to leave.[22] A similar pattern led the Spanish Company to welcome members of the East India Company into the corporation. After a motion by its members to precisely define the status of investors in the joint-stock organisation, the Spanish Company 'resolved and fully agreed that the said company of East India is dissolved and not to be any longer accounted as a company'. From the perspective of their regulations, therefore, 'any such freedom of itself [in the East India Company] is not thought sufficient to bar or hinder any merchant being otherwise lawfully qualified' from joining.[23] This workaround, mentally dissolving the competing company for the purposes of their members, allowed the corporation to maintain strict rules relating to its members joining direct competitors (such as the Merchant Adventurers) without denying them access to profitable opportunities. Maintaining strict boundaries only made sense when it benefited the corporation.

The crew and officers on ships employed by merchants also represented a necessary partnership between merchants and outsiders, and it,

– 139 –

too, presented a challenge – how could they restrain these individuals from trading on their own accounts once in port overseas?[24] For some merchants, such as Mr Bell and Mr Hall who were trading in France, the common practice of allowing mariners to carry some small number of goods was seen as a key reason why English shipping was uncompetitive against 'other nations by cheapness of their freight'. They recommended the adoption of a new policy that would either limit foreign competition or stop mariners 'from being merchants'.[25] From Bell's and Hall's perspective, ensuring that merchants alone could conduct trade was the only way they could effectively participate in competitive international markets. In a similar attempt to restrain their employees from brokering trade on their own behalf, the Eastland Company insisted that all ship masters enter into a £50 bond before travelling east, which was reimbursed on their return so long as they could show 'true payment of the tolls of the King of Denmark, and of the King of Poland and Duke of Prussia' and that they had not carried any strangers' goods without consent from the company.[26] When this proved insufficient, the bond was increased to £300 in a desperate attempt to stop the 'excessive trade of mariners and masters of ships', who were seen to 'cloy the markets and in their sales abase the commodities of this kingdom'.[27] Mariners were necessary partners but they were also potential competitors, and their disorderly trading was eventually damaging not only to the profitability of trades overseas but also to the reputation and relationships of English merchants overseas.

To maintain their monopolies, corporations depended on internal regulations and support from the state, but they also relied on local officials across England who collected impositions or dues and monitored potentially illicit activities.[28] For instance, when the French trader Daniel Angebauld and London merchant John Holland 'bought and sold' French wine in Portsmouth 'contrary to the ancient order, custom and privilege of the town', city authorities seized the offending beverage. Holland, pleading ignorance, promised to pay any fine demanded and to never commit the same offence again; £3 10s was levied, the wine

– 140 –

MONOPOLISTS AND INTERLOPERS

released, and Portsmouth's privileges effectively enforced.[29] For companies with interests across England, the support of local officials was particularly important. Soon after receiving its charter, the Spanish Company wrote to customs officers across England requesting their assistance, as 'the mere merchants of England trading into Spain and Portugal' struggled to impose their privileges 'inhibiting all others to use any trade to those two realms'.[30] Port officers were expected to stop goods being shipped that did not belong to members of the company and were informed that this meant 'excluding all retailers, artificers, innholders, farmers, common mariners and handicrafts men' from the trade.[31] Similarly, during a dispute about the payment of dues for currant imports, the Levant Company 'thought fit to desire one Mr Willett, who is employed by the farmers of the customs, and resides at Bristol, that he would take care thereof on the company's behalf and demand and collect the same'. In essence, this meant that the company expected the unfortunate Willett to spy on his neighbours on its behalf.[32] Indeed, keeping track of competing claims was a chore for many customs officers, such as Thomas Heson, who complained from Southampton about the difficulties of collecting fees from merchants in the face of confusing, overlapping rights and privileges claimed by different groups.[33] Even when merchants did follow the rules they could find themselves running into conflicting claims of oversight, such as the mariner John Moody, who carefully sought permission from the Levant Company to unload currants purchased in Marseille only to be told he should treat with the Merchant Venturers of Bristol instead, 'for that it only concerned them and not this company'.[34]

Overseeing trading activities in English ports could be difficult enough, but for companies seeking to regulate their members overseas the challenge was even greater. The Merchant Adventurers maintained the right to seize the property of any Englishman trading to the mart towns in opposition to their monopoly – and to do so kept officials and half of the senior management of the company resident overseas.[35] Similar efforts were made by the Eastland Company after it was discovered that

– 141 –

certain members were 'endeavouring by new devises and collusions (with evil examples of others), so cunningly to deal that neither themselves nor their goods can conveniently be met' on their return to England. The corporation decided it had no other option but to send their representatives to search trader's goods while they were still in Poland.[36] Despite these efforts, the challenges of enforcing a monopoly over goods returning from the Baltic remained and were exacerbated by the risk of these same goods being carried within Europe, by non-English merchants, to places where English merchants belonging to other companies were resident – such as Hamburg. To overcome this challenge, the company elected to operate by the spirit of their charter in the hope that others would follow their lead. The Eastland merchants were ordered 'that from henceforth no commodity of the Eastland country grown shall be imported into this kingdom by any brethren of this fellowship, other than from the places of their own privilege, and that in English bottoms only'.[37] Of course, this action was only helpful if merchants in other corporations were willing to operate under similar principles. In the end, if merchants did not follow the accepted and expected rules of behaviour that underpinned commercial activity in early modern England, there was only so much that corporations could do.

When merchants were not successful in restraining interloping actors who acted in opposition to the tenants and practices of the wider community, they often vilified these figures for undermining the profitability of trade and threatening the very fabric of early modern commercial society. For example, after the Moroccan ruler Abu Marwan Abd a-Malik I encouraged English traders to 'enter in league as well for the quiet traffic of your ships and subjects in to this country of Barbary' in the same way 'as through the straights into the Levant Seas', merchants had high hopes for establishing a well-ordered trade.[38] However, reports about 'the trouble that we your factors and servants' were facing in the region highlighted the 'sinister and undirect dealing of John Symcotte and his adherents', and complained that 'every unruly person shall there stand free at his own liberty, whether he will be ruled or no'.[39] Without a patent to

– 142 –

regulate the trade and strong corporate representation to enforce it, the Barbary merchants had little ability to impeach Symcotte. Similarly, when a series of interlopers sought to circumvent the Levant Company's monopolistic control over currant imports by carrying currants 'pretended to be for account of the masters and mariners', the corporation quickly took action in England.[40] First, Henry Hide and Mr Hobson, merchants from Yarmouth, saw their smuggled currants seized and faced heavy fines for their action as the Levant Company was able to 'insist upon the power and strength of the charter'.[41] Concerns remained, however, about the ease with which interlopers had gained access to markets in Zante, where Levant Company factors were stationed. In particular, there were 'many bitter complaints against Simon Whitcombe', whose 'cunning and malicious practices' had undermined the corporation. Recriminations followed: in order to 'restore that trade of currants in a better order for the future', a decision was taken 'for the punishing of those delinquents'.[42] Whether Symcotte in North Africa or Whitcombe in Zante, interlopers threatened the communal structures of early modern English merchants.

Working out how to stop interlopers entering into regions or trades theoretically under their control was a near-constant pressure for early modern corporations.[43] Complaints from companies about such threats were common, whether in Germany, where the Merchant Adventurers were frustrated by 'interlopers and stragglers' who undermined their activities in the mart towns, or in North Africa, where the Barbary Company complained that Richard Thompson had beaten them to market for the purchase of almonds, dates, capers and molasses.[44] Stopping private traders, ship captains or gentlemen adventurers from travelling to a region notionally restricted to members of a particular corporation was almost impossible, especially in extensive maritime regions like the East Indies or Atlantic. That is not to say that challenges to corporate, monopolistic authority were limited to distant oceans.[45] For example, within the City of London's plantation project in Ireland disputes arose as different livery companies sought to manage their own lands independently. In one instance, a contested series of hedges were made and torn down

– 143 –

during a disagreement between the Drapers' agent Robert Russell and the Salters' Mr Gayer about who was permitted access to the town of Moneymore.[46] Even in England, Southampton's corporate privileges were impinged on when the Earl of Southampton constructed new ironworks at Bewley and Titchfield that engrossed 'the woods and under-woods thereabouts which were formerly vented to this place'.[47] Overcoming such threats, despite all the advantages their corporate privileges offered, was often difficult, and corporations employed numerous strategies to see off these unwanted competitors.

At their heart, concerns about interlopers rested on the effectiveness and efficacy of privileges rewarded to corporations to stop outsiders from trading (or undertaking other activities) without permission. To be successful, stopping interlopers required two things – clear privileges that could be enforced and support from the state to enforce them.[48] In the North Atlantic, for instance, when the Muscovy Company complained it was 'disturbed in their said whale fishing by their own nation', interloping English whalers objected to the very idea of monopolising the seas that were, after all, 'not under the government of any king, prince or potentate'.[49] Whalers from Hull went further still and argued that it was they, not the Muscovy Company, who had first discovered Greenland – meaning they, rather than the corporation, should have privileged access to the northern waters.[50] The Muscovy Company was forced to turn to the privy council for support, asking for strict measures to be imposed on interlopers.[51] Without aid, they feared the company would lose investment, 'for merchants will not adventure where they know an assured loss to follow', and questioned whether they would be able to fund English diplomatic efforts in Russia if the state failed to back their position.[52] Although the Muscovy Company was in this case able to obtain assistance from the privy council, to the great frustration of many corporations in early modern England this support was not always forthcoming, and even when it was it could not necessarily be depended on for long.

In the early decades of the seventeenth century, the East India Company faced numerous threats from interloping individuals and organisation that threatened its trade in Asia, thereby demonstrating the potential weakness of its monopoly and its ongoing need for state support. Some of these attempts to breach the company's monopoly were easily overcome. For instance, when the former Levant Company merchant John Mildenhall sought to use his experience of travelling to India to entice investors and the state to support a proposed voyage to India, he was quickly shot down. Not only was Mildenhall denied a patent for his voyage, but the state soon issued a 'proclamation inhibiting the importation of pepper from foreign parts except by the East India Company' and orders that no pepper was 'unloaded in any port or creek' except by the company followed.[53] Similarly, when a number of English merchants sought to establish a competing enterprise in France, it too was quashed with support from the state, and when Eustace Man, a key figure in the proposed scheme, sought to move to Flushing to launch the proposed voyage, a warrant was issued for his arrest.[54] More concerning for the East India Company were well-connected competitors. When Sir Henry Thynne sought to send ships to Asia, there were no proclamations of support from the state, and the corporation faced a growing backlash – first from Sir Thomas Roe, who warned that it would cause a scandal if the voyage was stopped, and then from Sir Carew Raleigh, who admonished them for presuming to demand that all gentlemen, when beginning a voyage, 'must yield an account unto them, whither they go, and what they carry'. In the end, the ship Thynne had purchased and provisioned was deemed unsuitable for the demands of the transoceanic voyage, but the threat was clear – the monopoly so carefully maintained by the East India Company could only go so far if support from the state was lacking.[55]

Reliance on state support against interlopers left many corporations with only limited recourse for enforcing their monopolies, especially in cases where there were competing claims for access. For example, when the Guinea Company gave one of their members, Mr Davis, 'sole trading to the said places of Guinea and Benin', its efforts to enforce the narrow monopoly quickly proved unsustainable. Another member, Humphrey Slany, quickly opposed the validity of the corporation's decision, pointing out that he had personally sent 'two or three ships' to the region already, not only 'to trade there' but also 'to search out and discover other new places of trade as not yet frequented by any English merchant'. He argued that his right to capitalise on his investment outweighed the company's new order, a position that was supported by the privy council, which declared that by 'excluding all those of the same company from trading to those parts' the company had acted in bad faith. The corporation was instructed that it would no longer 'molest and hinder the said Humphrey Slany', as even though he had interloped on Davis's monopoly, his ventures had been 'well used, both for the enlargement of trade, employment of mariners and increase of his majesty's customs' and were therefore more in keeping with the aims of the corporation's charter.[56] By attempting to impose a strict monopoly in Africa, the Guinea Company had pushed its privileges too far beyond the purpose for which they had been granted; in the end, it was not only unable to stop the interloper but also faced an unpalatable situation where the state actively encouraged the interloping attempt.

As this suggests, the state could sometimes exacerbate, rather than mitigate, the challenges companies faced. The Muscovy Company, as well as facing competition over its whaling privileges, was similarly distraught to discover that a certain Richard Finch and other interlopers who had been expelled from Russia had been granted permission to return by James I. The Russian emperor, Michael I, had ejected the interlopers for 'being opposers and hinderers of the said company's trade', and the corporation desperately sought to ensure they remained barred, hoping that the English king had made a mistake as a consequence of 'misinformation to your highness'.[57] Yet, despite their efforts, more interlopers followed and three years later Nicholas Gatenbie and Robert Coldcole were given licence to 'part and come without further trouble' in spite of the Muscovy Company's monopoly.[58] Unable to stop interlopers returning to Russia, the corporation risked damaging their relationship with Michael I – if it could not control merchants from its own country, how useful a partner was the corporation after all?

Letters from Henry Lello, 'her majesty's ambassador with the Grand Signor in Constantinople', to the Levant Company similarly highlighted the damage that interlopers could cause to a corporate reputation overseas. Complaining that English privateers in the Mediterranean were causing 'great disturbance to the quiet trade we ought or at least should have', Lello lamented the company's inability to enforce its monopoly.[59] Beyond requesting assistance from Marino Grimani, the Doge of Venice, to seize interloping English ships, there was little the corporation could do.[60] To make matters worse, Venetian and French residents in Constantinople had protested about the rogue English actors and Ottoman officials had made their displeasure known. While Lello assured local authorities that the privateers were not the company's friends but its enemies, he could do nothing to undo 'the great dishonour and not profit to our country and countrymen' already caused.[61] As attacks on shipping continued, the ambassador was called before the Ottoman Sultan Mehmed III, who 'wished me to take notice and see these abuses reformed'.[62] Lello advised the company to obtain a warrant from the privy council to supress the interlopers before the company's relationship with the Ottoman court was damaged beyond repair.[63]

The East India Company was similarly aware of the risks interlopers posed. It argued that a voyage planned from Ireland in contravention of its monopoly should be stopped, telling the privy council that while its own activities 'proceed in peaceable manner like merchants', the same could not be said of the proposed Irish voyage, which was violent and piratical and would bring 'great dishonour unto this nation'.[64] Having armed shipping of its own, the corporation was better positioned than most to police interlopers. Thus, when Lord Rich seized 'a great junk richly laden being the goods of the mother of that prince [the Mughal Emperor Jahangir]' worth an estimated £100,000, an East India Company captain was able to recapture the vessel and return it, earning 'the ambassador and merchants ... great thanks, and for the present have purchased themselves great favour'.[65] Yet, despite its efforts, the corporation was unable to stop English privateering in the Indian Ocean

– 147 –

world. Nor was it the only corporation whose reputation was at risk – attacks on Ottoman shipping in the Red Sea led to complaints from Aden and Mocha that reflected poorly on the Levant Company, whose representatives were present in Constantinople.[66] In the connected world of early modern trade interloping privateers represented a threat far and wide as they damaged the commercial community's reputation in the eyes of overseas parties.

COMPETING CORPORATE CLAIMS

Outsiders, interlopers and renegade members were common threats to monopolistic practices, but they were by no means the only form of competition between merchants and their corporations in early modern England. The privileges of different organisations were often ill-defined and failed to take into account overlapping claims about who had the right to participate in overseas trade and empire. As more corporations and individuals sought to restrain the access of competitors to specific markets, English merchants were faced with a challenging environment where barriers to their access to markets were being erected at the very same time that their commercial interests were becoming more connected. The markets identified in corporate charters were not really representative of discrete trading regions, and it was not uncommon for new privileges obtained by one company to impinge on those of another. Unsurprisingly, this situation led to numerous instances where competing corporations sought to demonstrate that their specific privileges, old or new, should take precedence.[67] In most circumstances, merchants were able to operate in different companies and markets without issues arising, but this was not always the case and disputes between different corporations for control over particular commodities could become fraught as merchants found themselves on opposing sides of disputes with people they would normally see as trusted and essential partners.

Some saw access to new markets and the increasingly international activities of merchants as a threat to the traditional corporate order.

– 148 –

John More, a York merchant and member of the Eastland and Merchant Adventurers companies, for instance, argued that fellow members of Merchant Adventurers participating in the newly open trade with Spain 'doth greatly at this time hurt the generality'. He warned that although the trade was 'being beneficial unto themselves', it was 'hurtful to the company'. By selling goods in Antwerp early in the season to reach Spain in time for seasonal markets, they pushed down prices for English cloth sold by other members of the company. More suggested that in cases where markets were connected it was wrong for merchants to shuttle goods directly from one to another. In his opinion, only by ensuring all goods were returned to England for re-export could domestic cloth manufacturing be supported, exports sustained and customs revenues increased.[68]

Concerns about the impact on domestic production, and the impact of competition on wider constituencies of these companies in England, were a common theme in many of these disputes.[69] Thus, when the Skinners' livery company petitioned the king demanding that the Eastland Company respect the spirit of its charter and only purchase skins from its members in future, rather than going directly to suppliers, it was as concerned with domestic trade as with the Eastland merchants' activities overseas.[70] Conversely, when the Spanish Company complained that the members of the Haberdashers' livery company produced 'felts and hats [made] of English wool, instead of wool imported by them, which are alone fit for purpose', it was concerned poor domestic production would harm its overseas trade. Arguing that 'such unlawful workmen' likely included those who had 'run away from their masters' and were operating in 'remote places', the Spanish Company demanded the livery company effectively impose regulations related to the manufacturing of these goods. Without such regulations, workers were likely to 'make but deceitful ware', and if left to continue would leave the 'honest workmen or felt maker much decayed and discredited', as well as 'all merchants, clothiers, drapers and others trading in any manner of cloth or woollen drapery', who would no longer be trusted as purveyors of high-quality product.[71] For merchants importing Spanish wool, the threat was not just a declining market for their goods in England, but that by attempting to circumvent the traditional practices of felt and hat production, these workers were challenging the corporate structures that regulated England's export trade. In each of these cases, competition between trading companies and domestic manufacturers led to moments where accepted practices of supply, production and sale broke down.

Efforts to maintain local control over domestic or international commercial relationships were also a common theme in early modern England. In London, successful attempts to impose the City of London's corporate regulation on visiting merchants was strengthened both by the importance of the city as a port and commercial centre, and through the long-term efforts of the city's urban corporation to ensure its citizens were best positioned to take advantage of global opportunities. For example, traders from Norwich, who were 'from time out of mind accustomed to have their several warehouses in this city of London', were just one group who felt the bite of these efforts. In the 1570s, they discovered that the mayor and council of London 'have by their proclamations' forbidden Norwich merchants 'to let any such warehouses or to harbour any of their commodities'. From now on, they would have to trade at the city's cloth market, Blackwell Hall, a highly regulated space at the heart of the city where impositions and fees could be strictly levied.[72] Thirty years later, despite sending aldermen to London to argue against the imposition, restrictions had only strengthened and goods from the Norfolk city were required to leave on Sunday to arrive at the Monday market.[73] Over the following years, regulations that all goods 'made of wool or mixed with wool', flax, or silk, must be sold at 'the common market place or places thereunto appointed, in, at or near Blackwell Hall' were carefully enforced. Thus, when London's authorities were concerned that these items were being 'bought and sold in secret and private houses' they imposed stricter requirements still, demanding that fees at Blackwell Hall must be paid in full, and goods registered, before being taken anywhere else in the city. Clerks caught

– 150 –

MONOPOLISTS AND INTERLOPERS

acting as brokers, stopping clothiers selling goods directly to merchants, would be heavily fined for a first offence and fired for a second.[74] Through these efforts, London's commercial regulators sought not only to integrate the national economy more effectively into the city's markets but also to have the opportunity to enforce other regulations related to quality control, a common concern for merchants transporting such goods overseas.

London's position at the centre of England's emerging global trading networks was further strengthened by the activities of many trading companies that, even when nominally nationally bodies, were predominantly geared towards serving the capital's commercial community. For example, when merchants from Newcastle obtained permission to trade with Norway as a means of obtaining essential supplies for their shipping industry, the Eastland Company quickly quashed their efforts by offering assurances that their trade provided the needed goods in abundance and that these would be made available in Newcastle – at a profit of course.[75] Similarly, following the chartering of the French Company, merchants from Yarmouth petitioned the newly empowered corporation to lift restrictions on the port's 'transporting of fish, herring and corn' to France. They were unsuccessful. Six years later the same town sent Nicholas Youngs to London to try to obtain a 'licence to transport herring in strangers' bottoms', but it was another four years until this was granted and even then foreign shipping could only be used to carry herring 'dried, salted and finished in this town [Yarmouth]'.[76] Petitions 'for the merchants of this town to be free to import their goods returned out of France', however, were not successful.[77] It was not Yarmouth's fishing industry that was the target of the French Company but its potential role as a competing marketplace to London. In each case, corporations led by and heavily representing merchants in London sought to carefully balance their control of commerce against the demands of local productive industries. Towns beyond London provided an important domestic market and contributed to the domestic economy, but their merchants were not to take international trade away from the capital.

– 151 –

As the power of London's merchants also became increasingly clear, merchants in towns across England sought to limit the imposition of external regulation. During a long-running dispute about conflicting privileges related to the import of sweet wines, the Levant Company struggled to impose the corporation's regulations on traders outside London. At first, efforts by 'those of Southampton' to bring 'wines of Candy' into the southern port were quelled when the Levant Company claimed the plans would be damaging to the state.[78] For the Levant Company, Southampton's merchants' 'refusal of payment' of dues to the London-based company was a key sticking point.[79] Yet, having spent 'above seven hundred pounds ... since the obtaining of the [Levant Company's] last charter' lobbying for the renewal of the town's privileges, Southampton's merchants were desperate to 'free the mayor, bailiffs and burgesses of this town from paying' further impositions on sweet wine.[80] In the face of the Levant Company's intransigence, fractures within the southern port's commercial community came to the surface. While the town's mayor and senior merchant William Neven decided to 'absolutely refuse to pay any money', the wider generality supported efforts to 'put an end to all manner of controversies concerning the wines'.[81] Concerned that Neven's previous representation 'had in some point neglected the report of the said business', the 'wine merchants of this town (one excepted)' were desperate for 'relief touching the benefit of sweet wines taken from this town by the practice of the company of the Levant merchants'.[82] Armed with 'all such charters, acts of parliament and other papers and writing as you have in your hands concerning that matter', the town's new representative went to London once more.[83] The efforts were in vain – the Levant Company was too well supported. Southampton's merchants continued to rail against the impositions that syphoned profits from its most important trade into the pockets of the London company, but there was little they could do.[84]

Resisting the centralising authority of London's new trading companies was an expensive and often fruitless task. Unable to sustain a presence in court and lacking in access to senior decision makers, the provincial merchants' attempts to maintain former privileges were often untenable. This was particularly threating where corporations obtained monopoly rights covering regions and goods that had long been staples of other groups. For instance, Bristol's merchants petitioned the privy council for support during a period where, to their 'great misery and calamity', their export of 'woollen cloths heretofore usually dyed and wrought in this part' to Spain and Portugal had declined. They claimed unemployment was rising as a consequence, increasing poverty in the city and severely reducing the customs obtained in a port 'which have heretofore been the greatest in England saving London'. Without 'licencing the citizens of Bristol to trade yearly to the seigneuries of Venice and Turkey' the petitioners warned that competition from the London companies would only lead to further decline.[85] A few years later, Bristol's merchants again found themselves facing difficulties as a consequence of a London-centred company's privileges. The French Company had recently been granted privileges to levy impositions on sweet wine, a product that Bristol's Merchant Venturers had long trafficked in – a suit was quickly made against the new corporation.[86] However, despite drawing on their members to fund multiple delegations to London each year, often led by aldermen of Bristol, they were unable to overturn the new privileges.[87] Despite their ancient rights, the merchants of Bristol struggled to oppose the centralising authorities of London's powerful new companies.

The challenges of navigating a competitive commercial landscape were equally clear in early modern Hull, the predominant port-market on the river Humber, where ensuring the town's status as an entrepôt within England's domestic economy was seen as vital for its success. The challenge for the northern town was how to maintain its position as a meeting point for numerous commercial networks without damaging the role its own merchants played as interlocutors, or leaving them to face the costs of providing essential infrastructure alone. This dynamic was clear during a long dispute with York regarding 'the maintenance of the haven at Hull', upkeep that the 'incorporation of Hull is only charged and the city of or

– 153 –

the citizens of York nothing'.[88] Hull's merchant leaders argued that without dues from visiting merchants, the town's economic viability was at risk and would cause both local decay and damage the cloth and lead trade across the whole of northern England.[89] Eventually, an agreement was concluded whereby York's merchants could import goods from Spain or Bordeaux without charge, but they were excluded from participating in the vital cloth and lead trade from the town.[90] Furthermore, York merchants would have to unload goods at a regulated warehouse where they would pay relevant charges for using port facilities.[91]

Unfortunately for Hull, merchants from nearby York were not the only outsiders seeking to take advantage of the vibrant markets in northern England, and pressure from London was harder to shake off. Thus, when London merchants William Walthall, Lambert Osberton, Edward Bagshaw, Edward Sleighton and Robert Godwolston were caught trading Derbyshire lead, Hull's merchants had little option but to turn to the state for support.[92] Petitioning Elizabeth I, Hull's corporation insisted that the port's charters made clear that Derbyshire lead could only be exported via the town, meaning that the commodity must be 'brought into this said town, weighed and sold there, and from thence shipping into the parts beyond the seas'. This structure enabled the collection of customs for outward traffic as well as imports, thus supporting Hull's ability to maintain 'many good and serviceable ships' and keep 'the whole country adjoining well-furnished in foreign commodities'.[93] A further petition to the Lord Treasurer asked 'what grief and pity, yea what loss and damage' might be caused if London's merchants were not brought to heel.[94] Yet, as they sought to reconfirm their privileges, Hull's misfortune was seen as an opportunity by merchants in nearby Gainsborough, who re-opened their town's market and specifically encouraged London merchants to bring hops, pitch, tar, flax and other goods directly to the town.[95] Grimsby, too, welcomed the capital's traders, who 'carried and conveyed sundry merchandises of iron and other wares unto Grimsby', and 'from hence have transported the same unto diverse towns' across the region. After two years, Hull's privileges were reconfirmed by the privy council, which announced that the town's merchants should be able to enjoy their 'ancient and usual trades without impeachment'.[96] However, the move was ill-advised – without London traders' willingness to work with the northern traders, Hull simply could not function as an effective entrepôt. Only four years later Hull's merchants weakened their monopoly and the capital's merchants returned, paying port-dues but otherwise able to take advantage of many of the northern markets Hull had tried so hard to monopolise.[97]

Competition could also be fierce across different corporations for control of specific commodities. For example, currants, a valuable product from the eastern Mediterranean, were particularly important for the Levant Company, which sought to maintain a dominant position in the trade in the face of considerable opposition.[98] While the company's charter granted its members alone the right to carry currants directly from the Mediterranean, there was nothing to stop English merchants purchasing them from markets in other parts of Europe.[99] In these conditions, it was not long before competition between the Levant Company and other English merchants had become intense, especially with members of the Merchant Adventurers, who obtained currants in northern Europe. On the recommendation of Sir Clement Edmonds, who was well known in the commercial community after working in the United Provinces regarding the East India trade, the Levant merchants sought advice about their charter from leading legal figure Sir Edward Coke.[100] But, when the company's deputy went to meet with Coke, they ran into Mr Towerson, a representative of the Merchant Adventurers, who had also sought advice. The next day, both companies sent delegates to appear before the privy council, which declared a desire for 'a friendly and peaceable union betwixt the two companies'. Despite advice from Coke about their charters neither side could persuade the lords, who refused to pass judgement and encouraged the merchants to 'treat betwixt themselves of the matter'. With little help from the state, both companies were forced back to the negotiating table, and the next day the Merchant Adventurers agreed in principle to the cessation of

– 155 –

importing currants. However, they did ask that any currants bought by their 'brothers and brethren' in Germany and the Low Countries before news of the agreement reached them should be allowed into England without facing any fines. Second, they insisted that no member of the Levant Company who was also a Merchant Adventurer would be permitted to import currants from these regions either. The Levant Company agreed to these parameters and to enforce the agreement, approved regulations that any members breaking the new restrictions would face a 'penalty of the loss of his freedom for that offence'.[101]

However, while these two companies were able, in the end, to find common ground regarding currants, the same was not true of Levant Company and Merchant Venturers of Bristol. For these Bristol merchants, the Levant Company's enforcement of restrictions on the currant trade targeted a much more important part of their revenues than it had for the Merchant Adventurers in London. Indeed, the western port town had long held privileges to trade into the Mediterranean – it had launched perhaps the earliest English voyage to the region in 1457 – and the Merchant Venturers saw the London-based Levant Company's prohibitions as an attempt to strip away these historic privileges.[102] Considering the seriousness of the threat, two Bristol aldermen, John Barker and John Whitson, were 'employed to solicit the Lords of His Majesty's most honourable privy council concerning their free trade to the Levant'.[103] Upon reaching London, they sought 'a speedy and favourable hearing' but were not optimistic, writing how 'we do observe by the passage of our business that we are in danger to be overruled'. Suggesting in a letter back to the Merchant Venturers that it might be better to 'subscribe to the ancient English proverb (it is better to incur inconvenience than mischief)', Barker and Whitson proposed a new approach that would accept some impositions.[104] However, responding six days later, the Bristol company stated that its members were 'all of the same resolution that they were of when you were present at the hall' and demanded that the charter be upheld; if the privy council proved unaccommodating, they were happy to turn to parliament for support.[105] In an attempt to

MONOPOLISTS AND INTERLOPERS

resolve the dispute, the Levant Company wrote to 'those of Bristol' offering reduced fees, but this was rejected and the Levant Company requested the privy council to 'constrain those of Bristol to pay 4d upon every pound of currants brought unto that port'.[106] Almost six weeks passed before Bristol's merchants received an order directly from privy council informing them that the Levant Company's charter would be upheld. Bristol's Merchant Venturers would only be granted a licence – on a three-year trial – to import a maximum of 200 tons of currants each year, but only from islands not belonging to Venice. These currants would also not be permitted to be transported to southern England but only 'for the provision of the City of Bristol and of those parts thereabouts'. Fees paid to the Levant Company for every currant imported would also be preserved.[107] With their legal access to currant-producing islands under Venetian governance having been effectively removed, the trial did little to assuage the Merchant Venturers concerns about the threat posed by the Levant Company. Nevertheless, the trial did at least provide a legal means for it to send ships to the Mediterranean – and two ships soon left Bristol to trade in the region. Unbeknown to the Levant Company, the ships' intended destinations were islands within 'the seignory of Venice', where they would trade for currants and return two years later carrying £5,400 of goods. They even left two factors in the Mediterranean, in expectation of a further voyage.[108] The Levant Company might have won the battle in England, but overseas there was only so much they could do to stop the Merchant Venturers interloping and trading as they always had.

The success of Bristol's merchants in resisting the demands of the Levant Company meant that the dispute was still ongoing over a decade later. Now, following another attempt by the London-based corporation to impose its privileges, the merchants of Bristol that traded in currants sent a letter confirming that they would continue to 'refuse to be obser-vant of the [Levant] company's order [that] touch the price of currants and the time of coming in of their ships to the islands, and refusing to pay the arrear of the duty of 4d per cent' – they were confident they were

– 157 –

protected 'according to an order of the Lords long since made on that behalf'. The Levant Company responded by petitioning the privy council to enforce its claims and to ensure the 'conformity of those merchants to the orders of the company, being made for the general good of the trade and kingdom'.[109] Lacking the ability to influence Westminster decision making, but confident that its own charter, first obtained in 1373, gave them privileges that preceded the new Levant Company, the Merchant Venturers were more than willing to ignore the regulations imposed upon them. They would not have seen these actions as dishonourable; on the contrary, the leaders of the Merchant Venturers were fulfilling their corporate obligations to their members and their city.

Competing claims about who could conduct trades like that in currants were not uncommon for merchants in early modern England. Even where a corporation had a clear claim to being the first company to obtain privileges to trade with a particular region, it could still face challenges by competitors with alternative claims. For example, the East India Company's monopoly was challenged by Isaac Le Maire on the basis that he had discovered an alternative route to Asia, via the southwest, and should therefore be able to capitalise on his finding. Arguing that his new route would enable him to circumvent the Dutch presence in the region, Le Maire insisted that he had already used the southern passage successfully and that the existing company was failing to live up to its charter by ignoring the opportunity presented.[110] Unfortunately for Le Maire, James I's enthusiasm for the southern route did not match his support for its supposed discoverer. He was quickly sidelined as the king pressured the governor of the East India Company, Thomas Smith, to lead a new corporation that would take advantage of the opportunity (an odd situation where two competing organisations would be led by the same merchant).[111] As the discussion continued within the East India Company, Smith weighed in, informing the generality that he was aware of 'the reports of a new discovery lately made, called the South passage' and that James I had shared the information with them after observing 'how commodious it may be for his subjects to enjoy the same'. As Smith

– 158 –

put it, the company had been presented with the decision of the new passage, either to undertake it on its own account or for Smith to take charge of an independent company for this purpose. He also warned that it seemed likely that the voyage would take place whether the generality agreed or not, as James I was particularly enthusiastic about the venture, believing 'that it will prove a great benefit to his subjects'.[112] In the end, with the presentation of new evidence on behalf of one of the company's employees, Richard Hawkins, who claimed he had discovered the passage himself years before, the East India Company claimed the southern passage was only known because of its own activities.[113] This temporarily relieved the corporation of the risk of a competing organisation, but their victory was only half won – James I warned them that he had not divided the world entirely for them, and that new discoveries were open for exploitation.[114] This episode demonstrated that even if a corporation had an ironclad claim, its ability to regulate and enforce privileges were under constant challenge from competitors.

THE CLOTH TRADE

Fears about the decline or stagnation of woollen cloths exports were pervasive in early modern England, and competition about where, when, in what form and in whose hands the trade should take place endemic.[115] Woollen cloth had risen to prominence in England's export trades over the course of the sixteenth century, leading one commentator to ardently express their admiration for the 'noble man, gentleman, yeoman, husbandman [and] merchants' who had made the wool trade 'her Majesty's Indies, mint and treasure house'.[116] Between 1485 and 1614, the sale of undressed woollen cloth by London's merchants had risen from around 20,000 to 127,000 pieces per year, and it was manufactured and exported within strictly regulated boundaries.[117] Early seventeenth-century observers reflected on the origins of the rich trade in Edward III's reforms over a hundred years before, who, by 'inviting all strangers and foreigners that were clothworkers to come into England'

– 159 –

so 'that the clothworkers of England (which were then but a few) might be instructed by foreigners which were then more skilful than Englishmen', had revolutionised the industry.[118] Yet, whereas the original aim had been for domestic manufacturers to produce high-quality finished cloth, later statutes by Henry VII and Henry VIII had weakened these provisions and undressed cloth had become the staple export of England's merchants. By the end of the sixteenth century, long-standing models for regulating both cloth manufacture and export were challenged by merchants seeking to take advantage of new markets across Europe and further afield.

Having been founded in 1407 by Henry IV and re-chartered by both Henry VII in 1505 and Elizabeth I in 1564, the company of Merchant Adventurers had long dominated the export of English cloth.[119] Relying on mart towns in northern Europe, where English merchants and manufactures could be carefully monitored and regulated, the corporation maintained a strong grip over where, when and how English woollens could be sold overseas.[120] By the early seventeenth century, in the face of pressure from competitors seeking to reduce their influence 'by means of new corporations, as the companies of Eastland and Tripoli merchants', the Merchant Adventurers' leadership sought to highlight the benefits of their organisation overseeing the wool trade.[121] Not only had the corporation (according to its governor Christopher Hoddesdon at least) initiated exports directly to Germany, thereby ending the dominance of Hanse merchants in England, but, by overseeing the massive export of over 100,000 cloths per year, the company effectively 'do by their orderly trading and selling themselves in a Mart Town gain many privileges'.[122] Without the Merchant Adventurers' regulation, they warned, the cloth trade would descend into a 'straggling trade' that would face similar challenges to those faced by English merchants in liberalised markets like France and Barbary, where local rulers had imposed severe duties on English goods.[123]

Despite warnings by the Merchant Adventurers, which, quite clearly, had its own motives for monopolising such a large part of England's trade into their hands, many merchants sought to break down the barriers that

MONOPOLISTS AND INTERLOPERS

had long constrained the trade.[124] Even the secretary of the Merchant Adventurers, John Wheeler, could not help but recognise the opportunities that were becoming available to English merchants across the globe. Expressing his belief that 'there is nothing in the world so ordinary, and natural unto men, as to contract, truck, merchandise and traffic one with another', Wheeler concluded that 'all the world chops and changes, runs and raves after marts, markets and merchandising, so that all things come into commerce, and pass into traffic (in a manner) in all times, and in all places'.[125] He even recommended that a wise ruler 'may use this kind of men, I mean merchants, to the great benefit, and good of his state, either for foreign intelligence, or exploration, or for the opening of an entry and passage unto unknown and fair distant parts'.[126] Although it was probably not his intention, many English merchants would have been happy to take this advice – if trade was a universal phenomenon, it only made sense for them to try to take advantage of new markets.

Seizing these opportunities was not so simple. The privileges of the Merchant Adventurers especially limited many merchants' room for manoeuvre, but this was not the only challenge. In Bristol, the city's corporate leadership complained about 'the great misery and calamity' that had been caused 'by reason of the want of trade into the ports of Spain and Portugal for the venting of woollen cloths heretofore usually dyed and wrought in this part'. Renewed conflict between the Iberian and English states, they claimed, had put many dyers and clothworkers out of business, or forced them to cut costs and employees. To make matters worse, they highlighted that 'the Londoners of late time have monopolised ... the greatest parts of foreign places and commerce', giving Bristol's merchants no way to find new markets for locally produced cloth or other important commodities, such as Welsh iron, lead from Mendip and calamine stone. Without the state 'licencing the citizens of Bristol to trade yearly to the Seigneuries of Venice and Turkey', the city's leaders worried that their downturn of fortunes would only get worse.[127] In the northeast of England, too, 'we the merchants of York, Newcastle and Hull' railed against attempts to limit their access to

– 161 –

traditional markets in the Baltic, in this case in the form of higher rates for customs on cloth exports from the towns.[128]

Even for merchants who had access to different markets overseas, strict regulation in England about what types of cloth could be manufactured and exported often did little to meet the demands of potential buyers in places ranging from Russia to North Africa or the Baltic to the Mediterranean. This led to changing attitudes about how the vital commodity should be produced and where it should be traded, and, by the turn of the seventeenth century, debates about whether or not production methods should be altered to cater to new markets were heating up.[129] As one author put it, wools were the most abundant 'staple commodity of this land and by transporting the same great benefit hath come to this land and the crown', and any changes risked damaging this.[130]

Two long-standing restrictions over the structure of England's wool trade were challenged. First, the Merchant Adventurers' monopoly over the export of undressed, undyed broadcloth was challenged by the Eastland Company, which sought to sell the same in Poland. When the Earl of Cumberland had obtained a licence to transport undressed cloth in 1602, he clearly believed that such old draperies were still in demand in markets where finished cloth was not, suggesting that if the Merchant Adventurers' monopoly was lifted then domestic production might benefit from a boost. The Eastland Company was quick to make this point and asserted their right to the same privileges as the Merchant Adventurers, specifically the right to transport undressed cloth to their mart town of Elbing.[131] The following year, the Eastland merchants who 'heretofore vented dressed cloths' were reported to 'now vent great part of their cloths undressed'.[132] Second, the limited production of 'new draperies' (finished and often dyed woollen cloth that was lighter and better suited for warmer climates) was questioned by merchants, who deemed these items more suitable to export to places such as Morocco, the Ottoman Empire or the Indian Ocean.[133] In the sixteenth century, the manufacture of new draperies had been 'in Newcastle and

– 162 –

Norfolk only', but new demands in markets overseas meant 'now they be set up in a hundred several towns and places within many counties of the realm'.[134] The success of merchants exporting dressed and dyed cloth was a driving force behind debates about whether older statutes restricting the export of finished cloth were still valid. In 1606, a bill in parliament sought to provide succour to clothworkers by allowing them to finish and dye cloth before export. This was deemed necessary because 'the Netherlander and Hamburger bring from their countries no commodity that yields labour or maintenance to this nation', while undressed English woollens 'set their [Dutch and German] countrymen a work, when the workmen of this land are ready to perish for want of labour'. Furthermore, the bill argued, 'in Dansk and Elbing under the King of Poland the people desire our English cloth undressed, to the intent to set their poor to work'.[135] In contrast, finishing cloth in England would support domestic manufacture, and English merchants could surely instead supplant foreign merchants in international markets where finished cloths were in demand. The demands of consumers in increasingly global, connected marketplaces were driving changes both in the regulation of cloth exports and in the types of cloth that English manufacturers were producing.

By connecting overseas markets with domestic industry, proponents of increasing the production and export of new draperies had hit on a winning strategy. Plans to export dyed, finished cloth were endorsed by some of the leading merchants in London as well as manufacturers who believed these additional processes would provide more jobs and more opportunities for profit. In 1607, the chief justice, concerned that the Eastland trade would decline without a greater acceptance of dressing cloth before export, proposed a conference between merchants and clothiers to discuss the issue.[136] The following year merchants trading to the 'Eastland countries', Russia and North Africa were given permission to export 28,000 finished cloths from Suffolk, Gloucester, Essex and Coventry.[137] Five years later, the Muscovy Company began to purchase cloths in Worcester, Gloucester, Hampshire and Manchester to 'dye and dress in London' before export.[138] Exporters of 'new draperies' and other finished cloth were not alone in encouraging this expansion of domestic industry dedicated towards the popular new commodities. Producers arguing for less strict regulations regarding cloth suggested that the movement towards dressing and dyeing cloth in England would increase both the total output of cloth and the number of people employed.[139] One author went so far as to recommend 'that all manufactures made of wool should be truly made and truly dyed' and that bans on the import of dyed woollens should be imposed.[140] This position was supported by 'some of the artisan clothworkers of this [Clothworkers' livery] company and by some of the company of dyers', who wrote to James I in 1613 'craving that all manner of cloths made in England might receive full manufacture before they be transported'.[141] It was not only clothworkers and dyers who were keen on reform: efforts to maintain demand for raw wool were supported by 'a great part of the clothiers of his kingdom' as well as 'the wool growers of the realm, being many noblemen, gentlemen and others of good quality'.[142] By presenting the benefits of dressing and dyeing cloths before export as beneficial to such a broad range of English constituents, the arguments for change were hard to ignore.

As the woollen cloth trade system changed in response to England becoming a more globally interested commercial player, debates centred the country within a connected web of markets and commercial chains. For the more forgiving observers, a comparison between new and old markets suggested that it was lack of demand, not lack of skill, that meant undressed white broadcloths remained the key export of the Merchant Adventurers to Germany.[143] For the less forgiving, existing prescriptive regulations were damaging English merchants who would greatly benefit from having new draperies as a more suitable commodity for new trades to more exotic climates.[144] For example, when the East India Company had undertaken 'a little trial in this kind' – that is, exporting dressed cloths – they had struggled to obtain stock in England.[145] Yet, their efforts were not entirely unsuccessful, and they soon obtained specific instructions from Muqarrab Khan, the governor of Surat and a senior figure within the Mughal administration, that the 'finest' yellow, red or green woollen cloth would find buyers at court. The company's senior factor in Surat, Nicholas Downton, reiterated the need for 'very fine cloth' dyed in 'perfect colours' if the company was to have any success in exporting English woollens to northern India.[146] Boosting domestic production to meet such demands was not the only benefit of these new trades for England's wider economy. Advocates of the Levant Company highlighted how the trade enabled 'superfluous commodities' to be exported in return for the import of essential commodities, which increased customs revenue, increased the shipping of the realm, maintained mariners, merchants, clothiers and fishermen, and they claimed had even contributed to '20,000 persons' being 'set to work by spinning and making' cotton purchased from the region.[147]

Presenting new trades like these as a way for England to establish itself as an entrepôt for international trade were touching on a raw nerve. In 1613, a 'brief remonstrance' against the Merchant Adventurers detailed how Dutch wealth was in fact built on an extractive relationship with England. The author argued that the sale of unfinished commodities to Dutch manufacturers and merchants undercut the opportunities for English actors. Noting how 'we raise wools ... they drape with our wools', 'we make tin ... they work our tin' and 'we make cloth ... they dress our cloth', the failure of England to capitalise on its rich supply of commodities was made clear.[148] The implication was obvious: only by bringing cloth finishing and advanced manufacturing to England could it compete with the Dutch in European markets. Fearmongering about the ill-effects of foreigners on England's economy did not stop there, and protests against 'the strangers and foreigners that dwell' in London criticised how they 'do drive the one half of the trade of this city'. The Mercers' livery company publicly condemned this state of affairs, arguing that 'their [the foreigners] exportation of our native commodities is far short of the importation of foreign many hundred thousands of pounds per annum', a situation 'which cannot but turn to the great loss of the common wealth'.[149] Numerous influential figures

– 165 –

weighed in, condemning the state of England's wool trade and laying the blame on the excessive influence of foreign merchants. Sir Walter Cope insisted that repatriating the production of finished products and restricting foreigners from carrying goods to or from England would renew the country's fortunes, while John Keymer argued that only through the 'full manufacturing of our homeland commodities' would English merchants be able to compete with the Dutch, who would otherwise continue to profit from finishing English cloth.[150]

Together, these pressures on the Merchant Adventurers' command of England's cloth exports quickly solidified into ongoing, well-supported attacks on the company's position. With so many possible opportunities for English cloth, of many different types, the continued concentration of the trade into the hands of only two hundred or so merchants was argued to be deeply damaging to the wider commercial community. Worse still, much of the Merchant Adventurers' trade was only in fine cloth, which, while profitable, did not provide the necessary scale of exports required to satisfy England's huge manufacturing sector.[151] The Merchant Adventurers also faced accusations that many of its members were less interested in exporting cloth than they were in ensuring their own access to foreign commodities that could be imported into England.[152] Indeed, members of the company seemed unable to provide an attractive enough proposition to foreign merchants, who had started exporting silk directly to England for cash, 'quick sale and speedy returns', rather than exchanging it for English wool in the mart towns.[153] Furthermore, the Merchant Adventurers were blamed for creating laws that were 'to the prejudice of the younger sort of their own company', forcing them to trade only to Middelburg alongside senior merchants who could operate at scale, meaning younger merchants were unable to foster their opportunities elsewhere.[154] At the heart of complaints against the long-standing corporation was William Cockayne, a London merchant whose own commercial interests expanded across Spain, France, the Baltic, and the Indian and Atlantic oceans, and who was at the time governor of the Eastland Company.[155] Cockayne proposed a

– 166 –

MONOPOLISTS AND INTERLOPERS

radical change in the way English cloth was exported and argued that the Merchant Adventurers were 'very idle and unskilful merchants in their business', suggesting that the lack of market for new draperies was because they were 'unskilful in dyeing and dressing of cloth for that they have not practiced the same'.[156] Regarded as damaging to domestic industry, as hypocritical monopolists of luxury imports, and as failing to provide training and development opportunities for young merchants, the Merchant Adventurers found little support in the wider commercial community.

The triple challenge of ensuring high-quality cloth production, increasing exports of woollens and not undermining the staple trade of undressed woollens into Europe by the Merchant Adventurers led to furious debates as merchants, clothiers, wool growers and the state sought solutions. Efforts to reform the wool trade and the Merchant Adventurers started in earnest in 1613, with the appointment of Sir Thomas Middleton by James I to oversee a committee tasked with examining a petition 'delivered unto us by the clothworkers and dyers, craving that all manner of cloths made in England might receive full manufacture before they be transported'. Middleton, the Lord Mayor of London, had been at the forefront of a number of new commercial projects, including the East India, New River, Virginia and Guiana companies, and had little time for the restrictive practices of the Merchant Adventurers. Bringing together representatives from 'all the companies of merchants', Middleton's committee concluded that the problem was not manufacturing capacity or quality in England, but that trade had been damaged because cloths were exported by strangers, causing a 'loss of employment of many thousands of our poor subjects'. Yet, without having properly trained and ordered merchants overseeing the trade, the committee was concerned that standards would not be maintained and even more ground would be lost to foreign competition.[157] Taking this recommendation to heart, in 1614 the king granted a royal licence for merchants to export dressed and dyed woollens to locations that were in contravention of the Merchant Adventurers

– 167 –

monopoly, creating a new corporation – the New Merchant Adventurers – that was invested with powers to oversee and regulate the trade.[158]

While merchants debated the pros and cons of the proposed trade and went about establishing the new corporation, wool growers and clothiers across the country approached the king to ensure their own interests were not forgotten. Although there was some enthusiasm for new draperies, many were also concerned that the trend would undermine England's long-standing trade in undressed white cloth – and that new regulations would be used to diminish their position. For example, a petition from the 'poor handy crafts men of the Company of Clothworkers in London' claimed that new regulations on the export of dressed and dyed cloths was driving 'at the least 10,000 who live only upon the said trade of cloth working' into 'extreme beggary'. It also said that cloth making was also work suitable for the young, old and lame, while dyeing required 'strong and able men'.[159] The clothworkers needed the trade in high-volume commodities to flourish – and for prices of all cloth to remain high. The company's statutes ensured the export of undressed white cloth carried a value above £4, but they worried that members 'through want of work were like to perish', and so suggested no coloured cloths should be made anywhere within 'his majesty's dominions'. In particular, they called for the immediate cessation of dyeing and dressing cloth in Suffolk, Kent, Essex and Somerset, claiming that producers in those counties had no right to ignore regulations that had stopped them from doing the same in the past.[160] The Merchant Adventurers argued that the clothworkers' interpretation was faulty, and that for 'time out of mind there have been coloured cloths made in diverse counties, especially in Somerset, Essex, Yorkshire, Reading'.[161] They also pointed out that 'dressing cloth does not advantage us [the Merchant Adventurers]', and that it was 'merchants trading [in] Barbary, Turkey, Muscovy, the East Countries, France, Hungary, Italy' and 'the East Indies' who had pushed for changes in manufacturing regulations.[162] This, understandably, did little to reassure the clothworkers of London or, indeed, those of Norwich, who wrote to Sir Julius Caesar requesting that 'new draperies' and other 'new inventions' should be classified as the same 'species' as traditional products and therefore fall under the same regulation as other cloth.[163] Supportive commentators suggested that the New Merchant Adventurers should buy at least the same amount of cloth as the old company, so that 'clothiers have no just cause to complain'. Without maintaining the same volume of cloth, employment would fall even if merchants' profits rose, because 'more people set on work about the making of one cloth than there be in dying and dressing of them'.[164] This was a common concern, but so long as total cloth exports increased, it was concluded that new draperies could only increase the wealth of the kingdom.[165]

Meeting this challenge was the key requirement for the New Merchant Adventurers, and the corporation sought to ship both the innovative new product and large quantities of the more traditional, undressed white cloth that had characterised the trade. In the first year of operation, the new company shipped only 2,091 dyed cloths (mostly blue, black and red).[166] The following year 25,335 cloths were sent to Hamburg and Middelburg, just over 6,000 of which were finished cloths. Shipped by 140 different merchants, including many members of the old Merchant Adventurers who had joined the new organisation, new draperies were attractive as a supplementary product alongside undressed white cloth. This was clearly the case for merchants like John Wase, Clement Underhill, Robert Curtin and Abraham Cartwrights, who shipped only twelve, thirteen, two and nine dyed cloths respectively. Some merchants did ship larger numbers, including John Kendrick (1,260 cloths), Edmund Scott (450), Robert Angel (450), Robert Palmer (180), William Robinson (180) and Anthony Stubbs (306), and these were mostly merchants (apart from Kendrick) with experience selling this product in markets in Spain and the Mediterranean.[167]

Despite quick uptake by some members of the new company, other merchants remained unconvinced. Senior merchants like Richard Gore, a Merchant Adventurer who had refused to join the new company and who had experience in both the Spanish and French trade, had already made known their concerns that the new corporation would be unable to sustain England's long-standing, prominent position in the German cloth market. Gore believed that dressing and dyeing cloth in England would ruin England's hard-won reputation as a supplier of high-quality white cloth. He queried whether the risk of damaging the German market for English cloth was worth it considering that by shipping finished English cloths, the New Merchant Adventurers might impinge on the re-exports of Levant and Spanish company merchants. Gore also suspected that 'to imagine to vent much cloth in the East Indies is idle, the climate considered and that they are an ingenious people and provided with variety of their own country commodities as silks'.[168] In the connected international markets that English merchants were now taking part in, competing demands in different regions were hard to predict, and the New Merchant Adventurers were caught up in a very complex web.

Even where merchants did agree that new draperies were a positive addition to their stocklist, they were unsure about precisely how and where to market them. The argument went that if the New Merchant Adventurers could export dressed and undressed cloth together, then it no longer made sense to restrict the sale of either commodity from any other company. The Eastland Company, especially, pushed for the weakening of restrictions on the export of undressed cloth, which it argued would benefit the common wealth not only by increasing cloth exports but also by obtaining commodities useful for the state like soap ash, cordage, copper, canvas, linen, hides, staves, 'timber of all sorts', hemp, iron, wax, gunpowder, tar, masts, tallow and 'corn in great abundance'.[169] Without deregulation, the Eastland Company warned that its highly beneficial trade might fall into decay, leaving the English army and navy unsupplied and the Baltic open to domination by the Dutch.[170] The Merchant Adventurers objected to the claims, suggesting that the Eastland merchants would gain nothing from exporting undressed cloth because their competitors were not exporting dressed cloth either. Instead, German and Dutch merchants sold dressed and dyed cloth, which was why 'the people of the East Countries do take better liking to the cloths which the Netherlanders and Germans do bring unto them' in the first place. Considering the expansion of dyeing and dressing cloth in England currently under way, the Merchant Adventurers recommended the Eastland Company purchase undressed cloth in England that its members could then dye and dress themselves before export. In doing so, 'they would be able in short time not only to recover their trade, but also caste the strangers out'.[171] The Eastland Company countered that 'the greatest cause of our decay of trade cometh from them [the Merchant Adventurers]', whose control of the market left them with little room for manoeuvre. It argued it was the very lack of competition that made their proposal so appealing, and that because people in 'East Countries' were already skilled in dyeing and dressing cloth, there was great demand for undyed cloth in the region. Only by shipping undressed cloth could merchants hope to compete with Dutch and German merchants who shipped dressed cloth of a better quality than that produced in England.[172] The company also claimed that its proposal would benefit 'the poor workmen' who manufactured cloth by replacing lost export opportunities to Germany, and that the dyeing and dressing industry would be better aided by exports to Muscovy and Barbary in any case.[173] For William Cockayne, the Eastland Company governor who had launched the New Merchant Adventurers as a competitor to the old Merchant Adventurers in Germany, it would not do for England's cloth trade to be so strictly prescribed. Global opportunities could only be taken – whether in Asia, Africa, America or Europe – if merchants were given the freedom to carry the products they wished.

The New Merchant Adventurers were, in the end, only a short-lived blip on the corporate landscape of early modern England: the company was dissolved in 1617. Yet, despite failing to remake the English woollen cloth manufacturing sector or drastically change the English products most popular in German markets, the corporation did reflect a sustained drive by merchants to diversify exports in reflection of the international markets of which they were now part. The export of old draperies would

– 171 –

never again reach the same peaks as in the early seventeenth century, as detractors of the scheme had warned, but the decline was more than made up for through sales of new draperies and other goods that found ready markets across the world.[174] It became increasingly clear that carrying re-exports – such as oil, spices and silks – alongside woollen cloth could only benefit the country's trade balance and its merchants' bottom lines.[175] Before long, merchants in organisations like the Levant Company were arguing that they now 'exported great quantity of the woollen manufactures and other commodities of the growth of England' for 'the great enriching of this nation'.[176] Together, new goods and new types of manufacturing helped drive English participation in new markets and reveal the power of the commercial community, not just as drivers of international but also of domestic economic development. Goods for new markets beat demands for sustaining domestic production and tradition. In this instance, innovation beat stability. As England's merchants came to depend, more and more, on serving the needs of newly opened markets across the world, they were caught in a web of domestic and international interests that increasingly made traditional structures of the cloth trade untenable. By the first decades of the seventeenth century, it was no longer widely accepted that so much of England's manufacturing should be tied so closely with a single, oft-threatened and declining export market. It made no sense for merchants in the Baltic and the Mediterranean, or the Indian or Atlantic oceans, to carry goods no one wanted. If England was to sit at the heart of an international commercial network, contemporaries recognised that the long-standing privileges and monopolies of some of its most established companies would have to fall away.

FIVE

THE CITY AND THE COURT

In May 1624, shocking news reached England – the Dutch agent on Amboyna, Herman van Speult, had imprisoned, brutally tortured and executed ten English merchants who had been resident on the island. Immediately informing James I of this attack, which they decried as 'without all humanity', the East India Company's directors sought desperately to try to work out exactly what had happened, who was to blame and how the state could 'force them [the Dutch] to reparation'. However, their efforts were seemingly in vain – hopes that the crown would act soon faded and the company became increasingly concerned that public opinion was not in its favour – and so the company decided to try to force the king's hand.[1]

As the first survivors began to return to England in the aftermath of the massacre, the East India Company collected evidence and prepared to make its case. Having been presented to the company's members in advance, witnesses' accounts were 'set down in writing to be published' as early as 2 July 1624, whereby it was hoped 'the cruelties of the Dutch towards the English' would be laid bare. When printed, *A true relation of the unjust, cruel, and barbarous proceedings against the English at Amboyna* was branded with the company's coat of arms to show 'them to be true' and widely distributed in England and the United Provinces.[2]

Although *A true relation* presented a careful legal argument, at its core was a graphic, highly emotive and politically charged story. England's merchants were cast as moral and law-abiding heroes facing Dutch villainy. The brutal interrogation of each merchant was described in detail, and readers would learn, for instance, that John Clarke was forced to inhale water 'till his body was swollen twice or thrice as big as before, his cheeks like great bladders, and his eyes staring and strutting out beyond his forehead'. When Clarke still refused to confess, the Dutch, 'saying his was a Devil, and no man, or surely was a witch', cut off his hair to reveal signs of witchcraft and left him 'five or six days without any chirurgion to dress him, until (his flesh being putrefied) great maggots dropped and crept from him in a most loathsome & noisome manner'. What king would not step forward and help them right this wrong?[3]

In case this explicit account was insufficient to win support, and to reach a wider audience still, the East India Company continued its public campaign through other means. A painting by Richard Greenbury portraying the event (now lost) was hung publicly in central London, the pastor Robert Wilkinson condemned the Dutch for being 'ignorant of the law of nature and nations' during a sermon at Whitehall, and a ballad was produced that recounted these tales of torture to the accompaniment of a popular tune.[4]

In the months following news of the massacre, the East India Company took careful control of the collection, interpretation and distribution of news of the event. The corporation's campaign was highly successful in motivating public support – so successful in fact that the growing threat of anti-Dutch violence in London led the privy council to ask the company to cease its publishing activities – and yet the state remained unmoved. The merchant corporation was told that 'it was not clear if they [its printed accounts] were politically acceptable'. For the moment at least, the state had other priorities, and England's merchants would be left to fend for themselves.[5]

– 174 –

THE CITY AND THE COURT

MERCHANT INFLUENCE AND STATE POLICY

For many early modern merchants, their ability to operate effectively at home and abroad depended on the tacit or practical support of the state. In some cases, this involved the delegation of state authority to individuals and organisations, and in others it involved direct action on the part of the state in court, by diplomats, or even militarily.[6] Indeed, for many companies, their relationship with the state was central to their foundation as a corporate entity. Reliance on privileges conferred by means of royal charter or letters patent, while placing many corporations in a position of strength relative to their competitors in England, also created a level of dependency between these companies and the state.[7] For the East India Company, for instance, it was not only during times of stress, such as in the aftermath of the Amboyna massacre, that reliance on the state for support was challenging, and the corporation was kept in a position of relative unease about its privileges for much of the early seventeenth century.[8] Even though the company's charter was renewed and sustained throughout the reigns of James I and Charles I, the environment in which it was enforced was much less stable.[9] Throughout this period, companies were forced to negotiate the scope and authority of their charters and privileges with the crown, and these could change depending on the political or economic context. Even when merchants were able to obtain support from the crown or parliament, these privileges were mutable in their effect due to the reliance of corporations on the state to enforce them.[10]

However, the early modern state was 'very much in formation, coexisting and sharing power with a range of allies and rivals', which granted merchants significant leeway of their own when it came to developing new means of controlling, organising and ordering people.[11] To obtain, maintain or resist state-issued privileges, merchants negotiated with the state on a continuous basis, and it was not uncommon for their position to suddenly weaken when they found themselves in opposition to more influential groups within the networks surrounding the crown

– 175 –

or parliament.[12] To overcome this challenge, merchants and corporations brokered relationships with powerful figures outside the commercial community who could facilitate access or encourage favour within the avenues of power.[13] In a period where state institutions remained weak, effective networks that could draw on people within the state apparatus were an important way to develop safeguards for support. Through these connections, which could be with members of the court, including lawyers, courtiers, the privy council or even the monarch,[14] merchants sought to influence state policy and obtain aid when necessary. '[T]he *marriage de convenance* between the government and big business . . . had been a central feature of royal commercial policy' since Elizabeth I had ascended the throne and would remain so throughout the early seventeenth century.[15] However, while the state benefited from mercantile activity in a number of respects, and provided many English companies with support, 'the common vision of a mercantile system premised upon a coherent, strong, and expansive nation state is simply unsustainable'.[16] Mercantile projects for trade and empire developed outside the apparatus of the state, even if they required support from the state on occasion, and the relationship between the two was far from consistent.

For much of the early modern period, the state operated with an awareness of this flexible association with the commercial community and was careful to positively promote relations rather than callously imposing restrictions on, or seeking to command, their activities. For example, when James I ascended to the English throne he wrote to London's mayor and aldermen to ensure them he was aware of their 'ancient fidelity and reputation hereditary to that our City of London being the chamber of our imperial crown and ever free from all shadows of tumultuous and unlawful courses'. Alongside a flattering assessment of the capital, James I wrote that the city's merchants should be assured that if they 'crave anything of us fit for the maintenance of all in general and every one of you in particular . . . it will be most willingly performed'. He promised that he would give special favour to the city's urban government and 'in the mean time to go constantly forward in doing all and whatever thing yourselves shall find necessary and expedient for the good government of the said city'.[17] Similarly, when the lord chancellor appeared before the City of London's elite at the Royal Exchange, he was at pains to show his appreciation for corporate activities that assisted the state – specifically the plantation in Ireland and hosting foreign ambassadors. He also promised not to meddle with the 'ordering of trades' and to allow merchants the same liberty as his predecessor.[18] It was, for the most part, a relationship between state and merchant community that reflected the benefits each could offer to the other.

No amount of kind words, however, could mask the power imbalances in the relationship – the state could, if it chose, retract or refuse to renew privileges, or introduce new regulations that would damage merchants' business. For example, merchants' complaints in 1616 about an imposition that increased customs paid by some traders more than others were summarily dismissed. They were told that if they 'refuse to conform themselves to the continuation of the payments', the king saw no reason not to take back the benefits and favours that he had granted to them in the past. The only option was acquiescence: the threat against their privileges was too great to ignore and they could only hope Lionel Cranfield, the surveyor general of customs, might help James I 'understand the trade of our kingdom and be better prepared for the disposing of our customs and subsidies hereafter'.[19] Lacking means for direct confrontation or avoidance, the merchant community could do little in the face of sudden alterations of policy.

Not even the richest and most powerful corporations were necessarily protected. As one disparaging account of the East India Company made clear, there was nothing stopping James I from overlooking the company in favour of other ventures when it suited him. Although it is unclear who penned the document, it was likely intended to be presented to James I, as it sought to show 'what benefit his Majesty may make by the trade to the East Indies' and suggested that the existing corporation was not functioning as effectively as it could, arguing that its privileges could be withdrawn if it did not refocus on the crown's priorities – and those of its closest courtiers. Reminding James I that 'the said company and their stock are at his majesty's grace and pleasure', the author was unsubtle in their assessment of where the power lay in the relationship. Though offering little by way of alternative, the author's main complaint was that the company was dominated by 'rich gentleman, merchants and usurers', with only a small number of lords inducted into the company.[20] While James I seems to have taken no special interest in the document (if it even reached him), the focus on the East India Company's social make-up reveals a significant challenge facing many, corporations in England. While many members of a company might have personal relationships with people around the king, privy council or the wider court, merchants themselves were not from these social strata and this could seriously affect the effectiveness of their lobbying.

The distance between merchants (whether within corporations or independently) and the state apparatus meant that the relationship was 'the product of constant negotiation, lobbying, and even at times outright hostility and suspicion.'[21] At times, organisations could play an important role in strengthening merchant groups by constraining the power of the state, and they undertook numerous strategies for ensuring the relationship was as effective as possible. On the least subtle level, this could include flattering the crown, parliament or a particularly important ally at court with all the pomp and circumstance that an early modern corporation could muster. For instance, after James I's coronation, he was welcomed into London with a triumphal procession, including a series of specially made arches to honour the occasion – and the hoped-for positive relationship between the city and the court (Plate 8).[22] Likewise, when the Mercers' livery company received news that James I intended to come to St Paul's Cathedral to listen to a sermon, it made sure members were ready 'with their livery hoods attired in their best apparel to wait and attend his majesties coming'. The company even organised 'whistlers in coats of velvet and chains of gold, ten at the least' to welcome the king.[23] Likewise, in honour of James I joining the Clothworkers' livery

– 178 –

THE CITY AND THE COURT

company, it was thought 'fit for the worship and credit of the company' that the company's hall in London 'be enlarged in length one bay at the upper and more windows for light be made on the sides', with 1,000 marks set aside to fund renovation.[24] The East India Company, which lacked the opportunity to host the king in such a manner, through 'gifts and gratuities in cash and kind, lobbying, petitions, and vigorous print campaigns secured its relationship with the state through hard work and strategic deployment of both political and financial capital'.[25] This might have taken the form of physical gifts or favours, such as the company choosing neither to call in debts from members of the privy council, nor demand late payments from members of the court 'whose favours the company may have present use of '.[26] Nor was it alone in doing so. The Levant Company's new year's gifts for 1624 included 'silver cups for the lord keeper, lord admiral, lord treasurer, secretary Calvert, secretary Conway' and 'a tun of claret wine for the archbishop of Canterbury and lord president'.[27] Corporations ranging from the Drapers' livery company, which gave Abraham Speckart preferential treatment to lease the Black Raven in Cheapside on consideration 'of his wife, being a servant unto the Queen', to Southampton's city corporation, which 'ordered that a new year's gift to the value of £40 or £50' would be given to the Earl of Hartford, likewise saw gifts and flattery as a useful means of building stronger links with well-connected patrons.[28] By spending time and money in these ways, corporations were able to strengthen bonds that stemmed from often long-standing, mutually beneficial arrangements.

Merchants understood that their continued hold on charters and patents depended, in part, on the effective delivery of promised benefits to the state, and it was not uncommon for companies to justify their continued receipt of privileges by publicly demonstrating this beneficial role.[29] For instance, when the East India Company came under attack in a number of printed texts as a drain on England's resources, the corporation decided 'to have a book set forth in defence of the East Indies trade, and to make known the benefit that it brings to the commonwealth'.[30] In their soon published defence, the company's member Sir Dudley

– 179 –

Digges highlighted the various contributions made by the company – from training mariners and employing the poor to building ships 'that round the world disperse the honour of the crown they serve, and then return with wealth for the kingdom'. 'By fetching from the wellhead' Asian commodities, Digges estimated that the trade did 'save the land £69666 13s 4d' at the expense of foreign competitors.[31] The corporation continued to draw on its merchants for supportive publications when attacks were renewed a few years later.[32] On this occasion, Thomas Mun argued that trade was a 'laudable practice whereby the intercourse of nations is so worthily performed' and 'the very touchstone of a kingdom's prosperity'. As well as defending the import of luxury products, he reasoned that bringing commodities such as silk and cotton to England provided 'maintenance of so many hundreds of poor people, who are continually employed in the winding, twisting, and weaving of the same'. He calculated that the company's activities now saved England £953,543 4s 4d each year.[33] As Digges and Mun would have it, the privileges accrued by corporate actors were more than paid for by their positive contributions to the wider economy. This argument could have been effective during negotiations with the state, and when James I sought to purchase the East India Company's entire shipment of pepper (and inadvertently undermine the corporation's profits), its members argued that as it was 'the merchant that bear the dangers of sea and land', so too should their company benefit from a rising market. Being 'unwilling to do that which might be distasteful unto them', James I altered his plans and withdrew his offer – there was little to be gained by threatening or harming a company that was providing him with income and the country with commodities.[34] In the *quid pro quo* relationship between state and corporation, the main expectation on companies was that they function well, regulate effectively and increase the wealth of the kingdom and its subjects.

The state, however, was not always satisfied with these returns and often supported projects that were deemed likely to increase its revenue through customs, taxes and other fees despite opposition from

THE CITY AND THE COURT

merchants.[35] For example, when the 'merchants of York, Newcastle and Hull', alongside the 'merchants of the western counties', complained about the introduction of a new book of rates by James I, suggesting that higher rates would damage the export of English cloth, the privy council was unmoved. Insisting that the rates reflected 'the enhancement of our money, as the measure of all things, both the rents of lands, and all other goods and merchandises', the council was in no mind to listen to the merchants' complaints.[36] Similarly, after the liberalisation of cloth production in the 1610s, whereby finished, dyed cloth became an increasingly important export to markets such as the Baltic or North Africa, a report by Henry Yelverton and Thomas Coventree – the attorney general and solicitor general – recalled that customs on wool had traditionally been paid by weight, meaning that James I could claim equal customs for broadcloth, narrow cloth and new draperies. Without doing so, they warned the crown 'should lose a great revenue yearly'.[37] The following year Yelverton reiterated these recommendations and suggested that woollen cloth should be charged for custom at 40s per sack, irrespective of the type of cloth.[38] Following Yelverton's report, the attorney general concluded that customs for long and narrow cloth was being claimed at too low a rate. Attempting to rectify the perceived error, it was proposed that the 'governors of the companies of the merchants of London trading in cloth' should present evidence regarding the issue. Despite the merchants' evidence, the crown's representatives concluded that 'whereas the merchants did allege that that payment of this duty might be an hindrance to the vent of cloth, we see no sound reason of that fear'.[39] As English merchants took advantage of global markets to diversify their trades, long-standing regulations regarding customs could quickly become obsolete and the state made sure to adapt its policies to reflect changing conditions.

Mercantile opposition to state impositions such as these could be successful but required considerable support across the commercial community and from powerful political allies. When James I imposed a high levy on foreign commodities in order to raise funds, for instance,

– 181 –

widespread concerns about 'the overthrow of merchants and shipping, the raising of general dearth and the decay of all wealth' were widely debated, and further charges were seen by detractors of the scheme as deleterious for commerce and liable to make English merchants less competitive.[40] The king was told that unless he removed the levy, he risked damaging London's role as an international port to the 'great discouragement both unto merchants and mariners' and also to the hurt of the whole common wealth'. One commentator even opposed the levy from the perspective that it contravened the thirteenth-century Magna Carta and demanded the king 'allow for the free traffic of merchants by their old and right customs' without excessive tolls.[41] The king was also warned that customs revenue would not increase, as 'merchants shall be forced [as some have done already] . . . to send their ships with currants to some other place upon the other side of the seas where they may land their currants' without ever bringing them to England.[42] The levy was not just seen as a threat to the livelihood of merchants, but as an attempt to contravene parliament's authority to oversee taxation in England. Outraged that the king 'without consent of parliament' had set impositions 'upon commodities exported or imported by the merchants', support was quickly obtained in the commons, where MPs demanded the levy should be immediately lifted, for the 'great satisfaction' and 'exceeding joy' of the merchants.[43] Finding himself in a sticky situation, James I quickly agreed to discuss the unforeseen 'inconveniences' to commerce.[44] Merchants understood and accepted that customs payments had long been, and always would be, part of their day-to-day business, but they considered additional, unexpected and large levies as unacceptable.

The early modern state also drew on the commercial community as a source of direct and immediate funding through loans. Although these were theoretically obtained with the expectation that they would be repaid, this was not expected quickly, and many merchants objected to the burden, refused to pay or sought to negotiate.[45] When companies were levied to finance these large loans, they were often forced to

1. Thomas Gresham, pictured here in Anthonis Mor's imposing portrait, was the most successful merchant of his day, sending ships and goods to destinations across Europe. A businessman, ambassador and royal adviser, Gresham used his wealth to modernise London's commercial infrastructure by founding the Royal Exchange.

2. In the sixteenth century, new corporations such as the Levant Company helped connect English consumers with goods from across the world. Some items, like this beautiful İznik ware jug, were embellished by craftsmen in England to create prominent display pieces – in this case with a silver cover, mount and spout.

3. Peter Mundy, an English merchant visiting Constantinople in 1618, collected this image of 'a Greek that sells vinegar'. It was added to a carefully annotated album of paintings that commemorated his time in the Ottoman capital and shared his insights about commercial life in the Mediterranean.

4. This richly decorated carpet was made in Lahore for William Fremlin, an East India Company employee who served as its president in Surat. As well as bearing traditional animal scenes, it prominently displays his family coat of arms.

5. Alongside gifts of silver and gold, the East India Company gave the Mughal Emperor Jahangir a portrait of King James I. It was copied by the Indian artist Bichitr (himself pictured second from the bottom) to showcase the emperor's relationships with the wider world.

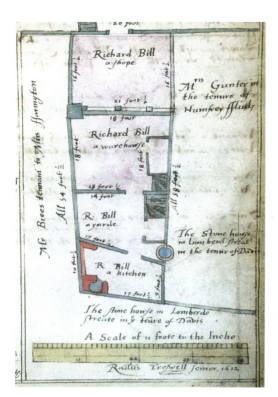

6. In this plan of Richard Bill's shop and home, we can see how life and work were tightly intertwined in early modern England. The grocer's shop, with an entrance onto Cornhill Street, fronted a four-storey complex that included a warehouse, kitchen, counting house and living chambers.

7. This nineteenth-century photograph shows the house of Levant Company merchant Sir Paul Pindar. Originally built around 1599, it was a rare survivor of the Great Fire of London. Pindar's home was in a neighbourhood popular with merchants, with close links to sites like the Guildhall and the Royal Exchange.

8. In 1604, King James I made his royal entry into London. The ensuing pageant included a procession through seven sumptuously adorned triumphal arches designed by architect Stephen Harrison. The first, seen here, celebrated 'Londinium' and the city's *Genius Urbis* – the spirit of the city.

9. In 1623, Dutch authorities in Amboyna tortured and executed ten English merchants. Pamphlets, paintings, engravings, sermons and ballads were produced that condemned the Dutch, often portraying graphic details to shock their public audience. Such images were reproduced throughout the seventeenth century during periods of Anglo-Dutch rivalry.

10. William Windover was a merchant who wanted his portrait to celebrate his life in business. Grasping a letter from Hamburg, where he traded woollen cloth, he is surrounded by emblems representing the important communities in his life – his family, the Merchant Adventurers, and the Drapers' livery company.

11. In Jamestown, the Virginia Company's colonial capital, the size of vessels for eating and cooking increased as these activities became more communal, reflecting corporate practices in London. The larger pipkin and dish on the right show how life was changing in the nascent colony.

12. In 1619, this ballot box was presented to the East India Company in an attempt to change the way the corporation elected its leaders. Despite the efforts of the box's London maker to evoke the riches of Asia, it was condemned and rejected for being subversive and dangerous.

13. Wenceslaus Hollar's evocative illustration of the Royal Exchange, founded by Thomas Gresham in 1571, shows the bustle of business in England's capital. Not only a site for trade and business, this was a space where merchants could gossip and share news, make plans and meet partners, and witness the fruits of their labour.

THE CITY AND THE COURT

monitor and punish members for failure to comply, or offer support or guidance to ensure payment.[46] For example, the Drapers' livery company, when requested to loan £1,152, made sure to record each member who failed to contribute to the payment or 'made absolute refusal' to do so and passed their names onto the Lord Mayor.[47] In other cases, corporations sought to mitigate the burden on the members when they were asked for funds, such as the Haberdashers' livery company that offered low-interest loans to members to enable them to make payments to the company that would then be loaned to the crown.[48] Only on rare occasions were companies able to avoid payment entirely. For instance, after the East India Company and Merchant Adventurers came together to fashion a loan of £50,000 for the crown, each corporation probably felt like it had paid its due.[49] Yet, later the same year, the privy council returned to the East India Company seeking further loans. As the 'greatest, rightest and most flourishing in the land, and the very column of the kingdom', the corporation was believed to be 'of best ability to do his majesty a pleasure'. Unwilling to reject the request outright, the company responded by thanking James I for his continued support and that they were happy to offer a 'retribution, for his care and good will towards them'. However, the company's directors were careful to state that they would be obliged to discuss the issue with the generality, a situation that meant the king's request would likely 'be published abroad throughout the land' and that a possible rejection of the loan would reflect dishonourably on the crown. Unwilling to allow a public discussion, the privy council withdrew its request.[50] Concerns that members would be unwilling or unable to fund loans required the adoption of strategies by corporations that might prove detrimental to their relationship either to the state, or, perhaps worse, with their own generality.

Despite this challenge, and widespread mercantile objections, requests from the crown for loans soared over the course of the early seventeenth century and companies increasingly struggled to comply, often seeking to negotiate in order to reduce demands upon them. The Mercers' livery company recorded, for instance, detail demands from the crown for loan after loan – and its difficulties in meeting them. Soon after James I ascended the throne, the company was forced to compel members – many of whom were merchants – to pay their dues to cover a £1,200 loan.[51] Almost a decade later, in an attempt to avoid the same necessity, the company responded to demands that they contribute towards a £100,000 levy that James I sought from London's urban corporation by offering to give £310 'by way of benevolence' that would not require repayment.[52] Later, when approached for further funds 'towards the charge of the wars for preserving of the Palatinate', the company sought to negotiate again. It argued that 'this company be found to be above £3000 in debt by reason of many extraordinary charges lately come upon them, and especially by the plantation in Ireland' – another expense forced upon them by the state – and offered only £200 towards the loan. This was turned down by the Lord Mayor, who insisted they pay £310, a sum that equalled earlier payments and those of other livery companies in the city. The Mercers' acquiesced 'but with all protestation to be made that this shall be no precedent for the future'.[53] Demands only increased further under Charles I, with a request for a new £60,000 loan from the City of London (taking the total owed by the crown to £100,000) that was quickly followed by a call for the city to furnish twenty ships intended to challenge 'the vast ambition and malice of his declared enemy the King of Spain' – at the cost of another £18,000.[54] When Charles I returned the following year requesting £60,000, London's commercial community was no longer willing to acquiesce and demanded that surety was offered in the form of crown lands across England, 'for this and other money formerly lent unto his majesty and his noble father' to the value of £120,000.[55] Exacting surety was a significant shift in policy, recognising the 'great debt owed by his majesty to the city'.[56] It went some way to assuaging the concerns of members contributing to the new loan, and the company eventually agreed to contribute their share towards the loan in return for 'valuable portion of the land now to be purchased off his majesty . . . for their security' and 6 per cent interest.[57] To raise the sum required,

THE CITY AND THE COURT

£3,720, the Mercers' sought to ensure neither their members nor the corporation would be too inconvenienced by making the payment from the company's common stock, using 'ready money' obtained from external sources, including a loan from Sir Baptiste Hicks, who agreed to 'furnish £2700 upon security of the company's bond under the company's seal' and '£600 due by the East India Company' that was 'being now offered by the treasurer of that company'.[58] Pressure from the state was hard to resist as corporations continued to depend on it for their privileges and other forms of support. If companies wanted influence at court, they had few options but find a way to pay up.

As well as giving gifts, publicising their benefits, paying customs and funding loans, corporations made efforts to influence the state by drawing on the networks of their members, which sometimes included the wealthiest and most powerful merchants in England.[59] This by no means immediately translated into influence with the state, and although sometimes merchants did reach positions of considerable authority, such as Lionel Cranfield, 'the merchant earl of Middlesex', who became chancellor of the exchequer, this was not a common experience.[60] More usually, rather than having direct access, corporations remained dependent on relationships between company members and the crown, parliament or members of the court when it needed support from the state.[61] Many merchants had, of course, collaborated with numerous individuals from the gentry and nobility in activities including commerce and colonisation, and these relationships would have been important when seeking support in court circles. This was easiest for participants in colonial activities, where merchants worked closely with non-merchants in terms of investing and managing the companies involved, and also on the ground, as gentry participants took positions of authority through their presumed expertise in military and land-management issues.[62] In the Irish Society, for example, over a quarter of members were identifiable as gentry or nobility, a figure that rose to just under half in the Virginia Company. For companies limited to professional merchants, the figure was much lower, with less than 2 per cent of

– 185 –

members in the Levant or Spanish companies drawn from such backgrounds. The East India Company stood between these extremes, with almost one in eight members identifiable as gentry, although here, too, merchants alone were able to join the highest echelons of corporate government.[63] A corporation's members might provide some degree of influence with the state, but this could hardly be relied upon by those desperate to maintain or improve their position.

In some cases, corporations would actively extend their membership to courtiers and influential figures as a means of improving their position. For instance, in 1609 the East India Company altered its membership criteria to admit a number of 'lords, knights, and gentlemen', including the Lord Treasurer Robert Cecil, the Earl of Salisbury and the Lord Admiral Charles Howard – influential figures all with wide interests in colonial and trading ventures.[64] Membership of the company was gratefully received by such figures, and the Earl of Southampton showed his thanks by delivering a 'brace of bucks' as a gift to the corporation.[65] Over the following decade, opening the membership of the company became a common strategy for increasing influence at court. Whether through Sir James Stonehouse, who was admitted specifically because he attended the king on a daily basis and the company wanted 'such of their friends about the king, that should be tied unto them', or Sir Julius Caesar, 'a person of that eminency and place' who happily announced that he was 'willing and ready to do as great kindness for the company as others are' if they allowed him to join, the company's network in court grew considerably.[66] The most notable investor among the non-merchants brought into the company was Prince Charles, who invested a substantial sum in the company in 1619.[67] Through such relationships, and the careful management of ongoing relations with members of the court, the East India Company hoped it would be in a better position to influence the crown.

The merchant John Watts employed a similar strategy within the context of the Clothworkers' livery company to try to maintain support from the court during a difficult decade for the corporation.[68] In June

THE CITY AND THE COURT

1607, for instance, when Watts was Lord Mayor of London, James I visited his house where he was 'joyfully received and royally feasted'. During the event, the Clothworkers' urged the king to take the freedom of the company. He consented and immediately travelled with them to the company's hall, which happened to be next door, where 'his highness was pleased openly to publish that he would from thenceforth be a free brother of the said company of clothworkers'. To celebrate, the king promised to send two bucks to the company each year for a feast and the company ordered 'a fair table to remain in the common hall of the said company for ever' in commemoration of the event.[69] Following James I's admittance into the company, a lobbying coup in many respects, John Watts initiated a policy of building further networks with influential figures, both English and foreign. These included Patrick Stewart the 'Earl of Orquency', John Ramsay Viscount Hedington, the Italians Marchese Ferrante, Bentinogli the Marchese di Gualtiere and Lord Cavaliere 'Mari Stimini', 'diverse Gentlemen strangers' from Bohemia, Picardy and Hesse, and even an Ottoman visitor called 'Cotti Seg Zu'.[70] By welcoming such esteemed personages into these highly restrictive organisations, even if only on an honorary basis, corporations were able to interact, and ingratiate themselves, with figures whose influence might benefit them in the future.

Whether or not a corporation had such esteemed company to wield influence on its behalf, the arduous process of petitioning the state for the renewal or obtaining of privileges was a challenge that many senior merchants came to experience, whether through roles in livery, urban or trading corporations.[71] Indeed, it is likely that the common experience across these different organisations helped ensure as smooth a process as possible, and to highlight common interests and economic benefits during the petitioning process. For example, when the Drapers' livery company sought a new charter, the corporation appointed its members John Jolles, Thomas Hayes, James Deane, John Hall, William Megges and Mr Quarles to meet with the privy council and discuss the matter.[72] As well as their roles within the Drapers', Jolles was an experienced alderman in the City of London, Hayes was a Merchant Adventurer and Deane was a founding member of the East India Company, while Hall was a member of the Spanish company and would be part of the French company alongside Megges when it was founded a few years later. All of these organisations had been through processes to obtain charters, and interlocutors like this group of merchants helped to ensure that each organisation was able to draw on the experience of others. In a similar vein, merchants might act together to pressure the state more effectively. In Southampton, for instance, the city's corporation allowed 'Mr Robert Chambers Alderman, who has a lease for the forfeiture of the sweet wines, to make petition or petitions to such lords and others in the town's name'. Rather than acting alone, Chambers was able to depend on the wider community for backing during negotiations regarding 'the better advancement of his said farm of sweet wines'.[73] Multiple companies, too, might join forces during a particular dispute. For example, when a new patent was offered monopolising the tanning of cony skins, the Skinners' livery company argued that the proposal would damage both its own and the Eastland Company's business.[74] The skinners were soon joined by representatives of the Eastland and French companies in opposition to the patent.[75] Together, the three organisations persuaded the privy council that the potential damages to overseas trade and domestic manufacturing were too great, and the patent was revoked.[76] With the state involved in so many parts of merchants' lives, the know-how and expertise required for effectively negotiating was an important skill to have.

When seeking support from the state, merchants often highlighted their experience of international commerce. This allowed them to distance themselves from detractors and to show that their skills and practices had developed within the stabilising, orderly world of corporate life.[77] This was clear during the public dispute between the East India Company and its detractors detailed above: Thomas Mun dismissed the opposition as 'not participating in the society', inexperienced and likely to 'willingly run into these errors'; while Edward Misselden reminded his

– 188 –

readers that it was essential for trade to be entrusted to men of 'approved credit and trust' rather than 'novices and new-made merchants, by whose inexperience the trade might be subject to be betrayed into the hands of foreign nations'.[78] Dudley Digges, too, made sure to explain that his own material had been 'taken out of the custom-books, out of the East India Company's books, out of Grocers, Warehouse-keepers, merchant's books, and conference with men of best experience' – he was simply better positioned and better able to understand the trade, so it made sense for the state to support his position.[79] Merchants sought to leverage these skills and considerable experience during negotiations with the state. For instance, when critics of corporate management 'said that there are not any companies in foreign countries' as evidence that companies should be abolished, they were countered by merchants familiar with a range of examples. Not only were they told how 'the Hanse towns have been a society of long continuance, and in Italy, Germany, Spain and Portugal there are diverse companies very ancient', but it was also highlighted how 'the United Provinces very lately were forced to follow this example of England for the trade to the East Indies'.[80] Similarly, when proponents of a monopolistic corporation to oversee fishing presented their case, they stressed that their project would 'imitate the example of other great kingdoms and states', and even presented a copy of the King of Denmark's proclamation against fishing on the coast of Iceland as a means of demonstrating the viability of their proposal.[81] When drawn into dialogue with the state, it was always good to have evidence and expertise ready to back you up.

Approaching the privy council, crown or parliament was a drawn-out, expensive business and companies took care to ensure their efforts were not wasted. This might take the form of pre-negotiation research, such as the Clothworkers' livery company electing to spend 15s to assess 'how the lords stand affected towards their late suit' before committing themselves further, or the Spanish Company's choice to levy 20s from its members to fund directors of the organisation to attend the chancellor in person.[82] As negotiations continued, costs would only rise.

When the Clothworkers' livery company sought new privileges to reflect changing overseas conditions for the wool trade, for instance, it paid £20 on three separate occasions between 1599 and 1600 for members to oversee the negotiation effectively. A further payment of £4 was made to Mr Altham, a councillor who had advised the company and written on its behalf during the process, and another 14s 4d to the scrivener who had drawn up the petitions.[83] Similarly, when the Drapers' livery company employed Sir Christopher Hatton to defend the company's privileges regarding land ownership in London, it was soon joined by other livery companies in defence of their common rights, including the Mercers' livery company who agreed to 'disburse £200 toward the passage of a bill in the Parliament'.[84] Influencing the state was both a tough and expensive business.

Organisations outside London were disadvantaged additionally in this respect, as their lack of presence in Westminster made it difficult for them to lobby effectively, and they faced higher expenses for representatives' maintenance, writing and sending letters, and paying messengers. Some, such as Bristol's Merchant Venturers, sought to have a semi-regular presence in London, and members could be sent to attend 'his Majesty and the Lords of his Privy Council in such things as shall concern this company', but this arrangement was unsuitable during long-term negotiations and disputes – which might easily last months if not longer.[85] For these organisations, cost pressures could build up. During disputes over the cloth trade, Norwich's merchants were forced to pay upkeep for Thomas Pettus during his long stay in London, and similar charges to the value of £40 were faced by the Merchant Venturers of Bristol as they lobbied for the renewal of their charter.[86] Costs included much more than maintenance for representatives: Nottingham's city council, when seeking a renewal of their corporate charter, detailed costs including payments to the Queen's attorney 'for examining the paper', to clerks for copying the document, and even charges for parchment and paper.[87] Similarly, the Merchant Adventurers of York recorded money 'paid to Mr William Allyn for letters concerning Spain'.[88] Simply paying

– 190 –

THE LIMITS OF STATE SUPPORT

for a messenger to the capital cost Portsmouth's merchants 25s 6d for 'charges riding to London in the town business'.[89] Obtaining support from the state was expensive, difficult and by no means guaranteed. In England and overseas, the state could be an influential arbiter, a powerful backer, a useful partner or an implacable barrier, and for early modern merchants it was a relationship that they could not choose to ignore.

THE LIMITS OF STATE SUPPORT

Even when support was forthcoming, it could take an age to come into force at a practical level, and during negotiations the goal posts could suddenly shift as the state sought to use its negotiating power to impose its own policy objectives. During one episode, soon after peace was announced between England and Spain in 1604, the Spanish Company was rudely awakened to the limitations of relying on state backing when the corporation sought a new charter that would allow it to take advantage of the new opportunities that peace represented. Delivering the old charter to the lord chancellor, who it was hoped 'would presently give order for the engrossing of a charter of confirmation ready to be sealed, which in a few days might be procured under the great seal of England', the company expected a quick turnaround and ready support on the part of the state. It was not to be. Ten months later it was still awaiting full confirmation of its privileges in the face of resistance from detractors who sought the full deregulation of the trade. Opponents to the new charter argued that the company's charter 'became void by *non user* during the long time of the continuance of the war' with Spain, 'which doth therefore dissolve the said corporation unless the same be restored again by a new creation'. While the privy council offered encouraging support to the company's interpretation – that the case of *non user* was not applicable, as the corporation had been unable rather than unwilling to prosecute the trade as stipulated in their old charter due to the war – the state did not support the renewal until there had been further consideration. It took another six months for the charter to be confirmed.[90]

As the Spanish Company had discovered, support from the state was not always something that could be relied upon.

For merchants, whose profits often depended on meeting the demands of quick changing market conditions, the time and cost of consulting with the state was an unfortunate but necessary part of their day-to-day lives. For example, one merchant, William Stallenge, found himself in the unenviable position of waiting for permission from the privy council to sell corn and fish from Newfoundland he had already shipped to Bayonne and Saint-Jean-de-Luz. The two Basque towns were access points to Spanish markets that currently faced a blanket ban on English entry while hostilities between the states continued. Without the council's permission to move forward, Stallenge could do nothing but watch as his livelihood rotted away on the Biscay coast.[91] Similarly, urgent petitions from the East India Company revealed how dependence on the state for permission to act could upend even the most powerful commercial organisations. In one case, the corporation required clearance to purchase 200 barrels of gunpowder 'without the which' it 'dare not adventure to set [its ship] to sea in these dangerous times of rovers'. If its petition was not quickly approved, it warned, it would not be able to send its fleet to Asia until the following year.[92] In each case, the risks of changeable conditions overseas were often exacerbated by state regulation as much as assisted by state support.

In part, corporations were intended to function as a regulator to oversee the day-to-day business of trade without constant recourse to the state, but when opposed by competitors, organisations were forced to seek confirmation that their privileges should and could be enforced. This was a clear dilemma for the Clothworkers' livery company, whose oversight of woollen cloth production had been undermined by new state regulations that sought to promote new manufacturing processes in the 1610s. Thus, towards the end of the decade, the corporation petitioned the privy council to 'be assisted by their lordships favourable directions and authority for the settling of their company under an orderly rule and government for the preventing of such abuses and

THE CITY AND THE COURT

inconveniences as do daily arise for want thereof'. To keep regulating the cloth industry, the company needed to be able to enforce the company's own regulations backed up by the state. After seeking advice from the king's attorney and the City of London, the privy council agreed that 'all artisan clothworkers of what company so ever they be free shall be subject to such orders and government of the Company of Clothworkers for so much as concerns their trade'. Furthermore, in the future all artisan clothworkers would have to be made free of the corporation. In future, it was hoped, the corporation would be able to take on the responsibility of regulating cloth manufacture effectively, reducing the need for state involvement on a regular basis.[93] In a similar vein, almost a decade later, the Merchant Adventurers complained to the privy council about 'the great trouble unto trade and the venting of the cloth of the kingdom' that had come about due to 'molestation done [to] them by the master and wardens of the Company of Clothworkers'. Claiming that its ancient privileges to export cloth were not only still in force but also that they were more important than ever before 'for diverse reasons of state, the times and conditions of trade', the company insisted that its oversight of the cloth trade should be respected. The privy council agreed and ordered that the liberties of the Merchant Adventurers must be respected and that all suits against it should be withdrawn.[94] With support from the state, in both instances the companies would continue in their roles as regulators. Yet, once again, this backing was mutable and uncertain, with each company obtaining privileges that contradicted those of the other. When collaborative and cooperative practices failed the commercial community, recourse to the court was by no means an assured way of resolving underlying problems.

While the state could be called upon to have the final say in resolving domestic disagreements, when merchants were caught up in disputes internationally, support from the court was especially important. While many companies and individual merchants did have some recourse to treating with officials overseas, these efforts were often limited and carried more weight when they were supported by, or in support of,

– 193 –

state-backed communications. For example, when English merchants to the Ottoman Empire sought to obtain greater commercial and legal rights from the Sultan, they expected that only through Elizabeth I's ambassador's demonstration that the queen was 'a prince absolute power, not inferior nor needy of help', would they have any hope of obtaining an improved grant.[95] Likewise, when English merchants were claimed to be 'accustomed to giving aid to the Turks, who are this time waging wars with the Christians' and refused access to the Holy Roman Empire, Elizabeth I defended them, insisting that her ambassador in Constantinople was merely there to ensure the 'protection of the free trading of our merchants in those parts' and threatened to have her complaints printed so that they could be communicated with ease to every one of the Princes of the Empire'.[96] Similarly, the merchant Richard Lee sought a formal appointment from the state as ambassador to Russia, a role that he admitted 'may seem partial for my private affairs' but that he argued would be beneficial for the country also.[97] His argument was backed by the Muscovy Company, which suggested that the Russian Emperor Feodor II might reduce or cancel its privileges if a formal ambassador was not sent immediately.[98] In each case, merchants were keen for representation that would recognise their specific demands and act on their behalf. When this was not the case, as experienced by the Eastland Company when it desperately sought to reduce Denmark's increased tolls at the Sound (the entrance to the Baltic) – fees that were suddenly higher than those paid by its Dutch competitors – it could do little on its own beyond drawing attention to its plight during negotiations between England's diplomats and the Scandinavian state.[99] In an international environment, drawing on the state for support while maintaining autonomy to act was a challenge that many merchants faced.

When corporate representatives were unable to intercede effectively in foreign courts, overseas merchants had to petition the English state for aid. For instance, when it became clear that local officials in Bordeaux were not following a new customs agreement made between the English and French states, a group of fourteen English merchants who were

THE CITY AND THE COURT

affected had little choice but to request assistance from the English crown, which they hoped would intercede on their behalf.[100] Similarly, when the Eastland Company faced problems conducting their trade to Sweden and Poland, concluding that the 'sending over of any cloth or woollen commodities before things were settled would quite overthrow the hope of success', the corporation ordered that no ships should depart until letters were 'procured for the better obtaining of this free trade' from James I.[101] Likewise, the East India Company carried highly decorated letters from the English monarch to present to rulers in Asia, in the hope that the presentation of royal authority would boost their chances of obtaining preferential commercial access to new markets.[102] The Muscovy Company was also dependent on supplying supporting documents from Charles I that promised 'trade will be no inconvenience to your country, but rather a benefit in venting commodity' before the Russian Emperor Michael I would grant its merchant Robert Sym permission to export corn.[103] In an extreme example, when the Holy Roman Emperor Rudolf II 'made an arrest of all the merchants goods and persons' that the Merchant Adventurers had in Germany, 'with so great animosity as shows his spleen', the company relied on James I for support – who retaliated by ordering the seizure of all Hanse ships passing through the English Channel.[104]

Merchants might also depend on the state for support during disputes relating to lost goods, compensation from foreign states or payments from erstwhile partners. For instance, when local authorities in France seized the estate of the merchant Richard Archdale in 1628, following an English attack on La Rochelle, he was quick to arrange for his wine, turpentine and other commodities to be transported to Holland, where he had had business dealings since at least 1623. Here, alongside those of fellow merchants Henry Lee, Martin Broadgate, Edward Browne, George Rouckes and Benjamin Wright, Archdale's goods could be kept safe – but by crossing the French–Dutch border these merchants had moved from one English regulatory framework to another and the group was forced to wait for the privy council to grant special permission before

– 195 –

the goods could be returned to England.[105] However, whereas Archdale only required permission from the English state to ship his goods home, others were less lucky and found themselves caught up in court battles overseas. For example, the ambassador to France, Thomas Edmonds, was asked to assist Thomas Thornell, a merchant from York, who had been locked in a long suit with the trader Pineau of Bordeaux 'in sundry courts of that realm, to his impoverishing and nigh utter undoing'. Pineau had been sentenced by the grand council in Paris, but Thornell was still waiting for compensation four years later. Through the ambassador the merchant hoped his case 'may be duly re-examined by good indifferent commissioners, and justice done'.[106] John Watts and Giles Flemming had been waiting even longer for recompense during another dispute, and the same ambassador was ordered to assist them in dealing with French courts over piracy committed 'by some of Rochelle' sixteen years earlier.[107] In Spain, too, numerous English merchants complained about the challenges of obtaining payments, sometimes over similarly long periods. For example, the two merchants William Green and Roger Corbett had been let down by poor contract enforcement in Spain. Their factors, John Mulis and Richard Bere, had made an agreement in Lisbon with Don Fernando de Toledo for 4,000 kintals of Muscovy cordage, worth over £4,400. They had shipped the Russian commodity to Portugal only for Toledo to renege on the contract. The situation was only made worse by their former partner's order that the cordage could not be sold to any third party.[108] Similarly, George Weaver reported that his factor, George Wiche, had 'been troubled, molested and hindered in the recovery of a great sum of money due for a parcel of copper sold there'. The debt, worth 20,000 ducats, was still unpaid 'to the great impoverishing of this deponent and one George Clerk'.[109] Another merchant, Roger Kilvert, was still waiting for £8,000 from Madrid in payment for lead he had been compelled to sell sixteen years before.[110]

Meeting the regulatory expectations of foreign states presented further challenges, and trading overseas could be fraught with the threat of seizure, expensive court battles and even the Inquisition.[111] For

THE CITY AND THE COURT

instance, in 1635, English merchants trading to Spain were invited to submit, under oath, their complaints regarding treatment in Spain over the past half decade and revealed a litany of concerns.[112] Many merchants complained of goods being seized by local authorities and of having to appeal to courts in Madrid that had overthrown positive outcomes they had obtained in local courts where English consuls had long built relationships. For the partners Roger Dunster and Jeremy Honeychurch who traded to Bilbao and Biscay, their troubles had begun when John Ortiz accused them of using a 'Holland built' ship. Adamant their vessel had been taken from the French as a lawful prize, they had appealed to the court in Bilbao where a local judge had taken their side. However, Ortiz had taken the case to the Admiralty Court in Madrid where, 'though there were no more things alleged nor proved', the ship and goods valued at £4,800 were ordered seized and their factors were arrested.[113] Ortiz had also proved the undoing of Robert Oxwick, Elias Roberts and Thomas Boyer who had seen £4,800 of English manufactured goods seized in 1631 following claims they were in fact Dutch made.[114] In Seville English merchants were no luckier, and Robert Oxwick and Michael Waring had lost £350 after local officials declared their shipment of hides and tin contraband. Their factor, Nathaniel Oxwick, had successfully argued their case in the local court, but this, too, had been overturned in Madrid.[115] For many English merchants, the dishonesty of local officials using new regulations against Dutch shipping for their own profit was deemed a likely cause of their troubles. According to Martin Broadgate and Robert Swinerton, this duplicity was not even subtle, and they claimed officials in the Canary Island increased fees at the port from 100 to 500 ryalls and threatened to denounce ships as Dutch built if the fees were not paid.[116] In each case, merchants could do little but record and report their problems to the English state, and hope that diplomatic resolutions might be found to help them overcome the difficulties they faced.

Nor did the challenges of Spanish regulations end in Europe. As English merchants became increasingly active across the world, they often

– 197 –

found themselves drawn into regions under the imperial jurisdiction – to one degree or another – of the Spanish Empire. When travelling back from successful trading in the Ottoman Empire, the merchant Richard Deane's ship was seized in Spanish waters, with losses valued at a career-changing £2,000.[117] Wider-ranging complaints were made in 1605, during a period of peace, as English merchants protested that imbalanced regulations in the two states disadvantaged them. Pointing out that Spanish merchants were able to transport English goods, including fish from Newfoundland, pilchards from Ireland and cloth, the English merchants thought it unfair that they faced steep charges for carrying Spanish goods and that, by 'keeping of the trade of Brazil and the West Indies to themselves', Spain was 'excluding our [English] nation from trading there'.[118] In each case, complaints rested on English merchants seeking to enter, or pass through, regions where Spanish traders held monopolistic privileges of their own, and they hoped that the English state would somehow obtain them access during diplomatic negotiations.

When merchants did enter restricted markets, such as in the Caribbean, Africa or the Indian Ocean, the delegation of authority to make war and peace held by some companies might supersede their reliance on the English state for support.[119] Thus, when the Guinea Company's 'pinnace called the *Intelligence* trading upon the coast of Guinea . . . to gain and discover that hopeful trade for gold' was captured, Nicholas Crispe and Humphrey Slany, two leading merchants in the Guinea trade to Africa, petitioned the privy council for assistance. The merchants maintained that they had sought only supplies from São Tomé after a longer than anticipated voyage left the ship 'in distress for wood and water', and although the island was in the possession of Portugal, the merchants' ship's master had been confident of peaceful trade, finding '2 or 3 English ships in trade' at the island and 'supposing that England and Spain were in peace and amity'. Yet, no sooner had he 'cast anchor in the harbour by the rest of the English ships' and gone ashore, the ship's master was imprisoned by the Portuguese governor and condemned as a pirate. The governor then seized the ship, crew and goods – valued at

THE CITY AND THE COURT

£20,000. Another of the company's ships, the 500-ton *Crispiano*, had also been mistreated at the Portuguese island of São Miguel in the Azores, where two of its crew had been imprisoned. Quickly escalating, this stand-off reached new heights when another larger Guinea Company ship, the *William*, 'being a ship of good force' was sent to São Tomé to retake the pinnace and demand satisfaction. The threat of using force to obtain satisfaction was likely intended to motivate the English king as much as the Portuguese governor, but before taking such extreme measures Crispe and Slany were willing to wait for Charles I to assist them in obtaining restitution and the release of their crew.[120] In spaces overseas where regulatory authority and legal opinion was contested, asking for support from the English state was often a matter of last resort. Indeed, as corporations were delegated greater authority to arm themselves, make war and even seize territory overseas, the diplomatic priorities of the English state were not necessarily their immediate concern.

While merchants trading into Spanish dominions might often find themselves at the mercy of the Spanish state, competition with other European merchants across the globe was an increasingly common theme.[121] Competition with the Dutch, especially, whose commercial expansion outpaced that of England during this period, was a familiar experience for English merchants, and complaints were common.[122] In Norway, Dutch merchants were accused of offering cheap credit to local merchants who would freight goods on their ships, then sell the commodities in England where they would be paid in coin. Commentators claimed the practice was so common that 'our English coin, both gold and silver, is as common payment in Holland and Zeeland as it is here in England'.[123] In the North Atlantic, English merchants often found their fishing voyages interrupted by Dutch vessels ranging far and wide in waters claimed by the Muscovy Company.[124] Not even the East India Company, often held up as the richest and most powerful corporation in England, was immune – not only did it face Dutch pressure so intense that it was 'eating up our prosperity', but its very foundation had been 'induced by the successes of the voyage performed by the Dutch nation'.[125]

– 199 –

In each case, merchants relied on the state for favour during disputes with their international competitor(s). The exceptional profits of Dutch merchants and the burgeoning wealth of the young state led to accusations that English trade had decayed as a result of their accomplishments.[126] Indeed, many attempts to persuade the state to restructure England's economy, such as by liberalising trade or promoting manufacture, made specific comparisons to practices in the United Provinces.[127] For instance, John Keymer's proposal to alter policies on taxation, monopolies and currency all rested on his analysis that, through 'smallness of custom and liberty of trade', the Dutch used to 'draw multitudes of merchants to trade with them and many other nations to inhabit amongst them' so that 'they make stockhouses of all foreign commodities'.[128] It was a model he saw only benefits in adopting.

England's merchants apparently saw no contradiction in praising the supposed openness of the Dutch market and demanding the state facilitate their own access to markets overseas, while insisting that their own domestic monopolies were supported and maintained. Thus, when Dutch envoys Pavius Bourghe, Bourell Bourghe and Macman Escherim, joined by Hugo Grotius, visited London for a conference 'for the avoiding of a misunderstanding' between the Dutch and English East India companies, there was only minimal room for manoeuvre.[129] The Dutch, for their part, were unhappy that the East India Company had involved the state at all, suggesting that complaints were 'but by some private men' rather than the corporations, and could have been handled privately.[130] Furthermore, they claimed that, like the English, they had intended 'to have applied themselves wholly to merchandizing' but had been forced to 'war upon the Portuguese' in response to attempts to 'drive both us out of the Indies and destroy those Indians who had trade with us'. They argued that great costs sustained during the conflict, and agreements with local rulers 'promising unto us only the sale of the spices', validated their monopoly over the region.[131] The first conference led to little in the way of agreement, and the following year senior merchants Robert Middleton and Maurice Abbott travelled to The

Hague to join the ambassador Sir Henry Wotton and continue the debate.[132] They sought 'all such mutual and friendly usage and treaty in all parts and places' where both English and Dutch merchants were active. However, at the same conference, Wotton was ordered to try to ensure that Dutch shipping to the North Atlantic stopped because it was already fished by the Muscovy Company.[133] With pressure from both the East India and Muscovy companies for support, the English state was torn between two opposing positions – insisting on free trade in Asia while imposing a monopoly in the Atlantic.

It was not only in distant oceans that English traders sought protection from international competition. Many merchants railed against the undue influence of goods being carried to and from England in non-English ships, and sought protectionist measures to protect domestic ship owners and merchants alike.[134] This was particularly targeted at Dutch ship owners, who offered to carry freight at rates far lower than the English. The Dutch employed ships with larger, broader dimensions, 'by which means they draw not so much water as our ships do, and yet be of greater burden than our ships be', and a more efficient design that required less crew. Thus, 'by the advantage they gain of us in burden, and by the charge they save in mariners, wages, and victuals, they are able to carry their freight better cheap than we'.[135] It was not only Dutch merchants who benefited from this lower freight, and commentators in England complained how 'the lamentable estate that our navigation is fallen into' was a direct result of 'the Flemings that are daily employed by our English merchants'. Without immediate redress, they claimed Dutch competition would erode English participation in markets across Europe. The merchants further argued that policies restricting foreign shipping were not an uncommon strategy. They highlighted how Venice imposed restrictions on foreigners transporting coral and how Spain banned its subjects from freighting on behalf of foreign merchants, 'which law is very severely executed'. Even the Dutch, it was claimed, insisted that all goods were brought into the country before re-export and ensured native shipping would be given priority over strangers' ships.[136]

– 201 –

MERCHANTS

Not all merchants agreed, however, and many depended on Dutch shipping to carry their goods, but the trend towards more protectionist policies would not be halted. For example, following a petition from the Eastland Company, the privy council refused to accept that 'many great inconveniences [were] like to fall upon their trade by the late restraint of bringing in commodities in strangers' bottoms'. The council saw no reason why the offer of ship owners 'to furnish the said merchants with sufficient shipping at such reasonable rates as shall give contentment unto them' would not be acceptable. Acting as arbitrators between the English merchants and freighters, the council helped the two groups reach an agreement regarding fees and wrote to the Levant, Muscovy, French and Spanish companies urging them to do the same.[137] Eventually an agreement was reached, whereby rates would be adjusted depending on the destination of ships and commodities transported.[138] In an attempt to mitigate concerns about foreign shipping, numerous proclamations were issued by the state during the early modern period to regulate against the practice of using 'strangers' bottoms' for carrying goods to or from England, usually in relation to a specific commodity or region, but these were only intermittently successful.[139] As England's commerce became more international, it proved near impossible for the state to effectively impose itself over every ship coming or going from its ports.

Together, concerns about monopoly, international competition and the encouragement of protectionist policies contributed towards a general shift in the state's relationship towards trade – and encouraged novel arrangements for overcoming a perceived decline in England's trade during the latter 1610s and 1620s.[140] The causes suggested for the decay were numerous: unwarranted exports of bullion, excessive imports of luxuries, a disregard for English manufacturing or undue reliance on Dutch shipping. When the Merchant Venturers of Bristol weighed in on the debate, the company offered an array of reasons for the decline that reflected its own experience: impositions on lead, Turkish piracy, wars in France, restrictions on the import of alum, export of bullion to the East Indies, the 'extraordinary importation and use of tobacco', the excessive

– 202 –

THE CITY AND THE COURT

wearing of gold and silver, silk and velvet, and the curtailing of fishing near Virginia and Newfoundland.[141] For Bristol's merchants, these pressures reflected England's changing commercial landscape rather than local issues or a policy of the state, and they understood the challenging commercial environment caused by overlapping, interconnected and international markets that they believed cumulatively undermined the efficacy of the English economy. Another author even targeted climatic variation, suggesting that poor harvest years drained money from the country and 'doth cause a general misery to the tradesmen' – a challenge they believed would be overcome through the cultivation of common land and the suppression of alehouses.[142] Some commentators suggested more radical ideas still. An anonymous author recommended banning merchants buying high-value property until after the birth of their third child, arguing that the policy would 'be no discouragement to their industry' and after 'having raised their estates they may live as plentifully and as fairly as any gentleman of this Kingdom'.[143] As more and more commentators sent their recommendations to the court, it became increasingly clear that starkly opposing views of different interest groups would not be brought into agreement.

Fractures between the court and commercial community were quick to appear. When the influential writer John Keymer recommended that a commission should be established to oversee trade policy, only two of his suggested eleven members were merchants.[144] It was a sign of shifting influence in court about how trade should be understood and regulated, and Keymer's proposals were quickly followed by further criticism aimed at current commercial practices. Henry Montagu, the newly minted Viscount Mandeville, presented an analysis that rested on his understanding of the 'nature of exchange of money by bills' and argued that imposing standardised rates of exchange between English and foreign currency would re-balance the country's trading deficit. Montagu recommended the king should 'restrain the vast and immoderate expense of foreign needless wares' that were imported, by which domestic industry would 'be daily improved, and the outward trade of

– 203 –

your merchants be restored again'.[145] Another author, Gerard Malynes, took this argument further still and suggested that increasing exports was unlikely without developing new regulations for currency exchange, without which 'we shall never find any such effect but still hunt our own shadow and augment the said causes' of the balance of trade.[146] Sir Ralph Madison supported Malynes' position, condemning merchants who did not export commodities for weakening the wider economy.[147] Claiming that 'I have seen in my time a dearth of corn without need, and a famine without dearth' due to the profiteering of merchants who stripped the country of coin, he believed that the only option was to impose rates of exchange 'lest the general overbalance of trade happening by decay of prices enforce a general want and poverty in the kingdom'.[148] Resting their interpretation on a widespread acceptance that the 'state is most perfect which has all wants either for necessity or commodity supplied within itself', these commentators refused to accept a commercial world where such visions of autarky butted against the reality of interconnected, global trade.[149]

The merchant response to the recommendations of these influential figures was, for the most part, livid and emphasised what they perceived as a lack of understanding on the part of individuals unskilled and inexperienced in the practice of trade. Robert Bell, Thomas Mun, George Kendrick, Henry Wood, Thomas Jennings and John Skinner – merchants who had been recommended by Montagu as suitable assessors of his proposals – presented a response after they 'had sundry meetings, and seriously debated the matter amongst ourselves, according to our best skill and understanding'. It was not the response Montagu was hoping for. The merchants used their greater knowledge of practical trading to show that his proposals were unsuitable for application in complex trading environments like Hamburg or the Low Countries. They argued that to compensate for Montagu's proposed increase in rates merchants would be forced to raise prices, making them uncompetitive. They further scoffed at his poor understanding of trade by suggesting that the proposal would invalidate English bills of exchange and force foreign

– 204 –

merchants to carry more currency from England, not less. They concluded that the king should let 'the exchange go free, at the pleasure of the merchants contracting it' and it was important that 'as the balance of the trade sways so necessarily' merchants should be allowed to export coin 'for the evening of the same'.[150] While the merchants' response was quickly dismissed by Montagu, their approach to the argument – demonstrating their practical experience as merchants as a source of knowledge and wisdom – would become a mainstay of their argumentation against state interference with trade.[151] Indeed, as detractors of import-heavy trades attacked the activities of organisations like the East India or Levant companies, merchants struck back by using their unique knowledge of trading in distant lands. Thomas Mun's response to the recommendations of Montagu and Malynes was furious, condemning 'arguments of this kind which I have lately seen' as no more than 'mere fallacies and froth'.[152] Presenting his counterargument as a five-point analysis considering the trade balance in a comparative, global perspective, Mun drew together commercial activities in the East Indies, Baltic and Levant to show how the balance of trade should not be examined as any single trade but all of them together.[153] From the perspective of this mercantile position, the English economy was inextricably connected with global trading networks and only through commerce could the proceeds of domestic industry and demands for overseas goods be effectively balanced.

As debates about trade policy began to break down long-standing assumptions about merchants' pre-eminent professional position at the head of England's commercial activity, a weakening relationship between the state and the commercial community contributed to more and more overseas activities being undertaken by individuals who had not been raised and trained as merchants.[154] In colonial projects, especially, merchants had little expectation of maintaining their role in managing overseas activity, although their prominence within these ventures differed across the emerging English empire.[155] A considerable proportion of trade remained in merchant hands, whether to Europe or

– 205 –

further-flung markets, but their stranglehold was weakening even as their wealth increased.[156] By the middle of the seventeenth century, England's merchants were increasingly weakened in terms of their influence at court, partly because gentry and noble competitors were keen to break into the valuable opportunities offered overseas and partly because of the state's increasing willingness to overlook English merchants in favour of traders from outside this community. Thus, in 1642, when Scottish merchants presented proposals for 'laws, liberties and continual practices' to allow Scottish ships to travel unmolested 'in any part of the Kingdoms of England or Ireland', they argued that commerce would 'run through the veins of all his majesty's dominions for the greater fullness and better nourishing the whole body'. While many English merchants might have supported the sentiments, and even been excited by the possibility of accessing Scottish markets, a final suggestion would have caused dread for many – that the same rules should apply universally.[157] Scottish merchants sought access to long monopolised markets in Asia, the Mediterranean and Europe. In one fell swoop, the state could undo privileges that English companies had sought so carefully to maintain and thus undermine the practices of commercial governance that had sustained English merchants across the world for the previous century. A globally connected England had been theirs to profit from, but a more closely united Britain represented a threat to the very behaviours, practices, regulations and institutions that they had relied upon while conducting trade across the world.

CONCLUSION
The Business of Empire

Sitting down in the early seventeenth century to discuss how to increase England's naval might and commercial wealth, a group of merchants and other interested parties came up with a bold idea – it was time to colonise Russia. They were not expecting to extract gold or silver from the frigid lands to the East, nor to extract taxes from local farmers. Instead, these commercial conspirators hoped to create and govern a new entrepôt that would give England a monopoly over locally produced commodities and dominion over trade routes to Persia and Turkey. In doing so, they would re-write the map of global trade.

These merchants were not ruminating on the impossible: they had encouraging political and commercial intelligence from their factors across Russia, and through links with English merchants came across the Baltic and northern Europe. They learned that after Polish and Swedish occupation, the Russian people had been left 'without a head and in great confusion', desperate for aid. They believed that the people would be 'able enough to offer resistance [to the occupiers] if they were heartened and well directed' and would willingly 'cast themselves into the arms of some prince that will protect them'. They even heard that their agents had been approached by Russians who wanted to offer James I the crown.

MERCHANTS

The offer of the crown was deemed a step too far, but with the Muscovy Company now a predominant commercial body in this distant empire, its members reckoned their well-governed trading outposts might be an excellent basis for a colony along the Russian coast, where James I would be sovereign or protector. They determined to send a specially appointed diplomat to engage with the Russian people, backed up with 'so much in treasure and commodities as will defray the charge of the arming and transporting the number of men' needed to secure the colony against the Polish threat and secure Russian support. The company's members considered the cost well worth it: the project would provide 'much glory to his majesty, much charity towards those oppressed people' as well as 'the increase of our shipping and trade'. In their minds, success would result in 'the greatest and happiest overture that ever was made to any king of this realm, since Columbus offered King Henry VII the discovery of the West Indies'. For this group of merchants, they saw no reason whatsoever why they should not shift from being international traders to empire builders.[1]

By the middle of the seventeenth century, England's merchants would claim that in 'every kingdom and great city of the world, and every petty port and creek of the same' you could 'find in each some English prying after the trade and commerce thereof'. Through their efforts, the country had grown richer and London, they boasted, had become 'the prime city of trading this day in the world'.[2] Experience trading in conditions ranging from the icy North of Russia to the balmy climes of the Moluccas, dealing with people as diverse as the Mughal emperor, Dutch burghers and Algonquian fishermen, and exchanging goods as varied as Norfolk cloth, Persian silks, Akan gold or Virginian tobacco, had led merchants to conceive of a globally connected commercial world. Carefully constructed and maintained institutional structures were designed to keep them safe, secure and profitable as they pursued these ventures – rather than depending on luck. These institutions rested on learned

CONCLUSION

behaviours, shared skills, common values, collaborative practices and corporate forms of governance. Drawing on a distinct professional, social and cultural identity, merchants were able to function effectively in numerous commercial environments, and as England's overseas interests began to encapsulate imperial ambitions, this same identity and set of values continued to underpin how merchants conducted themselves. In England's global trade and empire, the shared cultural values held by participating merchants helped them form deeply interconnected communities, and it was through this cooperative, corporate and collaborative ecosystem that they drove England's commercial expansion. Through these efforts, merchants had brought the world to England and, from their perspective, it was also through their efforts that this tiny island on the periphery of Europe had become an entrepôt for global commodities. As Thomas Johnson put it, the 'terrestrial globe is cut out into islands and continents', and 'although they be severed by the work of nature, yet they may be said to be joined together by commerce'.[3]

In connecting England to the world, merchants had come to participate in imperial and commercial projects, and each new venture built on its predecessors. Trade, exploration, colonisation, privateering and more were undertaken within a communal and connected setting, and whether they took place in the Atlantic, in Asia, or just across the English Channel in Europe, merchants could draw on their own experiences or those of associates to understand and plan their next endeavour. Their working lives were just as much social as economic, and merchants pursued careers that ran through local, national and global scales of activity, and within various corporate bodies and business pursuits. The networks of merchants and their agents crisscrossed empires, oceans and continents, and these international links were sustained through the same sets of relationships – including family, business and corporate ties – that enabled commercial activities within England. To be successful in this environment, they depended on a painstakingly calibrated and enforced cultural system that made it possible for them to effectively work and live together – at home and overseas. Consequently, on an institutional level, the commercial

– 209 –

community can be viewed through a single lens, revealing global connections across England's overseas activities that, as Johnson suggested, drew these together through commerce. These connections by no means dissipated with increased interest in colonisation and, for England's merchants, their expertise in doing business 'beyond the seas' would seem equally applicable to imperial as much as commercial activities.[4] Why should they not be the ones to realise the possibilities of empire?

MERCHANT COLONIAL LEADERSHIP

The behavioural practices merchants learned during their training, alongside their experience of overseeing distant agents and the rigorous reporting standards imposed by private merchant and corporation alike, were valuable assets that merchants could repurpose to organise activities other than commerce. It was in this vein that Thomas Mun confidently stated that oversight of England's global interests should be left 'only to them, who have had an education thereunto' – that is to say, merchants.[5] For Mun and others, this was not just about merchants' behavioural and governance practices, but their greater understanding of how to act effectively in overseas environments. According to Edward Misselden, merchants were uniquely 'acquainted with the manners, customs, languages, laws of foreign nations'; he warned that handing governance to 'novices and new-made merchants' risked England's commercial power being 'betrayed into the hands of foreign nations'.[6] Or, as Lewes Roberts put it, through merchandising and learning the skills of the merchant overseas, individuals could 'perform the greatest employments that are incident to the service of a state or kingdom' – 'those that have had their education thus ... have proved not only good commonwealth's men, but also excellent statesmen'. Whether it was the 'ancient policies and present flourishing continuance of the state of Venice, the politic and rich estates of the Netherlands, the opulent and eminent quality of the Duke of Tuscany' or 'the wealthy well governed Hanse towns in Germany', Roberts believed 'merchandising is found to be the school from whence

– 210 –

they gather their first principles, and indeed the chief foundation upon which their fabric of political government is raised'.[7]

As well as their professional aptitude, mercantile government of colonial enterprises could draw on a range of innovative corporate models for managing people and places overseas. In early modern England, corporations had a prominent role in the daily lives of the commercial community and members acted together towards common goals, employing the framework and structure that the corporation provided to serve the public communities that these companies represented. Merchants depended on unwritten rules, social norms and a regularity of behaviour to work together, and corporate ties reinforced these.[8] As well as drawing merchants together (with their experience and capital), corporations regulated their behaviour and were able to impose their own laws and orders over populations that fell under their jurisdiction. Through corporate organisation, merchants had become familiar with the challenges of governing people at home and overseas. They understood them as practical structures of authority and order, and frameworks for collaborating effectively and functioning as an English society, even when far from home, and as exercising a disciplinary function.[9] The Somers Island Company, for example, was granted 'full and absolute power and authority to correct, punish, pardon, govern and rule' anyone either on a voyage to or from the island of, as well as all inhabitants on, Bermuda.[10] As merchants came to have deeper involvement in colonial enterprises, corporate practices were maintained and given yet more authority, and their practices became integral to 'the institutions and ideologies that [would] condition political authority, obedience, coercion, and negotiation' in England's trade and empire.[11]

When the lessons learned by merchants were not followed, even the most keenly supported colonial organisations could fall apart. For example, when, with much fanfare, 'a great project' was announced 'for an adventure and plantation upon the river of the Amazons near Guiana, and a company to be erected whereof Captain North the Lord North's brother is to be governor', a number of prominent figures quickly

– 211 –

invested. Captain North could happily report that the Duke of Lennox, Earl of Arundel, Earl of Warwick and 'others of great estate are adventurers' were together contributing £1,728 8s 2d, but there was little in the way of mercantile involvement.[12] Consequently, trade, or questions of shipping, supply or long-term financing, were perhaps not as prominent in the new company's plans as might otherwise have been the case. After less than four years, the plantation had effectively failed, but the limitations of the corporation's organisation were only just becoming known.[13] North, having spent £2,300 on the venture, complained that he had received only a third of promised investment from investors and was heavily indebted as a consequence. Lord Paget refused to pay, not because he had not agreed to participate, but because North's accounting practices were so lax that he did not believe there was conclusive evidence that the erstwhile adventurer had actually suffered damages. Paget claimed the precise sums promised were 'remembered not, neither does he remember what agreement was made as to the disposing of the residue of every adventurers sum'. North had not thought to keep a written record. Furthermore, North had returned with commodities from the voyage, but the details were again not well accounted for. Indeed, Paget was so unsure of the sum that he had crossed out a numerical value for the goods obtained and merely written 'a good value'. Without proof of investments promised, costs endured and profits accrued, North had little to fall back on during disputes with his former partners.[14] Lacking common standards for undertaking such a complex scheme, the accounting practices needed to underpin it, or the dispute resolution mechanisms in place to mitigate its failures – institutions which were so common in the commercial community – North could do little as his colonial scheme fell apart around him.

Colonisation might well have been a departure from the typical commercial business that defined the day-to-day activities of most English merchants, but they represented a professional group with skills, experience and institutional practices that were deemed well suited to the task. In the Virginia Company and Irish Society, especially,

– 212 –

CONCLUSION

merchants would contribute to the establishment of large, territorial settlements, managed and supported from England – in the former as investors in a joint stock and in the latter through levies imposed by their respective livery companies that would oversee the management of the Ulster plantation. Both in Virginia and Ireland, these organisations saw colonisation as their main purpose and merchants took part in these imperial designs without any doubt as to their function.[15] These activities would have been extensions to merchants' normal activities and they participated with a keen awareness of what was expected of them. When James I presented numerous 'motives and reasons', 'to induce the City of London to undertake a plantation in the North of Ireland' in 1609, the project was pitched with commercial as well as imperial interests in mind. The city's urban and livery companies would spend an initial £20,000 towards building 200 houses in Derry and 400 in Coleraine (leaving room for 500 more to be constructed later) and be responsible for erecting and maintaining fortifications. In return, they would receive all customs income from the plantation for ninety-nine years, the rights to fish in the rivers for perpetuity and off the coasts, and privileges to 'transport all prohibited wares growing upon their own land'. The most enticing part of the proposal was northern Ireland's extensive farmland, which was supposed to easily supply enough food for the growing colony as well as become a source of supplies for the ever-growing English capital. Furthermore, the lands of the plantation reportedly grew 'hemp and flax better than anywhere', promising a ready supply of ship-building materials, while 'great fishing' in the region and its geographical position opened new possibilities of commerce from Ireland into Scotland, England, Spain and Newfoundland.[16]

The Virginia colony was pitched in similar terms.[17] Although the Virginia Company had been established three years earlier, a series of disasters in 1609 meant 'gentleman adventurers ... withdrew themselves, in despair of the enterprise, and so gave it over, not enduring to repair the ruins, nor to supply what themselves had underwritten', to merchants and others who continued to support, manage and fund the

– 213 –

plantation.[18] Merchants were encouraged to participate in the enterprise by promises that it would 'augment your glory, or increase your wealth, or purchase your eternity'.[19] Detailed texts were distributed that outlined how the colony would be managed.[20] They assured readers that the company would spread the gospel, alleviate overpopulation, increase England's might and wealth, and 'furnish and provide this Kingdom with all such necessities'.[21] The colony was also presented as a natural extension of merchants' existing commercial interests: merchants could import ship-building supplies from Virginia that would 'yield gold or silver in any our bordering nations' and cater to markets in 'Hamburg, Holland, or other places', produce Virginian wines to compete with French markets, or even grow Virginian silk that might replace 'that of Persia, Turkey or any other place'. Through investment, 'art and industry', and 'a little patience to bring these things to pass', proponents also hoped the plantation might help England overtake the Dutch, who currently 'surpass and go beyond us in continual plenty of corn and shipping'.[22] In colonisation, the possibilities for profit were deemed substantial, and merchants understood them within a framework of both domestic demands and international competition.[23]

In England's developing empire, the commercial community provided an important means of connecting new activities with traditional practices and experience obtained across the world. Merchants served as vital brokers between overlapping, intersecting networks of colonial and commercial enterprise, making up for limited, practical state involvement or centralisation by enabling different ventures to draw on each other.[24] To organise their colonies in Ireland and Virginia, as was so often the case elsewhere, investors drew on a corporate organisational form and employed trusted and experienced representatives to act as agents overseas.[25] In Ireland, the draper John Rowley was appointed to oversee the colony, with clear instructions as to the tasks that were required.[26] Much like merchant factors employed overseas, Rowley reported the local situation in detail when he reached Ulster, describing challenges obtaining timber, stone and lime for building work, and how navigation by sea and

CONCLUSION

river was problematic.[27] Having been encouraged to 'keep your selves continually in our affairs' by the City of London, Rowley was expected to not only follow instructions but also use his 'good discretions' to make decisions about issues they had not foreseen. Furthermore, Rowley was instructed to inform them of income or expenditure related to their properties within three months and to carefully survey the existing local economy in advance of further orders – especially in relation to rent from existing properties and the state of industry in the region. Manufacturing in neighbouring counties was especially of interest so that the company's representatives 'may think of a course to have the said [goods] wrought in that country to set our people a work'.[28] The Virginia Company likewise appointed carefully selected officers to oversee the settlements and execute its strategic vision, but its primary concern was to build a colony in America that would no longer depend on England for basic supplies and had the necessary organisation in place to welcome new colonists without disruption. These priorities were made clear to Thomas West, the newly appointed governor, who was instructed that only after securing food and other basic supplies should he start looking for 'proofs of some valuable commodities' that might encourage further support.[29]

As well as drawing on corporate structures in their efforts to build profitable colonies overseas, the Irish Society and Virginia Company took steps to ensure that their long-term colonial activities were managed with the same dedication to order and discipline that was shown by their corporate forebears in England. In Ireland, for example, Rowley was instructed to ensure the colony was well governed and orderly by limiting the number of taverns and alehouses, and having a newly built prison 'set in the market place' to punish infractions – it was of course carefully managed so as not to 'be offensive or noisome' to other residents.[30] Meanwhile, the Virginia Company actively encouraged the adoption of practices that recreated, to one degree or another, London's urban civility.[31] It urged 'persons be appointed as officers in every company to see that their cabins and lodgings be kept cleanly and healthily' and suggested introducing communal arrangements for meals, proposing 'they have their diet at communal tables by companies after the fashion of the old world' (Plate 11).[32]

Following these prescriptions and drawing on decades of experience in managing people and resources overseas, by the middle of the 1610s, each corporate colony was taking shape. When London alderman Peter Proby visited the Irish colony, he painted a positive picture. Houses had been built and rented, fortifications improved and the plantation's maritime trade seemed to be growing apace. Confidence in the security of the towns encouraged one Mr Haywood to pay £180 to build nine large stone houses in Coleraine in return for an eighty-year lease, and Proby was hopeful that 'in a short time more will be encouraged upon the same offer to build'. Fishing, too, remained profitable, and suitors from Coleraine and Derry had offered £800 for privileges over the plantation's rivers, a sum its current holders, Mr Nugent and Mr Fitzsimons, topped with a counter-offer of £1,000 per year.[33] As they came to take control of their share of the colony, many livery companies fielded offers from individuals keen to rent these properties in Ireland – whether in part or in full – and others soon started to collect rents.[34] Activities in Virginia had been more successful still, and towns across both banks of the James River had been established and fortified.[35] Improvements were soon noted in London and, in keeping with the company's expectations, colonists confidently reported 'this main objection of wanting food is utterly removed'.[36] By 1616, six settlements had been built: Henrico, Bermuda City, West and Sherley, Jamestown, Kequought and Dales Gift (at Cape Comfort). Each had a specific role to play: one was 'maintained by the colony' in return for processing salt; another focused on tobacco; and settlers in a third 'labour generally for the colony, amongst whom, some make pitch and tar, pot-ashes, charcoal, and other works'.[37] These towns were more than simple farmsteads. In Henrico, reports described how 'they have built competent and decent houses, the first story of all bricks' and that 'there is within this town 3 streets of well framed houses'.[38] Jamestown, too, had been 'reduced into a handsome form, and has in it two fair rows of houses, all of framed timber, two stories and an upper garret, or corn

CONCLUSION

loft high' and near the town were 'some very pleasant and beautiful houses' and 'certain other farmhouses' that now occupied most of the island.[39] Large structures with 'cobblestone foundations', 'brick chimney bases' and wooden floors had also been constructed.[40] Jamestown was likely built around an extensive marketplace, designed to facilitate intra-plantation trade and the company's mercantile enterprises.[41] In recognition of their officers' achievements, merchants in London praised the colony's governor, Thomas Dale, widely in print and showed their appreciation by appointing him admiral of a fleet sent to the East Indies.[42] The Virginian plantation had not only survived, which had been doubtful only six years before, but it also thrived: it was predicted (perhaps a little too ambitiously) to become 'one of the goodliest and richest kingdoms of the world'.[43] Colonial governance depended on effective organisation of people and goods, and the practices that merchants relied on to manage trade across the world could be drawn on by English colonists as they sought to impose themselves in newly seized territories overseas.

CONFLICT AND THE MILITARISATION OF TRADE

England's merchants had not become colonisers overnight. Over the course of the sixteenth and early seventeenth century, 'the global imagination of English writers was given urgency by economic and political competition', with commercial practice shifting in response to threats to England's growing international ambitions.[44] As they engaged more in competitive overseas environments, merchants increasingly required a strong military or colonial edge: to defend them from attack, force their way into closed markets, initiate raids or protect newly seized and occupied territory.[45] For the Muscovy Company, in the face of Dutch competition in the North Atlantic, where the corporation had extensive interests in fishing (especially for whales), the company's merchants sought to impose its territorial claim over the seas and lands it had discovered. In 1612, the Muscovy Company was reported to have found 700 whales in the northern seas, killing seventeen and returning to

– 217 –

England with a rich stock.[46] The next year the company had elected to defend the Greenland fisheries by force from Dutch, French and Spanish ships.[47] Three years later, the corporation was launching a veritable navy of fourteen ships. Three were lost in conflict with the Dutch and, to boost its strength, the company offered £1,000 to the king to send his own ships with the fleet.[48] The trade war continued to escalate. In 1617, the company 'furnished sixteen good ships in warlike manner well provided' and 'at its own charge maintain his majesty's right against the French, Spaniards, Hollanders and all other nations whatsoever'.[49] For a while, at least, the company's attempts seemed to be successful and the need to deploy heavily armed fleets began to diminish.[50]

However, the Muscovy Company did not believe it could hold on to the region, despite its application of naval power, without colonies to claim possession of the seas. Its merchants had noted how Spanish and Dutch power in the West and East Indies rested on seizure of territory, and that the company had faced increased competition from the French after the establishment of a French plantation on a 'river in Canada'.[51] The Muscovy Company therefore endeavoured to gain state support for its own colonial plans to exploit the North Atlantic more effectively, by arguing that fishing and whaling around Greenland had been 'first begun and continued by the singular industry and charge of the Company of Muscovy Merchants of London'.[52] The company had 'endeavoured to discover the unknown part of those northern seas and by sending forth of ships and pinnaces from year to year', and 'by their incessant industry, labour and travail, and a continual freighting through those seas, at their expensive charge ... discovered a land called Greenland'. The English court supported these claims, and the privy council encouraged the merchants 'to proceed in their course of trade' as was their due *jura natura*, according to a rule of law'. With support from the state secured, the company focused on the newly claimed Greenland ('nominated by King James his Newland') and sent further exploratory ventures 'to find out what the continent of Greenland is or what commodities might grow from thence'. Confident in the viability of a colony, the merchants

CONCLUSION

approached the Russian emperor and obtained his agreement to build a collaborative plantation – the company would transport 'Lapps, a people living in a very cold climate and a barren soil' to Greenland 'with some English to inhabit there'.[53] There is no evidence to suggest that the Muscovy Company's Lapp settlers ever reached Greenland, but the planning of such an elaborate colonisation scheme alone demonstrates the willingness of English merchants to move far beyond traditional activities to protect their wealth.

The Muscovy Company was not alone in blending its economic activities with violence, conquest and territorial acquisitions. The East India Company was founded with this in mind and even its earliest voyages had been conducted with ships more than capable of defending themselves (and attacking others) in distant seas.[54] It did not take long for thoughts to turn towards using this military capability directly to further the corporation's interests in the region. When Edward Connock wrote to the company from Isfahan in 1617 that the Persian shah Abbas I had offered 'a grant for the Spaniards to fortify on the Persian shore', the company was concerned that the deal would be catastrophic for 'the trade of silks from China' and would damage the East India Company as well as English, French, Dutch and Italian merchants in the Mediterranean. It also meant the Iberian Empire would 'yearly grow rich, strong and yet prouder in these seas', allowing them to encroach on the English trade in India. Connock hoped, however, that if the English demonstrated their 'great strength and absolute power by sea', Abbas I would be willing to reach an agreement whereby they, and not the Spanish, might be granted special permission to trade in Persia. Connock argued that by working with the East India Company, perhaps even by 'taking Ormuz into his possession', Abbas I could open Persia's ports to 'be supplied with spices and other commodities of India' that could be carried by English ships in collaboration with 'Moor and Banyam merchants' in Surat.[55]

Plans were pushed ahead when reports reached the English in 1621 that Portuguese efforts to restrict English access to the Persian Gulf were part of a broader strategy 'for the rooting out of the English out of India'. The East India Company ordered its fleet to engage with Portuguese ships that had been harassing trade in the Indian Ocean, but the commanders of the fleet re-evaluated after receiving news that 'the Persian had lain siege [to a Portuguese fortress at Ormuz] unto some seven or eight months, and lost some eight or nine thousand men in siege of it'. Whereas previously the company had been supplicants with little to offer Persia in return for greater commercial access, the commanders considered that the Persian commander now 'required our aid in these wars': they recognised that the company's naval strength could shift the balance of power in the conflict. The Persian commander told the English that 'it was our enemy as well as his' and offered 'great privileges for the future good of our masters'. An agreement was reached for 'the castle of Ormuz to be delivered to the possession of the English' and the English offered naval support to the Persian forces who soon gained possession of the town.[56] Although the attack was beyond the remit of the company's orders to its officers, there was no suggestion of returning Ormuz to the Portuguese or paying reparations. Indeed, some advocated retaining the settlement as a company fortress because if they left, the Dutch might 'take advantage of the English refusal to aid the Persian in his warlike designs'.[57] For these merchants, if possessing territory and taking military action was necessary for dominating trade, then so be it. Commercial ends would be achieved with violent means. Such practices lent new meaning to practices of commercial power – as one commentator noted, quoting Themistocles, 'he that possesses the seas possesses the whole world'.[58]

THE SINEWS OF EMPIRE

Whereas the state had encouraged the commercial community to drive forward its imperial ambitions in Ireland and Virginia, the limitations of state support and authority encouraged the Muscovy and East India companies to take matters into their own hands. The corporate form

– 220 –

CONCLUSION

had proved adaptable once more and seemed perfectly suitable as a means for establishing an English empire. As state interest and involvement in such activities increased, and it sought to impose structure across England's activities, proponents of the corporate form pushed for further reaching employment of the organisational structure.[59] For example, proposals for an English West India Company, first mooted in 1621, with a joint-stock funding model and corporate structure similar to its East India counterpart, gained increasing traction in courtly and mercantile circles.[60] As well as providing corporate oversight to colonial activities in the Americas, the proposed organisation would also balance England's global commercial interests – as Thomas Crew noted, 'we have an East India to carry out; we want a West India to import'.[61] In 1625, Sir John Coke insisted that such a company could 'invade his [Spanish] countries: to fortify and plant there: and to establish government, confederacy and trade', and eventually end 'the pride and terror of the Spanish pretended empire'. This would be funded 'at the common charge of the kingdom by a company incorporated for the west, as there is already for the east', with an estimated initial cost of £361,200.[62] A decade later, Sir Thomas Roe, the former ambassador to the Ottoman and Mughal empires and one-time adventurer to Guiana, wrote to the privy council in response to Charles I's 'generous resolution of erecting a West India Company'. With rare experience within the East India and Levant companies, and of colonisation in the Atlantic, Roe took it upon himself 'to send your lordships a rude model of my conceptions that they may be polished by your wisdom'. In time, he hoped the new company 'may prove a seed of a kingdom in India for England'.[63] Roe's model for the English company rested on charters and regulations relating to the Dutch West India Company that he had 'gotten from Holland, and set to translate', which revealed 'the whole structure and forms of government of that society, which will give a great light in the composure and distribution of a company [planned] at home and save us many errors'.[64] From the perspective of Crew, Coke and Roe, if England was going to challenge the Spanish Empire successfully in

– 221 –

America, it was not the haphazard approach of Captain North and others that would make it possible – corporate organisation was the key.

The state had other ideas, and the limits of mercantile influence, and that of supporters like Crew, Coke and Roe, were soon laid bare. Even as merchants adapted their institutions to imperial ends, the crown turned towards alternative arrangements, potentially denying mercantile participation in new ventures even as investors or partners. Facing competition from courtiers, gentry and nobles with imperial aspirations of their own, the validity and security of merchant-led corporate activity at the heart of England's growing empire was increasingly in doubt. While the East India, Virginia, Irish, Somers Island, Muscovy and other companies were pushing their territorial agendas, plans for new colonial ventures came thick and fast and were by no means restricted to merchant participation.[65] Non-merchants seeking to impose their will on the commercial activities of colonial enterprises often posed significant challenges for merchants. A flexible approach to business and willingness (at times) to collaborate meant that compromises could sometimes be made, such as when Bristol's Merchant Venturers agreed to transport one settler with provisions to the New England Company's colony for each of the town's ships that travelled to the region. However, this type of arrangement could be revoked at will (in this case only eight years later) and hardly contributed to making a secure and stable trading environment.[66] In other cases, merchants were simply excluded from decision-making processes. Colonies in the Atlantic and Indian oceans were proposed and executed without merchant involvement or in opposition to the privileges of existing corporations.[67]

Over time, more and more colonial activities fell under the government of non-mercantile leadership, and as new privileges were extended to governing individuals or bodies, merchants were often excluded. Even where they participated as investors or traders, their ability to self-govern was often limited. Thus, when James Hay, the Earl of Carlisle, obtained letters patent to govern 'a certain region or country commonly called or known by the name of the Caribee Islands, containing in them the islands of St Christopher, Granado, St Vincent, Barbados and other islands',

CONCLUSION

merchants could be confident they would play a considerable role – but the colony's ultimate government was out of their hands. Hay 'granted to Marmaduke Rawdon, William Parkin, Alexander Bannister, Robert Wheatley, Edmond Forster, Robert Swinnerton, Henry Wheatley, John Sharpes and John Farrington of London merchants, privilege and authority to settle a plantation' on Barbados.[68] In turn, the merchants appointed Charles Wolverston as governor of their plantation. After less than a year, Wolverston was reporting 'many mutinies and rebellions', resulting in losses amounting to '30,000 weight of tobacco', and having already cost four or five thousand pounds, he warned that without further supplies they would 'hazard to lose their whole plantation'.[69] Yet, the merchants' plantation remained under the broader authority of the island's governor, Sir William Tufton, whom Hay expected to ensure the authority of the earl's own officers over the island, especially regarding issues such as defence.[70] The merchants were left with little recourse for securing their own property. By 1641, the merchants' complaints 'concerning the ten thousand acres of land belonging to the Londoners plantation' claimed that they 'have been much wronged by some we trusted who have sold most if not all of our lands and given us no account'.[71] During the Civil War, this situation only worsened, as the earls of Carlisle and Warwick claimed authority of the Caribee islands with support from Charles I and parliament respectively, and each sent representatives to try to enforce their rule.[72] The commercial community had no option but to wait for resolution. Lacking the state support that had underpinned the explosion of corporate activity in the earlier seventeenth century, merchants could often do little but look on as their authority across England's emerging empire diminished. Despite their best efforts, they would, it seemed, be relegated to their former position – merely merchants.

In this role, however, the merchant community that had proven so influential in the expansion and structure of England's overseas commerce would continue to flourish.[73] The challenges of civil war and the emergence of colonial activities that they could not control might have diminished their influence as territorial governors, but the expansion of England's

– 223 –

imperial footprint brought with it new opportunities for trade. In the Atlantic world, for instance, the Muscongus patent gave two gentlemen – John Beauchamp and Thomas Leverett – the rights to 'all profits, commodities, etc from the lands and rivers' within a region of New England that spread 10 leagues to the North of the Penobscott river, while efforts to colonise St Lucia were enthusiastically undertaken with hopes of producing lucrative exports such as sugar, indigo and ginger.[74] By connecting these ventures into the commercial world of early modern England, merchants ensured that the wheels of commerce kept turning, even when excluded from leadership, and they maintained their own processes of organisation and oversight in regarding to colonial trade. For instance, in 1634 a group of London merchants including Gregory Clement, Robert South and Maurice Thompson transported £15,500 worth of tobacco from the colony in Virginia – although on that occasion they lost their ship to pirates.[75] Two years later, thirteen merchants from Bristol were more successful in profiting from Barbados's burgeoning tobacco production after they agreed to establish a joint stock between themselves, sent two ships to the island and shared returns of £38,900, most of which went to the principal investors, Richard Young and James Matthew.[76] Activities like these contributed to rapidly growing commercial activity in the Caribbean during the 1630s and 1640s, as merchants established themselves as the key link between the new colonies and England.

The expansion of English territories in North America and the Caribbean, even if merchants could not hope to oversee these activities directly, served to generate demand for new commercial enterprises to supply and carry produce to and from the new colonies, and merchants were quick to fill this role. By the middle of the seventeenth century, over a million pounds of tobacco and around five thousand tons of sugar were shipped from these colonies to England – an increase of production that owed much to the exploitation of new territory with cheap or unfree labour, creating a profitable circuit for participating merchants.[77]

New demands for labour in these regions also led merchants to participate in the most inhumane of ventures: the traffic of enslaved

CONCLUSION

captives from Africa. In the 1640s, English merchants began to take part in the trans-Atlantic slave trade and within a decade had contributed to forty-one voyages between Africa and the Caribbean.[78] Most of these voyages were destined for the growing English plantation on Barbados, which sat at the heart of an emerging commercial web that would come to offer so much opportunity for English merchants over the coming decades. Among the merchants involved were individuals such as Nicholas Crispe and John Wood who had been leading figures of London's merchant community in the previous decades.[79] They brought with them experience and ways of doing business they had gained from participating in privateering, colonisation in Ireland, Virginia, Bermuda and Massachusetts, and through their activities in companies responsible for trade to the Levant, East Indies, northern Europe and Africa. Other early slave traders, like the Bristol merchant William Pennoyer, had similarly broad corporate laurels and was involved in local livery company organisation in England as well as holding wide-ranging commercial interests. Others again, like Samuel Vassall, the son of a Huguenot refugee, had not grown up in the merchant community but had still learned their trade in corporate environments like the Massachusetts Bay and Guinea companies. Through these links, through merchants and their corporations, the networks of experience that underpinned and facilitated England's trade and empire also came to underpin activities including colonisation and the slave trade even where merchant leadership was no longer paramount.

Having spent decades developing their trading presence in markets across the world, and now leading the development of colonies overseas, the confident, powerful and hugely wealthy commercial community in England had increasingly come to see the potential of activities that were outside its usual wheelhouse – the application of violence, the conquest of new lands and the governance of territory and people.[80] This is not to say that visions of empire dimmed interest in trade. Rather, the conceptual framework of merchant empire came to rest on an understanding that colonies and commerce could develop hand in hand.

– 225 –

Personal relationships within and across corporations, as well as the dissemination of printed, oral and manuscript news, helped early modern merchants 'perceive in its entirety a world once experienced only in fragments', and helped bring together the 'overlapping and intersecting worlds of commercial and colonial enterprises'.[81] One anonymous commentator reflecting on the wealth of nations made this clear: Genoa's former riches had been stripped away when 'the Portuguese, had discoveries [*sic*], the way to the East Indies by the cape', leading to conquests that allowed them to dominate the trade in Asian commodities and, in doing so, become 'masters likewise of all our staple commodities here in England'.[82] The fate of Genoa was not one that England's merchants wished to suffer, and if empire could reshape global trade overnight, then these same merchants were keen to make sure it was reshaped in their favour.

What, though, did this mean for the merchant community? In what ways had they shaped England's trade and empire during a century of expansion? How far had the practices and institutions of these 'mere merchants' come to dominate the way business was conducted in England? As we have seen across this volume, merchants had a distinct professional identity, built on common training and their place in deeply interconnected commercial communities. England's merchants shaped the country's trade and empire not just by taking a leading role, but by creating the frameworks in which commerce and colonisation could take place. Central to their success was the creation of conditions in which they could depend on each other, irrespective of the distance or complexity in their trades. Trust was essential for lubricating the wheels of commerce, and merchants needed to believe that contracts and agreements would be honoured, and that partners and agents would act towards shared interests. To achieve this, in the century after 1550, merchants had reinforced and popularised what was expected from

CONCLUSION

commercial partners and enforced strict requirements for participation in commerce that demanded adherence to common values and practices. Young merchants were expected to have spent years working and living overseas, or as the servants of senior figures in the community, learning not just the practical skills of merchandising but also the behaviours that went along with it. In time, shared commercial experiences, education and participation in corporations contributed to the development of a common commercial culture that generated a regularity of behaviour through rules, beliefs, norms and organisational practices that made it easier for merchants to work together. Through these means, what emerged from the merchant community was an expansion of commercial activity that depended as much on social and cultural factors as on strictly economic ones. Although English merchants and corporations were often in competition, business depended on the effective execution of activities that were connected and collaborative.

As England's imperial ambitions expanded, merchants lost their automatic place at the head of the table when it came to leading English ventures to distant shores. Yet, whether as suppliers or traders, or as collaborators and partners within institutional structures that had their roots in the corporate models that had been utilised so widely in England's commercial development, merchants maintained an essential role within the mechanics of the emerging empire. Colonial activities kept their commercial aspects, and non-merchant leaders would seek to sell profitable exports and continue to require essential imports. Before long, colonial commerce would make up almost one-eighth of England's imports and one-twelfth of exports, surpassing the East India Company in each respect.[83] Together, traders in the Atlantic and Indian Ocean worlds added to the vast increases in England's trade in the early modern period, building on, learning from and contributing to the ongoing success of trade with Europe that remained by far England's largest market. Across these activities, merchants continued to depend on the institutions that they had honed and developed over the preceding century, which had helped to forge and strengthen the networks of trust,

– 227 –

credit and information that were so important for profitable international trade. By 1650, the commercial community's approach to global trade had become so ingrained in the English empire that their approach was no longer confined to London, its corporations or even to merchants themselves. It had become the foundation of a system of international trade and empire that would have global consequences in the centuries to come.

NOTES

ABBREVIATIONS

BA	Bristol Archive, Bristol
SMV	Society of Merchant Venturers
BerkRO	Berkshire Record Office
AC	Trumbull Ms, Alphabetical Correspondence
MC	Trumbull Ms, Miscellaneous Correspondence
BL	British Library, London
Add Ms	Additional Manuscripts
IOR	India Office Records
BLO	Bodleian Library
CC	Clothworkers' Company Hall, London
CMAY	Company of the Merchant Adventurers of York
DAB	Department of Archives Barbados
DC	Drapers' Company Hall
MB	Court of Assistants Minute Books
RA	Renter Warden's Accounts
GL	Guildhall Library, London
HHC	Hull History Centre
HL	Huntingdon Library

HRO	Hampshire Record Office
KHLC	Kent History and Library Centre
LMA	London Metropolitan Archive
MC	Mercers' Company Hall
AoC	Acts of Court
MHS	Massachusetts Historical Society, Boston
NorthRO	Northampton Record Office
NRO	Norfolk Record Office
NRS	National Records of Scotland
PLMC	Pepys Library at Magdalene College
FP	Ferrar Papers
PRONI	Public Record Office for Northern Ireland
SA	Southampton Archive
StaffRO	Staffordshire Record Office
TNA	The National Archives, UK
C	Chancery
CO	Colonial
PC	Privy Council
PROB	Probate
SP	State Papers

INTRODUCTION

1. PLMC, FP 11. William Turner to John Collett, 30 December 1606.
2. 'Mere merchant' and 'merchant' are used interchangeably. Where a non-merchant who participated in trading activities is considered, they will be identified specifically depending on their role (trader, investor, ship owner, etc.).
3. The training of merchants is examined in detail in chapter 1, while their professional identity and efforts by corporations to secure this are considered in chapter 2.
4. Eliga H. Gould has highlighted the steep learning curve experienced by English merchants operating on the fringes of other

NOTES to pp. 4–5

European empires in 'Entangled histories, entangled worlds: The English-speaking Atlantic as a Spanish periphery', *American Historical Review* 112, 3 (2007), pp. 1415–22. England was by no means the world's predominant imperial power during this period, and in terms of commercial success, it lagged behind some competitors, including the Dutch. See Jan de Vries and Ad van der Woude, *The First Modern Economy: Success, Failure, and Perseverance of the Dutch Economy, 1500–1815* (Cambridge, 1997).

5. For traditional interpretations, see Robert Brenner, *Merchants and Revolution: Commercial Change, Political Conflict, and London's Overseas Traders, 1550–1663* (London, 1993); Nicholas Canny, 'Introduction', in Nicholas Canny (ed.), *The Origins of Empire: British Overseas Empire to the Close of the Seventeenth Century* (Oxford, 1998), pp. 1–32. A global perspective has already shown some of the connections between English activities in North America and the rest of the world. See, for example: Huw V. Bowen, Elizabeth Mancke and John G. Reid (eds), *Britain's Oceanic Empire: Atlantic and Indian Ocean World, c. 1550–1850* (Cambridge, 2012); Jonathan Eacott, *Selling Empire: India in the Making of Britain and America, 1600–1830* (Williamsburg, VA, 2016); Alison Games, *The Web of Empire: English Cosmopolitans in an Age of Expansion, 1560–1660* (Oxford, 2008). Similarly, a connected corporate perspective is presented in Edmond Smith, 'The global interests of London's commercial community, 1599–1625: Investment in the East India Company', *Economic History Review* 71, 4 (2018), pp. 1118–46; Henry S. Turner, *The Corporate Commonwealth: Pluralism and Political Fictions in England, 1516–1651* (Chicago, 2016). For the implications of global history methodology for the study of England's trade and empire, see James Belich, John Darwin, Margret Frenz and Chris Wickham (eds), *The Prospect of Global History* (Oxford, 2016), pp. 4–5; Sebastian Conrad, *What Is Global History?* (Princeton, NJ, 2016), p. 5.

– 231 –

NOTES to pp. 6–7

6. A typical and essential part of doing business in cross-cultural contexts. See Philip Curtin, *Cross-cultural Trade in World History* (Cambridge University Press, 1984), pp. 5–11.

7. Lauren Benton, *Law and Colonial Cultures: Legal Regimes in World History, 1400–1900* (Cambridge, 2002), p. 22.

8. For how another merchant community depended on these common practices, see Francesca Trivellato, *The Familiarity of Strangers: The Sephardic Diaspora, Livorno, and Cross-cultural Trade in the Early Modern Period* (New Haven, CT, 2012), pp. 4, 13.

9. Anver Greif, *Institutions and the Path to the Modern Economy: Lessons from Medieval Trade* (Cambridge, 2006), pp. 30, 382–3.

10. TNA, PROB 11/135. For more information about the role of apprenticeships in early modern society, see Tim Leunig, Chris Minns and Patrick Wallis, 'Networks in the premodern economy: The market for London apprenticeships, 1600–1749', *Journal of Economic History* 71, 2 (2011), pp. 413–43.

11. English merchants adapted to the rigours of travel, cultural encounter and living overseas in numerous ways, and their experiences were often passed on to other merchants. For example, Margaret Jacob, *Strangers Nowhere in the World: The Rise of Cosmopolitanism in Early Modern Europe* (Philadelphia, PA, 2006); Games, *Web of Empire.*

12. Douglas North, 'Institutions', *Journal of Economic Perspectives* 5, 1 (1991), pp. 97–9. English merchants were not alone in this practice, for an international comparison see Ron Harris, *Going the Distance: Eurasian Trade and the Rise of the Business Corporation, 1400–1700* (Princeton, NJ, 2020).

13. Phil Withington, 'Public discourse, corporate citizenship, and state formation in early modern England', *American Historical Review* 112, 4 (2007), p. 1017.

14. S.R.H. Jones and Simon P. Ville, 'Efficient transactors or rent-seeking monopolists: The rationale for early chartered companies', *Journal of Economic History* 56, 4 (1996), pp. 898–915.

– 232 –

NOTES to pp. 7–8

15. Philip Stern, 'Companies: Monopoly, sovereignty, and the East Indies', in Philip Stern and Carl Wennerlind (eds), *Mercantilism Reimagined: Political Economy in Early Modern Britain and Its Empire* (New York, 2013), p. 179.

16. William Scott, *The Constitution and Finance of English, Scottish, and Irish Joint-stock Companies to 1720* (Cambridge, 1910), pp. ix, 1–7. For the broader European context of the guild system, see Stephan Epstein and Maarten Prak (eds), *Guilds, Innovation and the European Economy, 1400–1800* (Cambridge, 2008); Oscar Gelderblom and Regina Grafe, 'The rise and fall of the merchant guilds: Re-thinking the comparative study of commercial institutions in premodern Europe', *Journal of Interdisciplinary History* 40, 4 (2010), pp. 477–512; Carlo Taviani, 'Confraternities, citizenship and factionalism: Genoa in the early sixteenth century', in Nicholas Terpstra, Adriano Prosperi and Stefiana Pastore (eds), *Faith's Boundaries: Laity and Clergy in Early Modern Confraternities* (Turnhout, 2013), pp. 41–57.

17. Joshua Barkan, *Corporate Sovereignty: Law and Government under Capitalism* (Minneapolis, MN, 2013); Withington, 'Public discourse, corporate citizenship'.

18. Steve Rappaport, *Worlds within Worlds: Structures of Life in Sixteenth-century London* (Cambridge, 1989); Edward Cavanagh, 'A company with sovereignty and subjects of its own? The case of the Hudson's Bay Company, 1670–1763', *Canadian Journal of Law and Society* 26, 1 (2011), pp. 25–50; Anne Goldgar and Robert L. Frost (eds), *Institutional Culture in Early Modern Society* (Leiden, 2004).

19. Many of these activities were restricted to professional merchants and a number of companies were careful to exclude other people from participating. The different opportunities available to merchants and gentry are discussed in Theodore Rabb, *Enterprise and Empire: Merchant and Gentry Investment in the Expansion of England, 1575–1630* (Cambridge, MA, 1967).

20. Richard Grassby, *The Business Community of Seventeenth-century England* (Cambridge, 1995).

– 233 –

NOTES to pp. 8–9

21. M.S. Giuseppi (ed.), *Calendar of the Manuscripts of the Most Honourable the Marquis of Salisbury*, vol. 18 (London, 1923–40), p. 329.

22. Craig Muldrew, *The Economy of Obligation: The Culture of Credit and Social Relations in Early Modern England* (Basingstoke, 1998). In relation to international trade, see Ceri Sullivan, *The Rhetoric of Credit: Merchants in Early Modern Writing* (London, 2002); Nuala Zahedieh, 'Credit, risk and reputation in late seventeenth-century colonial trade', *Research in Maritime History* 15 (1998), pp. 53–74.

23. Muldrew, *Economy of Obligation*, p. 2.

24. LMA, Inquisitions Post Mortem, City of London, 1577–1603. Ref. William Ridgley; TNA, PROB 11/135. William Turner's Will, 7 February 1620.

25. This growth was sustained by increasing connections between London and other parts of England too, and merchants from across the country would come to work together to take advantage of new opportunities. The population of the city grew from approximately 100,000 in 1570 to nearly 400,000 in 1640. Jeremy Boulton, 'London, 1540–1700', in Peter Clark (ed.), *The Cambridge Urban History of Britain*, vol. ii: *1540–1700* (Cambridge, 2000). This included the movement of prominent merchants from other towns to the city; see David Harris Sacks, *The Widening Gate: Bristol and the Atlantic Economy, 1450–1700* (Berkeley, CA, 1991), pp. 29–32.

26. Giuseppi (ed.), *Calendar*, vol. 18, p. 329.

27. Douglas Bisson, *The Merchant Adventurers of England: The Company and the Crown, 1474–1564* (Newark, 1993).

28. Some of the new companies were modelled closely on the Merchant Adventurers; so-called regulated companies, where a central organisation would facilitate trade. These included the Spanish, Levant and Barbary companies, which allowed members to trade to specific regions on their own account while receiving fees that they used to support diplomatic efforts overseas. Others, most

– 234 –

NOTES to pp. 9–10

prominently the East India Company, collected investment from members and directly managed trade overseas, actively constraining members and others from trading of their own volition. In the case of both regulated and joint-stock organisations, companies were 'bureaucratic economic organisations' that provided essential structure and institutional support for overcoming the considerable strains of complex overseas activities. See William Pettigrew and Tristan Stein, 'The public rivalry between regulated and joint stock corporations and the development of seventeenth-century corporate constitutions', *Historical Research* 90, 248 (2016), pp. 341–62; Pauline Croft, *The Spanish Company* (London, 1973); Mortimer Epstein, *The Early History of the Levant Company* (London, 1908); Kirti N. Chaudhuri, *The English East India Company: The Study of an Early Joint-stock Company* (London, 1964) and *The Trading World of Asia and the English East India Company, 1660–1760* (Cambridge, 1978), p. 82; T.S. Willan, *The Early History of the Russia Company* (Manchester, 1956). There was considerable contemporary debate about how to regulate overseas trade and what role these companies should take. See Tom Leng, 'Commercial conflict and regulation in the discourse of trade in seventeenth-century England', *Historical Journal* 48, 4 (2005), pp. 933–54.

29. KHLC, U269/1/B82/14, m. 689. List of New Merchant Adventurers, 1616–17.

30. BL, IOR/B/1, 22 September 1599.

31. BL, Add Ms 20031. Patent of James I to the merchants of England trading in the Levant, 9 November 1605; TNA, C66/2313, f. 7. Patent for Newfoundland Company; TNA, SP 63/228, f. 32. Patent for the Irish Society.

32. Giuseppi, *Calendar*, vol. 21, p. 271. TNA, PROB 11/135.

33. Brenner, *Merchants and Revolution*, pp. 14, 48–51, 61–74. Brenner's analysis remains influential in this field and has been widely used as a means to explain 'the significant differences between Atlantic "new

NOTES to pp. 10–11

merchants" and the entrenched monopoly traders' in works covering both the seventeenth century and later periods. For example, Paul Slack, *The Invention of Improvement: Information and Material Progress in Seventeenth-century England* (Oxford, 2015), p. 70; Brian Cowan, *The Social Life of Coffee: The Emergence of the British Coffeehouse* (New Haven, CT, 2005), p. 276. For ideology in context of British imperial development, see David Armitage, *The Ideological Origins of the British Empire* (Cambridge, 2000), pp. 71–81.

34. Phil Withington and Alexandra Shepard (eds), *Communities in Early Modern England: Networks, Place, Rhetoric* (Manchester, 2001); Phil Withington, *The Politics of Commonwealth: Citizens and Freemen in Early Modern England* (Cambridge, 2005) and 'Company and sociability in early modern England', *Social History* 32, 3 (2007) pp. 291–307; Rappaport, *Worlds within Worlds*.

35. Keith Wrightson, 'The Politics of the Parish in Early Modern England', in Paul Griffiths, Steve Hindle and Adam Fox (eds), *The Experience of Authority in Early Modern England* (Basingstoke, 1996), p. 11.

36. The symbiotic relationship that could develop between corporate bodies and private traders is examined in Emily Erikson, *Between Monopoly and Free Trade: The English East India Company, 1600–1757* (Princeton, NJ, 2014).

37. Natasha Glaisyer, *The Culture of Commerce in England, 1660–1720* (Woodbridge, 2006).

38. The relationship between the commercial community and the state is considered in Robert Ashton, *The City and the Court, 1603–1643* (Cambridge, 1979); John Brewer, *The Sinews of Power: War, Money, and the English State, 1688–1783* (Oxford, 1989); Bruce G. Carruthers, *City of Capital: Politics and Markets in the English Financial Revolution* (Princeton, NJ, 1993).

39. Philip Stern, *The Company-state: Corporate Sovereignty and the Early Modern Foundation of the British Empire in India* (Oxford, 2011), p. 130.

NOTES to pp. 11–12

40. Oscar Gelderblom, *Cities of Commerce: The Institutional Foundations of International Trade in the Low Countries, 1250–1650* (Princeton, NJ, 2013), p. 3.

41. Michael Braddick, *State Formation in Early Modern England, c. 1550–1770* (Cambridge, 2000).

42. Ibid., p. 4.

43. Games, *Web of Empire*, pp. 6–15.

44. Canny, *The Origins of Empire*, p. 32. Similar accounts are found in Kenneth Andrews, *Trade, Plunder and Settlement: Maritime Enterprise and the Genesis of the British Empire, 1480–1630* (Cambridge, 1984). William Pettigrew has recently suggested that it was the very flexibility of the corporate form that made trading companies successful in a changeable international environment: 'Corporate constitutionalism and the dialogue between global and local in seventeenth-century English history', *Itinerario* 39, 3 (2015), pp. 487–501.

45. J. Rose, A.P. Newton and E.A. Benians (eds), *The Cambridge History of the British Empire*, vol. 1: *The Old Empire from the Beginnings to 1783* (Cambridge, 1929), pp. 57.

46. Atlantic history has many advocates and serves as the thematic foundations for numerous historical works. For example, Daron Acemoglu, Simon Johnson and James Robinson, 'The rise of Europe: Atlantic trade, institutional change, and economic growth', *American Historical Review* 95, 3 (2005), pp. 546–79; David Armitage and Michael J. Braddick (eds), *The British Atlantic World, 1500–1800* (Basingstoke, 2009); L.H. Roper and B. Van Ruymbeke (eds), *Constructing Early Modern Empires: Proprietary Ventures in the Atlantic World* (Leiden, 2007). However, the limitations of Atlantic history have also been explored in depth, in particular the ways in which it has constrained studies from embedding 'Atlantic' activities within wider, global topics. See: Peter A. Coclanis, Alison Games, Paul W. Mapp and Philip J. Stern, 'Forum: Beyond the Atlantic', *William and Mary Quarterly* 53 (2006), pp. 675–742;

– 237 –

Jack P. Greene and Philip Morgan (eds), *Atlantic History: A Critical Appraisal* (Oxford, 2009).

47. Irish Society, *A Concise View of the Origin, Constitution, and Proceedings of the Honourable Society of the Governor and Assistants of London of the New Plantation in Ulster, within the Realm of Ireland, Commonly Called the Irish Society* (London, 1842).

48. This is particularly clear in attempts to integrate Atlantic history with English activities in Asia. See Lauren Benton, 'The British Atlantic in a global context', in Armitage and Braddick (eds), *The British Atlantic World*, pp. 271–89; Nicholas Canny, 'Asia, the Atlantic and the subjects of the British monarchy', in Barry Coward (ed.), *A Companion to Stuart Britain* (Oxford, 2003), pp. 45–66.

49. Slack, *The Invention of Improvement*; Joel Mokyr, *The Culture of Growth: The Origins of the Modern Economy* (Princeton, NJ, 2016).

1 THE ART OF MERCHANDISING

1. A 'Description of the Two Voyages Made out of England into Guinea in Africa' was printed as an addendum to Richard Eden's translation of Pietro Martire d'Angiera, *The Decades of the New World or West India Containing the Navigations and Conquests of the Spaniards* (London, 1555), pp. 343–60.

2. Curtin, *Cross-cultural Trade*, pp. 38–59; Trivellato, *Familiarity of Strangers*, pp. 1–2.

3. A range of institutional frameworks that were adopted by merchant communities to cater to specific conditions. For example, Catia Antunes and Amelia Polónia (eds), *Beyond Empires: Global, Self-organising, Cross-imperial Networks, 1500–1800* (Leiden, 2015); Sebouh Aslanian, *From the Indian Ocean to the Mediterranean: The Global Trade Networks of Armenian Merchants from New Julfa* (Berkeley, CA, 2011).

4. Trivellato has led the way in this approach, see *Familiarity of Strangers*, p. 1. For a more traditional approach to institutional development, see Paul Milgrom, Douglas North and Barry

NOTES to pp. 17–18

Weingast, 'The role of institutions in the revival of trade: The law merchant, private judges, and the Champagne fairs', *Economics and Politics* 2, 1 (1990), pp. 1–23.

5. On female apprentices, see Ilana Krausman Ben-Amos, 'Women apprentices in the trade and crafts of early modern Bristol', *Continuity and Change* 6, 2 (1991), pp. 227–53; Laura Gowing, 'Girls on forms: Apprenticing young women in seventeenth-century London', *Journal of British Studies* 55, 3 (2016), pp. 447–73.

6. The structure of the apprenticeship system has been examined by Stephan Epstein, 'Craft guilds, apprenticeship, and technological change in preindustrial Europe', *Journal of Economic History* 58, 3 (1998), pp. 684–713; Jane Humphries, 'English apprenticeship: A neglected factor in the first Industrial Revolution', in Paul David and Mark Thomas (eds), *The Economic Future in Historical Perspective* (Oxford, 2003), pp. 73–102; Patrick Wallis, 'Apprenticeship and training in premodern England', *Journal of Economic History* 68, 3 (2008), pp. 832–61.

7. Olive Dunlop and Richard Denman, *English Apprenticeship and Child Labour* (London, 1912), pp. 81–2.

8. The average age for someone to start an apprenticeship was 19.5 years old in late-sixteenth-century London, meaning they would usually have completed some schooling (including essential skills like writing and arithmetic) and had some experienced the operations of their family's businesses. See Rappaport, *Worlds within Worlds*, p. 295; Wallis, 'Apprenticeship and training', pp. 846–7.

9. Dunlop and Denman, *English Apprenticeship*; Christopher W. Brooks, 'Apprenticeship, social mobility, and the middling sort, 1550–1800', in Jonathan Barry and Christopher W. Brooks (eds), *The Middling Sort of People: Culture, Society, and Politics in England, 1550–1800* (Basingstoke, 1994), pp. 52–83; Joan Lane, *Apprenticeship in England, 1600–1914* (London, 1996).

10. For a detailed quantitative analysis of relationships between apprentices, their masters and the leadership of England's trading

– 239 –

NOTES to pp. 18–20

companies, see Aske Brock, 'The Company Director: Commerce, State and Society', PhD thesis, University of Kent, 2017.

11. Dianne Berry and Paul Dienes Zoltan, *Implicit Learning: Theoretical and Empirical Issues, Essays in Cognitive Psychology* (Hove, 1993), pp. 26–8; Wallis, 'Apprenticeship and training', p. 847.

12. Lewes Roberts, *The Marchants Mapp of Commerce: necessarie for all such as shall be imployed in the publique afaires of Princes in foraine partes, for all gentlemen & others that travell abroad for delight & plesure, and for al marchants or their factors that exercise the art off marchandiseinge in any parte of the habitable world* (London, 1638).

13. Sheilagh Ogilvie, 'Guilds, efficiency, and social capital: Evidence from German proto-industry', *Economic History Review* 57, 2 (2004), p. 312.

14. CMAY, Acts and Ordinances of Eastland Merchants, ff. 5–7. 18 March 1617.

15. BL, Cotton Nero B XI, f. 115. Articles exhibited to the lord treasurer against the Levant Company's new charter, 1591.

16. Rates of apprenticeship remained fairly consistent throughout the sixteenth and seventeenth centuries. See Rappaport, *Worlds within Worlds*, pp. 232, 294; Leonard Schwartz, 'London apprentices in the seventeenth century: Some problems', *Local Population Studies* 38 (1987), p. 21.

17. Probably less than half of all apprentices, see Wallis, 'Apprenticeship and training', pp. 838–9.

18. For a detailed assessment of joining trading companies specifically, see chapter 3.

19. Humphries, 'English apprenticeship', p. 90.

20. Greater Manchester County Archives, GB127.L1/10/125. Apprentice indenture of John Clayton to John Bolton, 29 September 1647.

21. John Browne, *The Merchants Avizo: verie necessarie for their sonnes and seruants, when they first send them beyond the seas, as to Spayne and Portingale or other countreyes* (London, 1590), dedication and pp. 3–5.

– 240 –

NOTES to pp. 20–23

22. BL, Cotton Nero B XI, ff. 296, 299. Petition from merchants trading to Barbary to the Earl of Leicester, 1574; An account of imports from Barbary and Portugal, 1574–5.

23. Wendy R. Childs, *Anglo-Castilian Trade in the later Middle Ages* (Manchester, 1978).

24. Gigliola Pagano de Divitiis, *English Merchants in Seventeenth-century Italy*, trans. Stephen Parkin (Cambridge, 1990), pp. 23–35; Gerald MacLean and Nabil Matar, *Britain and the Islamic World, 1558–1713* (Oxford, 2011), pp. 79–123.

25. Trivellato, *Familiarity of Strangers*, p. 4. In these circumstances, as well as corporate training, merchants might also rely on shared religious, familial, or national identities to help sustain trust between each other. See Harris, *Going the Distance*, pp. 198–225.

26. TNA, Patent Rolls, 9 Jac. 1, 35. Charter of the French Company, 1611.

27. TNA, SP 105/149. Levant Company minutes, 2 June 1632.

28. NorthRO, C/2484. William Cockayne junior to William Cockayne senior, 28 October 1624.

29. KHLC, U269/1/B141, m. 1357. Note by [John Tucker], [undated, *c.* 1618]; SA, SC9/3/11, f. 219. Voluntary deposition of George Gregory, 19 March 1629.

30. The apprenticeships were administered by the Drapers' livery company. See Percival Boyd, *Roll of the Drapers' Company* (London, 1934); Records of London's Livery Companies Online (ROLLCO) [https://www.londonroll.org/home].

31. TNA, PROB 11, 174. Will of Richard Archdale, 1638.

32. KHLC, U269/1/AB1. A journal book for the account of my master Richard Sheppard and for the account of William Cranfield and William Halliday, 29 July–6 November 1594.

33. NorthRO, C/2493. Deed of appointment for Simon Fryer, 24 February 1590.

34. KHLC, U269/1/B191. List of goods seized by Edward Wollaston, December 1620.

– 241 –

NOTES to pp. 23–25

35. TNA, E 190/18/10. Port Book London, leather and wool exports under licence of Arthur Basano, 1615.

36. LMA, CLC/B/227/MS35025a. Subsidiary accounts of Daniel Harvey's agent in Rouen, 1632–3.

37. BL, IOR/B/1, 22 November 1600. Learning languages in early modern Europe was a practical, hands-on experience and employees would have travelled widely learning the languages required. See Eric R. Dursteler, 'Speaking in tongues: Language and communication in the early modern Mediterranean', *Past & Present* 217, 1 (2012), pp. 47–77; Games, *Web of Empire*, pp. 84–115; John Gallagher, *Learning Languages in Early Modern England* (Oxford, 2019).

38. BL, IOR/B/1, 22 November; 13 December 1600. In the end, Oliver Stile's influence and wealth made the offer redundant: another factor, Richard Collymore, was persuaded to relinquish his position in favour of Roger, in return for Oliver investing £200 on Roger's behalf in the Company. BL, IOR/B/1, 24 December 1600.

39. BL, IOR/B/1, 17 December 1600.

40. BL, IOR/B/9, 29 October 1624.

41. Ibid., 3 November 1624.

42. Ibid., 17 November 1624.

43. Ibid., 3 December 1624.

44. NorthRO, C/2427. Hatton Farmor to William Cockayne, 18 January 1623.

45. HHC, C DDBH/22/23. Bond between Humphrey Thompson and Arthur Robinson, 19 May 1615 [Latin]; GD226/18/21/3–4. Henry Shanks will, 24 April 1625; Translation of Shanks' will by a Dutch notary in Batavia, 1625 [Dutch].

46. CMAY, 2/7/14. Bond between William Robynson, Andrew Trewe, Robert Brooke and Anthony Pulley and Edward Robertson, 1579; BA, 26389/5. Bond between Roger Watkins and William Jones, 30 August 1614; NRO, NCR/17/D/11. Orders Concerning Wool, 1577; NRO, NCR/17/D/12. A Book of Dutch Orders, 1582.

NOTES to pp. 25–27

47. BA, JAdm/4/37. Wannoir la Nord to Mayor of Bristol, October 1590.

48. TNA, SP 71/13, ff. 40–56. General observation of the Barbary trade, 4 April 1638.

49. BL, IOR/E/3/1/1, f. 218. Richard Cocks to William Adams, 24 December 1613; BL, Cotton Nero B XI, ff. 79–82. Letter from Mehmed III to Elizabeth I, 1602.

50. BL, IOR/E/3/1, ff. 198–9. Thomas Aldworth to East India Company, 9 November 1613.

51. By providing unique expertise individuals could obtain considerable influence within communities. See Eric H. Ash, *Power, Knowledge and Expertise in Elizabethan England* (Baltimore, MD, 2005).

52. BL, IOR/B/1, General Court, 8 December 1600.

53. Ibid., 10 December 1600.

54. BL, IOR/B/9, 22 October 1624.

55. BL, Sloane Ms 1622, f. 98. William Strachey's *The Historie of Travaile into Virginia Britannia*; Gotthard Arthus, *Dialogues in the English and Malaiane languages: or, certaine common formes of speech, first written in Latin, Malaian, and Madagascar tongues, by the diligence and painfull endeuour of Master Gotardus Arthusius, a Dantisker, and now faithfully translated into the English tongue by Augustine Spalding merchant, for their sakes, who happily shall hereafter vndertake a voyage to the East-Indies* (London, 1614); BL, IOR/B/5, 22 January 1614.

56. SA, Southampton Register of Apprentices, 1609–1740, p. 3, no. 17; TNA, SP 105/149. Levant Company minutes, 17 July 1632.

57. SA, SC9/3/11, ff. 274–5. Voluntary depositions by Lewes Jackson, 17 September 1630.

58. George Best, *A True Discourse of the Late Voyages of Discovery, for the finding of a passage to Cathaya, by the Northwest* (London, 1578), p. i.

59. MHS, Miscellaneous Bound 1629–1658. Promissory note from Richard Foxwell to Francis Johnson, July 1632.

NOTES to pp. 28–29

60. BL, Add Ms 9366, f. 35. Journal of John Kerridge.

61. John Bruce (ed.), *Letters and Papers of the Verney Family Down to the End of the Year 1639* (London, 1853), p. 197.

62. Ann Carlos, 'Principal–agent problems in early trading companies: A tale of two firms', *American Historical Review* 82, 2 (1992), pp. 140–5; B. Sobek, '"After my Humble Dutie Remembered": Factors and/versus merchants', in B. Charry and G. Shahani (eds), *Emissaries in Early Modern Literature and Culture: Mediation, Transmission, Traffic, 1550–1700* (Farnham, 2009), pp. 113–28.

63. Edmond Smith, 'Governance', in William Pettigrew and David Veevers (eds), *The Corporation as a Protagonist in Global History, c. 1550–1750* (Leiden, 2018), pp. 163–86.

64. Lauren Benton, *A Search for Sovereignty: Law and Geography in European Empires, 1400–1900* (Cambridge, 2010); Lauren Benton and Richard Ross (eds), *Legal Pluralism and Empires, 1500–1850* (New York, 2013).

65. BL, IOR/A/2/1, Charter of the East India Company, 31 December 1600.

66. Edmond Smith, 'Reporting and interpreting legal violence in Asia: The East India Company's printed accounts of torture, 1603–1624', *Journal of Imperial and Commonwealth History* 46, 4 (2018), pp. 603–26.

67. Stern, *The Company-state*, p. 135.

68. BL, Add Ms 18913, f. 15. The Lawes, Customs, and Ordinances, of the Fellowship of Merchant Adventurers, 1608.

69. BLO, Ms Bankes 8, ff. 1–4. Lord Baltimore's patent for New England, [undated, *c.* 1629].

70. TNA, SP 105/148. Levant Company General Court, 11 March 1618; 15 April 1618.

71. CMAY, Acts and Ordinances of Eastland Merchants, f. 10. 18 March 1617.

NOTES to pp. 30–33

72. SA, SC2/1/1, f. 3. Southampton Mayor's Book, 24 October 1606; BL, Add Ms 9365, pp. 27–9, 101. Register Book of the Spanish Company.

73. CMAY, Acts and Ordinances of Eastland Merchants, f. v. Oath of the secretary, [undated].

74. BL, Lansdowne 213, ff. 394–7. The case for a legal reforming of one of the greatest home-trades within the commonwealth of England, [undated, *c.* 1625–49].

75. CMAY, Acts and Ordinances of Eastland Merchants, f. 24. 18 March 1617; CMAY, Book of Acts and Copies of Several Wills and Bequests, ff. 207–11. Will of William Harte, 1632.

76. BL, IOR/A/5, Charter of the East India Company, 1609; BL, IOR/B/1, 24 December 1600.

77. MC, AoC 1595–1629, f. 236. 5 November 1622.

78. NRO, YC/19/5, f. 32. Great Yarmouth Assembly Book, 5 November 1602.

79. HL, EL2352. William Chancellor's petition to Lord Chancellor Ellesmere, [*c.* 1598–9].

80. LMA, COL/AD/01/030, f. 159. Corporation of London Letter Book, 12 October 1613.

81. SA, SC2/1/1, f. 2. Southampton Mayor's Book, 17 October 1606.

82. SA, SC2/1/6, f. 124. Southampton Assembly Book, 29 November 1611.

83. LMA, COL/AD/01/030, f. 24. Corporation of London Letter Book, 8 January 1612.

84. LMA, COL/AD/01/030, f. 59. Corporation of London Letter Book, 5 May 1612.

85. CC, CL/B/1/4. Orders of Court, f. 37. 1 August 1608.

86. BL, Add Ms 18913, f. 167. The Lawes, Customs, and Ordinances, of the Fellowship of Merchant Adventurers, 1608.

87. Philip Stern, '"A Politie of Civill and Military Power": Political thought and the late seventeenth-century foundations of the

– 245 –

East India Company-state', *Journal of British Studies* 47, 2 (2008), pp. 253–83.

88. BL, IOR/A/2/1. Charter of the East India Company, 31 December 1600.

89. BL, IOR/A/1/6. Royal Commission for the Sixth Voyage, 1610; Mary Anne Everett Green (ed.), *Calendar of State Papers Domestic, James I, 1603–1625* (London: 1857–59): vol. 1, p. 400; vol. 2, pp. 229–32, 269–71, 335–41.

90. His Majesty's Stationery Office, *Acts of the Privy Council of England*, vol. 33: *1613–1614* (London, 1921), p. 233.

91. BL, IOR/A/1/8. Commission of James I granting judicial powers to servants in India of the Governor and Company of Merchants of London trading into the East-Indies.

92. For the development of the East India Company as the ruler of indigenous population's overseas, see Stern, *The Company-state*. For wider mercantile practices of colonial governance, see the conclusion of this book.

93. As well as their practical uses, effective records could demonstrate the reputations and creditability of individuals and companies; see Muldrew, *Economy of Obligation*; Alexandra Shepard, *Accounting for Oneself: Worth, Status and the Social Order in Early Modern England* (Oxford, 2015). For corporate writing and accounting practices, see Vahé Baladouni, 'Accounting in the early years of the East India Company', *Accounting Historians Journal* 10, 2 (1983), pp. 63–80.

94. Jan de Vries, 'Understanding Eurasian trade in the era of trading companies', in Maxine Berg, Felicia Gottman, Hanna Hodacs and Chris Nierstraz (eds), *Goods from the East, 1600–1800: Trading Eurasia* (Basingstoke, 2015), pp. 7–39.

95. NorthRO, Finch Hatton Manuscripts, m. 2257. Agreement between Henry Addes and George Mortimer, 6 July 1615.

96. Miles Ogborn, *Indian Ink: Script and Print in the Making of the English East India Company* (Chicago, 2007) and 'Writing travels:

NOTES to pp. 35–37

Power, knowledge and ritual on the English East India Company's early voyages', *Transactions of the Institute of British Geographers* 27, 2 (2002), pp. 155–71.

97. BA, DC/A/6/3, f. 38. Fragment of Merchant's [probably William Appowell] Day Book, 1558–9.

98. For the importance of common accounting standards in both national and imperial economic development, see Jacob Soll, *The Reckoning: Financial Accountability and the Making and Breaking of Nations* (London, 2014).

99. Nottinghamshire Archives, DD/P/7/2. Accounts of Jarvis Wylde, 1586.

100. For a detailed examination of Gresham's accounting practices, see James Winjum, 'The journal of Thomas Gresham', *Accounting Review* 46, 1 (1971), pp. 149–55.

101. MC, Gresham Day Book.

102. LMA, COL/SJ/08/015. Account of Mr Martin from Stood, 13 November 1610.

103. LMA, CLC/B/013/Ms23953. Richard Archdale's *Journal of Receipts and Payments*, 1623–30.

104. Ibid., ff. 1–79.

105. This included voyages to Amsterdam, Malaga, the Canary Islands, Bordeaux, 'Terceraes', Madeira, Cadiz and Lisbon. Ibid., ff. 4, 5, 12, 39, 54, 57, 58, 69.

106. Ibid., ff. 2–3.

107. Ibid., ff. 10–11.

108. NRO, AYL/825. Indenture between Nicholas Osborne and John Osborne, 5 September 1621.

109. StaffRO, D339/52/13/29. Article of agreement between Benedict Webb and George Mole, 19 February 1624.

110. BL, Add Ms 9365, p. 11. Register Book of the Spanish Company, 8 June 1604.

111. CC, CL/B/1/4, Orders of Court, ff. 3, 5, 13. 17 January; 10 February; 6 November 1606.

– 247 –

NOTES to pp. 37–42

112. East India Company, *The Lawes or Standing Orders of the East India Company* (London, 1621), p. 9.

113. BL, IOR/B/3, 19 July 1607; BL, IOR/B/5, 16 July 1614.

114. StaffRO, D(W)1761/C/12. Agreement between the executors of William Buckley, 11 January 1639.

115. NRS, GD34/924/3. Case regarding tobacco, [*c.* 1640].

116. BL, Add Ms 12504, f. 132. Reasons wherefore William Harwarde and his wife desire to have use of the books of account in the hands of Robert Draper.

117. TNA, C 2/JASI/IANDJ10/29/1. Petition to the Chancery Court, 27 November 1622.

118. TNA, C 2/JASI/IANDJ10/29/3. Answers of Benjamin Discrowe, 6 December 1622.

119. TNA, C 2/ChasI/G22/31/1. Complaint of Greenland Company, 21 May 1634. Overman and Whitwell argued that they had not agreed to purchase the oil due to a proclamation prohibiting the use of whale oil for soap in June 1632, but that they would purchase the oil at the agreed price if the restriction was lifted. TNA, C 2/ChasI/G22/31/2, Answers to complaint of Greenland Company, 11 June 1634.

120. TNA, C 2/ChasI/G22/31/1. Complaint of Greenland Company, 21 May 1634.

121. CC, CL/B/1/4, Orders of Court, ff. 123, 131. 15 June 1613.

122. MC, AoC 1595–1629, ff. 200–1. 4 October 1619.

123. BL, IOR/B/6, General Court, 4 February 1620.

124. Ibid., 4 February 1620.

125. BL, IOR/B/8, 20 September 1624.

126. BL, IOR/B/6, 18 June 1619.

127. Ibid.

128. BL, IOR/B/6, 2 July 1619.

129. Accounting was an important a widely taught skill. See Margaret Hunt, 'Time management, writing and accounting in the eighteenth-century English trading family: A bourgeois

NOTES to pp. 42–45

enlightenment', *Business and Economic History* 18 (1989), pp. 150–9.

130. CMAY, Faults found by the auditors. 1575; 1581; 20 May 1584.

131. MC, AoC 1595–1629, f. 163. 5 November 1616.

132. TNA, PC 2/28, f. 289. Report from the Attorney General, 5 June 1616.

133. TNA, SP 105/148. General Court, 11 March 1618; BA, SMV/2/1/1/1, f. 52. Merchants' Hall Book of Proceedings, 4 April 1642.

134. DC, MB 10, 7 October 1588.

135. For example, the Merchant Venturers spent £15 13s 2d hiring Edmond Brown as auditor in 1619. BA, SMV/3/1/1/1, ff. 3–4. Treasurers Account Book.

136. MC, AoC 1595–1629, ff. 200–1. 8–10 February 1620.

137. Ibid., ff. 205, 216. 20 April 1620; 2 March 1621.

138. Ibid., f. 63. 10 July 1605.

139. Ibid., f. 137. 23 November 1614.

140. For example, see Cecil Carr (ed.), *Select Charters of Trading Companies, A. D. 1530–1707* (London, 1913).

141. BL, Add Ms 9365, pp. 37–8. Register Book of the Spanish Company, 12 June 1605.

142. BA, SMV/2/1/1/1, f. 56. Merchants' Hall Book of Proceedings, 6 August 1642.

143. BA, SMV/1/1/1/7, front page and ff. 3–30. Book of Charters.

144. CMAY, Acts and Ordinances of Eastland Merchants, ff. 35–6. 18 March 1617; CMAY, Faults found by the auditors, 1575.

145. For the uses of marks and seals in early modern England, see Edward Elmhirst, *Merchants' Marks* (London, 1959); F.A. Girling, *English Merchants' Marks: A Field Survey of Marks Made by Merchants and Tradesmen in England between 1400 and 1700* (London, 1962); Elizabeth New, 'Representation and identity in medieval London: The evidence of seals', in M. Davies and

– 249 –

NOTES to pp. 45–47

A. Prescott (eds), *London and the Kingdom: Essays in Honour of Caroline M. Barron* (Donnington, 2008), pp. 246–58.

146. NorthRO, C/2466. George Hyde to William Cockayne, 27 May 1612.

147. BL, Add Ms 9365, pp. 19, 23. Register Book of the Spanish Company, 31 August 1604; 7 September 1604.

148. HHC, DSN/1, Monthly Court, 17 April 1648; DC, MB 10, 20 November 1584.

149. BL, Add Ms 9365, p. 4. Register Book of the Spanish Company, 29 March 1604.

150. CMAY, Acts and Ordinances of Eastland Merchants, f. 27. 18 March 1617.

151. PRONI, D3632/A/27d. Drapers' Company to John Rowley, 28 March 1616.

152. TNA, SP 71/12, f. 14. Request of merchants trading in Barbary, 8 April 1583.

153. BL, Add Ms 18913, ff. 14, 144. The Lawes, Customs, and Ordinances, of the Fellowship of Merchant Adventurers, 1608.

154. CMAY, Acts and Ordinances of Eastland Merchants, ff. 19–20. 18 March 1617.

155. Correspondence was essential in most early modern commercial communities; see Sebouh Aslanian, '"The Salt in a Merchant's Letter": The culture of Julfan correspondence in the Indian Ocean and Mediterranean', *Journal of World History* 19, 2 (2008), pp. 127–88; Rene Barendese, 'The long road to Livorno: The overland messenger service of the Dutch East India Company in the seventeenth century', *Itinerario* 12, 2 (1988), pp. 25–45; Francesca Trivellato, 'Merchants' letters across geographical and social boundaries', in Francisco Bethencourt and Florike Egmond (eds), *Correspondence and Cultural Exchange in Europe, 1400–1700* (Cambridge, 2007), pp. 80–103.

156. StaffRO, D593/S/4/69/19. Thomas Smith to Sir John Leveson, 6 August 1604.

NOTES to pp. 47–50

157. NorthRO, C/2451. John Cockayne to William Cockayne, 23 September 1624.

158. BA, AC/C48/1. Elizabeth Smith to Thomas Smith, 14 May 1622.

159. Here, we see the development of writing practices that would remain useful and important in the organisation of England's overseas trade even as corporate oversight declined. See, for example, Eve Tavor Bannet, *Empire of Letters: Letter Manuals and Transatlantic Correspondence, 1680–1820* (Cambridge, 2006).

160. LMA, CLC/B/227/Ms 29393a. Thomas Rogers to William Hurt, 12 January 1633.

161. LMA, CLC/B/227/Ms 29393d. Thomas Rogers to William Hurt, 20 March 1636.

162. LMA, CLC/B/227/Ms 29393a. Thomas Rogers to William Hurt, 12 January 1633.

163. LMA, CLC/B/227/Ms 29393b. Thomas Rogers to William Hurt, 6 July 1633.

164. LMA, CLC/B/227/Ms 29393c. Thomas Rogers to William Hurt, 19 November 1635.

165. BL, Add Ms 12206, f. 4. William Baffin's *True Declaration of his Fourth Voyage for the Discovery of the North-West Passage*, 1615.

166. NRS, GD406/1/2386. Letter to James Gibson, 24 April [1648].

167. BL, IOR/E/3/1, ff. 198–9. Thomas Kerridge to the East India Company, 9 November 1613.

168. Alastair Bellany, *The Politics of Court Scandal in Early Modern England: News Culture and the Overbury Affair, 1603–1660* (Cambridge, 2002); Richard Cust, 'News and politics in early seventeenth-century England', *Past & Present* 112, 1 (1986), pp. 60–90; Adam Fox, 'Rumour, news, and popular political opinion in Elizabethan and early Stuart England', *Historical Journal* 40, 3 (1997), pp. 597–620; Joad Raymond (ed.), *News, Newspapers, and Society in Early Modern Britain* (London, 1999).

169. BL, IOR/B/5, 13 January 1614.

170. BL, IOR/B/7, 26 June 1622.

NOTES to pp. 50-53

171. Ibid.; BL, IOR/B/5, 16 July 1614.

172. BL, IOR/B/5, 4 July 1614.

173. Paul Griffiths, 'Secrecy and authority in late sixteenth- and seventeenth-century London', *Historical Journal* 40, 4 (1997), pp. 925–51.

174. Stern, *The Company-state*, pp. 135–6.

175. CMAY, Acts and Ordinances of Eastland Merchants, f. 41. 18 March 1617.

176. In 1608, this key was passed from Richard Staper, deceased, to Alderman Farrington. CC, CL/B/1/4, Orders of Court, f. 36. 22 July 1608.

177. SA, SC2/1/6, f. 184. Assembly Book, 8 July 1618.

178. MC, AoC 1595–1629, f. 352. 12 August 1629.

179. CMAY, Acts and Ordinances of Eastland Merchants, f. 41. 18 March 1617.

180. BL, IOR/B/5, 11 July 1615.

181. Ibid., 30 August 1615.

182. BL, IOR/B/6, 23 June 1619.

183. BL, IOR/B/7, 26 September 1622.

184. CMAY, Acts and Ordinances of Eastland Merchants, f. v. Oath of the secretary, [undated].

185. CMAY, Acts and Ordinances of Eastland Merchants, f. 14. 18 March 1617.

186. BA, SMV/1/1/1/7, f. 77. Book of Charters. Acts, Ordinances, and Decrees, [undated, *c.* 1617].

187. BL, Add Ms 18913, f. 69. The Lawes, Customs, and Ordinances, of the Fellowship of Merchant Adventurers, 1608.

188. East India Company, *Lawes and Standing Orders*, p. 4.

189. BL, IOR/B/6, 8 December 1619.

190. Ibid., 13 December 1619.

191. Ibid.

192. Ibid.

193. BL, Lansdowne 112, f. 134. Letter from the Muscovy Company to Lord Burghley, [undated, *c.* 1591]. Attached to their letter was a list of

NOTES to pp. 53–60

quotations and page numbers relating to the specific text they thought would be taken offensively by the Russian emperor. The book in question was Giles Fletcher, *Of the Russe Common Wealth* (London, 1591). This episode has been examined by Felicity Stout, *Exploring Russia in the Elizabethan Commonwealth: The Muscovy Company and Giles Fletcher, the Elder (1546–1611)* (Manchester, 2015), pp. 93–116.

194. SA, SC2/1/6, f. 112. Assembly Book, 20 July 1610.

195. BerkRO, D/ED/F6/1/16. Thomas Smith to Henry Neville, 18 August 1609.

196. MC, AoC 1595–1629, f. 194. 4 October 1619.

197. NRS, GD226/18/21/1. Account of Thomas Robinson, 5 March 1630.

198. NRS, GD226/18/25. Petition by Captain William Ramsey, [*c.* 1630].

199. MC, AoC 1595–1629, f. 269. 16 February 1625.

200. Witnesses included Sir James Lancaster, William Keeling, David Middleton, Christopher Vincent and Edmund Scott, whose printed account of the Bantam factory contained considerable material relating to English agreements with local authorities. BL, Add Ms 48155, ff. 5–8. Minutes of conference relating to the East Indies, 30 March–30 April 1613; Edmund Scott, *An Exact Discourse of the Subtilties, Fashishions, Pollicies, Religion, and Ceremonies of the East Indians as well Chyneses as Javans, there abiding and dwelling* (London, 1606).

201. The letter was written in Arabic and translated by Mr Bedwell. BL, Cotton Nero B XI, f. 302. Letter from Mulley Peydan to James I, 11 July 1609.

202. BL, Add Ms 36448, ff. 13–19. Complaints regarding treatment of merchants in Spain, 25 June–27 August 1635.

2 MANY BODIES CORPORATE

1. BL, IOR/B/6, 25 June 1619; 2 July 1619.

2. Corporations and other forms of communal governance provided an institutional framework for economic activity. Scott,

NOTES to pp. 60–61

Constitution and Finance; Leonard Blusse and Femme Gastra (eds), *Companies and Trade: Essays on Overseas Trading Companies during the Ancien Regime* (Leiden, 1981); Patrick Wallis, Justin Coulson and David Chilosi, 'Structural change and economic growth in the British economy before the Industrial Revolution, 1500–1800', *Journal of Economic History* 78, 3 (2018), pp. 862–903; Sheilagh Ogilvie, *The European Guilds: An Economic Analysis* (Princeton, NJ, 2019).

3. Stern, *The Company-state*, p. 6.
4. For a quantitative study of these networks, see Smith, 'Global interests'.
5. Philip Stern, ' "Bundles of hyphens": Corporations as legal communities in the early modern British Empire', in Benton and Ross, *Legal Pluralism and Empires*, pp. 21–48.
6. Rappaport, *Worlds within Worlds*; Withington, 'Company and sociability'; Jennifer Bishop, '*Utopia* and civic politics in mid-sixteenth-century London', *Historical Journal* 54, 4 (2011), pp. 933–53.
7. For details regarding the practical organisation of trading companies, see Gary W. Anderson, Robert E. McCormick and Robert D. Tollison, 'The economic organisation of the English East India Company', *Journal of Economic Behaviour and Organisation* 4 (1983), pp. 221–38; F.J. Fisher, 'Experiments in company organisation in the early seventeenth century', *Economic History Review* 4, 2 (1933), pp. 177–94; Harris, *Going the Distance*; Scott, *Constitution and Finance*.
8. Mary Campbell, *Wonder and Science: Imagining Worlds in Early Modern Europe* (New York, 1999); Benjamin Schmidt, *Innocence Abroad: The Dutch Imagination and the Representation of the New World, c. 1570–1670* (Cambridge, 2001); Kristina Bross, *Future History: Global Fantasies in Seventeenth-century American and British Writings* (Oxford, 2017).
9. Ian Archer, *The Pursuit of Stability: Social Relations in Elizabethan London* (Cambridge, 1991); Games, *Web of Empire*; Smith, 'Global interests'.

– 254 –

NOTES to pp. 61–62

10. Heather Dalton, *Merchants and Explorers: Roger Barlow, Sebastian Cabot, and Networks of Atlantic Exchange, 1500–1560* (Oxford, 2016); Justin Coulson, 'Negotiating merchant identities: The Stockfishmongers and London's companies merging and dividing, c. 1450–1550', in Martin Allen and Matthew Davis (eds), *Medieval Merchants and Money: Essays in Honour of James L. Bolton* (London, 2017), pp. 3–20.

11. BL, IOR/A/1/2, Letters Patent, 31 December 1600. For details regarding the social implication of operating as 'one body corporate and politique', see Withington, *Politics of Commonwealth*, p. 81. For information on the foundation and development of the East India Company, see Chaudhuri, *The English East India Company*.

12. Percival Griffiths, *A Licence to Trade: The History of the English Chartered Companies* (London, 1974).

13. The relationship between state and company could wax and wane as circumstances demanded. See chapter 5 and Rupali Mishra, *A Business of State: Commerce, Politics and the Birth of the East India Company* (Boston, MA, 2017).

14. HHC, C BRE/5/10, Ordinances of Company of Merchants Inhabiting in Kingston upon Hull, 30 July 15[76]; HHC, C BRS/1/3, Petition to Queen Elizabeth from Kingston upon Hull, 11 May 1577. Hull received letters patent reconfirming privileges or targeting specific goods, such as corn or herring, from Queen Elizabeth I in 1576, 1577, 1582 and 1598. See John R. Boyle (ed.), *Charters and Letters Patent Granted to Kingston upon Hull* (Hull, 1905), pp. 84–130.

15. Differences between the privileges of different corporations, especially those defined as 'regulated' or 'joint-stock' companies, are explored in Pettigrew and Stein, 'Public rivalry'.

16. For a range of corporate charters and the specific privileges they granted, see Carr, *Charters*.

17. BL, Add Ms 20031, f. 14. Charter of the Levant Company, 9 November 1605.

– 255 –

NOTES to pp. 62–63

18. CMAY, 1/5/3/5/1. Thomas Pullison and Thomas Russell to the Merchant Adventurers of York, 2 September 1579.

19. Anver Greif, Paul Milgrom and Barry Weingast, 'Coordination, commitment, and enforcement: The case of the merchant guild', *Journal of Political Economy* 102 (1994), pp. 745–76.

20. Female members of these organisations were rare, but they could be influential. See Misha Ewen, 'Women investors in the Virginia Company in the early seventeenth century', *Historical Journal* 62, 4 (2019), pp. 853–74; Aske Brock and Misha Ewen, 'Women's public lives: Navigating the East India Company, Parliament and courts in early modern England', *Gender and History* 33, 1 (2020), pp. 3–23.

21. These practices were widespread across early modern England, see Withington, *Politics of Commonwealth*, pp. 29–37.

22. BL, Add Ms 9365, pp. 16–17. Register Book of the Spanish Company, 31 August 1604.

23. As we saw at the start of the chapter, for joint-stock organisations such as the East India Company, non-merchants could purchase stock and become members but were then excluded from both leadership positions in England and acting as factors overseas.

24. TNA, Patent Rolls, 9 Jac. 1, 35. Charter of the French Company, 1611; BL, Add Ms 20031, ff. 9–10. Charter of the Levant Company, 9 November 1605.

25. BL, Add Ms 9365, p. 26. Register Book of the Spanish Company, 31 August 1604.

26. CMAY, Acts and Ordinances of Eastland Merchants, f. iii. The requirement for time spent overseas was reduced to two years in 1617. CMAY, Acts and Ordinances of Eastland Merchants, ff. 5–7. 18 March 1617.

27. BL, Add Ms 9365, p. 51. Register Book of the Spanish Company, 1 July 1605.

28. HHC, C BRS/1/3, Petition to Queen Elizabeth from Kingston upon Hull, 11 May 1577.

– 256 –

NOTES to pp. 64–67

29. Full lists of members were regularly updated. For example, BA, SMV/2/1/1/1, f. 8. Merchants' Hall Book of Proceedings, 22 July 1639.

30. BL, Add Ms 9365, pp. 38–9. Register Book of the Spanish Company, 13 June 1605.

31. BA, AB/B/63, 3 folios at end of volume. Ledger of John Smith, [1550].

32. BL, Add Ms 9365, p. 3. Register Book of the Spanish Company, 29 March 1604.

33. Ibid., pp. 16–17. 31 August 1604.

34. TNA, SP 105/148. General Court, 30 July 1622.

35. TNA, SP 105/149. Levant Company minutes, 13 April 1633.

36. BA, SMV/2/1/1/1, ff. 5, 99. Merchants' Hall Book of Proceedings, 20 April 1639; 6 April 1647.

37. DC, MB 10, 2 February 1585; 17 February 1585; 13 October 1585; 14 January 1586; 4 May 1586; 10 October 1586; 3 August 1587.

38. TNA, SP 105/149. Levant Company minutes, 20 March 1633.

39. BL, Add Ms 9365, pp. 18–19. Register Book of the Spanish Company, 31 August 1604.

40. Ibid., p. 10. 24 May 1604.

41. CMAY, Acts and Ordinances of Eastland Merchants, ff. 5–7. 18 March 1617.

42. HL, EL2361. Richard Cocks' petition to Lord Chancellor Ellesmere, [undated].

43. CMAY, Trade Correspondence, London. John More's Comments on the Eastland Company, Merchant Adventurers and Spanish Trade, 1579.

44. BA, SMV/1/1/1/7, f. 77. Book of Charters, Acts, Ordinances and Decrees, [undated].

45. BL, Add Ms 18913, f. 81. The Lawes, Customs, and Ordinances, of the Fellowship of Merchant Adventurers, 1608.

46. BL, Add Ms 20031, f. 20. Charter of the Levant Company, 9 November 1605.

– 257 –

NOTES to pp. 67–70

47. BL, Add Ms 9365, p, 40. Register Book of the Spanish Company, 14 January 1605.

48. Ibid., p. 25. 19 September 1604.

49. CMAY, Acts and Ordinances of Eastland Merchants, ff. 7–8. 18 March 1617.

50. R.A. Roberts (ed.), *Calendar of the Cecil Papers in Hatfield House*, vol. 12 (London, 1910), pp. 698–706.

51. TNA, SP 105/148, General Court, 21 November 1622.

52. Ibid., General Court, 23 September 1623.

53. BL, Add Ms 9365, p. 40. Register Book of the Spanish Company, 15 January 1606.

54. Joyce Appleby, *Economic Thought and Ideology in Seventeenth Century England* (Princeton, NJ, 1978). This is discussed in further detail in chapters 4 and 5.

55. BL, Add Ms 14027, f. 277. King James I to Thomas Lowe, 3 December 1613.

56. TNA, SP 105/148. General Court, 20 February 1623; General Court, 15 March 1623.

57. TNA, Patent Rolls, 9 Jac. 1, 35. Charter of the French Company, 1611. For ongoing efforts to regulate British traders active in France, see Siobhan Talbott, 'British commercial interests of the French Atlantic Coast, c. 1560–1713', *Historical Research* 85, 229 (2012), pp. 394–409.

58. The extent of this control by a small oligarchic elite has, however, been exaggerated. See Brenner, *Merchants and Revolution*, p. 14.

59. LMA, COL/AD/01/030, ff. 19–20, 35–6. Corporation of London Letter Books, November 1611; 15 February 1612.

60. Different companies employed different terms but the 'generality' was commonly used to refer to all members of a corporation.

61. Glaisyer, *Culture of Commerce;* Zahedieh, 'Credit, risk and reputation'; Sheryllyne Haggerty, *'Merely for Money': Business Culture in the British Atlantic, 1750–1815* (Liverpool, 2012), pp. 66–96.

62. Archer, *Pursuit of Stability.*

NOTES to pp. 70–75

63. Aske Brock, 'Networks', in Pettigrew and Veevers (eds), *The Corporation as a Protagonist*, pp. 91–115; Smith, 'Global interests'.

64. TNA, SP 105/148. General Court, 16 October 1623.

65. Company directors were variously known as committees, assistants and wardens. They took on roles such as managing employees, overseeing shipping, arbitrating disputes and interacting with the state.

66. BL, Add Ms 9365, pp. 46–7. Register Book of the Spanish Company, 27 June 1605; IOR/A/1/2, Letters Patent, 31 December 1600.

67. StaffRO, D(W)1778/V/277, pp. 15–19. Patent of the Somers Island Company, 29 June 1616.

68. BL, IOR/B/10, General Court, 1 July 1625.

69. DC, MB 10, 2 August 1592

70. MC, AoC 1560–95, ff. 348–9. 22 March 1581.

71. TNA, SP 105/148. General Court, 16 October 1623.

72. East India Company, *Lawes and Standing Orders*, p. 2.

73. BL, Add Ms 20031, f. 6. Charter of the Levant Company, 9 November 1605.

74. BA, SMV/2/1/1/1, f. 1. Merchants' Hall Book of Proceedings, 11 May 1639.

75. The company had hundreds of members at this point. BL, Add Ms 9365, p. 11. Register Book of the Spanish Company, 8 June 1604.

76. MC, AoC 1595–1629, f. 128. 19 May 1613.

77. BA, SMV/2/1/1/1, f. 9. Merchants' Hall Book of Proceedings, 22 July 1639; CMAY, Acts and Ordinances of Eastland Merchants, ff. 1–2. 18 March 1617.

78. BL, IOR/B/9, 4 April 1623.

79. BL, IOR/B/6, General Court, 4 February 1620.

80. East India Company, *Lawes and Standing Orders*, p. 6.

81. BL, IOR/B/6, 4 February 1620.

82. Ibid., 14 April 1620.

83. BA, SMV/1/1/1/7, f. 76. Book of Charters. Acts, Ordinances and Decrees, [undated].

– 259 –

NOTES to pp. 75–80

84. BL, Add Ms 18913, f. 10. The Lawes, Customs, and Ordinances, of the Fellowship of Merchant Adventurers, 1608.

85. East India Company, *Lawes and Standing Orders*, p. 7.

86. LMA, COL/AD/01/028, f. 162. Corporation of London Letter Books, 17 June 1606.

87. CC, CL/B/1/4, Orders of Court, f. 248. 30 November 1621.

88. GL, Ms 34010/5, ff. 93–4. Merchant Tailors' Court of Assistants, 28 August 1613.

89. BL, IOR/B/5, 8 September 1615.

90. MC, AoC 1595–1629, f. 138. 10 February 1615.

91. Ibid., f. 36. August 1601.

92. DC, MB 11, 2 March 1601.

93. BL, Add Ms 18913, f. 143. The Lawes, Customs, and Ordinances, of the Fellowship of Merchant Adventurers, 1608.

94. TNA, SP 105/148. General Court, 9 June 1618.

95. CMAY, Acts and Ordinances of Eastland Merchants, ff. 12–13. 18 March 1617.

96. BL, Add Ms 18913, ff. 5–6. The Lawes, Customs, and Ordinances, of the Fellowship of Merchant Adventurers, 1608.

97. BL, Add Ms 9365, p. 9. Register Book of the Spanish Company, 14 May 1604.

98. BA, AC/C45/1. Ferdinando Gorges to Hugh Smith, 8 July 1623. The launch of the New England colony was being supported by wide-ranging printed accounts of the plantation's suitability for settlement, expansion and profit. For example, Council for New England, *A Brief Relation of the Discovery and Plantation of New England and of Sundry Accidents Therein Occurring* (London, 1622); William Bradford, *A Relation or Journal of the Beginning and Proceedings of the English Plantation Settled in Plimoth in New England, by certain English adventurers both merchants and others* (London, 1622).

99. BA, AC/C45/1. Gorges to Smith, 8 July 1623.

100. BA, AC/C45/2. Ferdinando Gorges to Hugh Smith, 16 July 1623.

101. Stern, *The Company-state*, p. 135.

NOTES to pp. 80–84

102. BL, IOR/A/1/2, Letters Patent, 31 December 1600.

103. BA, SMV/1/1/1/7, ff. 69–73. Book of Charters.

104. BL, Add Ms 20031, f. 6. Charter of the Levant Company, 9 November 1605.

105. BL, Add Ms 9365, pp. 46–7. Register Book of the Spanish Company, 27 June 1605.

106. BL, Add Ms 18913, ff. 3–4. The Lawes, Customs, and Ordinances, of the Fellowship of Merchant Adventurers, 1608.

107. Brock, 'The Company Director'.

108. East India Company, *Lawes and Standing Orders*, p. 6; HHC, C BRE/5/10, Ordinances of Company of Merchants Inhabiting in Kingston upon Hull, 30 July 1557.

109. For the ways expertise was presented in courtly spaces, see Ash, *Power, Knowledge, and Expertise*.

110. BL, Add Ms 9365, p. 1. Register Book of the Spanish Company, 16 March 1604.

111. Kenneth Andrews, *Elizabethan Privateering: English Privateering during the Spanish War, 1585–1603* (London, 1964), appendix.

112. BL, IOR/B/1, 1 November 1600.

113. CC, CL/B/1/4, Orders of Court, f. 21.

114. BL, IOR/B/3, 23 August 1609.

115. BL, IOR/B/6, 25 November 1617.

116. Ibid., 5 December 1617.

117. Hugh Calvert, *A History of Kingston upon Hull: From the Earliest Times to the Present Day* (London, 1978), p. 143.

118. TNA, SP 14/103, f. 64. Letter from John Pory to Dudley Carleton, 25 October 1618.

119. BL, IOR/B/1, 3 October 1600.

120. BL, IOR/B/5, 31 January 1615.

121. Ibid., 10 March 1615.

122. TNA, SP 105/148. General Court, 17 July 1618.

123. Similar practices of oath taking also underpinned private mercantile transactions and networks. See Miles Ogborn, 'The power of

– 261 –

NOTES to pp. 84–87

speech: Orality, oaths and evidence in the British Atlantic world, 1650–1800', *Transactions of the Institute of British Geographers* 36, 1 (2011), pp. 109–25.

124. BL, Add Ms 18913, f. 4. The Lawes, Customs, and Ordinances, of the Fellowship of Merchant Adventurers, 1608.

125. HHC, C BRE/5/10, Ordinances of Company of Merchants Inhabiting in Kingston upon Hull, 30 July 1557.

126. BA, SMV/1/1/1/7, ff. 69–73. Book of Charters. Acts, Ordinances and Decrees.

127. CMAY, Acts and Ordinances of Eastland Merchants, f. v. Oath of the secretary.

128. BL, Add Ms 9365, p. 14. Register Book of the Spanish Company, 20 August 1604.

129. TNA, SP 105/148. General Court, 8 May 1623.

130. Ibid.

131. BL, IOR/B/1, 27 October 1600–31 January 1601.

132. BL, IOR/B/9, 29 August 1624–1 December 1624.

133. Ibid., 20 October 1624.

134. MC, AoC 1595–1629, f. 321. 24 December 1627.

135. CMAY, Acts and Ordinances of Eastland Merchants, ff. 1–2. 18 March 1617.

136. BL, Add Ms 9365, p. 25. Register Book of the Spanish Company, 20 September 1604.

137. TNA, SP 16/540/1, f. 149. Certificate by Richard Young, 26 May 1631.

138. CMAY, Acts and Ordinances of Eastland Merchants, ff. 10–11. 18 March 1617.

139. Ibid., f. 1. 18 March 1617.

140. NRO, NCR/17/B/7, f. 17. Society of Merchants of the Staple to the Mayor and City and Norwich, 14 May 1617.

141. BL, Add Ms 9365, p. 4. Register Book of the Spanish Company, 29 March 1604.

NOTES to pp. 87–90

142. In 1604, only Bristol, Chester and Exeter had representatives appointed. BL, Add Ms 9365, p. 8. Register Book of the Spanish Company, 14 May 1604.

143. BL, Add Ms 9365, p. 6. Register Book of the Spanish Company, 14 May 1604.

144. CMAY, 1/5/3/5/2. The Merchant Adventurers of York to Thomas Pullison and Thomas Russell, 25 October 1579.

145. CMAY, 1/5/3/5/3. Thomas Pullison and Thomas Russell to the Merchant Adventurers of York, 10 November 1579.

146. CMAY, 1/5/3/5/4. William Gee to William Robinson, 9 January 1580.

147. CMAY, 1/5/3/5/5. The Merchant Adventurers of York to the Merchants of Hull, 11 January 1580.

148. CMAY, 1/5/3/5/6. Roger Raw to the Merchant Adventurers of York, 15 January 1580.

149. CMAY, 1/5/3/5/7. Christopher Hoddstone to the Merchant Adventurers of York, 17 August 1580.

150. TNA, PC 2/28, f. 275. Letter from certain Eastland merchants to Lord Knollis, Sir Thomas Lake and the Master of Rolls, 26 May 1616.

151. TNA, PC 2/28, f. 289. Report of the Attorney General, 5 June 1616.

152. CMAY, Acts and Ordinances of Eastland Merchants, f. 47. Eastland Company General Court, 3 February 1631.

153. BL, Add Ms 9365, pp. 35–6. Register Book of the Spanish Company, 8 June 1605.

154. Ibid.

155. TNA, SP 105/148. General Court, 15 April 1618.

156. Smith, 'Global interests', pp. 1142–6.

157. TNA, SP 84/94, f. 96. For the company's account of the election see: BL, IOR/B/6, General Court, 2 July 1619.

158. BL, IOR/B/9, General Court, 1 July 1625. Each was a long-standing member of a more traditional trading corporation:

– 263 –

NOTES to pp. 90–93

Garraway (Levant Company), Harby (French Company), Ducie (Merchant Adventurers).

159. TNA, SP 71/13, ff. 40–56. General observation of the Barbary trade, 4 April 1638.

160. TNA, SP 71/12, ff. 235–6. Terms of treaty with Morocco, 1635.

161. Russell, along with William Clobery, George Fletcher and John Woods, had previously acted as a customs farmer in Morocco, as well as supplying the state with arms and other goods.

162. TNA, SP 71/12, ff. 237–8. 1635, Notes on Barbary trade and order for formation of company.

163. TNA, SP 71/12, f. 246. Answer to a remonstrance presented against Sir William Courteen and other merchants trading to Barbary, 1635.

164. TNA, SP 71/13, f. 37. Robert Black to the Privy Council, March 1638.

165. TNA, SP 71/13, f. 84. Representations of Barbary merchants to Privy Council, 1638.

166. Prominent commercial figures in London, Garraway, Pindar and Abdy all had over three decades' experience in the Levant Company, as well as participating in the East India (Garraway and Abdy), Muscovy (Garraway), Somers Island (Abdy) and Virginia (Abdy) companies.

167. TNA, SP 71/13, f. 89. Certificate concerning the trade of the Barbary merchants, 20 March 1639.

168. Before long, their relationship with Mohammed esh-Sheikh es-Seghir broke down too, when the Moroccan monarch reneged on contracts made with Russell. TNA, SP 71/13, f. 98. Letter from William Russel to Sir Henry Vane, 10 November 1640.

169. TNA, SP 71/13, f. 95. 15 September 1639, Order for Hearing Merchants about Trading with Morocco.

170. BA, SMV/2/1/1/34, f. 104. The Privy Council to the City of Bristol, 18 September 1621.

– 264 –

NOTES to pp. 94–99

171. BA, SMV/2/1/1/34, f. 105. List of Orders from the New England Company, 1621.
172. BA, SMV/2/1/1/34, f. 110. The Mayor of Bristol to Ferdinando Gorges, 13 October 1621.
173. BA, SMV/2/1/1/34, ff. 111–12. The Mayor of Bristol to Mr Whitson and Mr Guy in London, October 1621.
174. BA, SMV/2/1/1/34, f. 110. The Mayor of Bristol to Ferdinando Gorges, 13 October 1621.
175. BA, SMV/2/1/1/34, f. 123. The New England Company to the City of Bristol, 1622.
176. Julie Svalastog, *Mastering the Worst of Trades: England's Early Africa Companies and Their Traders, 1618–1672* (Leiden, 2021).
177. TNA, C 2/Jas1/G18/13. The answer of Michael Best, 1622.

3 LIVING TOGETHER, WORKING TOGETHER

1. Thomas Middleton, *The Triumphs of Truth: a solemnity vnparalleled for cost, art, and magnificence, at the confirmation and establishment of that worthy and true nobly-minded gentleman, Sir Thomas Middleton, knight, in the honorable office of his Maiesties lieutenant, the lord maior of the thrice famous citty of London* (London, 1613).
2. Tracey Hill, *Pageantry and Power: A Cultural History of the Early Modern Lord Mayor's Show, 1585–1639* (Manchester, 2011) and '"To the Honour of our Nation abroad": The merchant as adventurer in civic pageantry', in J. Caitlin Finlayson and Amrita Sen (eds), *Civic Performance: Pageantry and Entertainments in Early Modern London* (London, 2020), pp. 13–31.
3. For explorations of London as an 'imperial' city, see Richard Barbour, *Before Orientalism: London's Theatre of the East, 1576–1626* (Cambridge, 2003), pp. 88–9; Imtiaz Habib, *Black Lives in the English Archives, 1500–1677: Imprints of the Invisible* (London, 2008); Lauren Working, *The Making of an Imperial Polity: Civility and America in the Jacobean Metropolis* (Cambridge, 2020).

– 265 –

NOTES to pp. 99–100

4. MC, Gresham Day Book, ff. 1–7.

5. Overseas trade grew more quickly in the sixteenth century and was outpaced by (and contributed to) domestic trade in the seventeenth century. Stephen Broadberry et al., *British Economic Growth, 1270–1870* (Cambridge, 2015), pp. 165–72. Merchant shipping consequently increased, from 67,000 tons in 1582 to 115,000 tons in 1626 and 340,000 tons by 1686. Ralph Davies, *The Rise of the English Shipping Industry in the 17th and 18th Centuries* (Newton Abbott, 1962), pp. 10, 15, 17.

6. For changing balance of products traded, see E.M. Carus-Wilson and Olive Coleman, *England's Export Trade, 1275–1547* (Oxford, 1963); Childs, *Anglo-Castilian Trade*; F.J. Fisher, 'London's export trade in the seventeenth century', *Economic History Review* 3, 2 (1950), pp. 151–61.

7. Newer trades regulated by London-based trading corporations such as the Levant, East India or Muscovy companies contributed to this dominance.

8. Derek Keene, 'Cities in cultural exchange', in Donatella Calabi and Stephen Tark (eds), *Cultural Exchange in Early Modern Europe*, vol. 2: *Cities and Cultural Exchange in Europe, 1400–1700* (Cambridge, 2007), p. 17. For changing consumption in response to global trading encounter, see Lisa Jardine, *Worldly Goods: A New History of the Renaissance* (London, 1996); Beverley Lemire, *Global Trade and the Transformation of Consumer Cultures: The Material World Remade, c. 1500–1820* (Cambridge, 2018); Sara Pennell, 'Consumption and consumerism in early modern England', *Historical Journal* 42, 2 (1999), pp. 549–64; Joan Thirsk, *Economic Policy and Projects: The Development of a Consumer Society in Early Modern England* (Oxford, 1978).

9. Bristol imports, £12,500 (1562–3); £83,000 (1637–8), see Richard Stone, 'The overseas trade of Bristol before the Civil War', *International Journal of Maritime History* 23, 2 (2011), pp. 219–25. For London imports, see A.M. Millard, *The Import Trade of London, 1600–1640* (London, 1956), p. 316.

– 266 –

NOTES to pp. 100–102

10. For East India Company and Levant Company imports, see Brenner, *Merchants and Revolution*, p. 29.

11. David Frank Lamb, 'The Seaborne Trade of Southampton in the First Half of the Seventeenth Century', MPhil thesis, University of Southampton, 1971, pp. 19, 43–9.

12. SA, SC9/3/11, f. 103. Voluntary Depositions of Peter Priaulx and Paul Mercer, 7 July 1625; SA, SC9/3/11, f. 112. Voluntary Depositions of Peter Priaulx and Paul Mercer, 12 November 1625.

13. TNA, SP 71/13, ff. 40–56. General observation of the Barbary trade, 4 April 1638.

14. BA, SMV/10/1/2/1–3. List of Members, [undated].

15. KHLC, U269/1/B103, m. 276. Price list of groceries in London, 5 September 1601 [French].

16. In 1565, woollen cloth accounted for an estimated 86.6 per cent of the total value of exports. Broadberry et al., *British Economic Growth*, p. 166.

17. LMA, CLC/B/013/Ms23953. Richard Archdale's *Journal of Receipts and Payments*, 1623–30.

18. HHC, C BRX/4b, Articles betwixt York and Hull relating to tolls, 17 September 1622.

19. BerkRO, AC, vol. 22, f. 145. Sir John Digby to William Trumbull, 8 January 1615.

20. These exports were particularly vulnerable to changing market conditions and periods of stagnation or wildly fluctuating export volumes were common. B.E. Supple, *Commercial Crisis and Change in England, 1600–1642* (Cambridge, 1959), pp. 257–67. For disruption caused by the Civil War, see Ben Coates, *The Impact of the English Civil War on the Economy of London, 1642–50* (Farnham, 2004), chapter 7.

21. These volumes relate specifically to shortcloths from London by English merchants. See Brenner, *Merchants and Revolution*, p. 9; Supple, *Commercial Crisis*, p. 258. For further analysis of the cloth trade, see chapter 4.

NOTES to pp. 102–104

22. Supple, *Commercial Crisis*, pp. 136–62.

23. Ibid., p. 153.

24. Stone, 'The overseas trade of Bristol', pp. 219–26.

25. Whereas around 75 per cent of shortcloth exports were destined for Russian, Baltic or North Sea ports, more that 70 per cent of all other commodities were exported elsewhere. Fisher, 'London's export trade', p. 154. For the trading environment of the Baltic and Muscovy trades, see Artur Attman, *The Russian and Polish Markets in International Trade, 1500–1650* (Göteborg, 1973).

26. TNA, SP 63/254, f. 214. Letter from Henry de Laune to Secretary Nicholas, 20 January 1634.

27. HHC, C DMT/35/167, List of those trading between Hull and London, 1609.

28. BL, Cotton Nero B XI, f. 304. Statement of advantages of Levant trade, 1604.

29. BL, Lansdowne Ms 487, f. 94. Inconveniences from impositions on foreign commodities, 1610.

30. NRS, GD124/15/27/86. Earl of Fenton to Earl of Mar, 28 September 1620.

31. BL, IOR/E/3/2, ff. 165–9. Raphe Preston at Ahmedabad to East India Company, 1 January 1615.

32. TNA, 84/590, f. 36. List of cargo on *Affricane* of London when taken by Dutch ship off coast of Barbary, 20 March 1619; TNA, SP 71/12, f. 111. Note of goods laded in Transport of London for Barbary, 4 March 1626.

33. HL, EL2380. Petition from the Merchant Adventurers to the Privy Council, [undated].

34. BL, Add Ms 36448, ff. 13–19. Complaints regarding treatment of merchants in Spain, 25 June–27 August 1635.

35. TNA, SP 105/149. Levant Company minutes, 17 February 1632.

36. MC, Gresham Day Book, 29 August 1549.

37. SA, SC9/3/11, f. 146. Voluntary Depositions of Burrish Daniel and Adrian Fry, 1 May 1627.

NOTES to pp. 105–107

38. TNA, C 2/JASI/IANDJ10/29/1. Petition to the Chancery Court, 27 November 1622.

39. StaffRO, D(W)1761/C/12. Agreement between the executors of William Buckley, 11 January 1639.

40. NRO, AYL/825. Indenture between Nicholas Osborne and John Osborne, 5 September 1621.

41. BLO, Ms Tanner 103, f. 221. Sir Arthur Gorges' project for general commerce, [undated].

42. NorthRO, C/2567. William Cockayne and William Towerson's articles of agreement with Sir John Jolles, 1 April 1611.

43. R. Porter, 'The Crispe Family and the African trade in the seventeenth century', *Journal of African History* 9, 1 (1968), pp. 57–77.

44. TNA, SP 16/279, f. 147. Petition of diverse merchants to Newfoundland to the Privy Council, 1634.

45. BL, Cotton Nero B XI, f. 304. Statement of advantages of Levant trade, 1604.

46. Twenty thousand is almost certainly an exaggeration, but the argument is nonetheless indicative of mercantile recognition of how overseas trade related to domestic production. TNA, SP 14/72, ff. 127–32. Anonymous memorandum on the cloth trade, March 1613. For the early development of England's cotton industry, see Stanley D. Chapman, *The Cotton Industry in the Industrial Revolution* (London, 1987), pp. 11–16.

47. NRO, NCR/17/B/7, f. 33. Petition from the Mayor, Aldermen, Common Council, Burgesses and Inhabitants of Kings Lynn to the Privy Council, 27 May 1623.

48. StaffRO, D339/52/13/29. Article of agreement between Benedict Webb and George Mole, 19 February 1624.

49. TNA, SP 14/72, ff. 127–32. Anonymous memorandum on the cloth trade, March 1613.

50. For the scope, structure and significance of these networks, see Smith, 'Global interests of London's commercial community' and

NOTES to pp. 107–109

'The social networks of investment in early modern England', *Historical Journal* (2020).

51. Trivellato, *Familiarity of Strangers*, p. 155. As discussed in chapters 1 and 2, while religion did contribute in some cases to strengthening England's merchants' personal networks, common corporate and mercantile practices were more important for providing foundations for business relationships across this whole community. For an example of how religious strengthened one commercial network, see Esther Sahle, 'Law and gospel order: Resolving commercial disputes in colonial Philadelphia', *Continuity and Change* (2020).

52. Through their common networks, merchants were constrained by forms of 'communal' governance, see Smith, 'Governance'.

53. Tom Leng, 'Epistemology: Expertise and knowledge in the world of commerce', in Stern and Wennerlind (eds), *Mercantilism Reimagined*, pp. 97–116. For the role of credit, trust and reputation in early modern commercial networks, see Muldrew, *Economy of Obligation*; Zahedieh, 'Credit, risk and reputation'.

54. Trivellato, *Familiarity of Strangers*, p. 155.

55. Urban corporations were an increasingly common feature in early modern England. See Withington, *Politics of Commonwealth*, pp. 3–50.

56. Christopher Dyer, *An Age of Transition? Economy and Society in England in the Later Middle Ages* (Oxford, 2004), pp. 1–6.

57. Giuseppe Dari-Mattiaci et al., 'The emergence of the corporate form', *Journal of Law, Economics and Organisation* 33, 2 (2017), pp. 193–236.

58. For example, Southampton had welcomed Italian merchants since the thirteenth century and was a key conduit for Italian ideas and practices to enter England's merchants' skill set. See Alwyn Ruddock, *Italian Merchants and Shipping in Southampton, 1270–1600* (Southampton, 1951); Olive Coleman, 'Trade and prosperity in the fifteenth century: Some aspects of the trade of Southampton', *Economic History Review* 16, 1 (1963), pp. 9–22. Merchants from

– 270 –

NOTES to pp. 109–110

Bristol had engaged with the eastern Mediterranean as early as 1457 and sustained strong links across Spanish and Portuguese expansion into the Atlantic; see Dalton, *Merchants and Explorers*; Stuart Jenks, *Robert Sturmey's Commercial Expedition to the Mediterranean (1457–8): with editions of the trial of the Genoese before king and council and other sources* (Bristol, 2006).

59. Robert Batchelor, *London: The Selden Map and the Making of a Global City, 1549–1689* (Chicago, 2014).

60. This trend continued into the seventeenth century and the population of London has been estimated to have grown from 250,000 to 320,000 people between 1603 and 1625. Norman G. Brett-James, *The Growth of Stuart London* (London, 1935), p. 512.

61. Rabb, *Enterprise and Empire*, pp. 22–6.

62. In the Low Countries, cities were undergoing similar developments, and after the Dutch revolt, Amsterdam would rapidly develop and become London's major international competitor. See Gelderblom, *Cities of Commerce*.

63. Dyer, *An Age of Transition*, pp. 157–72.

64. A. Beier and Roger Finlay (eds), *London, 1500–1700: The Making of the Metropolis* (London, 1986); Keene, 'Cities in cultural exchange', in Calabi and Tark (eds), *Cultural Exchange*, p. 17.

65. Nuala Zahedieh, *The Capital and the Colonies: London and the Atlantic Economy, 1660–1700* (Cambridge, 2010), p. 15.

66. This was also part of a wider process in England during the seventeenth century towards investing in 'improvement'. Slack, *Invention of Improvement*.

67. For the relationship between livery companies and the East India Company, see Smith, 'Social networks of investment'; for the Virginia Company, see Terence O'Brien, 'The London livery companies and the Virginia Company', *Virginia Magazine of History and Biography* 68, 2 (1960), pp. 137–55.

68. Janelle Day Jenstad, 'Public glory, private gilt: The Goldsmiths' Company and the spectacle of punishment', in Anne Goldgar and

– 271 –

NOTES to pp. 110–112

Robert L. Frost (eds), *Institutional Culture in Early Modern Society*, pp. 191–217; Stephan Epstein and Maarten Prak (eds), *Guilds, Innovation, and the European Economy* (Cambridge, 2010); Rappaport, *Worlds within Worlds*; George Unwin, *The Gilds and Companies of London* (London, 1963).

69. During the period 1600 to 1615, the livery company affiliation of 302 members can be identified. Many are recorded in London's Livery Companies Online (ROLLCO).

70. Smith, 'Social networks of investment'.

71. For details of London's built environment, surveying techniques and plans of various properties, see John Schofield (ed.), *The London Surveys of Ralph Tresswell* (London, 1987); Dorian Gerhold, *London Plotted: Plans of London Buildings, c. 1450–1720* (London, 2016).

72. CC, CL/G/7/1, Treswell Survey, f. 21. 1617.

73. LMA, CLC/434/Ms14004/002. Indenture for Francis Hodgson to purchase property from Richard Chamblett, 1633.

74. CC, CL/G/7/1, Treswell Survey, f. 43. 1617.

75. Smith, 'Social networks of investment', p. 15.

76. John Stow, *A Survey of London. Reprinted from the Text of 1603*, ed. C.L. Kingsford (Oxford, 1908), pp. 129–38, 163–200.

77. These merchants all rented property from the Drapers' Company for between £2 and £14 per year; DC, RA 6/26, ff. 4–5 (a final property was rented to Sir Milton Lambard). They were members of the following overseas companies: William Cockayne (Spanish, Eastland, East India, French, Irish, North-West Passage, Baffin Island, and Virginia), Thomas Lowe (Merchant Adventurers, East India), Henry Garraway (Levant, East India, Muscovy), Isaac Jones (Merchant Adventurers), William Garraway (Levant, East India, North-West Passage, Virginia, Somers Island), William Towerson (Spanish, French, Irish, North-West Passage, Merchant Adventurers, East India), William Callie (Merchant Adventurers), John Williams (Levant, Irish, Muscovy, East India).

78. CC, CL/G/7/1, Treswell Survey, f. 15. 1617.

NOTES to pp. 112–115

79. Ibid., ff. 34–5.

80. Roger Leech, 'The symbolic hall: Historical context and merchant culture in the early modern city', *Vernacular Architecture* 31, 1 (2000), pp. 1–10.

81. Jean Vanes (ed.), *The Ledger of John Smythe, 1538–1550* (London, 1974), p. 79.

82. TNA, PROB 2/438. Probate Inventory of Richard Astell, 1658.

83. MC, AoC 1595–1629, f. 128. 11 August 1613. The same benefits were granted to Lionel Duckett and Halliday upon their elections to the office; ff. 141, 164. 16 August 1615; 28 May 1617.

84. Both events were described during a meeting of the Drapers' livery company. DC, MB 13, 20 January 1604.

85. MC, AoC 1595–1629, ff. 26–7. 27 August 1599.

86. HRO, 44M69/L35/5. Letter from Mayor of Southampton to Henry Sherfield, 19 December 1623.

87. BL, Add Ms 9365, p. 1. Register Book of the Spanish Company, 16 March 1604; TNA, SP 105/148. General Court, 11 December 1617.

88. LMA, CLA/008/EM/02/01/001/138V/08, City Land Estates, East India Company.

89. BL, IOR/B/6, 25 June 1619.

90. BL, Add Ms 48155, ff. 1–2. Minutes of conference relating to the East Indies, 30 March–30 April 1613.

91. BL, Add Ms 9365, p. 6. Register Book of the Spanish Company, 14 May 1604; HHC, DSN/1, Monthly Court, 4 October 1647.

92. Attendance at these dinners could also be enforced and directors fined for failing to participate. See GL, Ms 15842/1, f. 240. 8 February 1625.

93. GL, Ms 11571/010, ff. 271–2. Grocers' Company Wardens Accounts, 1601–11.

94. Consequently, the city regulated 'there shall not any fireworks be used at any Mayor's feast, either upon the day of the feast, the day before, nor after'. NRO, NCR/16/C/5, f. 417. Norwich Assembly Book, 2 March 1612.

95. DC, MB 13, 15 April 1605

NOTES to pp. 116–118

96. Ibid., 3 September 1606, 5 February 1629.
97. MC, AoC 1595–1629, ff. 49, 136, 144, 312. 11 August 1603; 7 September 1614; 3 November 1615; 15 August 1627.
98. Ibid., f. 299. 8 December 1626.
99. DC, MB 13, 4 June 1622; 4 April 1626.
100. Ibid., 5 August 1611
101. LMA, COL/AD/01/028, f. 49. Corporation of London Letter Books, 18 March 1605.
102. Derek Keene, 'The setting of the Royal Exchange: Continuity and change in the financial district of the City of London, 1300–1871', in Ann Saunders, *The Royal Exchange* (London, 1991).
103. A committee of London citizens undertook the management of the Royal Exchange, with equal members appointed by the City of London corporation and the Mercers' livery company.
104. MC, Gresham Repertory 1596–1625, ff. 18, 225, 240, 246, 259. 26 September 1597; 25 February 1617; 1621; 18 April 1622; 27 April 1625; LMA, COL/AD/01/032, f. 151. Corporation of London Letter Book, 20 May 1625.
105. MC, Gresham Repertory 1596–1625, f. 29. 2 February 1598.
106. Ibid., f. 25. 13 January 1598.
107. Ibid., f. 13. 13 July 1597.
108. BL, IOR/B/5, 15 September 1615.
109. Stow, *A Survey of London*, pp. 187–200.
110. Glaisyer, *Culture of Commerce*, pp. 27–68. Games, *Web of Empire*, pp. 81–2; Keene, 'Cities in cultural exchange' in Calabi and Tark (eds), *Cultural Exchange*.
111. BL, Add Ms 12497, f. 279. Speech by the Lord Treasurer to the Lord Mayor in the Exchange, 29–30 October 1609.
112. MC, Gresham Repertory 1596–1625, f. 188. 11 February 1608.
113. LMA, COL/AD/01/028, f. 47. Corporation of London Letter Books, 7 January 1605.
114. CC, CL/B/1/4, Orders of Court, f. 1. 16 September 1605; MC, AoC 1595–1629, f. 120. 8 November 1611.

NOTES to pp. 118–120

115. GL, Ms 15842/1, f. 92. 20 June 1597.

116. MC, AoC 1595–1629, ff. 257–8. 26 April; 12 May 1624.

117. LMA, CLA/008/EM/02/01/1, f. 50. Lease granted to the Haberdashers' Company, 1601; LMA, CLA/008/EM/02/01/1, f. 137. Muscovy Company's lease from the City of London for Botolph's Wharf, 1615.

118. NorthRO, C/2691. Payment of £26 from Henry Garraway to William Cockayne, Matthew Craddock and Jacob Price, 20 June 1635.

119. MC, AoC 1595–1629, ff. 37–8, 43, 46, 58, 60–2, 66, 69–70. 11 November 1601; 20 November 1602; 15 April 1603; 14 November 1604; 20 February 1605; 15 May 1605; 14 May 1606.

120. LMA, COL/AD/01/030, f. 52. Corporation of London Letter Book, 11 July 1612.

121. Supplying water had been a long-term problem for the City of London corporation, but efforts to fund the essential work independently had failed. LMA, COL/AD/01/028, ff. 174–5. Corporation of London Letter Books, 10 July 1605.

122. TNA, Patent Rolls, 17Jac1, 16. Charter of the New River Company, 1619.

123. BerkRO, D/EN/O24, ff. 3, 4. Payment to Hugh Middleton, 26 November 1610; Hugh Middleton to Henry Neville, 29 July 1613.

124. TNA, Patent Rolls, 17Jac1, 16. For further detail regarding this scheme and corporation, see Robert Ward, *London's New River* (Whitstable, 2003). The joint-stock model used by the New River Company had more in common with those used for mines and mills than with trading companies; see Harris, *Going the Distance*, pp. 267–9.

125. MC, Gresham Repertory 1596–1625, f. 209; BL, Add Ch 56224. Lease between Hugh Middleton and Hugh Merrick and Hugh Coloe, 17 March 1617.

126. LMA, COL/AD/01/032, f. 51. Corporation of London Letter Book, 13 November 1623; 16 March 1624.

NOTES to pp. 121–125

127. For link between communal and institutional governance, see Smith, 'Governance'.

128. NorthRO, C/2441. Gerard Malynes to William Cockayne, 8 July 1624.

129. Archer, *Pursuit of Stability*, pp. 100–30.

130. CMAY, Acts and Ordinances of Eastland Merchants, f. 37. 18 March 1617.

131. CC, CL/B/1/4, Orders of Court, f. 1. 4 October 1605.

132. DC, MB 10, 3 April 1586.

133. MC, AoC 1595–1629, f. 32. 6 August 1600.

134. BA, SMV/2/1/1/1, f. 9. Merchants' Hall Book of Proceedings, 22 July 1639.

135. NRO, YC/19/5, f. 5. Great Yarmouth Assembly Book, 8 December 1598.

136. LMA, CLC/B/227/Ms 29393. Thomas Rogers to William Hurt, 11 July 1636.

137. GL, Ms 15842/1, f. 152. 2 June 1606.

138. MC, Gresham Repertory 1596–1625, f. 3. 13 April 1597.

139. Ibid., f. 24. December 1597.

140. Calvin F. Senning, 'Piracy, politics, and plunder under James I: The voyage of the "Pearl" and its aftermath, 1611–1615', *Huntingdon Library Quarterly* 46, 3 (1983), pp. 187–222.

141. KHLC, U269/1/B28. List of goods received out of ships Godspeed (at Plymouth), Ann, Daisy and Dreadnought, 1614; KHLC, U269/1/B27, m. 280–285. Inventories of cargoes brought to London from Chester and Dover, 10 May 1614.

142. KHLC, U269/1/B20, m. 230. Anonymous deposition concerning Castleton's voyage, [undated, *c.* 1615].

143. KHLC, U269/1/B44, m. 313. Certificate of money ventured by John Ramsey, [undated, *c.* 1615].

144. Between March and August 1614 the goods were sold to Hugh Hamersley (who purchased £2,215 1s 8d of mace), William Drew (£678 2s 19d of cloves), Edward Beale (£231 18s of mace and

NOTES to pp. 125–126

£395 10s 2d of yellow shades), Philip Burlamachi (£1,303 2s of benjamin and £456 10s 2d of lignum aloe), Thomas Dalby (£3,571 12s 3d of nutmeg, £33 18s 10d of cloves, and £1,306 3s 9d of stalk of cloves), and £151 18s of raw silk were sold to James Trott, a silk man. Barring Trott and the rest of the buyers were all merchants with strong connections to the East India Company. KHLC, U269/1/B33, m. 288. Richard Perrott's account of sales of goods from the Pearl, March–August 1614.

145. Although Ellis and Sotherton would have to wait until 1621 until they actually received payment. KHLC, U269/1/B39, m. 235; 299; 263. Letter from Arthur Ingram to Lionel Cranfield, 1614; Account of transaction of Arthur Ingram, 1614; The Lord Treasurer's and Lionel Cranfield's certificate for £6,000, 1621.

146. TNA, SP 105/148. General Court, 11 December 1617; A Court at Whitehall, 21 December 1617.

147. Trivellato, *Familiarity of Strangers*, pp. 153–4.

148. DC, MB 10, 8 February 1585; CC, CL/B/1/4, Orders of Court, f. 101. 22 August 1612.

149. Leveson complained about the Bourmans' action to the Mercers' livery company who ordered the suit be staid should the debts be paid immediately. MC, AoC 1595–1629, f. 165. 30 July 1617.

150. TNA, PC 2/26, f. 239. Meeting of the Privy Council, 7 June 1601.

151. NorthRO, C/3215. Letter from John Swinnerton, William Cockayne, Richard Wheeler, Robert Smythe, Robert Offley to James Huishe, Richard Cooper, John Hanbury, John Hophins, John Bowater and John Blewett, 1 May 1612.

152. Tom Leng, 'Interlopers and disorderly brethren at the Stade Mart: Commercial regulations and practices among the Merchant Adventurers of England in the late Elizabethan period', *Economic History Review* 69, 3 (2016), pp. 823–43.

153. NRO, YC/19/5, f. 150. Great Yarmouth Assembly Book, 2 June 1615.

154. TNA, SP 105/148. General Court, 21 August 1623.

– 277 –

NOTES to pp. 127–133

155. BL, Add Ms 18913, f. 143–4. The Lawes, Customs, and Ordinances, of the Fellowship of Merchant Adventurers, 1608; CMAY, Acts and Ordinances of Eastland Merchants, f. 28. 18 March 1617.

156. TNA, SP 91/1, f. 185. Answer of the Muscovy merchants concerning Barne, 1602.

157. BA, SMV/2/1/1/1, ff. 61, 63. Merchants' Hall Book of Proceedings, 28 November 1643.

158. Ibid., f. 63. 7 December 1643.

159. BL, IOR/E/3/2, f. 161. 29 December 1614, William Edwards, John Aldworth and Edward Dadsworth at Ahmedabad to Mr Oxwick, Mr Farewell and Mr Ball at Bharuch.

160. TNA, SP 105/148. General Court, 14 February 1618; Levant Company minutes, 15 December 1618. For ongoing discussion of managed voyage with generality, see TNA, SP 105/148. General Court, 11 March 1618; 15 April 1618; 8 January 1619.

161. Ibid., General Court, 8 January 1619.

162. Ibid., General Court, 25 February 1619.

163. Ibid., General Court, 15 March 1619.

164. Ibid., General Court, 19 March 1619.

165. TNA, SP 105/149. Levant Company minutes, 7 March 1632.

166. Ibid., Levant Company minutes, 18 July 1632.

4 MONOPOLISTS AND INTERLOPERS

1. MHS, Ms N-760, ff. 3–7. William Pynchon Papers, 1640–7; MHS: Miscellaneous Bound 1629–1658. Notes Regarding Pynchon–Mason Dispute, 1639.

2. Jones and Ville, 'Efficient transactors or rent-seeking monopolists'.

3. BL, Cotton Nero B XI, f. 114. Reasons wherefore certain able merchants should be of the new corporation to Levant, October 1591. Other proposals supporting the new company also focused on the small number of current participants as a key weakness: BL,

– 278 –

NOTES to pp. 133–137

Lansdowne 112, f. 116. Proposal for regulations for merchants of Tripoli, [1591].

4. BL, Cotton Nero B XI, f. 116. Names of persons to be entered in her majesty's grant for the Turkey and Venice trade, 1591.

5. BL, Lansdowne Ms 150, f. 24. Petition from Merchant Adventurers to the Privy Council, 14 June 1601.

6. Robert Ashton, 'The parliamentary agitation for free trade in the opening years of the Reign of James I', *Past & Present* 38, 1 (1967), pp. 40–55; Theodore Rabb, 'Free trade and the gentry in the parliament of 1604', *Past & Present* 40, 1 (1968), pp. 165–73; David Harris Sacks, 'The countervailing of benefits: Monopoly, liberty and benevolence in Elizabethan England', in Dale Hoak (ed.), *Tudor Political Culture* (Cambridge, 1995), pp. 272–91.

7. BL, Lansdowne Ms 487, ff. 149–59. Instructions touching the bill for free trade, [undated, *c.* 1604–6].

8. HL, EL2389. Reasons restraint of cloth trade to Mart Towns is beneficial to the common wealth, [undated]. For the company's efforts to enforce its monopoly (and the limitations thereof), see Leng, 'Commercial conflict and regulation' and 'Interlopers and disorderly brethren'.

9. BL, Lansdowne Ms 487, ff. 146–8. Reasons on behalf of the Merchant Adventurers and other companies, showing their maintenance as at present is better for the state than such a liberty as the Lower House have agreed on, [*c.* 1604–6].

10. BL, Add Ms 20031, ff. 3–7. Charter of the Levant Company, 9 November 1605.

11. TNA, Patent Rolls, 9 Jac. 1, 35. Charter of the French Company, 1611.

12. HL, EL2463. Reasons for a joint-stock Muscovy Company, [*c.* 1603–18].

13. Anon., *A Discourse Consisting of Motives for the Enlargement and Freedom of Trade: especially that of cloth and other woollen manufactures* (London, 1645), pp. i–ii, 26–7.

NOTES to pp. 137–141

14. Greater Manchester County Archives, GB127.Tracts/P.2034.14. *A Brief Narration of the Present Estate of the Bilbao Trade*, 1648.
15. CC, CL/B/1/4, Orders of Court, f. 28. 17 November 1607.
16. CC, CL/B/1/4, Orders of Court, f. 2. 4 November 1605.
17. BA, SMV/1/1/1/7, f. 80. Book of Charters.
18. BL, Add Ms 9365, pp. 43–4. Register Book of the Spanish Company, 14 June 1605.
19. CMAY, Account Rolls, 1605–6.
20. NRO, YC/19/5, f. 17. Great Yarmouth Assembly Book, 5 September 1600.
21. NRO, NCR/17/B/7, ff. 21–2. Petition from Aldermen of City of Norwich to the Privy Council, 27 November 1618.
22. HL, EL2384. Merchant Adventurers to Privy Council, [*c.* 1581].
23. BL, Add Ms 9365, p. 100. Register Book of the Spanish Company, 6 September 1605.
24. Mariners used small-scale private trade as a common means for supplementing their wages, see Richard Blakemore, 'Pieces of eight, pieces of eight: Seamen's earnings and the venture economy of early modern seafaring', *Economic History Review* 70, 4 (2017), pp. 1153–84.
25. BL, Lansdowne Ms 142, f. 290. Recommendation of Mr Bell, Mr Hall and other merchants of London, 2 September 1609.
26. CMAY, Acts and Ordinances of Eastland Merchants, ff. 4–5, 25. 18 March 1617.
27. Ibid., f. 44. Eastland Company General Court, 10 February 1623.
28. Of course, in some situations local officials might assist the illicit traders, see Evan Jones, *Inside the Illicit Economy: Reconstructing the Smugglers' Trade of Sixteenth century Bristol* (Abingdon, 2012).
29. From Portsmouth's now lost Election and Sessions Books in Robert East (ed.), *Extracts from Records in Possession of the Municipal Corporation of the Borough of Portsmouth* (Portsmouth, 1891), p. 151.
30. BL, Add Ms 9365, pp. 45–6. Register Book of the Spanish Company, 27 June 1605.

NOTES to pp. 141–143

31. NRO, Ms 2650, 4A2. Thomas Sackville to the Port Officers of Great Yarmouth, 27 June 1605.
32. TNA, SP 105/149. Levant Company minutes, 26 July 1632.
33. BL, Lansdowne 69, f. 48. Letter from Thomas Heson to the Lord Treasurer, 8 January 1592.
34. TNA, SP 105/148. General Court, 25 February 1619.
35. BL, Add Ms 18913, f. 42. The Lawes, Customs, and Ordinances, of the Fellowship of Merchant Adventurers, 1608.
36. CMAY, Acts and Ordinances of Eastland Merchants, f. 31. 18 March 1617.
37. Ibid., f. 44. Eastland Company General Court, 10 February 1623.
38. TNA, SP 71/12, f. 2. Discourse of John Williams, March 1577.
39. TNA, SP 71/12, ff. 14, 19. Request of merchants trading in Barbary, 8 April 1583; Reasons to the contrary of incorporating merchants trading in Barbary, 1585.
40. TNA, SP 105/149. Levant Company minutes, 14 November 1632; 28 November 1632.
41. Ibid., 11 December 1632; 27 December 1632; 28 December 1632; 26 March 1633.
42. Ibid., 28 March 1633; 1 April 1633; 9 April 1633.
43. The role of private trade by members of corporate organisations has received considerable attention and recent work has demonstrated the positive benefits of such actors in filling the gaps between corporate activity and local market demands. See Erikson, *Between Monopoly and Free Trade*.
44. BL, Lansdowne Ms 86/81. Letter from Merchant Adventurers to Lord Burghley, 1598; BL, Lansdowne 112, f. 120. Letter from the Barbary Company, [1604–25].
45. For conflict between holders of patents or other privileges in England and domestic 'interlopers' and critics, see Koji Yamamoto, *Taming Capitalism before its Triumph: Public Service, Distrust, and 'Projecting' in Early Modern England* (Oxford, 2018), pp. 68–104.

– 281 –

NOTES to pp. 144–147

46. PRONI, D3632/A/45/2d. Robert Russell to the Drapers' Company, 17 October 1618.

47. SA, SC6/1/29. Leet Court, 1605.

48. The relationship between merchants and the state is the focus of chapter 5.

49. BL, Lansdowne Ms 142, ff. 389–90. Petition from the Muscovy Company, 22 January 1617.

50. TNA, SP 14/94, f. 113. Reasons why the inhabitants of Kingston upon Hull should prosecute the whale fishery in the northern seas, December 1617.

51. TNA, SP 14/94, f. 111. Petition from the Muscovy Company, 20 December 1617.

52. BL, Lansdowne Ms 142, ff. 389–90. Petition from the Muscovy Company, 22 January 1617; TNA, SP 14/94, f. 111. Petition from the Muscovy Company, 20 December 1617.

53. BL, IOR/B/3, 27 July 1609; Green, *Calendar of State Papers Domestic*, vol. 1, p. 565.

54. BL, IOR/B/5, 14 March, 1614; His Majesty's Stationery Office, *Acts of the Privy Council*, vol. 33, pp. 78–9, 375.

55. BL, IOR/B/5, 15 November 1614.

56. TNA, PC 2/31, f. 681. Meeting at Whitehall, 31 April 1623.

57. TNA, SP 91/2, f. 5. Petition from the Muscovy Company to James I, 1614.

58. TNA, PC 2/29, f. 141. Hearing of a complaint by the Muscovy Company, 14 October 1617.

59. BL, Cotton Nero B XI, f. 96. Letter from Henry Lello to the Levant Company, 4 July 1600.

60. BL, Lansdowne Ms 142, f. 67. Letter from Elizabeth I to the Doge of Venice, February 1600.

61. BL, Cotton Nero B XI, f. 96. Letter from Henry Lello to the Levant Company, 4 July 1600.

62. Ibid., ff. 97–8. Letter from Henry Lello to the Levant Company, 19 July 1600.

NOTES to pp. 147–151

63. Ibid., ff. 96, 97–8. Letter from Henry Lello to the Levant Company, 4 July 1600; 19 July 1600.

64. BL IOR B/5, 1 July 1614.

65. TNA, SP 14/103, f. 64. Letter from John Pory to Dudley Carleton, 25 October 1618. For more about Robert Rich's interests in piracy, see W. Craven, 'The Earl of Warwick, a speculator in piracy', *Hispanic American Historical Review* 10, 4 (1930), pp. 457–79.

66. BL, Cotton Nero B XI, f. 253. Letter from Sir Paul Pindar to the Lord Treasurer, 19 December 1612.

67. For the willingness of James I and Charles I to issue patents, see Yamamoto, *Taming Capitalism*, pp. 47–67.

68. CMAY, Trade Correspondence, London. John More's Comments on the Eastland Company, Merchant Adventurers and Spanish Trade, 1579.

69. Competition between the corporations and the state, too, could relate to broader domestic constituencies. See William Pettigrew and Edmond Smith, 'Corporate management, labor relations, and community building at the East India Company's Blackwall dockyard, 1600–57', *Journal of Social History* 53, 1 (2019), pp. 133–56.

70. Giuseppi, *Calendar*, vol. 17, p. 205.

71. TNA, SP 14/94, f. 208. Petition from the Eastland and Spanish companies to the Privy Council, 1617.

72. NRO, NCR/7/B/10. Petition to Queen Elizabeth I from the City of Norwich, *c.* 1570–80s.

73. NRO, NCR/16/C/5, ff. 263, 390. Norwich Assembly Book, 5 January 1608; 15 January 1610.

74. LMA, COL/AD/01/030, ff. 48–9. Corporation of London Letter Book, 11 July 1612.

75. KHLC, U269/1/OE239a, m. 5682. Petition from the Eastland Company, 1622.

76. NRO, YC/19/5, ff. 48, 90, 119, 142. Great Yarmouth Assembly Book, 14 August 1605; 30 September 1611; 17 October 1613; 7 October 1614.

NOTES to pp. 151–154

77. Ibid., f. 121. Great Yarmouth Assembly Book, 15 November 1613.

78. TNA, SP 105/148. General Courts, 17 July 1618; 19 October 1618.

79. SA, SC2/1/6, f. 159. Assembly Book, 31 May 1616; HRO, 44M69/L35/5. Letter from Mayor of Southampton to Henry Sherfield, 19 December 1623.

80. HRO, 44M69/L30/66. Letter from William Neven to Henry Sherfield, 21 January 1624.

81. HRO, 44M69/L35/16. Letter from Southampton Assembly to Henry Sherfield, 8 December 1624.

82. HRO, 44M69/L35/18. Letter from John Elleye to Henry Sherfield, 20 December 1624.

83. HRO, 44M69/L35/22. Letter from Southampton Assembly to Henry Sherfield, 26 August 1625.

84. After eight years the dispute reached the privy council, who were sympathetic, but the Levant Company's privileges were never revoked. HRO, 44M69/L35/51. Letter from Southampton Assembly to Henry Sherfield, 10 May 1633.

85. BL, Lansdowne Ms 86, f. 26. Petition from the City of Bristol to Lord Burghley, 20 January 1598.

86. BA, SMV/1/1/1/7, f, 45. Book of Charters. 1611.

87. Ibid., ff. 45–9. Book of Charters. 1611.

88. HHC, C BRS/46f, Articles declaring the causes why the merchants of York are not to be joined with the incorporation of Hull, [c. 1578].

89. HHC, C BRS/46g, Inconveniences that may arise and grow to her majesty's town and port of Kingston upon Hull, [c. 1578].

90. HHC, C BRX/4a, Agreement between York and Kingston upon Hull, 28 June 1578.

91. HHC, C BRS/46h, Articles between the City of York and Kingston upon Hull, 28 June 1578.

92. HHC, C BRS/2/1/1, A brief of complaints against London merchants, [c. 1590]; HHC, C BRS/2/1/2, Letter from Earl of Huntington to Mr Fanshaw, 18 December 1590.

– 284 –

NOTES to pp. 154–156

93. HHC, C BRS/2/1/3, Petition to Queen Elizabeth, [c. 1590].

94. HHC, C BRS/2/1/4, Petition to Lord Treasurer from Kingston upon Hull, 1590.

95. Edward Gillett and Kennet MacMahon, *A History of Hull* (Hull, 1980), pp. 136–7.

96. HHC, C BRS/2/2, Order of the Privy Council, 24 December 1592.

97. HHC, C BRV/44/1, Mayor and Burgesses of Hull v Robert Brooke and other merchants of London, 26 June 1596.

98. At the foundation of the Levant Company in 1591, 9,480 hundredweight of currants had been imported into England but over the course of the following five decades imports rose to a peak of 62,512 hundredweight in 1638. See Brenner, *Merchants and Revolution*, p. 27.

99. For negotiations between the Levant Company and the state regarding their chartered privileges, see Pauline Croft, 'Fresh light on Bate's case', *Historical Journal* 30, 3 (1987), pp. 523–39.

100. Edward Coke's influence on the legal constitution of England's emerging commercial empire was considerable. See Barbara Malament, 'The "economic liberalism" of Sir Edward Coke', *Yale Law Journal* 76, 7 (1987), pp. 1321–58; Daniel Hulsebosch, 'The ancient constitution and the expanding empire: Sir Edward Coke's British jurisprudence', *Law and History Review* 21, 3 (2003), pp. 439–82; Paul Raffield, 'Contract, classicism, and the commonweal: Coke's *Reports* and the foundations of the modern English constitution', *Law and Literature* 17, 1 (2005), pp. 69–96.

101. TNA, SP 105/148. General Court, 17 December 1617; TNA, SP 105/148. A Court at Whitehall, 21 December 1617.

102. Jenks, *Robert Sturmey's Expedition*.

103. BA, SMV/1/1/1/7, f. 57. Book of Charters. 1617.

104. BA, SMV/2/1/1/34, f. 51. John Whitson and John Barker to the Merchant Venturers, 10 February 1618.

105. BA, SMV/2/1/1/34, f. 52. The Merchant Venturers to John Whitson and John Barker, 16 February 1618.

NOTES to pp. 157–160

106. TNA, SP 105/148. General Court, 11 March 1618.

107. BA, SMV/2/1/1/34, ff. 53–4. The Privy Council to the Merchant Venturers, 15 March 1618. A later order did forbid the Levant Company from importing currants to Bristol, but this would hardly have mattered. BA, SMV/2/1/1/34, f. 55. The Privy Council to the Merchant Venturers, 20 March 1618.

108. BA, SMV/1/1/1/7, f. 86. Book of Charters. 1618.

109. TNA, SP 105/149. Levant Company minutes, 10 July 1632.

110. BL, IOR/B/6, 20 March 1618.

111. Ibid., 10 April 1618.

112. Ibid., General Court, 10 April 1618.

113. Ibid., 14 April 1618.

114. Ibid., 17 April 1618.

115. For the traditional cloth manufacture and trade, see Marie-Louise Nosch (ed.), *The Medieval Broadcloth: Changing Trends in Fashions, Manufacturing and Consumption* (Oxford, 2010).

116. NRO, MS21508/8/368X5. Memoranda of Matters to be Considered in Parliament, 9 February 1598.

117. See Brenner, *Merchants and Revolution*, p. 9; Supple, *Commercial Crisis*, p. 258. For further analysis of broader export trends, see chapter 3.

118. NRO, MC/3313/4/1067X4. Breviate for a Bill in Parliament Concerning Woollen Cloths, 1606.

119. Bisson, *Merchant Adventurers of England*; Anne Sutton, 'The Merchant Adventurers of England: Their origins and the Mercers' Company of London', *Historical Research* 75, 187 (2002), pp. 25–46.

120. Leng, 'Interlopers and disorderly brethren'.

121. TNA, SP 12/283a, f. 95. Letter from Christopher Hoddesdon to Secretary Cecil, 6 March 1602.

122. Ibid.; BL, Lansdowne Ms 487, ff. 146–8. Reasons on behalf of the Merchant Adventurers showing that their maintenance as at present is better for the state, [*c.* 1604–6].

NOTES to pp. 160–162

123. BL, Lansdowne Ms 487, ff. 146–8. Reasons on behalf of the Merchant Adventurers showing that their maintenance as at present is better for the state, [*c.* 1604–6].

124. The incentive for founding new trades, whether related to export of cloth or the import of 'luxuries' remains a matter of debate. For the export-focused argument, see F.J. Fisher, 'Commercial trends and policy in sixteenth-century England', *Economic History Review* 10, 2 (1940), pp. 95–117 and 'London's export trade', pp. 151–61; Supple, *Commercial Crisis*, pp. 258–9; G.D. Ramsay, *English Overseas Trade during the Centuries of Emergence* (London, 1957), pp. 20–30, as well as his *Tudor Economic Problems* (London, 1963), pp. 63–5 and *The City of London in International Politics at the Ascension of Elizabeth Tudor* (Manchester, 1975), p. 62. For the import-led argument, see Brenner, *Merchants and Revolution*, pp. 3–5, 51–61.

125. John Wheeler, *A Treatise of Commerce: wherein is shewed the commodities arising by a well ordered and ruled trade, such as that of the Society of Merchants Adventurers is proved to be* (London, 1601), p. 6.

126. Ibid., p. 8.

127. BL, Lansdowne Ms 86, f. 26. Mayor and Aldermen of Bristol to Lord Burghley, 20 January 1598.

128. BL, Add Ms 41613, ff. 2–4. Petition from the clothiers of the North to the privy council, 28 April 1605.

129. TNA, SP 15/34, ff. 41–2. Discussion of the impact of dressed cloths on the art of cloth working and dyeing, 1600.

130. BL, Add Ms 14027, f. 267. Papers relating to the manufacture of woollen cloth, [*c.* 1611–15].

131. KHLC, U269/1/B73a, m. 7147. Petition from the Eastland Merchants, [*c.* 1602].

132. Giuseppi, *Calendar*, vol. 14, p. 275.

133. For the many types of different woollen cloth produced in early modern England, see Negley Harte, *The New Draperies in the Low Countries and England, 1300–1800* (Oxford, 1997).

NOTES to pp. 163–165

134. NRO, MC/3313/4/1067X4. That it is a matter of good policy for to grant a licence to buy and sell some quantity (yearly) of wools, [undated, *c.* 1604–7].

135. NRO, MC/3313/4/1067X4. Breviate for a Bill in Parliament Concerning Woollen Cloths, 1606.

136. Giuseppi, *Calendar*, vol. 17, p. 327.

137. TNA, SP 14/40, f. 25. A toleration set down by the privy council, 1608.

138. TNA, SP 14/72, ff. 127–32. Anonymous memorandum on the cloth trade, March 1613.

139. BL, Add Ms 14027, f. 271. Papers relating to the manufacture of woollen cloth, [*c.* 1611–15].

140. BL, Add Ms 41667 G, f. 23. Tract on the decay of trade, 1610.

141. CC, CL/B/1/4, Orders of Court, f. 114. 8 March 1613; BL, Add Ms 14027, f. 273. King James I to the Lord Mayor of London, 3 December 1613.

142. BL, Add Ms 34324, f. 10. 23 June 1616.

143. TNA, SP 14/72, ff. 127–32. Anonymous memorandum on the cloth trade, March 1613.

144. BL, Add Ms 14027, f. 271. Papers relating to the manufacture of woollen cloth, [*c.* 1611–15].

145. TNA, SP 14/72, ff. 127–32. Anonymous memorandum on cloth trade, March 1613.

146. BL, IOR/E/3/2, f. 97. Mukarrab Khan to the East India Company, 1614.

147. BL, Cotton Nero B XI, f. 304. Statement of advantages of Levant Trade, 1604.

148. BL, Add Ms 48155, f. 60. Certain brief remonstrances offered unto His Majesty concerning diverse inconveniences grown in the commonwealth by the Netherlanders and the Merchant Adventurers, 1613.

149. MC, AoC 1595–1629, ff. 141–2. Certificate of the company of Mercers, 1615.

NOTES to pp. 166–168

150. BLO, Ms Tanner 103, ff. 206–10. John Keymer's *Book of Observations for your Most Excellent Majesty Touching Trade and Traffique Beyond the Seas*, [undated]; BL, Add Ms 48155, ff. 61–5. Certain brief remonstrances offered unto His Majesty concerning diverse inconveniences grown in the commonwealth by the Netherlanders and the Merchant Adventurers, 1613.

151. HL, EL2382. Remembrance touching the Merchant Adventurers, [undated, *c.* 1613–16].

152. HL, EL2379. Notes touching the Merchant Adventurers, [undated, *c.* 1613–16].

153. KHLC, U269/1/B77, m. 70. Lionel Cranfield's *The Original and True Cause of the Decay of the Trade of the Merchant Adventurers*, 1615.

154. HL, EL2386. Recommendations for reforming the Merchant Adventurers, [undated, *c.* 1613–16].

155. The scheme to export dressed cloth became known as the 'Cockayne Project' and William Cockayne was named governor of the New Merchant Adventurers, who were licensed to oversee this trade. See Astrid Friis, *Alderman Cockayne's Project and the Cloth Trade: The Commercial Policy of England in its Main Aspects, 1603–1625* (Copenhagen, 1927).

156. TNA, SP 14/72, ff. 127–32. Anonymous memorandum on the cloth trade, March 1613.

157. BL, Add Ms 14027, f. 273. James I to Thomas Middleton, 3 December 1613.

158. NorthRO, C/2532. Royal Licence for the export of woollens, 14 May 1614.

159. HL, EL2393. Petition from poor craftsmen of the Clothworkers' Company, [undated, *c.* 1615]; KHLC, U269/1/B82/9, m. 683. Letter from John Walker to James I, 1616.

160. KHLC, U269/1/B82/2, m. 61. Notes taken at Exchequer case between Merchant Adventurers and Clothworkers', 1615.

NOTES to pp. 168–171

161. KHLC, U269/1/B83/5, m. 64. Merchant Adventurers answer to the Clothworkers', 1615.

162. KHLC, U269/1/B82/2, m. 61. Notes taken at Exchequer case between Merchant Adventurers and Clothworkers' livery company, 1615.

163. BL, Add Ms 12504, f. 64(i). Petition from City of Norwich to Sir Julius Caesar, 31 January 1618.

164. KHLC, U269/1/B82/9, m. 683. Letter from John Walker to James I, 1616.

165. KHLC, U269/1/B83/4, m. 59. Answer of Merchant Adventurers to Clothworkers', 1616.

166. KHLC, U269/1/B82/14, m. 691. Cloths shipped by the new company, 1616.

167. KHLC, U269/1/B82/14, m. 689. List of New Merchant Adventurers, 1616–17. Kendrick was a long-time Merchant Adventurer who was clearly happy to take advantage of the new regulations, while the others had all participated in at least one of the Spanish, Levant, French or East India companies.

168. BL, Add Ms 14027, f. 287. Reasons to approve that the new Company of Merchant Adventurers cannot be able to go forward with the shipping to the market towns of white cloths undressed and dressed together, 18 January 1615.

169. TNA, SP 14/88, f. 144. Remarks on the places where the New Merchant Adventurers company and the Eastland merchants should sell dyed and undyed cloths, September 1616; KHLC, U269/1/B84, m. 42. Consideration why the merchants of Eastland should be permitted to ship white cloth unwrought, 1615.

170. KHLC, U269/1/B84, m. 996. Reasons why the merchants of Eastland should be permitted to ship white cloths undressed as well as the Merchant Adventurers, 1615.

171. KHLC, U269/1/B83/1, m. 45. Answer of Merchant Adventurers to Eastland Company, 1615.

NOTES to pp. 171–174

172. KHLC, U269/1/B84, m. 46. Answer of the Eastland Company to the Merchant Adventurers, 1615.

173. KHLC, U269/1/B84, m. 42. Consideration why the merchants of Eastland should be permitted to ship white cloth unwrought, 1615.

174. See Brenner, *Merchants and Revolution*, p. 9; Supple, *Commercial Crisis*, p. 136–62, 258; Stone, 'The overseas trade of Bristol', pp. 219–26; Fisher, 'London's export trade', p. 154.

175. KHLC, U269/1/B82/7, m. 685. Draft of memorandum for James I, 4 September 1616.

176. BLO, Ms Tanner 103, f. 226. The present state of trade between the company of merchants trading into the dominion of the Grand Signor and the company of merchants trading into the East Indies, [undated].

5 THE CITY AND THE COURT

1. TNA, SP 84/117, f. 235; TNA, CO 77/3, f. 20; BL, IOR/B/8, 31 May 1624; 16 June 1624; BL, IOR/B/9, General Court, 2 July 1624; 28 July 1624.

2. BL, Sloane Ms 3645. Anonymous manuscript account of the Amboyna massacre, [*c.* 1624]; BL, IOR/B/8, 23 June 1624; BL, IOR/B/9, General Court, 2 July 1624; General Court, 9 July 1624; 6 October 1624; 22 October 1624; General Court, 10 December 1624. The *True Relation* was printed twice in 1624, the second edition updated with a graphic image of the torture described within, that would be reproduced during other moments of Anglo-Dutch conflict later in the century (Plate 9).

3. John Skinner, *A true relation of the unjust, cruel, and barbarous proceedings against the English at Amboyna: in the East-Indies, by the Netherlandish governour & council there* (London, 1624), pp. 11–12.

4. BL, IOR/B/9, 18 February 1625; East India Company, *Newes out of East India of the Cruel and Bloody Usage of our English Merchants*

NOTES to pp. 174–175

and others at Amboyna, by the Netherlandish Governour and Councel There: to the tune of Braggendary (London, 1624); Robert Wilkinson, *The Stripping of Joseph, or the Cruelty of Brethren to a Brother* (London, 1626), p. 15. For further detail regarding the events at Amboyna, see Adam Clulow, *Amboina, 1623: Fear and Conspiracy on the Edge of Empire* (Columbia, NY, 2019).

5. BL, IOR/B/9, 21 February 1625. The Amboyna 'massacre' and other episodes involving English merchants overseas would radically alter how corporations and the English state understood international law in the early modern period. See Smith, 'Reporting and interpreting'.

6. For the delegation of state power to private individuals and corporations, see Janice Thompson, *Merchants, Pirates, and Sovereigns: State-building and Extraterritorial Violence in Early Modern Europe* (Princeton, NJ, 1994).

7. The leading analysis of economic thought and the role of the state in commercial enterprise during this period remains Appleby, *Economic Thought and Ideology*. For concepts of mercantilism and the role of monopolies, see Robert Ekelund and Robert D. Tollison, *Politicised Economies: Monarchy, Monopoly, and Mercantilism* (College Station, TX, 1997); Istvan Hont, *Jealousy of Trade: International Competition and the Nation-state in Historical Perspective* (Cambridge, MA, 2005); William Pettigrew and George van Cleve, 'Parting companies: The Glorious Revolution, company power and imperial mercantilism', *Historical Journal* 57, 3 (2014), pp. 617–38; Stern and Wennerlind, *Mercantilism Reimagined*.

8. Stern, *The Company-state*, pp. 19–41; Mishra, *A Business of State*.

9. BL, IOR/A/1/5, Copy letters patent of James I renewing privileges of the governor and company of merchants of London, trading into the East-Indies, 31 May 1609; BL, IOR/B/9, 28 March 1625.

10. Elizabeth Mancke, 'Empire and state', in Armitage and Braddick (eds), *The British Atlantic World*, pp. 193–213 and 'Negotiating an

NOTES to pp. 175–176

empire: Britain and its overseas peripheries, c. 1550–1780', in Christine Daniels and Michael Kennedy (eds), *Negotiated Empires: Centers and Peripheries in the Americas, 1500–1820* (New York, 2002), pp. 237–62.

11. Stern, 'Companies', in Stern and Wennerlind (eds), *Mercantilism Reimagined*, p. 178. Also see Braddick, *State Formation*; Hendrik Spruyt, *The Sovereign State and its Competitors: An Analysis of Systems Change* (Princeton, NJ, 1994).

12. Courtiers such as Endymion Porter and the Lord of Arundel, for example, successfully used their influence to obtain patents for the colonisation of Madagascar despite the East India Company's monopoly. See Edmond Smith, '"Canaanising Madagascar": Africa in the English imperial imagination', *Itinerario* 39, 2 (2015), pp. 277–98.

13. The self-interest of members of the court provided one avenue of communication between commercial groups and the court. See Ramsay, 'The Tudor state and economic problems', in Simon Groenveld (ed.), *State and Trade: Government and the Economy in Britain and the Netherlands since the Middle Ages* (Zutphen, 1992).

14. The commercial community's relationship with the state and involvement in politics has been examined in detail. See Ashton, *The City and the Court*; Valerie Pearl, *London and the Outbreak of the Puritan Revolution: City Government and National Politics, 1625–43* (Oxford, 1961); Brenner, *Merchants and Revolution*; Perry Gauci, *The Politics of Trade: The Overseas Merchant in State and Society, 1660–1720* (Oxford, 2001); Steven Pincus, 'Neither Machiavellian moment nor possessive individualism: Commercial society and the defenders of the English commonwealth', *American Historical Review* 103, 3 (1998), pp. 705–36; Mishra, *A Business of State*.

15. Ashton, *The City and the Court*, pp. 11–12.

16. Philip Stern and Carl Wennerlind, 'Introduction', in Stern and Wennerlind (eds), *Mercantilism Reimagined*, pp. 1–17.

– 293 –

NOTES to pp. 177–179

17. BL, Add Ms 225787, f. 18. Letter from King James I to the City of London, 1603.
18. BL, Add Ms 12497, f. 279. Speech by the Lord Treasurer to the Lord Mayor in the Exchange, 29–30 October 1609.
19. BL, Add Ms 34324, ff. 79–83. Royal declaration concerning the fees at the Port of London, 17 January 1616.
20. TNA, SP, 14/90, f. 54. Anonymous treatise, 1617; BL, IOR/A/1/5, Letters Patent, 31 May 1609.
21. Stern, 'Companies', p. 178.
22. Similar statements of the city's relationship to the crown were made during the 1605 Lord Mayor's show. Tracey Hill, '"Representing the awefull authoritie of soveraigne Majestie": Monarchs and mayors in Anthony Munday's *The Triumphs of re-united Britania*', in Glenn Burgess, Rowland Wymer and Jason Lawrence (eds), *The Accession of James I: Historical and Cultural Consequences* (Basingstoke, 2006), pp. 15–33.
23. MC, AoC 1595–1629, f. 204. 1 February 1620.
24. CC, CL/B/1/4, Orders of Court, f. 24. 28 July 1607.
25. Stern, 'Companies', pp. 179–80. The importance of these gifts was so great that before leaving his role, Thomas Smith, the influential governor of the East India Company, was specifically asked to provide a list of dependable people at court who should be sent gifts, see BL, IOR/B/7, 26 November 1621.
26. BL, IOR/B/6, 28 May 1619; BL, IOR/B/7, 3 December 1621.
27. TNA, SP 105/148. Levant Company minutes, 22 December 1623.
28. DC, MB 13, 13 June 1610; SA, SC2/1/1, f. 12. Mayor's Book, 30 December 1606.
29. Merchants presented numerous arguments justifying their receipt of such privileges, many of which appeared in printed form during debates about the 'decay' of England's trade in the 1610s and 1620s. For an extensive analysis of these debates, see Leng, 'Commercial conflict and regulation'.

– 294 –

NOTES to pp. 179–181

30. BL, IOR/B/5, 22 February 1615. Tobias Gentleman's *England's Way to Win Wealth and to Employ Ship's Mariners* (London, 1614), Edward Sharpe's *Britain's Busse* (London, 1615) and Robert Kayll's *The Trades Increase* (London, 1615) had each critiqued the company's losses and suggested it should be abolished in favour of renewed investment in fishing. Kayll's critique was deemed so damaging (and libellous) that it was condemned as 'very near unto treason' and he was imprisoned for two weeks before issuing an apology for the publication. BL IOR/B/5, 16 February 1615; 22 February 1615; His Majesty's Stationery Office, *Acts of the Privy Council*, vol. 34, pp. 99, 107–8.

31. Dudley Digges, *The Defence of Trade* (London, 1615), pp. 1–5, 17–22, 27, 33–4, 45. For the East India Company's wider use of printed material to obtain public and political support, see Ogborn, *Indian Ink*.

32. Detractors concerns now increasingly focused on the company's export of bullion and supposedly negative impact on England's 'balance of trade'. Many of these arguments were presented in print in Gerard Malynes' *The Maintainance of Free Trade* (London, 1622) and *The Centre of the Circle of Commerce* (London, 1623).

33. Thomas Mun, *A Discourse of Trade, from England unto the East-Indies answering to diverse objections which are usually made against the same* (London, 1621), pp. 1, 9, 12. Similar arguments were made in support of other merchant-led trading organisations in Edward Misselden's *Free Trade, or, the Means to Make Trade Flourish* (London, 1622) and *The Circle of Commerce, or the Ballance of Trade in Defence of Free Trade* (London, 1623).

34. BL, IOR/B/3, General Court, 28 September 1609; 29 September 1609; 6 October 1609; 18 October 1609.

35. John Cramsie, 'Commercial projects and the fiscal policy of James VI and I', *Historical Journal* 43, 2 (2000), pp. 345–64 and *Kingship and Crown Finance under James IV and I, 1603–1625* (Woodbridge, 2002); David Harris Sacks, 'The paradox of taxation: Fiscal crises, parliament, and liberty in England, 1450–1640', in Philip Hoffman

– 295 –

and Kathryn Norberg (eds), *Fiscal Crises, Liberty, and Representative Government, 1450–1789* (Stanford, CA, 1994), pp. 7–66.

36. BL, Add Ms 41613, ff. 2–5. Petition from the clothiers of the North, 28 April 1605; Petition from the merchants of the Western Counties, 28 April 1605; The privy council's answer to the clothiers of the North, 12 June 1605.

37. HRO, 44M69/G2/13/3/1a. Report by Henry Yelverton and Thomas Conventree, 12 December 1617.

38. HRO, 44M69/G2/13/3/1b. Report by Henry Yelverton, 27 August 1618.

39. HRO, 44M69/G2/13/3/2. Letter from archbishops of Canterbury and York and others to James I, 29 'September 1618.

40. BL, Lansdowne Ms 487, ff. 86–7, 94. Petition by House of Commons to James I, 1610; Inconveniences from impositions on foreign commodities, 1610.

41. Ibid., f. 94. Inconveniences from impositions on foreign commodities, 1610.

42. Ibid.

43. Ibid., ff. 86–7.

44. Ibid., f. 143. James I to the House of Commons, 1610.

45. Cramsie, 'Commercial projects'.

46. For earlier resistance from livery companies and their members to impositions by the crown, see Ian Archer, 'The burden of taxation on sixteenth-century London', *Historical Journal* 44, 3 (2001), pp. 599–627.

47. DC, MB 13, 28 August 1604; 6 September 1604.

48. GL, Ms 15842/1, ff. 251–2. 28 December 1627.

49. TNA, SP 14/95/3. Letters and Papers, January 1618.

50. BL, IOR/B/6, 22 December 1618.

51. MC, AoC 1595–1629, f. 59. 25 August 1604. Requested in August, this loan was specified as having a repayment date the following March, yet this promise of quick repayment seems to have done little to assuage the concerns of members.

NOTES to pp. 184–185

52. Ibid., f. 133. 24 July 1614.

53. Ibid., f. 214. 15 December 1620.

54. LMA, COL/AD/01/032, ff. 143–4, 269–71, 285. Corporation of London Letter Book, 16 April 1625; 7 August; 9 August; 10 August; 11 August; 5 September 1626. For opposition to Charles I's financial agenda across England, see Richard Cust, 'Charles I, the Privy Council, and the forced loan', *Journal of British Studies* 24, 2 (1985), pp. 208–35.

55. MC, AoC 1595–1629, ff. 320–1. 20 December 1627; DC, MB 13, 2 December 1627.

56. GL, Ms 15842/1, f. 251. 28 December 1627.

57. Ibid., f. 321. 24 December 1627.

58. Ibid., f. 324. 29 December 1627. Baptiste Hicks traded in silks and was a member of the Irish, Virginia and Somers Island companies. While the king might be increasingly uncreditable, the bonds and behaviours instilled among England's merchants meant that within this community, at least, financing was readily available.

59. Ashton, *The City and the Court*, pp. 2–3.

60. Bruce, *Letters and Papers of the Verney Family*, p. 275. A hugely wealthy Merchant Adventurer, Cranfield also held interests in the Levant, Irish, Virginia and Bermuda companies alongside his responsibilities at court. R.H. Tawney, *Business and Politics under James I: Lionel Cranfield as Merchant and Minister* (Cambridge, 1958).

61. The Elizabethan and Stuart court was a complex community and has received considerable attention from historians. See Ronald Asch and Adolf Birke (eds), *Princes, Patronage and the Nobility: The Court at the Beginning of the Modern Age, c. 1450–1650* (Oxford, 1990); Felicity Heal and Clive Holmes, 'The economic patronage of William Cecil', in Pauline Croft (ed.), *Patronage, Culture and Power: The Early Cecils* (New Haven, CT, 2002), pp. 199–229; Linda Levy Peck (ed.), *The Mental World of the Jacobean Court* (Cambridge, 1991).

62. Games, *Web of Empire*, pp. 117–46.

NOTES to pp. 186–189

63. Rabb, *Enterprise and Empire*, pp. 30, 104. Most companies restricted active membership to merchants, see chapter 2.

64. BL, IOR/B/3, 30 May 1609.

65. Ibid., 4 July 1609.

66. BL, IOR/B/5, 19 March 1614; 31 March 1614; BL, IOR/B/6, 23 January 1618.

67. BL, IOR/B/6, 23 July 1619.

68. Watts was a senior member of the Spanish and East India companies who had also used his own ships for privateering and had invested in Drake's voyages in the 1580s and 1590s. The challenges facing clothworkers and a rapidly changing woollen cloth trade are examined in chapter 4.

69. CC, CL/B/1/4, Orders of Court, f. 21. 8 June 1607.

70. Ibid., ff. 21, 23, 24. 15 June 1607; 26 July 1607; 28 July 1607.

71. Merchants had a long history of lobbying the state for favour, see Ramsay, 'The Tudor state and economic problems'; Arnold Sherman, 'Pressure from Leadenhall: The East India Company lobby', *Business History Review* 50, 3 (1976), pp. 1660–78.

72. DC, MB 13, 21 October 1605.

73. SA, SC2/1/6, f. 123. Assembly Book, 15 November 1611.

74. TNA, SP 14/86, f. 131. Arguments by the Skinners' Company against a proposed patent for the tanning of gray cony skins, February 1616.

75. TNA, PC 2/28, f. 521. Privy Council meeting, 29 January 1617.

76. Ibid., f. 565. Privy Council meeting, 26 February 1617.

77. The education and governance of merchants is discussed in chapters 1 and 2.

78. Mun, *Discourse of Trade*, pp. i, 3–4; Misselden, *Circle of Commerce*, p. 64.

79. Digges, *Defence of Trade*, p. 51.

80. BL, Lansdowne Ms 487, ff. 146–8. Reasons on behalf of the Merchant Adventurers and other companies, showing their maintenance as at present is better for the state than such a liberty as the Lower House have agreed on, [undated, *c.* 1604–6].

– 298 –

NOTES to pp. 189–194

81. BL, Lansdowne Ms 142, ff. 360, 480. Several projects how a great yearly revenue may be raised upon strangers fishing in his majesty's four seas, [undated, *c.* 1609]; The King of Denmark's proclamation against all strangers fishing on the coast of Iceland without his special licence, 6 October 1602.

82. CC, CL/B/1/4, Orders of Court, f. 20. 2 June 1607; BL, Add Ms 9365, p. 2. Register Book of the Spanish Company, 16 March 1604.

83. CC, CL/D/5/4, Accounts 1599–1600.

84. DC, MB 13, 11 February 1607; MC, AoC 1595–1629, f. 77. 21 May 1607.

85. BA, SMV/2/1/1/1, f. 11. Merchants' Hall Book of Proceedings, 14 August 1639.

86. NRO, NCR/7/H/8. Charges of Thomas Pettus in London, 1577; BA, SMV/3/1/1/1, f. 7. Treasurer's Account Book.

87. Nottinghamshire Archives, DC/NW/3/1/1, f. 31. Accounts of sums paid for renewal of Royal Charter, 1558.

88. CMAY, Faults found by the auditors, 1575.

89. Portsmouth History Centre and Records Office, CF1/3. Thomas Lardner's Book of Disbursements and Receipts, 1622.

90. BL, Add Ms 9365, pp. 2, 27–9, 35–6. Register Book of the Spanish Company, 16 March 1604; 30 January 1605; 6 June 1605.

91. TNA, SP 12/274, f. 36. Petition from William Stallenge to the Secretary Cecil, 31 January 1600.

92. KHLC, U269/1/OE238, m. 5874. Petition of the East India Company, 1623.

93. CC, CL/A/4/1, Meeting at Whitehall, 10 October 1619.

94. Ibid., Meeting at Whitehall, 24 October 1627.

95. BL, Lansdowne 112, f. 109. Questions related to the conduct of a nuncio, [undated, *c.* 1558–1603].

96. Folger Shakespeare Library, V.b.181. Queen Elizabeth to Prince John George of Anhalt, 19 December 1597.

97. TNA, SP 12/274, f. 186. Letter from Richard Lee to Secretary Cecil, 19 April 1600.

– 299 –

NOTES to pp. 194–197

98. TNA, SP 91/1, f. 194. Petition from the Muscovy Company to the Privy Council, 9 May 1604.

99. BL, Cotton Nero B/V, ff. 48, 55. A declaration of the grievances the company of Eastland merchants sustained in the Sound, August 1602; Request from the Eastland merchants trading in Bries, 1602.

100. BL, Add Ms 48126, f. 163. Complaint from English merchants trading to France, 1602.

101. CMAY, Acts and Ordinances of Eastland Merchants, f. 46. Eastland Company General Court, 3 February 1631.

102. This practice is discussed in Ogborn, *Indian Ink*, pp. 42–6.

103. BL, Egerton 1553, ff. 46–7. Charles I to Michael I, April 1629.

104. BL, Stowe Ms 171, f. 272. Lord Salisbury's comments on the emperor's arresting English merchants, 2 July 1610.

105. TNA, SP/16/124, f. 80. Petition of Richard Archdale, Henry Lee, Martin Broadgate, Edward Browne, George Rouckes, and Benjamin Wright merchants to the Council; TNA, PC/2/38, ff. 147, 301. Privy Council to Captain Hughes, 21 May 1628; Order about French commodities brought to Hollande and from thence hither by Richard Archdale, Henry Lee and others, 17 July 1638.

106. BL, Stowe Ms 171, f. 312. Letter from James I to Thomas Edmonds, 30 July 1610.

107. BL, Stowe Ms 171, f. 277. Letter from the Privy Council to Thomas Edmonds, 4 July 1610.

108. BL, Add Ms 36448, ff. 13–19. Complaint of Roger Corbett and William Green, 27 August 1635.

109. Ibid. Complaint of George Weaver, 17 July 1635.

110. Ibid. Complaint of Roger Kilvert, 25 June 1635.

111. Immunity from the inquisition was a common hope from English merchants trading to Spain. BL, Add Ms 48126, f. 77. Petition of merchants trading with Spain to the Privy Council, spring 1600.

112. BL, Add Ms 36448, ff. 13–19. Complaints regarding treatment of merchants in Spain, 25 June–27 August 1635.

– 300 –

NOTES to pp. 197–199

113. Ibid. Complaint of Roger Dunster and Jerman Honeychurch, 25 June 1635.
114. Ibid. Complaint of Roger Oxwick, Elias Roberts and Thomas Boyer, 7 August 1635.
115. Ibid. Complaint of Roger Oxwick and Michael Waring, 14 August 1635.
116. Ibid. Complaint of Martin Broadgate and Martin Swinerton, [1635].
117. BL, Add Ms 48126, f. 74. Letter from Richard Dane to Robert Beale, spring 1600.
118. TNA, SP/89/1, f. 62. A brief remonstrance of the trade with Spain, 1605.
119. The East India Company, especially, utilised military power during its activities, see Edmond Smith, 'Naval violence and trading privileges in early seventeenth-century Asia', *International Journal of Maritime History* 25, 2 (2013), pp. 147–58.
120. BL, Add Ms 36448, f. 20. Petition from Humphrey Slany and Nicholas Crispe to the Privy Council, 1635.
121. Douglas Irwin, 'Mercantilism as strategic trade policy: The Anglo-Dutch rivalry for the East India trade', *Journal of Political Economy* 99, 6 (1991), p. 1308.
122. For Dutch commercial, imperial and economic development, see Charles Boxer, *The Dutch Seaborne Empire, 1600–1800* (England, 1973 [1965]); Vries and Woude, *The First Modern Economy*; Claudia Schnurmann, ' "Wherever profit leads us, to every sea and shore . . .": The VOC, the WIC, and Dutch methods of globalisation in the seventeenth century', *Renaissance Studies* 17, 3 (2003), pp. 474–93.
123. BL, Lansdowne Ms 142, ff. 294–6. A complaint for want of employment for English shipping, 4 July 1609.
124. BL, Add Ms 14027, f. 172. Sir Julius Caesar's answer to the complaint of the Low Countries touching the fishing of whales upon the coast of Greenland, 13 January 1614.

– 301 –

NOTES to pp. 199–202

125. Digges, *Defence of Trade*, pp. 2–5; BL, IOR/B/1, 25 September 1599. For the violent consequences of this competition, see Vincent Loth, 'Armed incidents and unpaid bills: Anglo-Dutch rivalry in the Banda Islands in the seventeenth century', *Modern Asian Studies* 29 (1995), pp. 705–40.

126. BL, Add Ms 48155, f. 60. Certain brief remonstrances offered unto His Majesty concerning diverse inconveniences grown in the commonwealth by the Netherlanders and the Merchant Adventurers, 1613.

127. Sophus A. Reinhart, *Translating Empire: Emulation and the Origins of Political Economy* (Cambridge, MA, 2011).

128. BLO, Ms Tanner 103, ff. 206–10. John Keymer's *Book of Observations for your Most Excellent Majesty Touching Trade and Traffique Beyond the Seas*, [c. 1601–15].

129. BL, Add Ms 48155, f. 1. Minutes of conference relating to the East Indies, 30 March–30 April 1613.

130. Ibid., ff. 1–2.

131. Ibid., ff. 4–5.

132. BerkRO, AC, vol. 46, f. 9. Edward Waldegrave to William Trumbull, 30 December 1614.

133. BL, Add Ms 48155, f. 20. Memorandum for conference relating to the East Indies and fishing of whale in the northern seas, December 1614; BerkRO, AC, vol. 44, f. 76. Sir Henry Wotton to Sir Thomas Edmonds, 6 May 1615.

134. BL, Lansdowne Ms 142, f. 290. Recommendation of Mr Bell, Mr Hall and other merchants of London, 2 September 1609; BL, Add Ms 41667 G, f. 22. Tract on the decay of trade, 1610.

135. BL, Lansdowne Ms 142, f. 292. Reasons why the ships of the Low Countries carry freight at a cheaper rate, [undated, c. 1609].

136. BL, Lansdowne Ms 142, ff. 294–6. A complaint for want of employment for English shipping, 4 July 1609.

137. TNA, PC 2/28, f. 49. Privy Council to five companies, 12 July 1615.

– 302 –

NOTES to pp. 202–205

138. TNA, PC 2/28, f. 315. Meeting of the Privy Council, [June 1631].

139. See, for example, NRO, YC/19/5, f. 142. Great Yarmouth Assembly Book, 7 October 1614; James I, *A Proclamation Extending the Former Proclamation for the Restraint of Shipping any Commodity in Strangers Bottomes either into this Kingdome or out of the Same* (London, 1615); TNA, SP 105/148. General Court, 19 October 1618; SA, SC2/1/6, f. 184. Assembly Book, 8 July 1618; King James I, *A Proclamation Prohibiting the Bringing in of Any Commodities Traded by the Eastland Merchants into this Kingdom, As Well by Subjects as Strangers, Not Free of that Company* (London, 1622); KHLC, U269/1/OE239a, m. 5682. Petition from the Eastland Merchants, 1622; CMAY, Acts and Ordinances of Eastland Merchants, f. 44. Eastland Company General Court, 10 February 1623.

140. Supple, *Commercial Crisis*.

141. BA, SMV/2/1/1/34, f. 103. Book of Trade, 11 September 1621.

142. HRO, 44M69/G2/117. Anonymous treatise, [undated, *c.* 1618].

143. BL, Add Ms 41667 G, f. 21. Tract on the decay of trade, 1610.

144. BL, Add Ms 41613, f. 229. John Keymer's tract, 1622.

145. BL, Add Ms 34324, ff. 153–4. Henry Mandeville's *Remonstrance of the Business of Exchange*, 1 May 1622.

146. BL, Add Ms 34324, f. 167. Gerard Malynes' comments on the balancing of trade, 12 April 1623.

147. BL, Add Ms 34324, f. 173. Sir Ralph Madison condemning merchants who are just exchangers of money and carry no commodities, 12 April 1623.

148. BL, Add Ms 34324, f. 179. Sir Ralph Madison's response to Thomas Mun, 2 July 1623.

149. BLO, Ms Tanner 103, f. 221. What benefit may ensure to the common weale by forbidding the bringing in of all manufactures, [undated].

150. BL, Add Ms 34324, ff. 155–7. Response by Robert Bell, Thomas Mun, George Kendrick, Henry Wood, Thomas Jennings and John Skinner, 31 May 1622.

– 303 –

NOTES to pp. 205–208

151. BL, Add Ms 34324, ff. 159–2. Response by Henry Mandeville, [1622].

152. BL, Add Ms 34324, f. 169. Thomas Mun's comments of the balance of trade, 12 April 1623.

153. BL, Add Ms 34324, ff. 177–8. Thomas Mun's response, 6 May 1623.

154. An ongoing concern that shaped the training, oversight and governance of the merchant community, see chapters 1 and 2.

155. For mercantile involvement and interest in empire, see the conclusion of this book..

156. The wealth of merchants and their prominence in politics, including the House of Commons, continued to increase in the latter half of the seventeenth and into the eighteenth century, but they never regained the same dominance of England's major trading companies that they had enjoyed in the first decades of the seventeenth century. For the changing role of merchants in this latter period, see Gauci, *Politics of Trade*; Zahedieh, *Capital and the Colonies*.

157. NRS, GD1/1123/66. Proposals concerning commerce and trading, 29 March 1642.

CONCLUSION

1. BL, Cotton Nero B XI, ff. 382–4. Discussion of trade into the Baltic and Russia, [1609–10]. Information about Russia's 'soil and climate' as well as population, commodities and revenues was increasingly accessible in England. See, for example, Giovanni Botero, *A Travellers Breviat, or an historicall description of the most famous kingdomes in the world relating their situations, manners, customes, civill government, and other memorable matters*, trans. Anon. (London, 1601), pp. 79–80; Richard Hakluyt, *The Principall Navigations, Voyages, Traffiques and Discoveries of the English Nation by Sea or Over-Land, to the Remote and Farthest Distant Quarters of the Earth* (London, 1599–1600), pp. 290–510. For

– 304 –

NOTES to pp. 208–213

Muscovy Company activities in Russia during this period, see Maria Arel, *English Trade and Adventure to Russia in the Early Modern Era: The Muscovy Company, 1603–1649* (Lanham, MD, 2019), pp. 19–40.

2. Roberts, *Marchants Mapp of Commerce*, section II, pp. 234, 257.

3. Thomas Johnson, *A Discourse Concerning of Motives for the Enlargement and Freedom of Trade* (London, 1645).

4. In the later British Empire, merchants remained deeply involved in imperial activity, but rarely reached the same levels of authority as they aspired to in the seventeenth century. See, for instance, Huw Bowen, *The Business of Empire: The East India Company and Imperial Britain, 1756–1833* (Cambridge, 2005).

5. Mun, *Discourse of Trade*, pp. 54–5.

6. Misselden, *Circle of Commerce*, pp. 18, 64.

7. Roberts, *Marchants Mapp of Commerce*, p. 2.

8. Greif, *Institutions*, pp. 30, 382–3; Trivellato, *Familiarity of Strangers*, p. 4.

9. The life of factors overseas has been examined extensively in relation to the eighteenth century; see Lisa Hellman, *The House Is Not a Home: European Everyday Life in Canton and Macao, 1730–1830* (Leiden, 2019).

10. StaffRO, D(W)1778/V/277. Patent for the Somers Island Company, 29 June 1616.

11. Stern, 'Companies', p. 130.

12. StaffRO, D(W)1734/1/3/75c. Roger North's complaint to the Bishop of Lincoln, 1623; TNA, SP 14/108, f. 125. Thomas Locke to Dudley Carleton, 30 April 1619.

13. Joyce Lorimer (ed.), *English and Irish Settlement on the River Amazon, 1550–1646* (London, 1999), pp. 60–8.

14. StaffRO, D(W)1734/1/3/75b. The answer of William Lord Paget, 1623.

15. There was, of course, a range of reasons why merchants and others might positively engage in these activities. See Armitage, *Ideological*

NOTES to pp. 213–214

Origins, pp. 71–81; Andrew Fitzmaurice, 'The civic solution to the crisis of English colonisation, 1609–1625', *Historical Journal* 42, 1 (1999), pp. 25–51; Abigail Swingen, *Competing Visions of Empire: Labor, Slavery, and the Origins of the British Atlantic Empire* (New Haven, CT, 2015).

16. PRONI, D683, ff. 38–41.

17. Links between the two enterprises have been examined extensively in Audrey Horning, *Ireland in the Virginia Sea: Colonialism in the British Atlantic* (Chapel Hill, NC, 2013).

18. The Virginia Company was a collaborative enterprise that drew merchants together with a range of other actors to manage the colony – the corporate framework that was established would have been especially familiar to participants in England's existing urban, livery and trading companies. Virginia Company, *A Brief Declaration of the Present State of Things in Virginia* (London, 1616), pp. 2–3. The 1609 and 1612 charters detailed the precise privileges of the company. Library of Congress, Thomas Jefferson Papers, Series 8, Virginia Records Manuscripts, vol. 6.

19. Robert Gray, *A Good Speed to Virginia* (London, 1609), A1–2.

20. For corporate practices of pamphleteering, see Liam Haydon, *Corporate Culture: National and Transnational Corporations in Seventeenth-century Literature* (London, 2019), pp. 25–57.

21. Virginia Company, *A True and Sincere Declaration of the Purpose and Ends of the Plantation Begun in Virginia* (London, 1610), pp. 2–4.

22. Robert Johnson, *Nova Britannia: offering most excellent fruites by planting in Virginia* (London, 1609), pp. C3, C4, D1, D3.

23. Not all merchants were convinced. In relation to Ireland especially, where participation was imposed on all members of livery companies that were levied to pay for the plantation, complaints led to strict enforcement on the part of London's urban and livery companies, with some recalcitrant members being fined or even imprisoned for continued refusal to contribute. See, for example, CC,

– 306 –

NOTES to pp. 214–216

CL/B/1/4, Orders of Court, ff. 49, 51, 58. 11 July 1609; 16 July 1609; 27 June 1610.

24. Games, *Web of Empire*, pp. 6–15.

25. The use of experts is detailed in chapter 2. In Ireland and Virginia, colonial governance had strong military and religious dimensions, and these too were overseen by the companies' officers. See Horning, *Ireland in the Virginia Sea*; Haig Smith, 'Risky business: The seventeenth-century English company chaplain, and policing interaction and knowledge exchange', *Journal of Church and State* 60, 2 (2018), pp. 226–47.

26. PRONI, D3632/A/15. Petition from City of London to Drapers' Company, 15 February 1610.

27. PRONI, D3632/A/20. Report from John Rowley on the Plantation in Ireland, 20 October 1610.

28. PRONI, D683, ff. 90–103. Instructions for the City of London's Agent in Ulster John Rowley, 12 November 1612.

29. PLMC, FP 29. Remembrances to be sent to the Lord Delaware, March 1611.

30. PRONI, D683, ff. 90–103. Instructions for Rowley, 12 November 1612.

31. The relationship between urban planning and colonisation has been explored by Paul Musselwhite, *Urban Dreams, Rural Commonwealth: The Rise of Plantation Society in the Chesapeake* (Chicago, 2018).

32. PLMC, FP 30. Virginia Company to Thomas West, March 1611. As well as changing material culture in the colony, cooking was undertaken in larger complexes that fed larger groups of colonists at a time. For example, a large bakery (structure 183) was built in 1611. William M. Kelso, Beverly Straube and Daniel Schmidt (eds), *2007–2010 Interim Report on the Preservation Virginia Excavations at Jamestown, Virginia* (Richmond, VA, 2012), p. 6.

33. Concerns remained, especially in relation to ongoing difficulties with local people and only limited financial returns. PRONI,

– 307 –

D683, ff. 124–134. The Answer of Peter Proby, Alderman of the City of London and Governor of the Irish Society, 1616.

34. PRONI, D3632/A/34. Agreement between Grocers' Company and Edward Roane, 2 May 1615; PRONI, T520, ff. 3–4. Articles of Covenant between Tristram Beresford and John Cook, 26 May 1615; PRONI, T2208/1. Articles of Agreement between Sir Robert McLellan and Adrian Moore, 8 April 1616; PRONI, D3632/A/45/2a. Russell to Drapers', 16 July 1618; CC, CL/B/1/4, Orders of Court, f. 161. 1 April 1615; DC, MB 13, 13 May 1617; 17 September 1622; 1 August 1626.

35. TNA, CO 1/1, f. 26. Thomas Dale to Salisbury, 17 August 1611; BerkRO, Trumbull Ms, MC vol. 7, f. 49. John Woodall to William Trumbull, 6 July 1615

36. John More to William Trumbull, 11 July 1611. BerkRO, Trumbull Ms, AC vol. 32, f. 32; Robert Johnson, *The New Life of Virginea* (London, 1612), p. 14.

37. John Rolfe, *A True Relation of the State of Virginia Left by Sir Thomas Dale Knight in May Last 1616* (London, 1617), p. 39.

38. Johnson, *New Life of Virginea*, p. 14; Raphe Hamor, *A True Discourse of the Present Estate of Virginia* (London, 1615), p. 30.

39. Hamor, *A True Discourse*, p. 33. For 'fair rows of houses', see William M. Kelso and Beverly Straube (eds), *2000–2006 Interim Report on the APVA Excavations at Jamestown, Virginia* (Richmond, VA, 2008), pp. 49–51; Seth Mallios and Beverly Straube, *1999 Interim Report on the APVA Excavations at Jamestown, Virginia* (Richmond, VA, 2000), p. 32; John L. Cotter, *Archaeological Observations at Jamestown* (Washington, DC, 1958), p. 164.

40. See Kelso and Straube, *2000–2006 Interim Report*, pp. 49–51.

41. Kelso, Straube and Schmidt, *2007–2010 Interim Report*, p. 51.

42. As commander for the East India Company, he continued to impose strict discipline. BL, IOR/B/6, 30, 77, 156; A Court Held Aboard the Moon, 21 May 1618. BL, IOR/E/3/7, 22–3. Another

– 308 –

NOTES to pp. 217–218

officer, Christopher Newport had also been rewarded with a position in the East India Company, who sought to use experienced Atlantic seamen and colonists to advance their changing strategy for empire in Asia; see BL, IOR/B/5, 6.

43. TNA, CO 1/1, f. 34. Thomas Dale to Ralph Winwood, 3 June 1616. After the 1619 election the Virginia Company increasingly fell under the control of Edwin Sandys, who adopted a radically different approach to expansion and economic development. See Theodore Rabb, *Jacobean Gentleman: Sir Edwin Sandys, 1561–1629* (Princeton, NJ, 1998), pp. 353–86.

44. Bross, *Future History*, p. 2.

45. Such militarisation was not only practised in distant waters; threats to English shipping in the Channel, North Sea, Irish Sea and even the River Severn were met with calls for the deployment of military force. See, for example, TNA, SP 12/270, f. 166. Letter from John Blytheman to the Privy Council, 26 April 1599.

46. TNA, SP 14/70, f. 49. Letter from the Earl of Northampton to James I, 2 August 1612.

47. TNA, SP 14/74, f. 171. Letter from John Chamberlain to Dudley Carleton, 27 October 1613.

48. TNA, SP 91/2, f. 9. Proposal from the Muscovy Company, 22 April 1615.

49. BL, Lansdowne Ms 142, ff. 389–90. Petition from the Muscovy Company, 22 January 1617.

50. Not all English commentators were convinced by the success of the fleets, however, and interloping fishermen from Hull suggested they had done little to stop Dutch ships operating in the region. TNA, SP 14/94, f. 113. Reasons why the inhabitants of Kingston upon Hull should prosecute the whale fishery in the northern seas, December 1617.

51. BL, Add Ms 14027, f. 178. Sir Julius Caesar's answer to the complaint of the Low Countries touching the fishing of whales upon the coast of Greenland, 13 January 1614.

– 309 –

NOTES to pp. 218–220

52. Ibid.; TNA, SP 14/76, f. 100a. The Muscovy Company's *True declaration of the discovery of the many lands, islands, seas, ports, havens & creeks lying in the north-west, north, and north-east of the world*, 28 March 1614.

53. BL, Lansdowne Ms 142, ff. 389–90. Petition from the Muscovy Company, 22 January 1617.

54. Ian Bruce Watson, 'Fortifications and the "idea" of force in the early English East India Company relations with India', *Past & Present* 88, 1 (1980), pp. 70–87; Loth, 'Armed incidents and unpaid bills'; Gabriel Paquette, *The European Seaborne Empires: From the Thirty Years' War to the Age of Revolutions* (New Haven, CT, 2019).

55. BL, IOR/E/3/5, f. 11. Letter from Edward Connock to the East India Company, 2 April 1617. Ongoing plans to dominate shipping between Mughal and Safavid empires continued, see BL, IOR/E/3/5, f. 268. Instructions for the ship intended for the Red Sea, 1618.

56. Samuel Purchas, *Hakluytus Posthumus, or Purchas his Pilgrimes, containing a history of the world, in sea voyages & lande travels, by Englishmen and others* (London, 1625), pp. 1789–93. News of the company's new conquest slowly reached London over the coming months. The English state was not overly critical of the action, but the crown and Lord Buckingham did demand a huge £20,000 payment as their share for the company's 'prize'. TNA, SP 94/25, ff. 336, 339. A Letter Written from Madrid, 19 December 1622; Earl of Bristol to Secretary Calvert, 20/30 December 1622; TNA, SP 94/26, f. 6. Earl of Bristol to Secretary Calvert, 12/22 January 1623; TNA, SP 14/148, f. 5. Letter from Calvert, 1 July 1623; John Chamberlain, Norman Egbert McClure (ed.), *The Letters of John Chamberlain*, vol. 2 (Philadelphia, PA, 1939), p. 468; BL, IOR/B/8, 4 July 1623; 23 July 1623; 1 August 1623; 6 August 1623; 3 February 1624; 13 February 1624; 18 February 1624; 5 March 1624; 2 April 1624; 7 April 1624; 24 April 1624; TNA, CO 77/2/83, f. 199. 18 March 1624.

NOTES to pp. 220-222

57. BL, IOR/B/8, January 1624; 16 July 1624. BL, IOR/B/9, 24 November 1624.

58. BL, Add Ms 14027, f. 178. An answer to the complaint of the Low Countries touching the whale fishing upon the coast of Greenland, 13 January 1614.

59. From 1639, the East India Company had begun its own colonisation efforts at Fort St George, Madras in India. David Veevers, *The Origins of the British Empire in Asia, 1600–1750* (Cambridge, 2020).

60. John C. Appleby, 'An association for the West Indies? English plans for a West India Company', *Journal of Imperial and Commonwealth History*, 15, 3 (1987), pp. 214–15.

61. Wallace Notestein (ed.), *Commons Debates, 1621*, vol. 5 (New Haven, CT, 1935), pp. 262, 525.

62. TNA, SP/16/1, f. 77. Propositions for incorporating a company for defence and protection of the west Indies, and establishing a trade to the same, 14 April 1625.

63. That is, in the West Indies. NRS, GD406/1/1252. Thomas Roe to the Privy Council, 19 September 1637.

64. NRS, GD406/1/1252. Thomas Roe to the Privy Council, 19 September 1637.

65. For an overview of English colonial interests in America, see Louis H. Roper, *Advancing Empire: English Interests and Overseas Expansion, 1613–1688* (Cambridge, 2017), pp. 37–61.

66. BA, SMV/2/1/1/34, ff. 111–12. The Mayor of Bristol to Mr Whitson and Mr Guy in London, October 1621; BLO, Ms Bankes 8, ff. 1–4. Lord Baltimore's patent for New England, [undated, *c.* 1629].

67. For instance, merchants including William Courteen and Maurice Thompson were heavily involved in Caribbean commerce while simultaneously drawing on their close relationships with the state to obtain privileges for colonisation in Madagascar and trading voyages in the Indian Ocean. See Brenner, *Merchants and*

NOTES to pp. 222–224

Revolution, pp. 170–5; Games, *Web of Empire*, pp. 182–99; Smith, ' "Canaanising Madagascar" '.

68. DAB, X10/15a. The Earl of Carlisle's grant to Charles Wolverston to be governor of the merchant's plantations, 28 April 1629; DAB, X10/15e. The Earl of Carlisle's grant of 10,000 acres of land to the merchants, 22 February 1630.

69. DAB, X10/15b. Captain Wolverston's declaration of the merchants' losses, [*c.* 1630].

70. DAB, X10/15d. The Earl of Carlisle's patent unto Sir William Tufton, [*c.* 1630].

71. NRS, GD34/923/18. Mr Hastings to Archibald Hay, 6 February 1641.

72. NRS, GD34/941. James Hay to Captain Bell, 5 January 1643. By this time, the profit from Barbados to its patentee was estimated at £200,000 per annum, see NRS, GD34/943b. Thomas Morris to Thomas Chappell, 16 September 1643.

73. Merchants maintained a prominent role in the Atlantic world in what has been described as a 'trading empire'. See Sheryllyne Haggerty, 'Actors of maritime trade in the British Atlantic: From the "sea dogs" to a trading empire', in Christian Buchet and Gérard Le Bouëdec (eds), *The Sea in History: The Early Modern World* (London, 2017), pp. 350–9.

74. MHS, Ms N-2182 (XT). Muscongus patent, 1629; NRS, GD34/929/2. Archibald Hay to Andreas Judd, 20 April 1640.

75. TNA, SP 16/343, f. 120. Sir Henry Marten to the Lords of the Admiralty, 7 January 1637.

76. BA, 12964/1, f. 13. Account of Tobacco out of the Eagle of Bristol and Fortune of Wexford, November 1636.

77. For practices of plantation economies during this period, see Russell Menard, 'Plantation empire: How sugar and tobacco planters built their industries and raised an empire', *Agricultural History*, 81, 3 (2007), pp. 309–32.

NOTES to pp. 225–227

78. Data from the Transatlantic Slave Trade Database [https://www.slavevoyages.org/voyage/database]. There were 1,013 voyages under the British flag in the following 50 years, many under the command of the Royal African Company, which had a membership, corporate model and directorship that closely mirrored that of the East India Company. See Brock, 'The Company Director'; Zahedieh, *Capital and the Colonies*.

79. For the most extensive examination of this community, see Svalastog, *Mastering the Worst of Trades*.

80. By 1630, merchants had made almost 10,000 investments in overseas activities. Of these, almost 34 per cent had not been primarily focused on trading. At least 1,027 merchants had participated in privateering ventures, and at least 1,457 had funded merchant-led colonisation in Ireland or Virginia. Of course, trading remained the most important activity for merchants, and no colonial corporation maintained the enduring engagement of the Spanish, French, Merchant Adventurer, East India, Eastland or Levant trades.

81. Games, *Web of Empire*, pp. 6–7.

82. BL, Add Ms 41667 G, f. 19. Tract on the decay of trade, 1610. Portuguese, Spanish and Dutch colonial activities were likewise viewed as a threat to England's commerce.

83. Imports in the 1660s totalled £3,495,000 (colonies £421,000, East India Company £409,000, Europe £2,638,000), exports totalled £2,039,000 (colonies £163,000, East India Company £30,000, Europe £1,809,000). Zahedieh, *Capital and the Colonies*, p. 11.

BIBLIOGRAPHY

ARCHIVES CONSULTED

Barbados National Archives (Department of Archives), Bridgetown
Berkshire Record Office, Reading
Bodleian Library, Oxford
Bristol Archive, Bristol
British Library, London
Clothworkers' Company Hall, London
Company of the Merchant Adventurers of York, York
Drapers' Company Hall, London
Folger Shakespeare Library, Washington, DC
Greater Manchester County Archives, Manchester
Guildhall Library, London
Hampshire Record Office, Winchester
Hull History Centre, Hull
Kent History and Library Centre, Medway
Library of Congress, Washington, DC
London Metropolitan Archive, London
Massachusetts Historical Society, Boston
Mercers' Company Hall, London

BIBLIOGRAPHY

National Records of Scotland, Edinburgh
Norfolk Record Office, Norwich
Northamptonshire Archives, Northampton
Nottinghamshire Archives, Nottingham
Pepys Library at Magdalene College, Cambridge
Portsmouth History Centre and Records Office, Portsmouth
Public Record Office for Northern Ireland, Belfast
Saddlers' Company Hall, London
Southampton Archives, Southampton
Staffordshire Record Office, Stafford
The Huntington Library, San Marino
The National Archive, London
West Yorkshire Archives Service, Leeds

PRINTED MANUSCRIPT SOURCES

Boyd, Percival, *Roll of the Drapers' Company* (London, 1934)

Boyle, John R. (ed.), *Charters and Letters Patent Granted to Kingston upon Hull* (Hull, 1905)

Bruce, John (ed.), *Letters and Papers of the Verney Family Down to the End of the Year 1639* (London, 1853)

Carr, Cecil (ed.), *Select Charters of Trading Companies, A.D. 1530–1707* (London, 1913)

East, Robert (ed.), *Extracts from Records in Possession of the Municipal Corporation of the Borough of Portsmouth* (Portsmouth, 1891)

Giuseppi, M.S. (ed.), *Calendar of the Manuscripts of the Most Honourable the Marquis of Salisbury*, vols 14, 17, 18, 21 (London, 1923–40)

Green, Mary Anne Everett (ed.), *Calendar of State Papers Domestic: James I, 1603–1625*, vols 1–4 (London, 1857–59)

His Majesty's Stationery Office, *Acts of the Privy Council of England*, vols 33 and 34 (London, 1921)

Irish Society, *A Concise View of the Origin, Constitution, and Proceedings of the Honourable Society of the Governor and Assistants of London of*

BIBLIOGRAPHY

the New Plantation in Ulster, within the Realm of Ireland, Commonly Called the Irish Society (London, 1842)

Jenks, Stuart (ed.), *Robert Sturmey's Commercial Expedition to the Mediterranean (1457–8): with editions of the trial of the Genoese before king and council and other sources* (Bristol, 2006)

Notestein, Wallace (ed.), *Commons Debates, 1621*, vol. 5 (New Haven, CT, 1935)

Roberts, R.A. (ed.), *Calendar of the Manuscripts of the Most Honourable the Marquis of Salisbury*, vol. 12 (London, 1910)

Roberts, R.A. (ed.), *Calendar of the Cecil Papers in Hatfield House*, vol. 12 (London, 1910)

Russell, C.W. and John P. Pendergast (eds), *Calendar of the State Papers Relating to Ireland of the Reign of James I*, vol. 3, *1608–1610* (London, 1874)

Vanes, Jean (ed.), *The Ledger of John Smythe, 1538–1550* (London, 1974)

PRIMARY PRINTED SOURCES

Angiera, Pietro Martire d', *The Decades of the New World or West India Containing the Navigations and Conquests of the Spaniards*, trans. Richard Eden (London, 1555)

Anon., *A Discourse Consisting of Motives for the Enlargement and Freedom of Trade: especially that of cloth and other woollen manufactures* (London, 1645)

Arthus, Gotthard, *Dialogues in the English and Malaiane languages: or, certaine common formes of speech, first written in Latin, Malaian, and Madagascar tongues, by the diligence and painfull endeuour of Master Gotardus Arthusius, a Dantisker, and now faithfully translated into the English tongue by Augustine Spalding merchant, for their sakes, who happily shall hereafter vndertake a voyage to the East-Indies* (London, 1614)

Best, George, *A True Discourse of the Late Voyages of Discovery, for the finding of a passage to Cathaya, by the Northwest* (London, 1578)

– 316 –

BIBLIOGRAPHY

Botero, Giovanni, *A Travellers Breviat, or an historicall description of the most famous kingdomes in the world relating their situations, manners, customes, civill government, and other memorable matters*, trans. Anon. (London, 1601)

Bradford, William, *A Relation or Journal of the Beginning and Proceedings of the English Plantation Settled in Plimoth in New England, by certain English adventurers both merchants and others* (London, 1622)

Browne, John, *The Merchants Avizo: verie necessarie for their sonnes and seruants, when they first send them beyond the seas, as to Spayne and Portingale or other countreyes* (London, 1590)

Charles I, *A Proclamation Inhibiting the Importation of Whale Finnes, or Whale Oil, into His Majesties Dominions by any but the Muscovy Company* (London, 1636)

Council for New England, *A Brief Relation of the Discovery and Plantation of New England and of Sundry Accidents Therein Occurring* (London, 1622)

Digges, Dudley, *The Defence of Trade* (London, 1615)

East India Company, *The Lawes or Standing Orders of the East India Company* (London, 1621)

East India Company, *Newes out of East India of the Cruel and Bloody Usage of our English Merchants and others at Amboyna, by the Netherlandish Governour and Councel There: to the tune of Braggendary* (London, 1624)

Fletcher, Giles, *Of the Russe Common Wealth* (London, 1591)

Gentleman, Tobias, *England's Way to Win Wealth and to Employ Ship's Mariners* (London, 1614)

Gray, Robert, *A Good Speed to Virginia* (London, 1609)

Hakluyt, Richard, *The Principall Navigations, Voyages, Traffiques and Discoveries of the English Nation by Sea or Over-Land, to the Remote and Farthest Distant Quarters of the Earth* (London, 1599–1600)

Hamor, Raphe, *A True Discourse of the Present Estate of Virginia* (London, 1615)

– 317 –

BIBLIOGRAPHY

James I, *A Proclamation Extending the Former Proclamation for the Restraint of Shipping any Commodity in Strangers Bottomes either into this Kingdome or out of the Same* (London, 1615)

James I, *A Proclamation Prohibiting the Bringing in of Any Commodities Traded by the Eastland Merchants into this Kingdom, As Well by Subjects as Strangers, Not Free of that Company* (London, 1622)

Johnson, Robert, *Nova Britannia: offering most excellent fruites by planting in Virginia* (London, 1609)

Johnson, Robert, *The New Life of Virginea* (London, 1612)

Johnson, Thomas, *A Discourse Concerning of Motives for the Enlargement and Freedom of Trade* (London, 1645)

Kayll, Robert, *The Trades Increase* (London, 1615)

Malynes, Gerard, *A Treatise of the Canker of England's Commonwealth* (London, 1601)

Malynes, Gerard, *Englands View in the Unmasking of Two Paradoxes* (London, 1603)

Malynes, Gerard, *The Maintainance of Free Trade* (London, 1622)

Malynes, Gerard, *The Centre of the Circle of Commerce* (London, 1623)

Middleton, Thomas, *The Triumphs of Truth: a solemnity vnparalleled for cost, art, and magnificence, at the confirmation and establishment of that worthy and true nobly-minded gentleman, Sir Thomas Middleton, knight, in the honorable office of his Maiesties lieutenant, the lord maior of the thrice famous citty of London* (London, 1613)

Misselden, Edward, *Free Trade, or, the Means to Make Trade Flourish* (London, 1622)

Misselden, Edward, *The Circle of Commerce, or the Ballance of Trade in Defence of Free Trade* (London, 1623)

Mun, Thomas, *A Discourse of Trade, from England unto the East-Indies answering to diverse objections which are usually made against the same* (London, 1621)

Purchas, Samuel, *Hakluytus Posthumus, or Purchas his Pilgrimes, containing a history of the world, in sea voyages & lande travels, by Englishmen and others* (London, 1625)

– 318 –

BIBLIOGRAPHY

Roberts, Lewes, *The Marchants Mapp of Commerce: necessarie for all such as shall be imployed in the publique afaires of Princes in foraine partes, for all gentlemen & others that travell abroade for delight & plesure, and for al marchants or their factors that exercise the art off marchandiseinge in any parte of the habitable world* (London, 1638)

Rolfe, John, *A True Relation of the State of Virginia Left by Sir Thomas Dale Knight in May Last 1616* (London, 1617)

Scott, Edmund, *An Exact Discourse of the Subtilties, Fashishions, Pollicies, Religion, and Ceremonies of the East Indians as well Chyneses as Javans, there abiding and dwelling* (London, 1606)

Sharpe, Edward, *Britain's Busse* (London, 1615)

Skinner, John, *A true relation of the unjust, cruel, and barbarous proceedings against the English at Amboyna: in the East-Indies, by the Netherlandish governour & council there* (London, 1624)

Stow, John C.L. Kingsford (ed.), *A Survey of London. Reprinted from the Text of 1603*, ed. C.L. Kingsford (Oxford, 1908)

Virginia Company, *A True and Sincere Declaration of the Purpose and Ends of the Plantation Begun in Virginia* (London, 1610)

Virginia Company, *A Brief Declaration of the Present State of Things in Virginia* (London, 1616)

Wheeler, John, *A Treatise of Commerce: wherein is shewed the commodities arising by a well ordered and ruled trade, such as that of the Society of Merchants Adventurers is proved to be* (London, 1601)

Wilkinson, Robert, *The Stripping of Joseph, or the Cruelty of Brethren to a Brother* (London, 1626)

SECONDARY LITERATURE

Acemoglu, Daron, Simon Johnson and James Robinson, 'The rise of Europe: Atlantic trade, institutional change, and economic growth', *American Historical Review* 95, 3 (2005), pp. 546–79

– 319 –

BIBLIOGRAPHY

Anderson, Gary W., Robert E. McCormick and Robert D. Tollison, 'The economic organisation of the English East India Company', *Journal of Economic Behaviour and Organisation* 4 (1983), pp. 221–38

Andrews, Kenneth, *Elizabethan Privateering: English Privateering during the Spanish War, 1585–1603* (London, 1964)

Andrews, Kenneth, *Trade, Plunder and Settlement: Maritime Enterprise and the Genesis of the British Empire, 1480–1630* (Cambridge, 1984)

Antunes, Catia and Amelia Polónia (eds), *Beyond Empires: Global, Self-organising, Cross-imperial Networks, 1500–1800* (Leiden, 2015)

Appleby, John C., 'An association for the West Indies? English plans for a West India Company', *Journal of Imperial and Commonwealth History* 15, 3 (1987), pp. 213–41

Appleby, Joyce, *Economic Thought and Ideology in Seventeenth-century England* (Princeton, NJ, 1978)

Archer, Ian, *The Pursuit of Stability: Social Relations in Elizabethan London* (Cambridge, 1991)

Archer, Ian, 'The Burden of Taxation on Sixteenth-century London', *Historical Journal* 44, 3 (2001), pp. 599–627

Arel, Maria, *English Trade and Adventure to Russia in the Early Modern Era: The Muscovy Company, 1603–1649* (Lanham, MD, 2019)

Armitage, David, *The Ideological Origins of the British Empire* (Cambridge, 2000)

Armitage, David and Michael J. Braddick (eds), *The British Atlantic World, 1500–1800* (Basingstoke, 2009)

Asch, Ronald and Adolf Birke (eds) *Princes, Patronage and the Nobility: The Court at the Beginning of the Modern Age, c. 1450–1650* (Oxford, 1990)

Ash, Eric H., *Power, Knowledge and Expertise in Elizabethan England* (Baltimore, MD, 2005)

Ashton, Robert, 'The parliamentary agitation for free trade in the opening years of the reign of James I', *Past & Present* 38, 1 (1967), pp. 40–55

BIBLIOGRAPHY

Ashton, Robert, *The City and the Court, 1603–1643* (Cambridge, 1979)

Aslanian, Sebouh, '"The salt in a merchant's letter": The culture of Julfan correspondence in the Indian Ocean and Mediterranean', *Journal of World History* 19, 2 (2008), pp. 127–88

Aslanian, Sebouh, *From the Indian Ocean to the Mediterranean: The Global Trade Networks of Armenian Merchants from New Julfa* (Berkeley, CA, 2011)

Attman, Artur, *The Russian and Polish Markets in International Trade, 1500–1650* (Göteborg, 1973)

Baladouni, Vahé, 'Accounting in the early years of the East India Company', *Accounting Historians Journal* 10, 2 (1983), pp. 63–80

Bannet, Eve Tavor, *Empire of Letters: Letter Manuals and Transatlantic Correspondence, 1680–1820* (Cambridge, 2006)

Barbour, Richard, *Before Orientalism: London's theatre of the East, 1576–1626* (Cambridge, 2003)

Barendese, Rene, 'The long road to Livorno: The overland messenger service of the Dutch East India Company in the seventeenth century', *Itinerario* 12, 2 (1988), pp. 25–45

Barkan, Joshua, *Corporate Sovereignty: Law and Government under Capitalism* (Minneapolis, MN, 2013)

Batchelor, Robert, *London: The Selden Map and the Making of a Global City, 1549–1689* (Chicago, 2014)

Beier, A. and Finlay, Roger (eds), *London, 1500–1700: The Making of the Metropolis* (London, 1986)

Belich, James, John Darwin, Margret Frenz and Chris Wickham (eds), *The Prospect of Global History* (Oxford, 2016)

Bellany, Alastair, *The Politics of Court Scandal in Early Modern England: News Culture and the Overbury Affair, 1603–1660* (Cambridge, 2002)

Ben-Amos, Ilana Krausman, 'Women apprentices in the trade and crafts of early modern Bristol', *Continuity and Change* 6, 2 (1991), pp. 227–53

Benton, Lauren, *Law and Colonial Cultures: Legal Regimes in World History, 1400–1900* (Cambridge, 2002)

BIBLIOGRAPHY

Benton, Lauren, 'The British Atlantic in a global context', in Armitage and Braddick, *British Atlantic World*, pp. 271–89

Benton, Lauren, *A Search for Sovereignty: Law and Geography in European Empires, 1400–1900* (Cambridge, 2010)

Benton, Lauren and Richard Ross (eds), *Legal Pluralism and Empires, 1500–1850* (New York, 2013)

Berry, Dianne and Paul Dienes Zoltan, *Implicit Learning: Theoretical and Empirical Issues, Essays in Cognitive Psychology* (Hove, 1993)

Bethencourt, Francisco and Florike Egmond (eds), *Correspondence and Cultural Exchange in Europe, 1400–1700* (Cambridge, 2007)

Bishop, Jennifer, '*Utopia* and civic politics in mid-sixteenth-century London', *Historical Journal* 54, 4 (2011), pp. 933–53

Bisson, Douglas, *The Merchant Adventurers of England: The Company and the Crown, 1474–1564* (Newark, 1993)

Blakemore, Richard. 'Pieces of eight, pieces of eight: Seamen's earnings and the venture economy of early modern seafaring', *Economic History Review* 70, 4 (2017), pp. 1153–84

Blusse, Leonard and Femme Gastra (eds), *Companies and Trade: Essays on Overseas Trading Companies during the Ancien Regime* (Leiden, 1981)

Boulton, Jeremy, 'London, 1540–1700', in Peter Clark (ed.), *The Cambridge Urban History of Britain*, vol. ii: *1540–1700* (Cambridge, 2000), pp. 315–46

Bowen, Huw, *The Business of Empire: The East India Company and imperial Britain, 1756–1833* (Cambridge, 2005)

Bowen, Huw, Elizabeth Mancke and John G. Reid (eds), *Britain's Oceanic Empire: Atlantic and Indian Ocean Worlds, c. 1550–1850* (Cambridge, 2012)

Boxer, Charles, *The Dutch Seaborne Empire, 1600–1800* (England, 1973 [1965])

Braddick, Michael, *State Formation in Early Modern England, c. 1550–1770* (Cambridge, 2000)

– 322 –

BIBLIOGRAPHY

Brenner, Robert, *Merchants and Revolution: Commercial Change, Political Conflict, and London's Overseas Traders, 1550–1662* (London, 1993)

Brett-James, Norman, G. *The Growth of Stuart London* (London, 1935)

Brewer, John, *The Sinews of Power: War, Money, and the English State, 1688–1783* (Oxford, 1989)

Broadberry, Stephen, Bruce Campbell, Alexander Klein, Mark Overton and Bas van Leeuwen, *British Economic Growth, 1270–1870* (Cambridge, 2015)

Brock, Aske, 'The Company Director: Commerce, State and Society', PhD thesis, University of Kent, 2017

Brock, Aske, 'Networks', in Pettigrew and Veevers (eds), *Corporation as a Protagonist*, pp. 91–115

Brock, Aske and Misha Ewen, 'Women's public lives: Navigating the East India Company, parliament and courts in early modern England', *Gender and History* 33, 1 (2020), pp. 3–23

Brooks, Christopher, 'Apprenticeship, social mobility, and the middling sort, 1550–1800', in Jonathan Barry and Christopher W. Brooks (eds), *The Middling Sort of People: Culture, Society, and Politics in England, 1550–1800* (Basingstoke, 1994), pp. 52–83

Brooks, Christopher, *Law, Politics and Society in Early Modern England* (Cambridge, 2008)

Bross, Kristina, *Future History: Global Fantasies in Seventeenth-century American and British Writings* (Oxford, 2017)

Bulut, Mehmet, 'The Ottoman approach to the Western Europeans in the Levant during the early modern period', *Middle Eastern Studies* 44, 2 (2008), pp. 259–74

Calvert, Hugh, *A History of Kingston upon Hull: From the Earliest Times to the Present Day* (London, 1978)

Campbell, Mary, *Wonder and Science: Imagining Worlds in Early Modern Europe* (New York, 1999)

Canny, Nicholas (ed.), *The Origins of Empire: British Overseas Enterprise to the Close of the Seventeenth Century* (Oxford, 1998)

BIBLIOGRAPHY

Canny, Nicholas, 'Asia, the Atlantic and the subjects of the British monarchy', in Barry Coward (ed.), *A Companion to Stuart Britain* (Oxford, 2003), pp. 45–66

Carlos, Ann M., 'Principal–agent problems in early trading companies: A tale of two firms', *American Historical Review* 82, 2 (1992), pp. 140–5

Carruthers, Bruce G., *City of Capital: Politics and Markets in the English Financial Revolution* (Princeton, NJ, 1993)

Carus-Wilson, E.M. and Olive Coleman, *England's Export Trade, 1275–1547* (Oxford, 1963)

Cavanagh, Edward, 'A company with sovereignty and subjects of its own? The case of the Hudson's Bay Company, 1670–1763', *Canadian Journal of Law and Society* 26, 1 (2011), pp. 25–50

Chapman, Stanley D., *The Cotton Industry in the Industrial Revolution* (London, 1987)

Chaudhuri, Kirti N., *The English East India Company: The Study of an Early Joint-stock Company* (London, 1964)

Chaudhuri, Kirti N., *The Trading World of Asia and the English East India Company, 1660–1760* (Cambridge, 1978)

Childs, Wendy R., *Anglo-Castilian Trade in the Later Middle Ages* (Manchester, 1978)

Clulow, Adam, *Amboina, 1623: Fear and Conspiracy on the Edge of Empire* (Columbia, NY, 2019)

Coates, Ben, *The Impact of the English Civil War on the Economy of London, 1642–50* (Farnham, 2004)

Coclanis, Peter A., Alison Games, Paul W. Mapp and Philip J. Stern, 'Forum: Beyond the Atlantic', *William and Mary Quarterly* 53 (2006), pp. 675–742

Coleman, Olive, 'Trade and prosperity in the fifteenth century: Some aspects of the trade of Southampton', *Economic History Review* 16, 1 (1963), pp. 9–22

Conrad, Sebastian, *What is Global History?* (Princeton, NJ, 2016)

BIBLIOGRAPHY

Cotter, John L., *Archaeological Observations at Jamestown* (Washington, DC, 1958)

Coulson, Justin, 'Negotiating merchant identities: The Stockfishmongers and London's companies merging and dividing, c. 1450–1550', in Martin Allen and Matthew Davis (eds), *Medieval Merchants and Money: Essays in Honour of James L. Bolton* (London, 2017) , pp. 3–20

Cowan, Brian, *The Social Life of Coffee: The Emergence of the British Coffeehouse* (New Haven, CT, 2005)

Cramsie, John, 'Commercial projects and the fiscal policy of James VI and I', *Historical Journal* 43, 2 (2000), p. 345–64

Cramsie, John, *Kingship and Crown Finance under James IV and I, 1603–1625* (Woodbridge, 2002)

Croft, Pauline, *The Spanish Company* (London, 1973)

Croft, Pauline, 'Fresh light on Bate's case', *Historical Journal* 30, 3 (1987), pp. 523–39

Curtin, Philip, *Cross-cultural Trade in World History* (Cambridge, 1984)

Cust, Richard, 'Charles I, the Privy Council, and the forced loan', *Journal of British Studies* 24, 2 (1985), pp. 208–35

Cust, Richard, 'News and politics in early seventeenth-century England', *Past & Present* 112, 1 (1986), pp. 60–90

Dalton, Heather, *Merchants and Explorers: Roger Barlow, Sebastian Cabot, and Networks of Atlantic Exchange, 1500–1560* (Oxford, 2016)

Dari-Mattiaci, Giuseppe, Oscar Gelderblom, Joost Jonker, Enrico Perotti, 'The emergence of the corporate form', *Journal of Law, Economics and Organisation* 33, 2 (2017), pp. 193–236

Davies, Ralph, *The Rise of the English Shipping Industry in the 17th and 18th Centuries* (Newton Abbott, 1962)

de Divitiis, Gigliola Pagano, *English Merchants in Seventeenth-Century Italy*, trans. Stephen Parkin (Cambridge, 1990)

Dunlop, Olive and Richard Denman, *English Apprenticeship and Child Labour* (London, 1912)

BIBLIOGRAPHY

Dursteler, Eric R., 'Speaking in tongues: Language and communication in the early modern Mediterranean', *Past & Present* 217, 1 (2012), pp. 47–77

Dyer, Christopher, *An Age of Transition? Economy and Society in England in the Later Middle Ages* (Oxford, 2004)

Dyer, Christopher, *A Country Merchant, 1495–1520: Trading and Farming at the End of the Middle Ages* (Oxford, 2012)

Eacott, Jonathan, *Selling Empire: India in the Making of Britain and America, 1600–1830* (Williamsburg, VA, 2016)

Ekelund, Robert and Robert D. Tollison, *Politicised Economies: Monarchy, Monopoly, and Mercantilism* (College Station, TX, 1997)

Elmhirst, Edward, *Merchants' Marks* (London, 1959)

Epstein, Mortimer, *The Early History of the Levant Company* (London, 1908)

Epstein, Stephan, 'Craft guilds, apprenticeship, and technological change in preindustrial Europe', *Journal of Economic History* 58, 3 (1998), pp. 684–713

Epstein, Stephan and Maarten Prak (eds), *Guilds, Innovation, and the European Economy, 1400–1800* (Cambridge, 2010)

Erikson, Emily, *Between Monopoly and Free Trade: the English East India Company, 1600–1757* (Princeton, NJ, 2014)

Ewen, Misha, 'Women investors in the Virginia Company in the early seventeenth century', *Historical Journal* 62, 4 (2019), pp. 853–74

Fisher, F.J., 'Experiments in company organisation in the early seventeenth century', *Economic History Review* 4, 2 (1933), pp. 177–94

Fisher, F.J. 'Commercial trends and policy in sixteenth-century England', *Economic History Review* 10, 2 (1940), pp. 95–117

Fisher, F.J. 'London's export trade in the seventeenth century', *Economic History Review* 3, 2 (1950), pp. 151–61

Fitzmaurice, Andrew, 'The civic solution to the crisis of English colonisation, 1609–1625', *Historical Journal* 42, 1 (1999), pp. 25–51

Fox, Adam, 'Rumour, news, and popular political opinion in Elizabethan and early Stuart England', *Historical Journal* 40, 3 (1997), pp. 597–620

BIBLIOGRAPHY

Friis, Astrid, *Alderman Cockayne's Project and the Cloth Trade: The Commercial Policy of England in Its Main Aspects, 1603–1625* (Copenhagen, 1927)

Gallagher, John, *Learning Languages in Early Modern England* (Oxford, 2019)

Games, Alison, *The Web of Empire: English Cosmopolitans in an Age of Expansion, 1560–1660* (Oxford, 2008)

Gauci, Perry, *The Politics of Trade: The Overseas Merchant in State and Society, 1660–1720* (Oxford, 2001)

Gelderblom, Oscar, *Cities of Commerce: The Institutional Foundations of International Trade in the Low Countries, 1250–1650* (Princeton, NJ, 2013)

Gelderblom, Oscar and Regina Grafe, 'The rise and fall of the merchant guilds: Re-thinking the comparative study of commercial institutions in premodern Europe', *Journal of Interdisciplinary History* 40, 4 (2010), pp. 477–512

Gerhold, Dorian, *London Plotted: Plans of London Buildings, c. 1450–1720* (London, 2016)

Gillett, Edward and Kennet MacMahon, *A History of Hull* (Hull, 1980)

Girling, F.A., *English Merchants' Marks: A Field Survey of Marks Made by Merchants and Tradesmen in England between 1400 and 1700* (London, 1962)

Glaisyer, Natasha, *The Culture of Commerce in England, 1660–1720* (Woodbridge, 2006)

Grassby, Richard, *The Business Community of Seventeenth-century England* (Cambridge, 1995)

Greene, Jack P. and Philip Morgan (eds), *Atlantic History: A Critical Appraisal* (Oxford, 2009)

Greif, Anver, *Institutions and the Path to the Modern Economy: Lessons from Medieval Trade* (Cambridge, 2006)

Greif, Anver, Paul Milgrom and Barry Weingast, 'Coordination, commitment, and enforcement: The case of the merchant guild', *Journal of Political Economy* 102 (1994), pp. 745–76

BIBLIOGRAPHY

Griffiths, Paul, 'Secrecy and authority in late sixteenth- and seventeenth-century London', *Historical Journal* 40, 4 (1997), pp. 925–51

Griffiths, Percival, *A Licence to Trade: The History of the English Chartered Companies* (London, 1974)

Goldgar, Anne and Robert L. Frost (eds), *Institutional Culture in Early Modern Society* (Leiden, 2004)

Gould, Eliga H., 'Entangled histories, entangled worlds: The English-speaking Atlantic as a Spanish periphery', *American Historical Review* 112, 3 (2007), pp. 1415–22

Gowing, Laura, 'Girls on forms: Apprenticing young women in seventeenth-century London', *Journal of British Studies* 55, 3 (2016), pp. 447–73

Habib, Imtiaz, *Black Lives in the English Archives, 1500–1677: Imprints of the Invisible* (London, 2008)

Haggerty, Sheryllyne, *'Merely for Money': Business Culture in the British Atlantic, 1750–1815* (Liverpool, 2012)

Haggerty, Sheryllyne, 'Actors of maritime trade in the British Atlantic: From the "sea dogs" to a trading empire', in Christian Buchet and Gérard Le Bouëdec (eds), *The Sea in History: The Early Modern World* (London, 2017), pp. 350–9.

Harris, Ron, *Going the Distance: Eurasian Trade and the Rise of the Business Corporation, 1400–1700* (Princeton, NJ, 2020)

Harte, Negley, *The New Draperies in the Low Countries and England, 1300–1800* (Oxford, 1997)

Haydon, Liam, *Corporate Culture: National and Transnational Corporations in Seventeenth-century Literature* (London, 2019)

Heal, Felicity and Clive Holmes, 'The economic patronage of William Cecil', in Pauline Croft (ed.), *Patronage, Culture and Power: The Early Cecils* (New Haven, CT, 2002), pp. 199–229

Hellman, Lisa, *The House Is Not a Home: European Everyday Life in Canton and Macao, 1730–1830* (Leiden, 2019)

Hill, Tracey, ' "Representing the awefull authoritie of soveraigne Majestie": Monarchs and mayors in Anthony Munday's *The*

BIBLIOGRAPHY

Triumphs of re-united Britania', in Glenn Burgess, Rowland Wymer and Jason Lawrence (eds), *The Accession of James I: Historical and Cultural Consequences* (Basingstoke, 2006), pp. 15–33

Hill, Tracey, *Pageantry and Power: A Cultural History of the Early Modern Lord Mayor's Show, 1585–1639* (Manchester, 2011)

Hill, Tracey, ' "To the Honour of our Nation abroad": The Merchant as Adventurer in Civic Pageantry', in J. Caitlin Finlayson and Amrita Sen (eds), *Civic Performance: Pageantry and Entertainments in Early Modern London* (London, 2020), pp. 13–31

Hont, Istvan, *Jealousy of Trade: International Competition and the Nation-state in Historical Perspective* (Cambridge, MA, 2005)

Horning, Audrey, *Ireland in the Virginia Sea: Colonialism in the British Atlantic* (Chapel Hill, NC, 2013)

Hulsebosch, Daniel, 'The ancient constitution and the expanding empire: Sir Edward Coke's British jurisprudence', *Law and History Review* 21, 3 (2003), pp. 439–82

Humphries, Jane, 'English apprenticeship: A neglected factor in the first Industrial Revolution', in Paul David and Mark Thomas (eds), *The Economic Future in Historical Perspective* (Oxford, 2003), pp. 73–102

Hunt, Margaret, 'Time management, writing and accounting in the eighteenth-century English trading family: A bourgeois enlightenment', *Business and Economic History* 18 (1989), pp. 150–9

Irwin, Douglas, 'Mercantilism as strategic trade policy: The Anglo-Dutch rivalry for the East India trade', *Journal of Political Economy* 99, 6 (1991), pp. 1296–314

Jacob, Margaret, *Strangers Nowhere in the World: The Rise of Cosmopolitanism in Early Modern Europe* (Philadelphia, PA, 2006)

Jardine, Lisa, *Worldly Goods: A New History of the Renaissance* (London, 1996)

Jenstad, Janelle Day, 'Public glory, private gilt: The Goldsmiths' Company and the spectacle of punishment', in Anne Goldgar and

BIBLIOGRAPHY

Robert L. Frost (eds), *Institutional Culture in Early Modern Society* (Leiden, 2004), pp. 191–217

Jones, Evan, *Inside the Illicit Economy: Reconstructing the Smugglers' Trade of Sixteenth Century Bristol* (Abingdon, 2012)

Jones, Norman, *God and the Moneylenders: Usury and Law in Early Modern England* (Oxford, 1989)

Jones, S.R.H. and Simon P. Ville, 'Efficient transactors or rent-seeking monopolists: The rationale for early chartered companies', *Journal of Economic History* 56, 4 (1996), pp. 898–915

Keene, Derek, 'The setting of the Royal Exchange: Continuity and change in the financial district of the City of London, 1300–1871', in Ann Saunders, *The Royal Exchange* (London, 1991)

Keene, Derek, 'Cities in cultural exchange', in Donatella Calabi and Stephen Tark (eds), *Cultural Exchange in Early Modern Europe*, vol. 2: *Cities and Cultural Exchange in Europe, 1400–1700* (Cambridge, 2007)

Kelso, William M. and Beverly Straube (eds), *2000–2006 Interim Report on the APVA Excavations at Jamestown, Virginia* (Richmond, VA, 2008)

Kelso, William M., Beverly Straube, Daniel Schmidt (eds), *2007–2010 Interim Report on the Preservation Virginia Excavations at Jamestown, Virginia* (Richmond, VA, 2012)

Lamb, David Frank, 'The Seaborne Trade of Southampton in the First Half of the Seventeenth Century', MPhil thesis, University of Southampton, 1971

Lane, Joan, *Apprenticeship in England, 1600–1914* (London, 1996)

Leech, Roger, 'The symbolic hall: Historical context and merchant culture in the early modern city', *Vernacular Architecture* 31, 1 (2000), pp. 1–10

Lemire, Beverley, *Global Trade and the Transformation of Consumer Cultures: The Material World Remade, c. 1500–1820* (Cambridge, 2018)

BIBLIOGRAPHY

Leng, Tom, 'Commercial conflict and regulation in the discourse of trade in seventeenth-century England', *Historical Journal* 48, 4 (2005), pp. 933–54

Leng, Tom, 'Epistemology: Expertise and knowledge in the world of commerce', in Stern and Wennerlind (eds), *Mercantilism Reimagined*, pp. 97–116

Leng, Tom, 'Interlopers and disorderly brethren at the Stade Mart: Commercial regulations and practices among the Merchant Adventurers of England in the late Elizabethan period', *Economic History Review* 69, 3 (2016), pp. 823–43

Leunig, Tim, Chris Minns and Patrick Wallis, 'Networks in the premodern economy: The market for London apprenticeships, 1600–1749', *Journal of Economic History* 71, 2 (2011), pp. 413–43

Loades, David, *England's Maritime Empire: Seapower, Commerce and Policy, 1490–1690* (New York, 2001)

Lorimer, Joyce (ed.), *English and Irish Settlement on the River Amazon, 1550–1646* (London, 1999)

Loth, Vincent, 'Armed incidents and unpaid bills: Anglo-Dutch rivalry in the Banda Islands in the seventeenth century', *Modern Asian Studies* 29 (1995), pp. 705–40

MacLean, Gerald and Nabil Matar, *Britain and the Islamic World, 1558–1713* (Oxford, 2011)

Malament, Barbara, 'The "economic liberalism" of Sir Edward Coke', *Yale Law Journal* 76, 7 (1987), pp. 1321–58

Mallios, Seth and Beverly Straube, *1999 Interim Report on the APVA Excavations at Jamestown, Virginia* (Richmond, VA, 2000)

Mancke, Elizabeth, 'Empire and state', in Armitage and Braddick (eds), *British Atlantic World*, pp. 193–213

Mancke, Elizabeth, 'Negotiating an empire: Britain and its overseas peripheries, c. 1550–1780', in Christine Daniels and Michael Kennedy (eds), *Negotiated Empires: Centers and Peripheries in the Americas, 1500–1820* (New York, 2002), pp. 237–62

– 331 –

BIBLIOGRAPHY

Menard, Russell, 'Plantation empire: How sugar and tobacco planters built their industries and raised an empire', *Agricultural History* 81, 3 (2007), pp. 309–32

Milgrom, Paul, Douglas North and Barry Weingast, 'The role of institutions in the revival of trade: The law merchant, private judges, and the Champagne Fairs', *Economics and Politics* 2, 1 (1990), pp. 1–23

Millard, A.M., *The Import Trade of London, 1600–1640* (London, 1956)

Mishra, Rupali, *A Business of State: Commerce, Politics and the Birth of the East India Company* (Boston, MA, 2017)

Mokyr, Joel, *The Culture of Growth: The Origins of the Modern Economy* (Princeton, NJ, 2016)

Muldrew, Craig, *The Economy of Obligation: The Culture of Credit and Social Relations in Early Modern England* (Basingstoke, 1998)

Musselwhite, Paul, *Urban Dreams, Rural Commonwealth: The Rise of Plantation Society in the Chesapeake* (Chicago, 2018)

New, Elizabeth, 'Representation and identity in medieval London: The evidence of seals', in M. Davies and A. Prescott (eds), *London and the Kingdom: Essays in Honour of Caroline M. Barron* (Donnington, 2008), pp. 246–58.

North, Douglas, 'Institutions', *Journal of Economic Perspectives* 5, 1 (1991), pp. 97–9

Nosch, Marie-Louise (ed.), *The Medieval Broadcloth: Changing Trends in Fashions, Manufacturing and Consumption* (Oxford, 2010)

O'Brien, Terence, 'The London livery companies and the Virginia Company', *Virginia Magazine of History and Biography* 68, 2 (1960), pp. 137–55

Ogborn, Miles, 'Writing travels: Power, knowledge and ritual on the English East India Company's early voyages', *Transactions of the Institute of British Geographers* 27, 2 (2002), pp. 155–71

Ogborn, Miles, *Indian Ink: Script and Print in the Making of the English East India Company* (Chicago, 2007)

BIBLIOGRAPHY

Ogborn, Miles, 'The power of speech: Orality, oaths and evidence in the British Atlantic world, 1650–1800', *Transactions of the Institute of British Geographers* 36, 1 (2011), pp. 109–25

Ogilvie, Sheilagh, 'Guilds, efficiency, and social capital: Evidence from German proto-industry', *Economic History Review* 57, 2 (2004), pp. 286–333

Ogilvie, Sheilagh, *The European Guilds: An Economic Analysis* (Princeton, NJ, 2019)

Paquette, Gabriel, *The European Seaborne Empires: From the Thirty Years' War to the Age of Revolutions* (New Haven, CT, 2019)

Pearl, Valerie, *London and the Oubreak of the Puritan Revolution: City Government and National Politics, 1625–43* (Oxford, 1961)

Peck, Linda Levy (ed.), *The Mental World of the Jacobean Court* (Cambridge, 1991)

Pennell, Sara, 'Consumption and consumerism in early modern England', *Historical Journal* 42, 2 (1999), pp. 549–64

Pettigrew, William and George van Cleve, 'Parting companies: The Glorious Revolution, company power and imperial mercantilism', *Historical Journal* 57, 3 (2014), pp. 617–38

Pettigrew, William, 'Corporate constitutionalism and the dialogue between global and local in seventeenth-century English history', *Itinerario* 39, 3 (2015), pp. 487–501

Pettigrew, William and Tristan Stein, 'The public rivalry between regulated and joint stock corporations and the development of seventeenth-century corporate constitutions', *Historical Research* 90, 248 (2016), pp. 341–62

Pettigrew, William and David Veevers (eds), *The Corporation as a Protagonist in Global History, c. 1550–1750* (Leiden, 2018)

Pettigrew, William and Edmond Smith, 'Corporate management, labor relations, and community building at the East India Company's Blackwall dockyard, 1600–57', *Journal of Social History* 53, 1 (2019), pp. 133–56

– 333 –

BIBLIOGRAPHY

Pincus, Steven, *Protestantism and Patriotism: Ideologies and the Making of English Foreign Policy, 1650–1668* (Cambridge, 1996)

Pincus, Steven, 'Neither Machiavellian moment nor possessive individualism: Commercial society and the defenders of the English commonwealth', *American Historical Review* 103, 3 (1998), pp. 705–36

Porter, R., 'The Crispe family and the African trade in the seventeenth century', *Journal of African History* 9, 1 (1968), pp. 57–77

Rabb, Theodore, *Enterprise and Empire: Merchant and Gentry Investment in the Expansion of England, 1575–1630* (Cambridge, MA, 1967)

Rabb, Theodore, 'Free trade and the gentry in the parliament of 1604', *Past & Present* 40, 1 (1968), pp. 165–73

Rabb, Theodore *Jacobean Gentleman: Sir Edwin Sandys, 1561–1629* (Princeton, NJ, 1998)

Raffield, Paul, 'Contract, classicism, and the common-weal: Coke's *Reports* and the foundations of the modern English constitution', *Law and Literature* 17, 1 (2005), pp. 69–96

Ramsay, G.D., *English Overseas Trade during the Centuries of Emergence* (London, 1957)

Ramsay, G.D., *Tudor Economic Problems* (London, 1963)

Ramsay, G.D., *The City of London in International Politics at the Ascension of Elizabeth Tudor* (Manchester, 1975)

Ramsay, G.D., 'The Tudor state and economic problems', in Simon Groenveld (ed.), *State and Trade: Government and the Economy in Britain and the Netherlands since the Middle Ages* (Zutphen, 1992)

Rappaport, Steve, *Worlds within Worlds: Structures of Life in Sixteenth-century London* (Cambridge, 1989)

Raymond, Joad (ed.) *News, Newspapers, and Society in Early Modern Britain* (London, 1999)

Reinhart, Sophus A., *Translating Empire: Emulation and the Origins of Political Economy* (Cambridge, MA, 2011)

Roper, Louis H., *Advancing Empire: English Interests and Overseas Expansion, 1613–1688* (Cambridge, 2017)

BIBLIOGRAPHY

Roper, Louis H. and Bertrand Van Ruymbeke (eds), *Constructing Early Modern Empires: Proprietary Ventures in the Atlantic World* (Leiden, 2007)

Rose, J., A.P. Newton and E.A. Benians (eds), *The Cambridge History of the British Empire*, vol. 1: *The Old Empire from the Beginnings to 1783* (Cambridge, 1929)

Rothschild, Emma, *The Inner Lives of Empire: An Eighteenth-century History* (Princeton, NJ, 2011)

Ruddock, Alwyn, *Italian Merchants and Shipping in Southampton, 1270–1600* (Southampton, 1951)

Sacks, David Harris, *The Widening Gate: Bristol and the Atlantic Economy, 1450–1700* (Berkeley, CA, 1991)

Sacks, David Harris, 'The paradox of taxation: Fiscal crises, parliament, and liberty in England, 1450–1640', in Philip Hoffman and Kathryn Norberg (eds), *Fiscal Crises, Liberty, and Representative Government, 1450–1789* (Stanford, CA, 1994), pp. 7–66

Sacks, David Harris, 'The countervailing of benefits: Monopoly, liberty and benevolence in Elizabethan England', in Dale Hoak (ed.), *Tudor Political Culture* (Cambridge, 1995), pp. 272–91

Sahle, Esther, 'Law and gospel order: Resolving commercial disputes in colonial Philadelphia', *Continuity and Change* (2020)

Scott, William, *The Constitution and Finance of English, Scottish, and Irish Joint-stock Companies to 1720* (Cambridge, 1910)

Schmidt, Benjamin, *Innocence Abroad: The Dutch Imagination and the Representation of the New World, c. 1570–1670* (Cambridge, 2001)

Schnurmann, Claudia, ' "Wherever profit leads us, to every sea and shore . . .': The VOC, the WIC, and Dutch methods of globalisation in the seventeenth century', *Renaissance Studies* 17, 3 (2003), pp. 474–93

Schofield, John (ed.), *The London Surveys of Ralph Tresswell* (London, 1987)

Schwartz, Leonard, 'London apprentices in the seventeenth century: Some problems', *Local Population Studies* 38 (1987), pp. 18–22

BIBLIOGRAPHY

Senning, Calvin F., 'Piracy, politics, and plunder under James I: The voyage of the "Pearl" and its aftermath, 1611–1615', *Huntingdon Library Quarterly* 46, 3 (1983), pp. 187–222

Shepard, Alexandra, *Accounting for Oneself: Worth, Status and the Social Order in Early Modern England* (Oxford, 2015)

Sherman, Arnold, 'Pressure from Leadenhall: The East India Company lobby', *Business History Review* 50, 3 (1976), pp. 1660–78

Slack, Paul, *The Invention of Improvement: Information and Material Progress in Seventeenth-century England* (Oxford, 2015)

Smith, Edmond, 'Naval violence and trading privileges in early seventeenth-century Asia', *International Journal of Maritime History* 25, 2 (2013), pp. 147–58

Smith, Edmond, ' "Canaanising Madagascar": Africa in the English imperial imagination', *Itinerario* 39, 2 (2015), pp. 277–98

Smith, Edmond, 'The global interests of London's commercial community, 1599–1625: Investment in the East India Company', *Economic History Review* 71, 4 (2018), pp. 1118–46

Smith, Edmond, 'Reporting and interpreting legal violence in Asia: The East India Company's printed accounts of torture, 1603–1624', *Journal of Imperial and Commonwealth History* 46, 4 (2018), pp. 603–26

Smith, Edmond, 'Governance', in Pettigrew and Veevers (eds), *Corporation as a Protagonist*, pp. 163–86

Smith, Edmond, 'The social networks of investment in early modern England', *Historical Journal* (2020)

Smith, Haig, 'Risky business: The seventeenth-century English company chaplain, and policing interaction and knowledge exchange', *Journal of Church and State* 60, 2 (2018), pp. 226–47

Sobek, B., ' "After my Humble Dutie Remembered": Factors and/versus merchants', in B. Charry and G. Shahani (eds), *Emissaries in Early Modern Literature and Culture: Mediation, Transmission, Traffic, 1550–1700* (Farnham, 2009), pp. 113–28

Soll, Jacob, *The Reckoning: Financial Accountability and the Making and Breaking of Nations* (London, 2014)

BIBLIOGRAPHY

Spruyt, Hendrik, *The Sovereign State and its Competitors: An Analysis of Systems Change* (Princeton, NJ, 1994)

Stern, Philip, ' "A Politie of Civill and Military Power": Political thought and the late seventeenth-century foundations of the East India Company-state', *Journal of British Studies* 47, 2 (2008), pp. 253–83

Stern, Philip, ' "Bundles of hyphens": Corporations as legal communities in the early modern British Empire', in Benton and Ross, *Legal Pluralism and Empires*, pp. 21–48

Stern, Philip, *The Company-state: Corporate Sovereignty and the Early Modern Foundation of the British Empire in India* (Oxford, 2011)

Stern, Philip, 'Companies: Monopoly, sovereignty, and the East Indies', in Stern and Wennerlind (eds), *Mercantilism Reimagined*

Stern, Philip and Carl Wennerlind, 'Introduction', in Stern and Wennerlind (eds), *Mercantilism Reimagined*, pp. 1–17

Stern, Philip and Carl Wennerlind (eds), *Mercantilism Reimagined: Political Economy in Early Modern Britain and Its Empire* (New York, 2013)

Stone, Richard, 'The overseas trade of Bristol before the Civil War', *International Journal of Maritime History* 23, 2 (2011), pp. 219–25

Stout, Felicity, *Exploring Russia in the Elizabethan Commonwealth: The Muscovy Company and Giles Fletcher, the Elder (1546–1611)* (Manchester, 2015), pp. 93–116

Sullivan, Ceri, *The Rhetoric of Credit: Merchants in Early Modern Writing* (London, 2002)

Supple, B.E., *Commercial Crisis and Change in England, 1600–1642* (Cambridge, 1959)

Sutton, Anne, 'The Merchant Adventurers of England: Their origins and the Mercers' Company of London', *Historical Research* 75, 187 (2002), pp. 25–46

Svalastog, Julie, *Mastering the Worst of Trades: England's Early Africa Companies and their Traders, 1618–1672* (Leiden, 2021)

– 337 –

BIBLIOGRAPHY

Swingen, Abigail, *Competing Visions of Empire: Labor, Slavery, and the Origins of the British Atlantic Empire* (New Haven, CT, 2015)

Talbott, Siobhan, 'British commercial interests on the French Atlantic coast, c. 1560–1713', *Historical Research* 85, 229 (2012), pp. 394–409

Tawney, R.H., *Business and Politics under James I: Lionel Cranfield as Merchant and Minister* (Cambridge, 1958)

Taviani, Carlo, 'Confraternities, citizenship and factionalism: Genoa in the early sixteenth century', in Nicholas Terpstra, Adriano Prosperi and Stefiana Pastore (eds), *Faith's Boundaries: Laity and Clergy in Early Modern Confraternities* (Turnhout, 2013), pp. 41–57

Thirsk, Joan, *Economic Policy and Projects: The Development of a Consumer Society in Early Modern England* (Oxford, 1978)

Thompson, Janice, *Merchants, Pirates, and Sovereigns: State-building and Extraterritorial Violence in Early Modern Europe* (Princeton, NJ, 1994)

Trivellato, Francesca, 'Merchants' letters across geographical and social boundaries', in Bethencourt and Egmond, *Correspondence and Cultural Exchange*, pp. 80–103

Trivellato, Francesca. *The Familiarity of Strangers: The Sephardic Diaspora, Livorno, and Cross-cultural Trade in the Early Modern Period* (New Haven, CT, 2012)

Turner, Henry S., *The Corporate Commonwealth: Pluralism and Political Fictions in England, 1516–1651* (Chicago, 2016)

Unwin, George, *The Gilds and Companies of London* (London, 1963)

Veevers, David, *The Origins of the British Empire in Asia, 1600–1750* (Cambridge, 2020)

Vries, Jan de, 'Understanding Eurasian trade in the era of trading companies', in Maxine Berg, Felicia Gottman, Hanna Hodacs and Chris Nierstraz (eds), *Goods from the East, 1600–1800: Trading Eurasia* (Basingstoke, 2015), pp. 7–39

Vries, Jan de and Ad van der Woude, *The First Modern Economy: Success, Failure, and Perseverance of the Dutch Economy, 1500–1815* (Cambridge, 1997)

BIBLIOGRAPHY

Wallis, Patrick, 'Apprenticeship and training in premodern England', *Journal of Economic History* 68, 3 (2008), pp. 832–61

Wallis, Patrick, Justin Coulson and David Chilosi, 'Structural change and economic growth in the British economy before the Industrial Revolution, 1500–1800', *Journal of Economic History* 78, 3 (2018), pp. 862–903

Ward, Robert, *London's New River* (Whitstable, 2003)

Watson, Ian Bruce, 'Fortifications and the "idea" of force in the early English East India Company relations with India', *Past & Present* 88, 1 (1980), pp. 70–87

Wennerlind, Carl, *Casualties of Credit: The English Financial Revolution, 1620–1720* (Cambridge, MA, 2011)

Willan, T.S., *The Early History of the Russia Company* (Manchester, 1956)

Winjum, James, 'The journal of Thomas Gresham', *Accounting Review* 46, 1 (1971), pp. 149–55

Withington, Phil, *The Politics of Commonwealth: Citizens and Freemen in Early Modern England* (Cambridge, 2005)

Withington, Phil, 'Company and sociability in early modern England', *Social History* 32, 3 (2007), pp. 291–307

Withington, Phil, 'Public discourse, corporate citizenship, and state formation in early modern England', *American Historical Review* 112, 4 (2007), pp. 1016–38

Withington, Phil and Alexandra Shepard (eds), *Communities in Early Modern England: Networks, Place, Rhetoric* (Manchester, 2001)

Working, Lauren, *The Making of an Imperial Polity: Civility and America in the Jacobean Metropolis* (Cambridge, 2020)

Wrightson, Keith, 'The Politics of the Parish in Early Modern England', in Paul Griffiths, Steve Hindle and Adam Fox (eds), *The Experience of Authority in Early Modern England* (Basingstoke, 1996), pp. 10–46

Yamamoto, Koji, *Taming Capitalism before its Triumph: Public Service, Distrust, and 'Projecting' in Early Modern England* (Oxford, 2018)

BIBLIOGRAPHY

Zahedieh, Nuala, 'Credit, risk and reputation in late seventeenth-century colonial trade', *Research in Maritime History* 15 (1998), pp. 53–74

Zahedieh, Nuala, *The Capital and the Colonies: London and the Atlantic Economy, 1660–1700* (Cambridge, 2010)

WEBSITES

Records of London's Livery Companies Online (ROLLCO): https://www.londonroll.org/home

Trans-Atlantic Slave Trade Database: https://www.slavevoyages.org/voyage/database

INDEX

Abbas I, Shah of Persia 48, 219
Abbott, Morris 128, 200–1
Abdy, Anthony 92
Abu Marwan Abd a-Malik I,
    King of Morocco 142
Adams, William 26
Addes, Henry 34
Aden 148
advice books 18, 20, 26–7, 34
Africa 14–16, 20, 46, 55, 82–3,
    91–3, 95, 101, 125, 135,
    142–6, 181, 198, 208, 224
Agadir 92
Agra 26
agriculture 203, 206–7, 213
Ahmadabad 49, 127
Aldworth, John 127
alehouses 203, 215
Alicante 23
alien 69

Allyn, William 190
almonds 91, 101, 103, 127, 143
Altham, Mr 190
alum 10, 106, 202
Alvie, Pope 22
ambergris 101
Amboyna 90, 173–4
Amsterdam 103, 195
Andalusia 35
Andrews, Thomas 99
Angebauld, Daniel 140
Angel, Robert 169
Antwerp 103, 139, 149
apes 28
ApJohn, John 77
Appowell, William 35
apprentices 6, 8, 17–20, 27, 30–2,
    34–5, 63–5, 88
Archbishop of Canterbury 179
Archdale, Matthew 22

– 341 –

INDEX

Archdale, Richard 22, 35–6, 101–2, 195
Arundel, Earl of 212
Ashwell, William 64
Asia 26, 33, 36, 48–9, 55, 57, 68, 83, 85, 90, 101, 103–4, 106, 110, 124–5, 127–8, 143, 145, 158–9, 162, 166, 180, 195, 198–202, 205, 208–9, 217, 219–20, 226
assistants *see* corporation, officers
Astell, Richard 113
Atlantic world 2, 10, 12, 22, 27, 29, 36, 39–40, 49, 78–9, 90, 93–5, 101–2, 106, 113, 130–2, 143–4, 166–7, 185, 192, 198–9, 201, 203, 208–9, 212–19, 221–5
auditors 41–3
Austin, Stephen 36
Azores 199

Backhouse, Rowland 77, 119
Bagshaw, Edward 154
balance of trade 202–5
Ball, Mr 127
Baltic 106, 142, 162, 166, 170, 172, 181, 194, 205, 207
Bannister, Alexander 223
Bantam 55
'Banyam' merchants 219
Barbados 27, 222–5

Barbary Company 55, 91–3, 142–3, 168, 170, 225
Barker, John 156
Barne, Richard 127
Barnstaple 87, 93, 102
Baron, Lord Chief 68
Barra, Robert de la 67
Barry, Mr 122
Batavia 25, 54
Bateman, Robert 38, 119
Bayley, Mr 82
Baynham, Edmond 26
Bayonne 192
Beadle, Edward 31
Beauchamp, John 224
beaver 27, 122
behaviour 4–8, 16–21, 23, 27–9, 31, 34, 40, 54–5, 62–4, 69, 74–9, 83–4, 121, 131–2, 142, 205, 208–10
Bell, Mr 140
Bell, Robert 204
Benin 14, 95, 125, 145
Bennet, John 119
Bennet, Mrs 55
Bennet, Thomas 113
Bentinogli, the Marchese di Gualtiere 187
Benzoin 103
Bere, Richard 196
Beresford, Richard 128
Bermuda 211, 225
Bermuda City 216

– 342 –

INDEX

Best, George 27

Best, Michael 95

Bharuch 103, 127

Bigges, John 31

Bilbao 23, 137

Bill, Richard 111

Bishop, Mr 43

Black, Robert 92

Bladwell, Mr 43

Bland, John 67

Blarkley, Thomas 65

Bodin, Peter 23

Bolton, John 19

Bond, Charles 65

Bordeaux 22, 101, 154, 194, 196

Boston (England) 22

Both, Richard 138

Boules, Robert 22

Bourghe, Bourell 200

Bourghe, Pavius 200

Bourman, John 126

Bourman, William 126

Bowdler, Henry 65

Bradshaw, Thomas 35

Brand, Joseph 55

Brazil 101, 198

Breerdy, Mr 138

Brimstone 106

Bristol 17, 25, 42, 44, 52, 64, 66, 72, 74–5, 80, 87, 93–4, 100–2, 104, 109, 113, 122, 127–8, 138, 141, 153, 156–8, 190, 202, 224–5

Broadgate, Martin 195

Brocket, Captain 82

Brown, Mr 27–8

Browne, Edward 195

Browne, John 20, 34

Bruen, George 54

Brund, Mr 26

Buckingham, Lord 83

Buckley, William 37, 105

bullion 85, 109, 199, 202–5

Burgh, Thomas 64

Burke, Mr 76

Burrish, Daniel 104

Butler, Henry 65

Byron, William 23

Cádiz 81, 102

Caesar, Sir Julius 168, 186

Calais 101

calfskins 23

calicos 103–4

Callie, William 112

Calvert, Secretary 179

camlet 99

Canada 218

Canary Islands 101

Canning, Paul 26

Caribbean 12, 22, 27, 101–2, 198, 208, 221–5

Carlisle, Earl of 37

Carpenter, John 117

carpets 48, 115–16

Cartwrights, Abraham 169

– 343 –

INDEX

Castleton, Captain 124
Caswell, William 75
Cecil, Robert 67, 186
Chambers, Robert 64, 188
Champion, Jerome 126
Chancery Court 40
Channel Islands 100
charity 54
Charles I, King 86, 91–2, 175, 184, 186, 195, 199, 221, 223
Chester 87
China 122, 219
City of London corporation 8, 31, 66, 75–6, 77, 96, 113–14, 118–19, 123–4, 150, 176, 183–4, 187–8, 213, 215
Clarke, Humphrey 31
Clarke, John 174
Clarke, Thomas 69
Clayton, John 19
Clement, Gregory 224
Clerk, George 196
climate 203
Clothworkers' livery company 32, 37, 40, 50, 66, 75–6, 81–2, 110, 112, 126, 137, 164, 168, 178–9, 186–7, 189–90, 192–3
cloves 104
coal 102
Cockayne, John 47

Cockayne, William junior 21, 47
Cockayne, William senior 21–2, 25, 39, 45, 47, 67, 106, 112, 118, 121, 166, 170
Cocks, Henry 66
Cocks, Richard 25
Cogram, Oliver 31
Coke, Sir Edward 155
Coke, Sir John 221
Coldcole, Robert 146
Coleraine 213, 216
collaboration between companies 88
Collett, John 1
Coloe, Hugh 120
colonisation 12, 29, 41, 78, 93, 130–1, 185–6, 207–26
committees *see* corporation, officers
Company of Merchants Inhabiting in Kingston upon Hull 45, 51, 63, 81, 84, 114, 154
Connock, Edward 219
Conquest, George 128
Constantinople 27, 129, 147–8
contracts 5, 17, 40, 64, 78–9, 123, 161, 196, 226
Conway, Secretary 179
Cooke, John 112
Cope, Sir Walter 166
copper 106, 196
coral 202

– 344 –

INDEX

Corbett, Roger 196
Cordell, Thomas 122
corn 43, 130, 151, 170, 192, 204, 214
Cornelius, Mr 2–3
corporation
  as arbiters of disputes 9, 32, 77, 121–7
  as colonial government 33, 93–4, 207
  as regulators of behaviour 8, 12, 17, 21, 28–32, 50–3, 62, 69, 72, 74–6, 89, 121–4, 132–4, 180, 208–9, 211
  as regulators of standards 29–31, 116, 118–19, 137–9, 149, 151, 192–3
  as social organisations 8–11, 17, 59–60, 69–70, 107–20, 209
  criticism of 19, 133, 136–7, 179–80, 188–9, 205
  defences of 134–7, 179–80, 188–9, 205
  employees 23–4, 26, 28, 30–2, 54, 82–3, 127, 139–41, 214
  factions 57–9
  joining a 6, 8, 17, 19, 62–9, 133
  joint-stock 7, 38–9, 78, 91–2, 120, 127–9, 133–4, 139, 213, 221
  members 8, 19, 26, 41, 44, 52, 57–9, 69–79, 89–95, 182–5

officers 24, 26, 31, 37–9, 40–1, 45–6, 51, 57–9, 73, 80–95
powers 4, 7–8, 11, 18–19, 21, 28–9, 33, 61–2, 135–6, 175, 192–3
cotton 22, 106, 165
Courteen, William 92
Coventree, Thomas 181
Coventry 163
Craddock, William 31
Cranfield, Lionel 22, 125, 177, 185
Cranfield, William 22
credit and debt 14, 22–3, 35–7, 66, 88–9, 99, 122–3, 126, 183–5, 199
creditability *see* trust
Crew, Thomas 221
Crispe, Ellis 106
Crispe, Nicholas 47, 106, 198, 225
Croft, James 64
Cross, Thomas 65
cross-cultural trade 4–5, 12, 16, 20–1, 23, 25, 27, 32, 99–101, 130–2
Cumberland, Earl of 162
currants 128, 141, 143, 155–6, 182
currency 203–4
Curtin, Robert 169

Dadsworth, Edward 127
Dalby, Thomas 31, 54, 67, 122, 124

INDEX

Dale, Thomas 216
Dales Gift 216
Damask 99
Daniel, Richard 65
Dansk 23, 163
Dartmouth 93
dates 91, 101, 143
Davenant, Edward 67
Davis, Mr 145
Davis, Samuel 22
Deane, James 187–8
Deane, Richard 198
decentred governance 80–1,
    86–9, 93, 135–6
Denmark 29, 100, 106, 140, 194
Derry 213, 216
Dickens, Nicholas 67
Digby, John 58
Digges, Dudley 90, 179–80, 189
diplomacy 7, 11, 25–7, 91, 114,
    134–6, 146–7, 175, 177,
    193–4, 208
directors *see* corporation, officers
discipline 8, 12, 15–16, 20–1,
    28–32, 50–2, 74, 95, 123,
    128, 215–16
Discrowe, Benjamin 38–9
disorderly behaviour 15, 21–2,
    30–2, 40, 46, 89, 95, 123,
    126–8, 134
disorderly trade 21, 29, 126–8,
    127, 132, 134–43, 146, 149,
    160, 167, 188–9

disputes between companies
    38–9, 50–1, 82, 84–5, 128,
    148–59, 164–72, 193
Dodan, Cidi Abdulla 25
Dominico, Signor 27
Downton, Nicholas 165
Draper, Robert 38
Drapers' livery company 42,
    45–6, 64–5, 77, 110,
    112–13, 115–16, 122, 126,
    144, 179, 183, 187–8, 190
Drummer, Mr 126
Dublin 19
Ducy, Robert 90
Dunn, Sir Daniel 33
Dutch *see* United Provinces
Dyers' livery company 164

East Indies *see* Asia
Eastford, Mr 138
Eastland Company 19, 29–30,
    42, 45–6, 50–2, 62–3,
    66–7, 77, 84, 86–9, 121,
    126–7, 140–2, 149, 151,
    160, 162, 166, 168, 170,
    188, 194–5, 202, 225
East India Company 10, 23–4,
    27–8, 30, 33–4, 36, 38–9,
    41, 48–54, 57–9, 61, 70,
    72–6, 80–3, 85–6, 90, 98,
    101, 103–6, 110–11, 114,
    117, 122, 124–5, 127–8,
    139, 144–7, 158–9, 164–5,

– 346 –

INDEX

167–8, 170, 173–4, 177–80, 183, 185–6, 188–9, 192, 195, 199–200, 205, 217, 219–22, 225

Edmonds, Sir Clement 155

Edmonds, Thomas 125, 196

Edmunds, Ralph 64

education *see* training

Edwards, William 127

Elbe 133

Elbing 29, 46, 162–3

elections 58, 70, 80, 90–1, 94

Elizabeth I, Queen 26, 62, 115, 132–4, 154, 160, 176, 194

Elliot, John 99

Ellis, Robert 138

Emden 65, 133

Escherim, Macman 200

excessive drinking 32

Exeter 87, 93

expertise 14–16, 24, 26, 60, 80–2, 95, 106–7, 204

factors

employment of 18, 22–5, 27–8, 34, 47–9, 83, 127–8, 214

oversight of 22, 28, 30, 34, 54, 122, 127–8, 141, 143, 214–15

family 6, 15, 18, 21–2, 24–5, 44, 47, 65, 79, 105–6, 111, 113, 119, 125–6, 209

Farewell, Mr 127

Farmor, Hatton 25

Farrington, John 223

Faulks, Mr 65

Favour, William 48

feathers 91, 101, 103

felt 22

Feodor II, Russian Emperor 194

Ferrante, Marchese 187

Fettiplace, Robert 64

Finch, Richard 146

Firth, Thomas 117

Fishbourne, Richard 112

fishing 2, 102, 137, 151, 189, 192, 198, 201, 203, 213, 216–17

Fishmongers' livery company 110

Fitzsimons, Mr 216

flax 154, 213

Flemming, Giles 196

Fletcher, Doctor 53

Flower, Thomas 65

Forster, Edmond 223

Fort St George 33

Fowle, Augustus 83

Foxwell, Richard 27

France 22–3, 25, 36, 62, 101, 103–4, 106, 126, 133, 135–6, 140, 151, 153–4, 160, 166, 168–9, 188, 194–6, 202, 214, 218

fraud 29, 31, 38–40, 42, 46, 54, 69, 124–6

freedom, of a corporation *see* corporation, joining a

– 347 –

INDEX

Freeman, Ralph 128
French Company 63, 68, 151, 153, 188, 202
fruit 127
Fry, Adrian 104
Fryer, Simon 22
fur 27, 122, 130

Gainsborough 154
Galicia 101
gambling 32
Gao 82, 101
Garrard, John 123
Garraway, Arthur 125
Garraway, Henry 77, 90, 92, 112, 118, 128
Garraway, William 42, 112, 116, 125
Garret, Thomas 45
Gatenbie, Nicholas 146
Gayer, Mr 144
General courts and meetings 71–5
generality *see* corporation, members
Genoa 226
gentlemen 57–9, 83, 93, 95, 145, 185, 211–13
Gerini, Ottavio 67
Germany (region) 22, 31, 44, 62, 100–3, 106, 127, 133–5, 141, 143, 155–6, 160, 163–4, 169–70, 194–5, 210

Gibson, James 49
ginger 101, 224
Gloucester 163
goatskins 91
Goddard, Richard 42, 65
Godwolston, Robert 154
Goff, Lawrence 65
Golconda 48, 122
gold 15, 22, 48, 82, 101, 198, 203, 206, 208, 214
Goldsmiths' livery company 110
Gore, Richard 133, 169
Gorges, Ferdinando 78, 94
Gorsuch, Mr 43
governance 79–95, 97–8, 175
Granado 222
Great Yarmouth 31, 122, 126, 138, 143, 151
Greek merchants 128
Green, William 196
Greenbury, Richard 174
Greenland 39, 144, 218–19
Gregory, John 22
Gresham, Thomas 35, 99–100, 104
Griffin, Mr 137
Griffiths, Hugh 122
Griffiths, John 36
Grimani, Marino 147
Grimsby 154–5
Grocers' livery company 110, 112, 115
Grosse, Samuel 31

– 348 –

INDEX

Grotius, Hugo 200

Guiana 113, 167, 211–12, 221

guild *see* livery company

Guillam, John 27

Guinea Company 82–3, 86, 95, 145–6, 198–9, 225

gum 91

Haberdashers' livery company 6, 8, 110, 118, 122–3, 149, 183

Hakluyt, Richard 27

Hall, John 187–8

Hall, Mr 140

Halliday, William 22

Hamburg 31, 55, 127, 133, 142, 169, 204, 214

Hamersley, Hugh 84

Hamor, Raph 69

Hampton, Francis 65

Hanger, George 64, 104

Hanse 160, 189, 195, 210

Harby, Job 90

Harrison, William 38–9

Harte, William 30

Hartford, Earl of 179

Harvey, Daniel 23

Harvey, Thomas 18

Harwarde, William 38

Hatton, Sir Christopher 190

Hawkins, Richard 159

hawks 103

Hay, James, Earl of Carlisle 222

Hayes, Thomas 187–8

Haywood, Mr 216

Heard, Mr 43

Heath, Nicholas 44

Heath, Sir Thomas 44

Hedington, Viscount 187

hemp 170, 213

Henrico 216

herring 31, 138, 151

Heson, Thomas 141

Hewett, Thomas 112

Hicks, Baptiste 122, 185

Hide, Henry 143

Hill, Richard 65

Hobart, Henry 82

Hobson, Mr 143

Hoddesdon, Christopher 160

Hodgson, Francis 111

Holland, John 140

Holworthy, Richard 64

Hooke, Mr 131

hops 154

Houbelon, Nicholas 67

Houghton, Simon 119

houses 112–20

Howard, Charles 186

Hull 22, 45, 51, 82, 86–8, 102–3, 114, 144, 153–5, 161–2, 181

Hunt, Michael 122

Hunter, William 40

Hurt, William 48

Hyde, George 45

– 349 –

INDEX

Iceland 189

India *see* Mughal Empire

indigo 49, 224

industry *see* manufacturing

information management 34–46, 49–54, 74, 85

Ingram, Thomas 126

interlopers 29–31, 92–5, 125, 132–48, 150, 157

investment 7, 10, 38–40

Ipswich 86–7

Ireland 12–13, 41, 46, 90, 106, 143–4, 147, 177, 184–5, 198, 212–17, 225

Irish Society 10, 13, 46, 185, 212–17, 222

iron 101, 103, 154, 161, 170

Ironmongers' livery company 110

Isfahan 219

Italian merchants 103

Italy (region) 22–3, 100–1, 128–9, 132, 135, 156, 161, 168, 201, 210

Jackson, Lewes 27

Jackson, Thomas 31

Jahangir, Mughal Emperor 26, 147

James, Edward 29

James I, King 55, 68, 135, 146, 149, 158–9, 164, 167, 173, 175–8, 180–1, 183–4, 187, 195, 207, 213

Jamestown 216

Jennings, Robert 77

Jennings, Thomas 204

Joanes, John 67

Johns, Alderman 112

Johnson, Francis 27

Johnson, Lancelot 112

Johnson, Robert 37, 64

Johnson, Thomas 209

Jolles, John 187–8

Jones, Isaac 112

Jones, Robert 84

Kendrick, George 204

Kendrick, John 169

Kentish, Martin 21

Kequought 216

Kerridge, Thomas 27–8, 49

Keymer, John 166, 200, 203

Kilvert, Roger 196

King's Bench 123

King's Lynn 22, 87, 106

Kingswood 37

Kirby, John 38–9

Lake, Edward 122

Lamott, John 69

Langhorne, William 128

Langley, Richard 81

language skills 14, 24–6

    Arabic 26

    Dutch 25–6

    French 25, 27

INDEX

Italian 25
Japanese 26
Latin 25, 28
Malay 27
mistakes 28
Portuguese 14, 26
Powhatan 26
Spanish 25–6
Wyapoko 27
Lanman, Christopher 37
'Lapp' people 219
Laune, Henry de 102
lawyer 81–2
Le Maire, Isaac 158–9
lead 99, 102–3, 154, 161, 202
Lee, Henry 195
Lee, Richard 194
Leghorn *see* Livorno
Lello, Henry 147
Lennox, Duke of 212
letter writing 18, 26–8, 34, 45–8,
        78, 195
Levant Company 10, 19, 21, 27,
        29, 42, 50–1, 63–8, 71–2,
        77, 80, 83–5, 89–90,
        103–4, 106, 114, 125–6,
        128–9, 132–3, 135–6,
        141–3, 145, 147–8, 152–3,
        155–8, 160, 165, 168–70,
        172, 179, 186, 202, 205,
        221, 225
Leverett, Thomas 224
Levesey, Richard 126

Levesey, Robert 126
Leveson, William 77
Leveson, Sir John 47
lewd behaviour 32
Lilly, Henry 116
lion tamer 10
Lisbon 23, 101, 196
livery company, function 7, 9, 59,
        99, 110, 115–16
Livorno 22–3, 129
loans 37, 86, 182–5
lobbying 114, 152–3, 156,
        175–91
local officials 140–1
Lodge, John 138
London
    Abchurch 112
    Aldersgate Ward 81
    All Hallows Barking 9
    apprentices in 19
    Bishopsgate 115
    Blackwall dockyard 114
    Blackwell Hall 150
    Botolph's wharf 118
    Bridewell 75
    Catteaton Street 111
    Cheapside 98, 179
    Cornhill 111, 118
    Drapers' Hall 115–16
    East Smithfield 118
    Finsbury Field 118
    Fleet Street 9
    Fresh Wharf 111

INDEX

Grocers' Hall 115
Guildhall 76, 96, 98, 111
Hammersmith 106
Katherine Wheel Alley 119
King's Arms 111
Leadenhall Market 112, 114
Maiden's Head 111
markets 67
New Fish Street 118
Newgate prison 31
Pewterers' Hall 114
Royal Exchange 50, 112,
    114–17, 123–4, 177
St Augustine 112
St Dunstan-in-the-East 111
St Katherine's 10
St Michael Bassishaw 111
St Nicholas Lane 112
St Paul's Cathedral 97–8, 178
St Paul's school 77
St Peter-le-Poer 112, 118
Strand 117
Throgmorton Street 112
Tower of London of 9–10
Worcester Hall 119
Long, Mr 50–1
Lord admiral 83, 179, 186
Lord chancellor 177, 185, 191
Lord mayor's show 96–8
Lord treasurer 83, 179, 186
Love, Philip 122
Low Countries 100–3, 106, 139,
    149, 156, 204, 208

Lowe, Thomas 112, 114
Lübeck 101
luxuries 103, 115, 167, 180,
    202–3

Madison, Sir Ralph 204
Madrid 196
Major, John 27
Málaga 23, 55, 101
Malynes, Gerard 121, 204
Mamotack 130–2
Man, Eustace 145
Manchester 37, 105, 163
Mansfield, Robert 125
manufacturing
    alum 10, 106
    bricks 106
    corn mill 130–2
    cotton spinning 106, 165, 180
    dyeing 119
    improvement of 202–4, 215
    iron 101, 144
    new draperies 25, 106
    rapeseed oil 37
    salt 101, 216
    soap 39–40, 106
    sugar refining 101
    woollen cloth 102, 105–6,
        139, 149–50, 153–4,
        159–72, 192–3, 202
Marseille 126, 141
Mason, Captain 131–2
Massachusetts 27, 130–2, 225

INDEX

Massachusetts Bay Company 225

Masulipatnam 48

Matthew, James 224

May, Arthur 65

May, Thomas 138

Mediterranean 16, 36, 100–1, 103–4, 109, 124, 133, 139, 147, 155–7, 162, 169, 172, 219

Megges, William 187–8

Mehmed III, Ottoman Sultan 26, 147

Mellyn, Mr 41, 73–4

Mercer, Paul 101

Mercers' livery company 30, 41–4, 51, 54–5, 70–2, 77, 86, 110, 113–14, 116–20, 122–4, 165, 178, 183–4, 190

Merchant Adventurers 8–10, 29, 31–2, 44, 46, 52, 61, 65–6, 75, 77, 81, 84, 103–4, 107, 116, 126–7, 133–6, 139, 141, 143, 149, 155–6, 160–71, 183, 188, 193, 195, 225

Merchant Adventurers of York 42, 45, 66, 102, 138, 154, 190

Merchant Adventurers to Greenland 39–40

Merchant Tailors' livery company 76, 110

Merchant Venturers of Bristol 42, 44, 52, 64, 66, 72, 74–5, 80, 84, 101, 122, 127, 138, 141, 153, 156–8, 160, 190, 202, 222

Merchants of the Staple 61, 87

'mere' merchants 3, 63–9, 134–5, 141, 185–6, 209–10

Merrick, Hugh 120

Merrick, William 31

Messina 23

Michael I, Russian Emperor 146, 195

Middelburg 31, 65, 103, 134, 166, 169

Middleton, Hugh 119–20

Middleton, Richard 55–6

Middleton, Robert 200–1

Middleton, Thomas (merchant) 96–8, 113, 119, 167

Middleton, Thomas (playwright) 96–8

Milan 101

Mildenhall, John 145

military 7, 175, 198, 200–1, 217–20

Misselden, Edward 188–9, 210

Mocha 148

Moffett, Peter 126

Mohammed esh-Sheikh es-Seghir, King of Morocco 91

Mole, Geoge 37, 106–7

– 353 –

INDEX

Moluccas 208

Moneymore 144

monopoly 7, 18, 29, 52, 68, 92–5, 124–5, 128–9, 130–48, 153–9, 198–201

Montague, Henry, Viscount Mandeville 203–4

Montomier, David le 23

Moody, John 141

Moore, John 42

Moors 97–8, 219

More, John 149

Morlaix (Brittany) 101

Morocco 20, 46, 55, 91–3, 101, 103, 135, 142–4, 160, 162–3, 181

Morris, John 125

Mortimer, George 34

Moyer, Mr 129

Mughal Empire, trade in 26, 28, 48–9, 103, 145, 147, 164–5, 208, 219, 221

Mulis, John 196

Mulley Pehdan, King of Morocco 55

Mun, Thomas 53, 180, 188–9, 204–5, 210

Muqarrab Khan, Governor of Surat 164–5

Muscovy Company 38–9, 47, 53–4, 61, 82, 84–5, 103–5, 107, 118, 126–7, 133, 144, 146, 163–4, 171, 194–5, 199, 201–2, 207–8, 217–20, 222

mutiny 15, 33, 223

Nantes 104

napkin thefts 30–1
    the butler did it 31

Naples 23

Navey, Mr 31

neighbourhood 9, 107–20

Nelson, Richard 75

Neven, William 152

Neville, Henry 54, 119

New Company of Soap Makers 106

New England (region) 222, 224

New England Company 29, 78–9, 93–5, 222

New Merchant Adventurers 10, 54, 168–72

New River Company 119–20, 167

Newcastle 86–8, 151, 161–2, 181

Newfoundland (region) 2, 10, 101–2, 106, 192, 203, 213

Newfoundland Company 10, 101

news 47–8, 104, 117, 173–4

Nord, Wannior la 25

North, Captain 211–12

North, Lord 211–12

North America 2, 10, 27, 29, 78–9, 90, 93–5, 101–2,

– 354 –

INDEX

106, 130–2, 167, 185, 192, 203, 208, 212–17, 222, 224–5
North West Passage Company 49
Norway, trade in 29, 100, 151, 199
Norwich 25, 105, 115, 125, 138, 150, 162, 168, 190
Nottingham 190
Nugent, Mr 216
nutmegs 104

oaths 83–4, 86–7, 138
Offley, Thomas 24
oil 101, 172
Olbolton, Lambert 122–3
opium 103
Ormuz 90, 219–20
Osberton, Lambert 154
Osborne, John 105
Osborne, Nicholas 37, 105
Ottoman Empire 26–7, 29, 36, 103–4, 115, 128–9, 132–3, 135, 139, 147–8, 153, 155–6, 161–2, 165, 169, 194, 198, 205, 214, 219, 221
Overman, Thomas 39
Oxwick, Mr 127

Paget, Lord 212
Palmer, John 9
Palmer, Robert 169

paper 103
Parker, Charles 22
Parkin, William 223
parliament 134, 137, 156, 163, 182, 189–90, 223
partnerships 1–10, 22–3, 37–8, 44, 47, 60, 104–6, 137–8
Peacock, Launcelot 122–3
pearls 47
Pechora 82
Pemstoy, Mitchell 122
Pennoyer, William 225
pepper 14–16, 100, 145, 180
Pernambuco 81
Persia 48, 206, 208, 214, 219–20
petitioning 187–91
Petra 29
Pettus, Thomas 190
Philip III, King of Spain 55
pilot 15, 82
Pindar, Paul 92
Pineau, merchant of Bordeaux 196
Pinteado, Antoniades 15
piracy 84–5, 192, 196, 198, 202, 224
pitch 154, 216
Plymouth 87, 93
Poland 23, 29, 47, 62, 100, 102–3, 106, 140–2, 162–3, 166, 170–1, 181, 195, 205, 207–8
Polonian cloth 103

– 355 –

INDEX

Polsted, Henry 53
Portsmouth 14, 140, 191
Portugal 23, 36, 49, 65, 90,
    100–1, 137–8, 141, 153,
    161, 196, 198, 200, 219–20,
    226
preacher 82, 86
Preston, Raphe 103
Pretty, Edmund 112
Price, Thomas 117
privateering 25, 81, 92, 147–8
Privy Council 46, 85, 125–6,
    133, 138–9, 144–7, 153,
    155–8, 174, 179, 181, 183,
    188–96, 198, 202, 218,
    221
Proby, Peter 216
Prussia 140
Prylaux, Peter 101
Puerto Rico 81
Pullison, Sir Thomas 62, 64
punishment
    corporal 31
    disenfranchisement 8, 32, 46,
        69, 74, 77, 128, 156
    dismissal 30–2, 86, 151
    execution 33
    fines 29–32, 46, 52, 72, 76–7,
        81, 137–8, 140, 143, 151
    imprisonment 30–1, 69, 75
    public acknowledgement of
        crime 40, 76
Pynchon, William 130–2

race 97–9
raisins 101
Raleigh, Sir Carew 145
Ramsey, John 125, 187
Rankin, Thomas 118
Raw, Roger 88
Rawdon, Marmaduke 119, 223
Reading 168
record keeping 8, 16, 18, 22–5,
    28, 34–56, 189, 212
recruitment 23–6
Red Sea 104, 148
refusing to serve in a corporation
    31, 81, 86
relationship with the English
    state 7, 11, 58–60, 81, 85,
    91, 125, 144, 153–4,
    173–206
retailers 52, 66–8, 118, 138, 141
Revel 29
rice 101
Rich, Lord 147
Roberts, Lewes 18, 210–11
Roberts, Mr 38
Robinson, Arthur 25
Robinson, John 31
Robinson, Mr 41
Robinson, Thomas 54
Robinson, William 169
Rode, Thomas 37, 105
Roe, Sir Thomas 145, 221
Rogers, Thomas 48, 122
Romney, William 113

INDEX

Rouen 23
Roukes, George 195
Rowley, John 46, 214–15
Rudolf II, Holy Roman Emperor 195
Russell, Robert 91, 144
Russel, Thomas 62
Russia 47, 53, 101, 103–5, 127, 144, 146, 162–3, 194, 196, 207–8, 219
Rye 29

Safi 92
Saint John, William 95
Saint-Malo 100
Salisbury, Earl of 186
salt 101
Salters' livery company 144
Samin, David 67
Samuel, associate of William Turner 2–3
Sanlúcar 101
São Miguel 199
São Tomé 101, 198–9
Sarsenet 99
satin 22, 99
Scotland 206, 213
Scott, Edmund 169
seals 45–6
secrecy 49–53, 137
Senegal 82
servants see factors
Seville 23, 55, 101

sexual relationships 32
Seye, Lyson 22
Shanks, Henry 25, 54
shareholders see corporation, members
Sharpes, John 223
Shepherd, Alexander 22
Sheppard, Richard 22
Sherfield, Henry 114
shipping 1, 7, 11, 85, 131, 140, 151, 170, 180, 184, 198, 201–2, 213–14
Shiraz 48
sickness 16, 48
Silesian linen 55
silk 22, 48, 99–100, 126, 150, 166, 170, 172, 180, 203, 208, 214, 219
silver 22, 99, 102, 203, 206, 214
Simpson, Henry 137
Simpson, Mr 118
Skinner, John 204
Skinners' livery company 110, 149, 188
Slany, Humphrey 145–6, 198
slave trade 224–5
Sleighton, Edward 154
Smith, Elizabeth 47
Smith, Henry 65
Smith, Hugh 78
Smith, John 64, 113
Smith, Jonathan 24
Smith, Mr 43

– 357 –

INDEX

Smith, Robert 65

Smith, Thomas 33, 47, 54, 58, 74, 82, 114, 158–9

Smith, William 77

Smyrna 29, 129

Somers Island Company 70, 105, 211, 222

Sotherton, Ellis 125

South, Robert 224

Southampton 29, 31, 50–1, 54, 68, 87, 100–1, 104, 114, 141, 144, 152, 179, 186, 188

Spain 1–3, 10, 13, 20, 23, 29–30, 36, 44, 54–5, 62, 65, 100–2, 104, 106, 113, 133, 135, 137–8, 141, 149–50, 153–4, 161, 166, 169–70, 184, 191–2, 196–8, 201, 213, 218–19, 221

Spanish Company 29, 44–5, 62–5, 67–8, 72, 77, 80–1, 84, 86–7, 89–90, 101, 114, 138–9, 141, 149, 170, 186, 188–9, 191–2, 202

Speckart, Abraham 179

speech 31, 49, 53, 74–6, 123

spices 97, 172, 200

St-Jean-de-Luz 192

St Kitts 22, 222

St Lucia 224

St Vincent 222

Stade 22, 103, 133

Stallenge, William 192

Stewart, Patrick 187

Stile, Oliver 24

Stile, Roger 24

Stimini, Mari 187

Stolt, Johan van 67

Stonehouse, Sir James 186

Stones, Andrew 66

Stow, John 111–12

Strachey, William 26

strangers 8, 15, 32, 82, 106, 138–40, 151, 159–60, 165, 167, 201

strangers' bottoms 200–2

Street, Humphrey 123–4

Stubbs, Anthony 169

sugar 101, 103, 224–5

Surat 28, 48, 164–5, 219

Sweden 29, 100, 195, 207

Swinnerton, Robert 223

Sym, Robert 195

Symcotte, John 46, 142–3

Talbot, Thomas 65

tapestry 99, 113, 115–16

tar 154, 170, 216

tax 180–2

Taxis, Don Jon de 64

Temple, Richard 26

Tench, Nicholas 22

Ternate 55

The Hague 201

Thompson, Humphrey 25

– 358 –

INDEX

Thompson, Maurice 22, 37, 224
Thompson, Richard 143
Thomson, Stephen 32
Thornell, Thomas 196
Thynne, Sir Henry 145
timber 29, 54, 101, 151, 170, 213–14
Timbuktu 82, 101
tin 67, 99, 128
Tiverton 93
tobacco 202, 208, 216, 224
Toledo, Don Fernando de 196
Towerson, William 106, 112, 155
trade volume and structure 99–107, 224, 227
training 6–8, 16–20, 24, 26–8, 59, 63–4, 69, 132, 205, 210
transparency 44, 46, 71–3, 89, 94
travel writing 26–7, 49, 53, 173–4
Troman, William 40
Trott, Mr 122
trust 8–9, 18–20, 24, 36–8, 40–5, 69–70, 76, 78–9, 90–2, 96–8, 130–2, 137, 148
Tucker, Mr 38
Tufton, Sir William 223
Turkey Company 62, 103, 139
Turner, William 1–13
Tuscany 210
Tyler, Mr 65

Ulster 13, 106, 213–14
unclear communication 27
Underhill, Clement 169
United Provinces
  commodities from 29, 55, 99, 103, 163, 214
  competition with 55, 90, 158, 163, 165, 170, 173–4, 194, 199–202, 210, 217–18, 220
  diplomacy with 26, 55, 114, 154, 173–4, 200–1
  Dutch West India Company 101, 221
urban corporation 17, 31, 59, 99, 110

Van Speult, Herman 173
Vassall, Samuel 225
Veale, Daniel 31
velvet 99, 115, 203
Venice 132, 135, 153, 156, 161, 201, 210
Vernon, Richard 41
Vintners' livery company 110
Virginia (region) 90, 101, 167, 203, 208, 212–17, 224–5
Virginia Company 101, 185, 212–17, 222

Walthall, William 154
Waltham, Richard 126
Ward, Edward 77

– 359 –

INDEX

wardens *see* corporation, officers

Warwick, Earl of 212, 223

Wase, John 169

Watts, John 81, 186–7, 196

wax 91, 101, 103, 170

Weaver, George 196

Webb, Benedict 37, 106–7

Weitts, Pedro de 55

Welsh cottons 36

Weser 133

West and Shirley 216

West India Company 221–3

West Indies *see* Caribbean

Westminster 96

Weymouth 93

whale 144, 217

whale oil 39, 106

Wheatley, Henry 223

Wheatley, Robert 223

Wheeler, John 65, 161

Whitcombe, Simon 143

Whitson, John 156

Whitwell, Edward 40

Whitwell, William 69

Wiche, George 196

Wilford, Thomas 114

Wilkinson, Robert 174

Willets, William 64

Willett, Mr 141

Williams, John 39, 112

Willis, Timothy 126

Wilson, Henry 36

Windover, William 18

wine 22, 50–1, 101, 114, 127, 140, 152–3, 188, 195, 214

Wiseman, Richard 128

Woleston, William 67

Wollaston, Edward 22

Wolostoy, Henry 122

Wolverston, Charles 223

Wood, Henry 204

Wood, John 225

Wood, Robert 118

Wood, William 138

Woodall, Mr 41

Woodrowe, Thomas 65

woollen cloth
 dyed 10, 106–7, 119, 153, 161–70
 Essex cloths 55–6, 163
 Kentish cloths 36
 Kerseys 31, 36, 99
 new draperies 25, 102, 106, 139, 162–4, 167–9
 old draperies 102, 162, 171–2
 Spanish wool 102, 149–50
 trade 9–10, 22, 29, 87, 99–102, 106–7, 133–4, 149–50, 153–4, 159–72, 181, 190, 198, 208
 undressed 102, 159, 162–3, 168, 170
 undyed 9, 99, 162–3, 170

Worcester 163

work spaces 111–20, 150–1

INDEX

Woronoto 131

Wotton, Sir Henry 201

Wright, Benjamin 195

Wright, Francis 111

Wright, John 137–8

Wright, William 76

Wylde, Jarvis 35

Wyndam, Mr 14–16

Yeamans, William 122

Yelverton, Henry 181

York 25, 42, 45, 62, 66, 72, 86, 88, 102, 138, 149, 153–4, 161–2, 181, 190, 196

Young, Anthony 65

Young, James 39

Young, Richard 224

Youngs, Nicholas 151

Zante 128–9, 143

Zeeland 65

Zu, Cotti Seg 187